THE ULTIMATE
VEGETARIAN
COLLECTION

THE ULTIMATE VEGETARIAN COLLECTION

ALISON **HOLST** & SIMON **HOLST**

NEW
HOLLAND

First published in 2012 by New Holland Publishers (NZ) Ltd
Auckland · Sydney · London · Cape Town

www.newhollandpublishers.co.nz

218 Lake Road, Northcote, Auckland 0627, New Zealand
Unit 1, 66 Gibbes Street, Chatswood, NSW 2067, Australia
86–88 Edgware Road, London W2 2EA, United Kingdom
Wembley Square, First Floor, Solan Road, Gardens, Cape Town 8001, South Africa

Publishing manager: Christine Thomson
Editor: Gillian Tewsley
Design: Sarah Elworthy
Photographer: Lindsay Keats (or as credited below)

Front cover: Oriental tofu & noodles

Photographic credits: David Bateman Ltd: 71, 265, 275; Chanel Publishers Ltd: 16, 16, 175, 189, 277; Hyndman Publishing: 9, 19, 20, 28, 31 (x2), 37, 41, 66, 67, 76, 78, 93, 111, 112, 126, 128, 135, 141, 164, 166, 190, 196, 213, 215, 225, 227, 246, 249, 252, 253, 257, 259, 261, 266, 268, 269, 271, 273, 281, 283; Sal Criscillo: 12, 59, 71, 75, 82, 96, 111 (top), 140, 145, 146, 161, 206, 208, 231, 232, 236, 272.

National Library of New Zealand Cataloguing-in-Publication Data

Holst, Alison, 1938–
The ultimate vegetarian collection / Alison Holst, Simon Holst.
Includes index.
ISBN: 978 1 86966 275 2
1. Vegetarian cooking. l. Holst, Simon. ll. Title.
641.5636—dc 23

10 9 8 7 6 5 4 3 2 1

Colour reproduction by SC (Sang Choy) International Pte Ltd, Singapore
Printed in China by Toppan Leefung Printing Ltd, on paper sourced from sustainable forests.

Contents

The vegetarian pantry

These are the basic items that we think a well-stocked kitchen should contain. You don't need to go out and buy them all at once, but if you just incorporate a few of them at a time into your weekly shopping (as they're needed for a particular recipe) you will find that over time they accumulate on the pantry/fridge/freezer shelves so the next time they feature in a recipe you've chosen to make, they'll already be there. In fact, once you've accumulated these items, you'll be surprised by how many different dishes you can make just by having a quick rummage round in the kitchen

Some of these items, the herbs and spices for example, aren't actually essential, and can be omitted from a recipe if you don't have them, but we think they are worth having on hand as they will make the food you cook more interesting and enjoyable.

- flour: all purpose, self-raising and high grade (bread)
- sugar: white & brown
- icing sugar
- cocoa powder
- rolled oats
- rice: short and long-grain
- pasta: assorted shapes
- noodles
- dried beans and/or lentils
- canned tomatoes: whole and diced
- tomato paste
- coconut cream
- canned beans
- canned fruit
- canola or other vegetable oil

- soy sauce, light and dark
- sweet chilli sauce
- wine vinegar
- sesame oil
- balsamic vinegar
- instant stock powder
- onions
- garlic
- potatoes
- salt and pepper
- basil
- thyme
- oregano
- marjoram
- paprika
- chilli powder
- curry powder
- ground cumin
- ground coriander
- cinnamon
- mixed spice
- vanilla essence

FRIDGE/FREEZER

eggs
mustard
tomato sauce
cheese
butter
frozen peas
frozen spinach

Eating well

As well as tasting and looking good, the food you eat should be good for you, keeping you healthy, strong, and in peak condition. It is really important to eat a good variety of foods. A wide range of foods in your diet keeps it interesting and well balanced, as nutrients that one food lacks are supplied by others.

Although you do not need to know the details of all the foods you eat, knowing a little about the four main food groups, and choosing foods from each group, each day, will ensure your diet is well balanced.

FRUITS & VEGETABLES
Make sure you have five servings (or more!) each day. Eat salads, cooked and canned vegetables, vegetable-based main courses, and canned fruit. Fresh fruit and dried fruit make good snacks.

BREADS & GRAINS
Each day, eat at least six servings of grain-based foods such as bread (1 slice is 1 serving), breakfast cereal, pasta, rice, couscous, and kibbled grains. (Include some whole-grain products.)

MILK & DAIRY PRODUCTS
Select at least two servings a day. Look for reduced-fat milk, yoghurt, cottage cheese, cheese, etc. (Vegans can replace milk with soy milk fortified with calcium and Vitamin B12.)

EGGS, NUTS, SEEDS AND DRIED BEANS, PEAS & LENTILS
Choose at least one serving a day from this group. Nuts and seeds make good snacks. (Non-vegetarians include meat, fish and poultry in this group, too.)

When you plan your daily food, remember that it is important not to eat too much fat, sugar and salt.

Keep a healthy weight with regular exercise as well as healthy eating.

Introduction

We find it hard to believe, but it is almost 25 years since we started work on our first vegetarian book, *Meals without Meat*.

While we were always confident that we would produce a good useful book that would be popular with Simon's student peers, the market beyond this was something of an unknown and it always seemed a slightly risky proposition.

We needn't have worried, as *Meals without Meat* was reprinted more than ten times over the next 20 years and has sold more than 250,000 copies – and we still get enquiries from people trying to get hold of copies!

It is always nice to get feedback on our books, and over the years we've had plenty of positive comments about *Meals without Meat* (and its subsequent companion volumes *Meals without Red Meat* and *Very Easy Vegetarian*). Not surprisingly, they've been very popular with vegetarians, but perhaps the most pleasing comments have been from those people who are not necessarily vegetarian themselves but are cooking for the family and a vegetarian family member. In these cases we're often told of the appeal of the recipes to the whole family, not just the vegetarian family members.

Likewise, we've also had lots of positive feedback from non-vegetarians who, for various reasons, are trying to eat meat less frequently.

The Ultimate Vegetarian Collection contains not only our favourite recipes from *Meals without Meat*, *Meals without Red Meat* and *Very Easy Vegetarian*, but also draws together our vegetarian recipes from our other books, magazine and newspaper columns. We think it looks great and has a nice fresh feel, but most importantly it sticks to the same 'basic recipe' we have used in all our books. Most of the recipes are reasonably simple, affordable and use only ingredients you will be able to find at your local supermarket. We've also tried to cover all occasions, from breakfasts and brunches, and quick after-work week-night meals to more elaborate dishes for entertaining, and also some sweet treats, desserts and baking because they're always nice to have.

We hope *The Ultimate Vegetarian Collection* will become the 'go to' book for a new generation.

Happy cooking!

ALISON HOLST & SIMON HOLST

When Alison was a child, she was taught that breakfast was the most important meal of the day, and without it she would not produce good work at school.

If you feel 'breakfast is boring' look at the following recipes. Your mouth will water once you see these interesting and delicious breakfasts. There are egg dishes, which can be made in less than five minutes, delicious smoothies, and when mornings are wintery, there are substantial cereal dishes to 'warm the cockles of your heart'.

Breakfasts

Bircher muesli plus

----

*This embellished Bircher muesli is really delicious!
It is the ideal breakfast food as it can be prepared
the night before.*

SERVES 2–3:

¼ cup whole unblanched almonds
¼ cup dried apricots
¼ cup sultanas (optional)
½ cup rolled oats, fine or regular
1 cup (or 2 x 150g pottles) natural or fruit-flavoured
   yoghurt
1 unpeeled apple
milk or fruit juice to thin (if required)

Roughly chop the almonds, apricots and sultanas either
by hand or in a food processor, then place in a medium-
sized bowl. Stir in the rolled oats and yoghurt. Coarsely
grate the apple, discarding the core, then add (with any
resulting juice) to the mixture and stir to combine.

   Leave to stand for 10–15 minutes (this allows the oats
to soften), or cover and refrigerate for up to 24 hours,
then thin to the desired consistency with milk or fruit
juice before serving.

VARIATIONS: *You can make almost limitless
variations on this simple theme using different nuts
(try walnuts, pecans or hazelnuts), dried fruit and
flavoured yoghurt combinations. Try using plain
unsweetened yoghurt and serving drizzled with a
little runny honey. The muesli looks particularly good
sprinkled with fresh berries.*

Swiss-style Bircher muesli

----

*This simple mix-in-a-bowl combination makes a
quick and easy meal.*

SERVES 1:

3 tablespoons rolled oats
3 tablespoons boiling water
1 tablespoon lemon juice
1 tablespoon sweetened condensed milk
1–2 tablespoons chopped or flaked nuts
1 unpeeled apple, grated (or other fresh fruit, sliced or
   chopped)

Measure the oats into a cereal bowl, and pour on the
boiling water. Leave to stand while you prepare the
other ingredients. Fold everything else into the oats and
eat immediately.

Swiss-style Bircher muesli

Mixed-grain apple porridge

SERVES 2:

3 tablespoons wholegrain rolled oats

3 tablespoons kibbled wheat or
 kibbled rye

3 tablespoons wheatgerm or
 wheatbran

3 tablespoons chopped dried apple

3 teaspoons cinnamon sugar (see
 page 14)

1¾ cups hot water

pinch of salt

Keep a selection of kibbled and flaked grains in jars, to make a quick and easy mixed-grain porridge.

Combine the cereals, apple and cinnamon sugar in a microwave-proof jug or deep bowl. Pour in the hot water, add the salt, and stir to mix. Microwave on High (100%) for 4–5 minutes, stirring after 1 and 3 minutes, or simmer on the stovetop for 5–10 minutes, until the porridge has a grainy texture.

Serve with milk or plain or fruity yoghurt.

Warm crunchy cereal

SERVES 2:

½ cup wholegrain rolled oats

2 tablespoons pumpkin or sunflower
 seeds

1–2 tablespoons chopped dried
 apricots

1–2 tablespoons chopped or flaked
 almonds

1–2 tablespoons sultanas

1½ cups hot water

Cooked seeds, dried fruit and nuts give this nutritious cereal a pleasant, slightly crunchy texture. Good at any time of the day!

Put the rolled oats, seeds, dried apricots, almonds and sultanas into a microwave-proof jug or deep bowl, or into a saucepan on the stove. Pour in the hot water and stir to mix well. Microwave on High (100%) for 4–5 minutes, stirring after 1 and 3 minutes; or simmer on the stovetop for 5–10 minutes, until the porridge is the texture you like. Stir before serving, adding a little extra water if it is too thick.

Serve warm rather than very hot, with milk, yoghurt and sliced bananas. Add a little sugar or golden syrup if you like.

Fruity porridge

SERVES 2–3:

1 cup rolled oats

¼ cup sultanas, chopped

¼ cup walnuts or pecans, chopped

3–4 tablespoons chopped dried apricots or mango

1 tablespoon wheatgerm (optional)

1¼ cups hot water

1 cup reduced-fat milk

¼ teaspoon cinnamon

pinch of salt

Adding extras such as dried fruit and nuts will transform porridge into an exciting and appealing breakfast.

In the microwave, combine all the ingredients in a 1–2 litre microwave-proof bowl. Microwave on High (100%) for 2 minutes, stir, then cook for a further 2 minutes on Medium (50%).

If you are using the stovetop, stir all the ingredients together in a medium-sized pot. Heat until boiling, stirring continuously, then reduce the heat and simmer for 2–3 minutes until thick.

Spoon into bowls and serve with milk and drizzled with honey or sprinkled with brown sugar and/or some additional chopped fruit and nuts.

Mixed-grain apple porridge and Warm crunchy cereal

Crunchy toasted muesli

SERVES 12–16:

2 cups wholegrain rolled oats

¼ cup wheatgerm

¼ cup oatbran

¼ cup fine or medium desiccated
   coconut

¼ cup pumpkin seeds

¼ cup sunflower seeds

¼ cup sliced almonds

¼ cup honey

1 tablespoon sugar

¼ teaspoon salt

1 tablespoon water

2 tablespoons canola or other light
   vegetable oil

½ cup chopped dried fruit (apricots,
   apples, pears, sultanas, raisins)

This muesli contains many 'goodies', has the right amount of crunch and tastes great!

Preheat the oven to 150°C. Mix the cereals, coconut, seeds and almonds together in a large bowl. Heat together the honey, sugar, salt, water and oil in a saucepan or microwave-proof dish, stirring occasionally, until the sugar has dissolved. Pour the hot liquid over the dry mixture in the bowl and stir to mix.

In the microwave, spread the mixture on a microwave turntable, leaving the centre uncovered. Microwave uncovered, on High (100%) for 6–10 minutes, or until lightly browned, checking after about 4 minutes and turning if necessary, to make sure the mixture is browning evenly.

If you're using the oven, spread the mixture in a large, shallow baking pan and bake for 20 minutes or until lightly browned. Stir if the edges darken.

Add the dried fruits. Cool and store in an airtight container.

Serve with fresh or stewed fruit and yoghurt or milk.

Tasty & light cranapple muesli

SERVES 8–12:

2 tablespoons canola oil

¼ cup honey

1 teaspoon cinnamon

2 cups puffed corn or puffed wheat

2 cups puffed rice or rice bubbles

2 cups cornflakes

1 cup extruded bran

½ cup shredded coconut (optional)

¼ cup wheatgerm

¼ cup sliced almonds

¼ cup pumpkin seeds

½ cup dried apple, chopped

½ cup dried cranberries, chopped

Sometimes it's hard to find exactly the right breakfast cereal: some are too light; and others, like toasted mueslis, can seem like too much hard work. This is somewhere in between!

Preheat the oven to 150°C. Measure the oil and honey together in a small bowl or saucepan and heat until easily pourable, then stir in the cinnamon.

Measure all the remaining ingredients except the dried apple and cranberries into a large roasting dish and stir to combine. Drizzle in the honey mixture and stir thoroughly again.

Place in the oven and bake for 12–15 minutes, removing and stirring thoroughly every 4–5 minutes, then remove from the oven. Stir in the dried apple and cranberries, then leave until completely cool before packing into an airtight container.

Serve with milk and/or yoghurt and fruit.

Microwave muesli

SERVES 12–16:

½ cup honey

¼ cup brown sugar

¼ cup oil

1 teaspoon cinnamon

1 teaspoon vanilla

½ teaspoon salt

3 cups whole grain oats

½ cup oat or wheat bran

½ cup coconut

½ cup wheatgerm

½ cup chopped nuts

This is, without a doubt, the easiest toasted muesli ever!

Mix the honey, brown sugar, oil, cinnamon, vanilla and salt in a microwave-proof bowl. Heat on High (100%) until the mixture bubbles, about 2 minutes.

Meanwhile, combine the remaining ingredients in a large, wide, shallow microwave-proof dish. Stir in the hot mixture.

Cook on High, stirring every minute after 4 minutes, until the mixture turns golden brown and starts to firm up, 6–10 minutes in total. Allow to cool. Break up if necessary.

VARIATIONS: *Heat the first six ingredients in a saucepan until the mixture bubbles. Combine with the rest of the ingredients and bake in a roasting pan at 150°C, stirring frequently until it browns lightly, about 30 minutes, or brown in a large shallow dish under a grill, turning frequently.*

Pain perdu

Pain perdu

- -

Stale bread dipped in an orange-flavoured custard mixture, then cooked gently on a hot surface until it has puffed up and is golden brown – a wonderful variation on French toast!

Place all ingredients except the French bread in a bowl, and whisk until well mixed. Place the bread in a large, shallow dish and cover with the egg mixture. Leave for 20–30 minutes, turning occasionally.

Heat a little butter in a large frying pan. Add the bread and cook over low heat for 5–10 minutes each side, turning when golden brown.

Serve immediately, topped with berries, a dusting of icing sugar, and a trickle of maple syrup, or serve with jam or jelly.

SERVES 4:

2 eggs
½ cup milk
2 tablespoons orange juice
1 teaspoon grated orange rind
2 tablespoons sugar
1 teaspoon vanilla
pinch of salt
1 tablespoon orange liqueur (optional)
8 slices French bread, cut diagonally, 1cm thick

French toast

- -

Even the most uninteresting stale slices of bread take on new life when dipped in an eggy mixture, then browned in a hot pan with a little butter.

Beat the egg together with the milk, orange juice or white wine until well mixed, but not frothy. Dip slices of bread into this mixture, turning to moisten both sides. Leave the coated bread slices to stand on a flat plate or tray for several minutes before cooking in a moderately hot frying pan, allowing about half a teaspoon of butter for each side. Cook long enough to brown evenly on both sides.

Serve hot, with honey, maple syrup or golden syrup, jam or jelly, and bananas, if you like sweet accompaniments. For savoury accompaniments, serve with grilled tomatoes, sautéed mushrooms, creamed corn, etc.

SERVES 1:

1 egg
1 tablespoon milk, orange juice or white wine
bread, fresh or stale, sliced*

* If using French bread, slice it diagonally.

Oaty pancakes

Even people who usually turn up their noses at rolled oats or porridge can't get enough of these pancakes, which contain a generous amount of those same oats!

SERVES 3-4:

¼ **cup milk**
¾ **cup rolled oats**
1 egg
½ **teaspoon salt**
2-3 tablespoons sugar
½ **cup self-raising flour**
25g butter, melted

Pour the milk over the rolled oats in a large mixing bowl (or food processor), add the rest of the ingredients and mix with a fork or process just enough to combine.

Lightly butter a frying pan or griddle (or spray with non-stick oil). Heat to a medium heat (180°C), or until a drop of water on the heated surface breaks up into several droplets that dance around. Spoon the batter onto the heated surface and cook until bubbles form and burst on the surface of the pancake. Slide a thin blade under the pancake and flip it over. Cook the second side until the centre springs back when pressed. Adjust the heat if necessary, until pancakes are golden when these stages are reached.

Stack several hot pancakes on a warmed plate, top with a little butter (so that it melts over the pancakes) and serve with maple syrup or golden syrup or honey.

Breakfast toppings for toast

A piece of toast spread with something tasty is a very useful snack at any time of the day or night. Some of these toppings can be made on the spot. Others may be prepared in the weekend and kept until you want a very easy snack. For variety, keep a selection of different sliced breads and split rolls in the freezer, toasting them from frozen if necessary.

Crunchy cashew butter

Warm 1 cup of roasted cashew nuts in a microwave or regular oven, then process in a food processor or blender with 2 tablespoons of olive, canola, or other oil. Spread generously on unbuttered toast. Eat like this or top with fresh pear slices.

VARIATION: *Use roasted (but never raw) peanuts or other nuts to make other flavourful nut butters.*

Peanut honey

Make crunchy peanut butter replacing the cashew nuts in Crunchy Cashew Butter with peanuts. Add about 2 tablespoons of honey to the warm nut mixture. Process until blended. Spread lavishly on warm, unbuttered toast and top with slices of crisp apple, pear or banana. Peanut Honey can be kept in a jar at room temperature for several weeks.

Chocolate hazelnut spread

Bake 1 cup hazelnuts at 180°C for about 10 minutes, or until the nut flesh is very lightly browned, then rub the nuts in a teatowel to remove their skins. While still hot, place the nuts in food processor with 2 tablespoons of caster sugar and mix until finely chopped.

In a saucepan, melt 100g cooking chocolate with 2 tablespoons canola or other light oil, taking care not to overheat. Add to the nuts and process until fairly smooth.

Spread thickly on unbuttered toast and top with slices of banana.

This spread will keep several weeks at room temperature.

NOTE: *Add more oil for a thinner spread. Try it with other nuts, too.*

Tutti-frutti spread

Heat ½ cup Fruit Medley in ¼ cup orange juice in the microwave for 2 minutes on High (100%). Stir in 2 tea-spoons sugar and cook 1 minute longer.

Stir in ½ cup of cream cheese, and ¼ cup chopped, roasted cashew nuts or almonds if you like. Serve on toasted bagels or bread. It can keep in the fridge up to 1 week.

NOTE: *You can buy fruit medley from the bulk foods department of some supermarkets. It contains chopped, dried apples, pears, peaches, raisins, and sultanas.*

Cinnamon sugar

Shake together in a screw-top jar ¼ cup brown sugar, ¼ cup white sugar and 1 tablespoon cinnamon. Sprinkle on hot buttered toast, plain, or spread with sliced bananas. Eat as is, or heat under grill until bubbly.

This keeps for a couple of months in an airtight jar.

Oaty pancakes

Blueberry pancakes

Blueberry pancakes

- -

SERVES 3–4:

1 cup milk
1 large egg
2 tablespoons canola oil
1½ cups self-raising flour
¼ cup sugar
pinch of salt
1 cup fresh or frozen blueberries

If you're not in a rush, what better way to start the day than with a pile of freshly made blueberry pancakes. Not only are they delicious, but blueberries are high in antioxidants.

Preheat the oven to a low heat (to keep cooked pancakes warm). Place the milk, egg and oil in a medium-sized bowl or large jug and whisk until smooth. Sprinkle in the flour, sugar and salt and mix gently until smooth. Add the blueberries and stir in gently.

Heat a large non-stick frying pan or griddle over medium heat. When the pan has heated, spray it lightly with non-stick spray. Carefully pour 2–3 quarter-cup 'lots' of the mixture into the pan and cook until bubbles form and burst on the upper side of the pancake, then carefully turn and cook until the second side is golden brown.

Stack the cooked pancakes on plates in a warm oven. (Place about a teaspoon of butter between each pancake as you stack them if you like.)

Repeat the cooking process until the mixture is all used, adjusting the heat of the pan as required.

Serve drizzled with maple syrup and with a fresh fruit salad or sliced banana if desired.

Pineapple waffles

- -

SERVES 3–4:

2 tablespoons butter
2 tablespoons sugar
1 egg
¼ cup milk
225g can crushed pineapple
**   (undrained)**
1 cup self-raising flour

This waffle mixture may also be cooked as pancakes or pikelets.

Melt the butter in a large bowl. Add the sugar, egg, milk and the contents of the can of pineapple. Beat lightly with a fork to combine all the ingredients. Fold in the flour, mixing just enough to combine – do not overmix. Heat a waffle iron according to the manufacturer's instructions. Spray with non-stick spray. Pour the batter into the prepared iron. Close the lid and cook at a moderate heat for 4–5 minutes, until evenly cooked and golden brown. (Cook longer at a lower temperature for crisper waffles.)

Serve warm or hot, plain or with fresh fruit and a dusting of icing sugar, with flavoured yoghurt or whipped cream.

Huevos rancheros

In the south-west of the United States and in Mexico this delicious dish is served for breakfast. It may sound unusual but it really does work well for something a little different for breakfast or brunch (or a light meal at any time of the day!).

Heat the oil in a large non-stick pan. Add the onion and garlic and cook, stirring frequently, for about 5 minutes until the onion is soft and clear. Add the spices and oregano and cook for about a minute longer, then stir in the tomatoes (break up whole tomatoes if necessary).

Simmer the tomato mixture for about 5 minutes, then season to taste with salt. Make 3 or 4 depressions in the tomato mixture, then carefully break an egg into each. Cover the pan and simmer gently for 3–5 minutes longer or until the eggs are as cooked as you like them. Remove the pan from the heat and sprinkle in the chopped coriander.

Spoon the eggs and sauce on to plates and serve immediately with the warmed tortillas on the side.

NOTES: *You can prepare the sauce in advance (the night before) then just heat it up again before adding the eggs.*

If you are catering for a larger group, make double the sauce mixture, pour it into an oven dish, add the eggs and bake in an oven preheated to 180°C until the eggs are cooked.

SERVES 3–4:

1 tablespoon olive oil or canola oil
1 medium onion, finely diced
1 clove garlic, crushed, peeled and chopped
1 teaspoon ground cumin
¼–½ teaspoon chilli powder, to taste
½ teaspoon oregano
400g can whole or diced tomatoes in juice
¼–½ teaspoon salt
3–4 eggs
2–3 tablespoons chopped coriander
3–6 flour tortillas, warmed

Huevos rancheros

Scrambled eggs

- -

SERVES 1:

1 teaspoon butter
1 egg
2 tablespoons milk
salt, freshly ground black pepper and
   fresh herbs

Scrambled eggs make a really fast meal, cooked in a pan or the microwave. We've given quantities for one serving here; you can multiply the recipe as required.

In the microwave: Melt the butter in a small microwave-proof bowl. Add the remaining ingredients, beat with a fork to mix the egg white and yolk, then microwave on High (100%) for 60–80 seconds, or until the mixture puffs, stirring after 30 seconds. Leave to stand for 30 seconds before serving.

On the stovetop: Melt the butter in a small frying pan or saucepan. Lightly mix the remaining ingredients and pour the mixture into the pan. Cook over moderate heat, running a small spatula or fish slice along the bottom of the pan to push the cooked mixture aside. Remove from the heat just before the last bit of egg sets. Serve on toast, bagels or fresh bread.

Hash browns

- -

SERVES 4–6:

600g floury or all-purpose potatoes
2–3 tablespoons oil or butter

Homemade hash browns and 'easy over' fried eggs, cooked on a large hotplate – just the best!

Boil or microwave as many large, floury potatoes as required until they are just tender (it's not necessary to peel them first). Refrigerate for at least 8 hours, then grate coarsely.

Heat a large frying pan with just enough butter to form a film. When the butter is a light straw colour, spoon in the grated potatoes. Fill the pan to form a layer of potato about 2cm thick. Pat down evenly with a fish slice so it forms a large, flat-topped cake. Brown over moderate heat for 10–15 minutes or until a crisp golden-brown crust forms underneath.

Slide the potato cake onto a plate, then flip it back into the pan, un-cooked side down. Add a little extra butter down the sides of the pan and cook until crisp underneath. Remove from the pan and cut into wedges.

Serve with tomatoes and/or mushrooms. Also good served with barbe-cued mushrooms and/or tomatoes and a green salad.

VARIATIONS: Cook the hash browns on a preheated, solid barbecue plate which has had a little oil drizzled onto it first.

Make individual hash browns – cook these in an electric frypan.

Smoothies

These smoothies have delicious fresh flavours, contain virtually no fat and yet are high in calcium, fibre and other 'goodies'. They are more substantial than you'd expect and make an excellent light meal on the run.

There are very few 'hard and fast' rules to smoothie making. You can use many different combinations of fruit. Try cubed fresh pineapple, sliced mango, peaches, nectarines, strawberries, raspberries or gold kiwifruit – or combinations of these – in place of the fruits suggested below.

For extra flavour variations, try adding a teaspoon of vanilla essence or, for something really different, a little grated fresh ginger really gives things a lift! For something more decadent, use ice cream in place of yoghurt.

Blueberry & banana smoothie

The berries give this an amazing colour.

SERVES 2:

1 medium banana
1 cup frozen (or fresh) blueberries
½ cup plain or fruit-flavoured low-fat yoghurt
3 dessertspoons honey
1 cup reduced-fat milk

Break the peeled banana into 3 or 4 pieces and place in a blender or food processor with the blueberries, yoghurt and honey. Process until smooth.

Add the milk and whiz again just enough to make a thick smooth drink (try to avoid processing for too long or you will crush up the blueberry seeds, making the drink gritty).

Pour into glasses and enjoy!

Zippy kiwi smoothie

A little fresh ginger makes this really refreshing.

SERVES 2:

1 medium banana
4 ice cubes (optional)
½ cup plain unsweetened low-fat yoghurt
2–3 dessertspoons honey
3 medium green kiwifruit
1 cup reduced-fat milk
1–2 teaspoons finely grated ginger

Peel the banana, break into 3 or 4 pieces and put into a blender or food processor. Add the ice cubes (if using), yoghurt and honey. Process until smooth.

Thinly peel the kiwifruit, then cut into quarters or chunks and add to the blender with the milk and grated ginger. Whiz again just enough to make a thick smooth drink (don't blend for too long after you've added the kiwifruit or you will crush up the seeds, making the drink unpleasantly gritty).

Pour into two tall glasses and enjoy!

Tofu shake

Here's a nutritious meal in a glass that is almost as quick to make as it is to drink!

SERVES 2:

125g tofu
1 banana
2 tablespoons brown sugar
1 cup orange juice or milk
½ teaspoon vanilla essence

Put the tofu and pieces of banana in a blender or food processor and process until well mixed. Add the sugar, orange juice or milk, and vanilla. Process again until the mixture is smooth and creamy.

Pour into one very large glass, or two medium-sized glasses. Serve with thick straws and/or long-handled spoons.

Orange Julia

Serve this as a 'breakfast in a glass'.

SERVES 1:

4 ice cubes
1 cup orange juice
½ cup skim milk powder
½ teaspoon vanilla essence
1–2 teaspoons sugar or honey

Process the ice cubes in a food processor (the loud noise will only last a few seconds). When the ice is chopped, and before it melts, add the orange juice, milk powder, vanilla essence and sugar or honey to taste and process until really frothy.

Serve immediately with a thick straw.

Although you may find some of these snacks and dips on the shelves in delis or supermarkets, the finger food & snacks that we have made over the years always seem to have more flavour than something similar in a jar which has travelled from the other side of the world.

Produce several of these tasty finger foods & snacks when you have friends for a drink, or make two or three different starters before your main course to impress your guests.

Finger foods & snacks

Pumpkin & peanut hummus (at back) and Hummus

Hummus

- -

Good old hummus is a delicious and versatile mixture. Served with vegetable crudités and wedges of pita bread it makes a delicious snack or light meal.

Use plain hummus or, if you feel like something a little different, try the Pumpkin & peanut version.

MAKES 1½ CUPS:

1 large clove garlic
300–400g can chickpeas, rinsed and drained*
2 tablespoons tahini
2 tablespoons lemon juice
2–3 tablespoons olive oil
¼–½ teaspoon salt
water to thin (if required)

Place the garlic and chickpeas in a blender or food processor, fitted with a metal chopping blade, and process until finely chopped. Add the tahini and lemon juice. Process until evenly mixed, then add 2 tablespoons of the oil and ¼ teaspoon of salt. Process until very smooth, stopping once or twice to scrape down the sides and adding the extra oil and/or water to thin to the desired consistency, if required. Taste and add a little extra salt if needed.

Serve immediately with warmed pita wedges, crackers and/or vegetable crudités (carrot, cucumber, celery and cauliflower), or transfer to an airtight container and store in the fridge for up to 1 week.

*Simon likes the convenience of canned chickpeas or beans, while Alison likes to start from scratch and cook her own. If you want to do this, use 1 cup dried chickpeas or other dried white beans, cover them with boiling water, leave to stand until nearly tender (1½–2 hours), add salt, then boil until completely tender. Drain, then proceed as above.

Pumpkin & peanut hummus

ingredients as above, except tahini
100g pumpkin, peeled and cubed
2 tablespoons peanut butter
¼ teaspoon curry powder

Place pumpkin in a small microwave-proof bowl, cover and microwave on High (100%) for 2 minutes. Add the cooked pumpkin to the food processor with the chickpeas and garlic. Replace the tahini with 2 tablespoons of peanut butter and, for a slight twist, add ¼ teaspoon curry powder as well, then proceed with the remaining ingredients and method described above.

Baba Ghanoush

This is a tasty Mediterranean dip made from aubergine.
Serve it with wedges of warmed pita bread or vegetable crudités, or as part of a mezze platter with some marinated feta and olives on the side.

MAKES 1½ CUPS:

1 medium aubergine (300–400g)
1 medium-large clove garlic, peeled
2–3 tablespoons lemon juice
2 tablespoons tahini
3–4 tablespoons olive oil
about ½ teaspoon salt

Prick the aubergine with a skewer in several places, then microwave it whole on high (100%) for 4–5 minutes, turning it over after 2 minutes, until it is soft and wrinkly. (Alternatively, place the aubergine in an oven preheated to 180°C and bake for 35–45 minutes, until soft and wrinkly.)

Once the aubergine is cool enough to handle, place on a chopping board, cut in half and scrape the flesh out of the skin. Place the flesh in a food processor, add the garlic, lemon juice and tahini and process until smooth.

With the motor running, drizzle in the olive oil and add the salt. Stop the processor, taste the mixture and add a little more salt if required.

Serve immediately, or transfer to an airtight container and refrigerate for up to 1 week.

Baba Ghanoush

Quick tapenade

This mixture has a very strong, concentrated colour, which varies depending on the colour of the olives used.

MAKES ¾ CUP:

1 cup black olives, pitted and sliced
2–4 cloves garlic, peeled
1 tablespoon capers
1 tablespoon caper liquid
1 tablespoon lemon or lime juice
2–3 tablespoons olive oil

In a food processor, finely chop (but do not purée) all ingredients, except the olive oil.

Add 2 tablespoons of the oil to the mixture, then spoon it into a jar, pour the remaining oil over the top, and close with a screw-top lid to form an airtight seal.

Use tapenade as a spread, toss through pasta with additional olive oil or pesto, or add to dressings and dips.

Store in the fridge for up to 1 month.

Alison's dukkah

A highly flavoured mixture of nuts and spices, served in shallow bowls. Dip pieces of good, firm, crusty bread in olive oil, then in dukkah, as a snack or a light meal.

MAKES 2¼ CUPS:

½ cup sesame seeds
½ cup sunflower seeds
½ cup pumpkin seeds
¼ cup cumin seeds
¼ cup coriander seeds
1 cup blanched almonds
1½ teaspoons rock salt
1 tablespoon ground paprika
1½ teaspoons ground turmeric

Heat the oven to 180°C. Put the seeds and almonds in to roast, in separate foil dishes or pie plates, in the order given; the first few ingredients take longer than those listed last. (As a guide, most will take about 10 minutes, but sesame and sunflower seeds may take 5 or so minutes longer.) Watch carefully, checking them at least every 5 minutes, and take out each container when the seeds have darkened a little (but not a lot) and have an appetising aroma.

Leave to cool, then grind in a food processor with the rock salt, paprika and turmeric, in one or two batches, using the pulse button. The final mixture should have a grainy texture – it should not be an oily powder.

Store in airtight jars in a cool cupboard. Although it will gradually lose some flavour on long storage, it will taste very good for 3 months.

NOTE: *Dukkah is delicious used in this way. It also makes a very easy last-minute flavouring for salads, soups, and plainly cooked vegetables. You can use it for a couple of months after it is initially made.*

Tzatziki

There is something cooling and soothing about the flavour of cucumber, so it is easy to understand how this smooth and creamy mixture evolved under the hot Mediterranean sun.

The combination of cucumber and yoghurt just seems to crop up again and again, so it's not surprising that tzatziki, despite its simple combination of grated cucumber and yoghurt, with a little garlic thrown in for good measure, is so good.

MAKES 1½ CUPS:

about ½ medium telegraph cucumber
1 cup thick unsweetened Greek-style yoghurt
1 large clove garlic, crushed, peeled and chopped
½ teaspoon salt
extra virgin olive oil to drizzle (optional)

Halve the cucumber lengthwise, then scrape out and discard the seeds using a teaspoon. Coarsely grate the cucumber flesh and squeeze gently to get rid of any excess liquid.

Combine the yoghurt, cucumber, garlic and salt in a medium-sized bowl. Stir gently to combine and it's ready to serve. The creamy white flecked with darker green mix looks – and tastes – good drizzled with extra virgin olive oil, if desired.

Serve the tzatziki as a dip or a spread with warmed pita or crusty bread, or with carrot and celery sticks.

Easy salsa fresca

MAKES 1½ CUPS:

¼ red onion or 2 spring onions
1 large clove garlic
1–2 tablespoons pickled jalapeno
    peppers
1 tablespoon liquid from jar of
    jalapeno peppers
½ teaspoon ground cumin
½ teaspoon dried oregano
400g can whole tomatoes in juice
    or 4 large fresh red tomatoes,
    roughly chopped
½–1 teaspoon salt
½–1 teaspoon sugar
2–3 tablespoons chopped coriander
    leaves (optional)

This fresh-tasting salsa is best the day it's made, but can be refrigerated for up to 3 days.

Chop the onion or spring onions, garlic, jalapenos and liquid, cumin and oregano in a food processor. (Use more peppers for extra hotness.) Add the tomatoes and process until mixed but still chunky. Add salt and sugar to taste (fresh tomatoes will need more than canned tomatoes) and add coriander leaves, if using.

Leave to sit for half an hour before using.

Use as a dip with corn chips, mix with mashed avocado to make an easy guacamole, or spoon over poached eggs (Alison's favourite!) and Mexican food.

NOTE: *Chop vegetables by hand if you don't have a food processor.*

Easy guacamole

MAKES ABOUT 1 CUP:

1 ripe avocado
2 tablespoons lemon juice
1 clove garlic, chopped
1 spring onion, finely chopped
¼ teaspoon salt
Tabasco sauce (optional)
chopped coriander leaves (optional)

This perennial favourite takes mere minutes to make.

Cut around the centre of the avocado lengthwise, then gently twist the two halves apart. Chop a sharp knife into the stone and twist it to remove the stone.

Spoon the flesh into a bowl. Mash with a fork, and add the remaining ingredients, using quantities to suit your taste.

Use immediately or cover with cling film, touching the surface, and leave for no longer than 1 hour before using.

Use as a dip with corn chips, as a topping for Mexican foods, crackers or crostini, and in other ways you like.

Good old onion dip

MAKES 1 CUP:

1 packet (about 55g) onion soup
250g low-fat or regular sour cream

Classic dips like this are quick, easy and still very popular.

Stir the soup mix and sour cream together with a fork until no lumps of powder remain. Leave to stand for at least half an hour, until the pieces of onion soften.

Use straight away or cover and refrigerate for up to 2 days, thinning with milk or yoghurt if necessary.

Serve with a colourful selection of crisp, cold vegetable crudités. Suitable vegetables include carrots, celery, red and green capsicums, cauliflower, young green beans, button mushrooms, radishes, daikon, young turnips, tender asparagus heads and snowpeas. To crisp vegetables, wash, cut up as desired, rinse with cold water, then refrigerate in sealed plastic bags until required.

VARIATIONS: *Replace half or more of the sour cream with plain, unsweetened yoghurt. Stir one or more of the following into the dip: chopped chives, spring onions, parsley or other fresh herbs, curry powder or paste, pesto, finely chopped walnuts, chopped roasted peanuts, chutney or Tabasco sauce.*

Easy salsa fresca, Easy guacamole, Good old onion dip

Green bean dip

MAKES 1½–2 CUPS:

500g green beans
3 hard-boiled eggs
½ cup cream cheese
1 small green capsicum, diced
1 teaspoon each: onion, garlic and
   mustard powder
1 teaspoon hot chilli sauce (or to taste)
½ teaspoon ground cumin
1 teaspoon sugar and salt
juice of 1 lemon
freshly ground black pepper
2 spring onions, sliced

If you are a guacamole addict but are put off by the price of off-season avocados, try this recipe – it is surprisingly good!

Cook the beans until tender, then drain as much water from them as possible. Put the beans and hard-boiled eggs into a food processor or blender, and process until smooth. Add the remaining ingredients and process again until well mixed. Pour into a bowl and refrigerate until ready to serve.

Red lentil dip

MAKES 2½ CUPS:

1 cup red lentils
1½ cups boiling water
1 teaspoon canola or other oil
1 medium onion, finely chopped
1 clove garlic, finely chopped
1 teaspoon ground cumin
½ teaspoon smoked or plain paprika
¼ teaspoon ground turmeric
3 tablespoons olive or canola oil
1 tablespoon tomato paste
1 tablespoon lemon or lime juice
¾–1 teaspoon salt

This smooth and delicious mixture makes a great dip, an excellent spread for sandwiches, crusty bread and toast, or even an interesting topping for baked potatoes and kumara.

Put the lentils and boiling water in a medium-sized microwave-proof bowl, cover loosely and microwave on Medium (50%) for 12 minutes, stirring after 6 minutes. If any lentils still look red after 12 minutes, stir again and cook for 5 minutes longer, until lentils are yellowish and tender. All the liquid should be soaked up by this time.

While the lentils cook, heat the oil in a frying pan, add the onion and garlic and cook gently, stirring occasionally, for about 6 minutes, until the onions are straw-coloured. Turn off heat and stir in the spices.

Put the cooled lentils, onion and spice mixture, and the remaining ingredients into a blender or food processor and whiz until smooth. Leave to cool. If the mixture thickens a lot during this time, add ¼–½ cup of extra water and mix well. Refrigerate in covered containers if not using immediately, and serve as a dip or spread – it's particularly good used to 'stuff' celery sticks cut into short lengths.

Red lentil dip

Zesty red bean dip

This lively dip is made in just a few minutes.

Peel and roughly chop the garlic and onion. If using spring onions, cut stems and green leaves in 2cm lengths. Put into a food processor with the parsley, coriander leaves, cumin and pickled jalapeno slices. Chop finely, then clean the sides of the processor and add the lime or lemon juice, tomato paste and olive oil and process again, briefly.

Drain the bean liquid into a separate container, then add the drained beans to the food processor and process until mixed but not completely smooth. Add enough bean liquid to thin the dip to the consistency you like, then taste to see if it needs more seasoning. It may not need any – it depends on the seasoning of the beans and the jalapeno peppers. If it's bland, add a little salt and more lime or lemon juice, or more tomato paste. If it is too zesty, add enough sour cream to 'soften' the flavours.

Serve with corn chips, crisp vegetable strips or toasted wedges of flour tortillas. Refrigerate for up to 3 days.

MAKES 1¾ CUPS:

1 large clove garlic
¼ red onion or 2 spring onions
¼ cup roughly chopped parsley
2 tablespoons coriander leaves, roughly chopped
1 teaspoon ground cumin
2 teaspoons pickled jalapeno peppers, sliced
2 teaspoons lime (or lemon) juice
1 tablespoon tomato paste
2 tablespoons olive oil (optional)
400g can kidney beans
sour cream (if required)

Green pea guacamole

Make this surprisingly good, brilliant green, nearly instant dip with frozen peas from the freezer.

Put all the ingredients except the peas and olive oil in a food processor.

Partly thaw the peas and get rid of any ice by putting them in a sieve (in several batches) and running hot water over them.

Process the nearly thawed peas with the other ingredients until evenly chopped and fairly smooth, adding the oil while processing. Taste and add more flavourings if you want a more highly seasoned dip.

Use immediately as a dip for corn chips, potato chips, wedges or toasted pita bread, or spread on crostini, crisp crackers, etc., and eat straight away. Refrigerate leftovers in a covered container for up to 24 hours.

MAKES 2 CUPS:

¼ cup roughly chopped coriander leaves
1 tablespoon chopped pickled jalapeno peppers (from a jar)
1 tablespoon liquid from the jar of peppers
½ teaspoon ground cumin
1 teaspoon herb, onion or garlic salt
2 spring onions, roughly chopped
1 tablespoon lime or lemon juice
400–500g frozen peas (baby peas if possible)
about 3 tablespoons olive oil

Layered festive dip

This spectacular layered dip can be prepared a day ahead, without the avocado discolouring.

Cook the garlic, chilli powder, cumin, oregano and salt in the oil for about 1 minute. Add the baked beans and tomato paste, mashing well as the mixture heats through. Remove from the heat and leave to cool. Spread evenly in one or more straight-sided glass dishes.

Mash the avocado with the lemon juice and spread evenly over the bean mixture. Season the sour cream with hot chilli sauce, then spread over the avocado. Cover and refrigerate until required.

Just before serving, decorate the top with chopped coriander leaves, sliced, pitted black olives and/or finely sliced spring onions and a dribble of hot chilli sauce.

Serve with corn chips or Crostini (pages 34 and 61), scooping deep to get several layers.

VARIATION: Stir 1 cup of grated tasty cheese into the hot bean mixture.

SERVES 6:

2 cloves garlic, finely chopped
¼ teaspoon chilli powder
1 teaspoon each: ground cumin and dried oregano
¼ teaspoon salt
1 tablespoon oil
440g can baked beans
2 tablespoons tomato paste
1 or 2 avocados
3–4 tablespoons lemon juice
½–1 cup low-fat sour cream
hot chilli sauce, to taste
coriander leaves, black olives, spring onions and hot chilli sauce, to garnish

Blue cheese dip or ball

This tasty mixture has the flavour of blue cheese and the texture of cream cheese. Add more liquid to make a good dip.

MAKES ABOUT 2 CUPS:

100g blue vein cheese
1 cup (250g) cream cheese
1 small onion
1 tablespoon Worcestershire sauce
about ¼ cup medium sherry
flaked almonds, chopped walnuts, sesame or sunflower
  seeds (to coat the ball)

For the dip: Put all ingredients into a food processor with metal chopping blade. Break or cut the blue vein cheese into small cubes. Put the cream cheese in on top in dessertspoon-sized blobs. Cut the onion into eighths before adding, then add the Worcestershire sauce and sherry. Process until smooth, wiping down the sides of the bowl with a rubber spatula when necessary. Thin the mixture with more sherry, cream or milk, if necessary. The mixture always thickens on standing.

Alternatively, mash the blue vein cheese into a large bowl with a fork. Add the cream cheese and beat with a wooden spoon until smooth. Grate the onion, or cut in half and scrape the cut surface with a teaspoon to get onion pulp and juice. Add to the cheese with the Worcestershire sauce and sherry. Thin as desired with extra sherry or cream.

For the ball: Mix as above but use only 2 tablespoons sherry and no extra liquid. Tip the mixture out of the bowl onto a piece of cling film on which you have spread the seeds and nuts. Lifting up the edges of the cling film, roll the cheese mixture in its coating until it is the shape you want. Although a ball looks lovely the first time it is served, it is hard to serve attractively a second time. A sausage or log shape is more practical.

Mexican cheese & tomato dip

This spicy and delicious hot dip is particularly welcome in cold weather.

MAKES 2 CUPS:

1 medium-sized onion
1 green capsicum
1 tablespoon canola or other oil
1 teaspoon ground cumin
½ teaspoon ground coriander seeds
½ teaspoon paprika or smoked paprika (optional)
1 tablespoon pickled jalapeno peppers (from a jar),
  finely chopped
425g can chopped tomatoes
1 tablespoon flour
2 cups tasty cheese, grated
¼–½ cup low-fat sour cream
coriander leaves or spring onions, to garnish

Halve then peel the onion. Halve the capsicum, and remove and discard all seeds and pith. Chop both into small cubes (about 5mm). Heat the oil in a saucepan and add the onion and capsicum. Cook for 3–4 minutes, taking care not to let them brown. Stir in the spices and cook for 1 minute longer.

Add the finely chopped jalapeno peppers, and 1–2 teaspoons of the liquid in the jar if you like an extra 'tang' to this dip. Bring to the boil and add the tomatoes. (If you use a can of whole tomatoes, break them up first.)

Toss the flour through the grated cheese, then stir into the hot tomato mixture until melted and smooth. Do not bring the mixture to the boil after adding the cheese.

Serve hot, in a shallow dipping bowl, topped with sour cream and garnished with chopped coriander leaves or finely chopped spring onions. Serve surrounded by corn chips for dipping.

VARIATION: *Make this dip without the green capsicum if desired. It is still very good! Replace the ground coriander with the same quantity of dried oregano if you like.*

Hot cream cheese dip

This can also be a delicious hot dip spread on rolls or English muffins and reheated under a grill.

MAKES 1½ CUPS:

250g cream cheese
1 spring onion, finely sliced
1 clove garlic, finely chopped
1 tablespoon tomato sauce
5 drops (or more) Tabasco sauce
¼ cup cheese, grated
1 tomato, finely chopped (optional)
¼ green capsicum, finely chopped (optional)

Soften the cream cheese by beating it with a wooden spoon until it is easily workable, or warm it briefly in a microwave. Add the finely sliced spring onion and garlic, then the tomato sauce, Tabasco sauce and grated cheese. Stir in the finely chopped tomato and capsicum, if desired.

Microwave on High (100%) for 2–3 minutes, stirring after each minute, until the cheese melts and the mixture is hot and bubbling round the edges. Alternatively, put the mixture in a flameproof container and heat under a grill, stirring once or twice as the mixture warms, then leaving it to brown in parts on the surface.

Serve hot with corn chips, raw vegetables or sliced French bread.

Blue cheese dip or ball (top); Mexican cheese & tomato dip

Herbed cream cheese pâté

MAKES 1½–2 CUPS:

100g soft butter
2 garlic cloves, chopped
¼ teaspoon each: salt and sugar
freshly ground pepper
¼ cup chives, chopped
¼ cup parsley, chopped
2 teaspoons thyme leaves
1 cup (250g) cream cheese
2 tablespoons lemon juice
2 tablespoons milk

This pâté is good by itself, or as a spread with tomatoes or other vegetables. Experiment by adding fresh herbs or chopped capers.

Soften (but do not melt) the butter. In a food processor, blend the butter until creamy. Add the other ingredients one at a time, in the given order, beating after each addition.

Line small pots or moulds with cling film and fill with the mixture. Refrigerate until required. When ready to serve, tip the pâté out of the moulds onto the serving platter.

Mushroom & almond pâté

MAKES 1½ CUPS:

1 cup whole, unblanched almonds
2 tablespoons olive oil
1 medium onion, peeled and finely
   chopped
2 cloves garlic, crushed, peeled and
   chopped
150g brown button mushrooms, sliced
2 tablespoons chopped basil
¼ teaspoon dried thyme
½ teaspoon salt
¼ cup sherry

The flavours of the almonds, mushrooms and onion merge to produce something quite different, slightly unexpected and delicious.

Preheat the oven to 180°C. Spread the almonds on a sponge-roll tin and cook in the oven for 10–12 minutes or until they just begin to colour.

While the almonds cook, heat the oil in a medium frying pan. Add the onion and garlic and cook, stirring occasionally, until the onion is soft and clear, then add the mushrooms. Continue to cook, stirring frequently, for 2–3 minutes longer until the mushrooms have softened and wilted, then remove from the heat and stir in the herbs, salt and sherry.

Cool the cooked nuts for a few minutes, then tip them into a food processor fitted with a metal chopping blade. Process until the nuts are finely chopped (about the size of breadcrumbs), then add the mushroom and onion mixture. Process again until the mixture is smooth and creamy.

Serve immediately as you would any pâté, or transfer to an airtight container and store in the fridge for up to a week.

Mushroom & walnut pâté

MAKES 2 CUPS:

1½ cups green beans
2 hard-boiled eggs
1 tablespoon oil
1 medium-sized onion, diced
¼ cup walnuts, chopped
100g mushrooms, sliced
1 teaspoon salt
½ teaspoon freshly ground black
   pepper
2 tablespoons dry sherry

This pâté really looks the part! It makes an elegant and delicious pre-dinner savoury, and is equally good piled on toast or crackers for a quick snack.

Cook the beans until tender, then drain well, squeezing out any excess water. Roughly chop the eggs.

Heat the oil and sauté the onion until it begins to soften. Add the walnuts and mushrooms and cook until the walnuts have darkened and the mushrooms are soft. Put the beans, eggs and mushroom mixture into a blender or food processor (if using a blender, purée in small amounts). Process with the metal blade until smooth. Add the seasonings and sherry, mixing in well. Transfer the pâté to a bowl and refrigerate before serving.

Crostini

Crostini

- -

Make these ahead of time and store in an airtight container to have on hand when guests arrive.

1 loaf French bread
¼ cup olive oil
flavourings: parmesan, pesto, tapenade, Dijon mustard, ground cumin, Tabasco sauce, etc.

Slice the loaf of bread diagonally into 1cm slices. Mix the flavourings of your choice with the olive oil in a shallow bowl and brush or spread evenly over the sliced bread.

Arrange on a baking tray that has been lightly sprayed with oil or lined with a non-stick liner and bake at 150°C for 5–10 minutes until golden brown and crisp. When cold, store in airtight containers for up to a week, until needed.

Serve with soups, dips, pâtés or nibbles with drinks.

Melba toast

- -

Cut stale bread rolls or French bread into very thin slices using a sharp serrated knife. Bake at 150–180°C in one layer on an oven tray until the bread browns very slightly. Cooking time will vary with the type of bread, its thickness and its staleness. Start to check after 3–4 minutes.

When cold, store in airtight jars or plastic bags. Refresh for 10 minutes at 150°C before serving, if you like.

Crisped flat breads

- -

The growing number of flat breads on the market, including pita bread, various tortillas, Middle Eastern flat breads, Indian naan, and mountain bread make interesting and varied snacks.

Fresh or not quite so fresh, they may be left flat, cut into smaller pieces and baked, grilled or heated in a pan until crisp. They then make great dippers, or crisp edible small 'plates' on which other foods may be piled.

Thin flour tortillas make excellent crisps, cut into squares, rectangles or wedge shapes, or sometimes heated in large rounds, then broken into small pieces for dipping.

Brush both surfaces lightly but evenly with a little (olive) oil, then crisp using one of the following methods:

1. Heat in a heavy, dry, preheated pan, about 3–4 minutes per side, until there are darker flecks on each side. (The tortilla will become crisper as it cools on a rack).
2. Heat for about 3–4 minutes under a grill until golden brown, turning after 2 minutes.
3. Heat on an oven tray at 180°C for about 3–4 minutes, until evenly golden brown, without turning.

Cool on a rack.

Garlic bread

- -

Simply the best and most satisfying party food! Prepare ahead then bake just before serving.

1 loaf French bread
50g butter
2 cloves garlic, finely chopped
2–4 tablespoons parsley or other fresh herbs, finely chopped

Cut the loaf into diagonal 1cm slices, without cutting through the bottom crust, so the loaf holds together.

Soften (but do not melt) the butter, then add the chopped garlic and herbs and mix to combine.

Spread the flavoured butter on the cut slices of bread, wrap the loaf in aluminium foil, leaving the top exposed, and bake at 200°C for about 10 minutes, or at a lower temperature for longer, until the top is crisp and the loaf has heated right through.

Roasting nuts & seeds

- -

Roasting or toasting nuts and seeds really improves their flavour and often their texture also. Uncooked sesame seeds, for example, are virtually tasteless when compared with their toasted counterparts, which also have a more attractive colour and aroma. Sunflower seeds benefit greatly from roasting, which transforms them into a crisp and delicious snack or topping.

To dry-roast seeds and nuts, cook them over a low heat in a heavy-bottomed pan; or spread them evenly over a baking tray and cook them in an oven heated to 180°C; or toast under a preheated grill, keeping the pan about 15cm away, until they are golden brown. Don't try to cook too many at once: a single layer will always cook most evenly. It is important to shake or stir the nuts or seeds frequently, as overcooking or burning will spoil the flavour.

If cooking seeds or nuts in a microwave, add a little oil or butter, but not too much as this will make them oily and unpleasant. One teaspoon of oil is enough for 1 cup of nuts. Microwave on High (100%) for about 6 minutes.

You may need to use more oil for smaller seeds. For sesame seeds, use about 1 teaspoon of oil per ¼ cup of seeds, and microwave on High for 4–6 minutes. Stir frequently to avoid burning. Remember that cooking will continue for a few minutes after the seeds or nuts have been removed from the oven.

Allow the seeds or nuts to cool, then salt lightly (try a variety of flavoured salts) if desired. Toasted nuts or seeds will keep fresh for weeks in an airtight container. Try toasting a whole packet of sesame or sunflower seeds as soon as you buy them, so that they are ready on hand when you want them.

NOTE: *If microwaving, make sure that the container you select is microwave-proof and heat-resistant. Nuts and seeds get very hot and will melt some plastics.*

Chilli soy roasted almonds

Nuts make a great snack to enjoy with drinks, or at any time of the day. Roasted like this they contain a minimal amount of added fat – relax and enjoy!.

2 cups whole, unblanched almonds
4 teaspoons Kikkoman or other light soy sauce
1 tablespoon sesame oil
1 teaspoon hot chilli sauce

Preheat the oven to 160°C.

Measure the almonds into a medium-sized bowl, add the soy sauce, oil and chilli sauce, then stir to combine.

Allow the nuts to stand for a few minutes, then spread them on a sponge-roll pan lined with baking paper or a Teflon non-stick liner. Place them in the oven (just above the middle) and cook, stirring once or twice to prevent burning, for 10–12 minutes or until lightly browned and plump-looking.

Remove from the oven and cool before storing in an airtight container until required.

Spiced sugared walnuts

These will keep for several weeks in an airtight jar.

2 cups walnut halves or large pieces
1 tablespoon egg white (use exact measure)
½ cup icing sugar
1 tablespoon cornflour
1 teaspoon cinnamon
½ teaspoon mixed spice
¼ teaspoon ground cloves (optional)
¼ teaspoon salt

Preheat the oven to 125°C. Put the walnuts in a bowl. Beat the egg white until light but not frothy, and tip onto the walnuts. Mix to coat the nuts thoroughly, using your fingers.

Shake the remaining ingredients through a fine sieve into a shallow dish, repeating several times if necessary, to mix thoroughly. Drop the nuts into the dry mixture and turn gently to coat evenly.

Line a shallow roasting pan with a non-stick liner or baking paper. Arrange the nuts on this so they do not touch, and bake for 10–15 minutes until lightly browned. They will become very crisp when cold.

Devilled almonds

These are particularly good when heated slowly so they don't brown before they heat through.

MAKES 1 CUP:

1 cup whole almonds, blanched or skin-on
1 teaspoon sesame oil or other oil
1 tablespoon icing sugar
⅛–¼ teaspoon chilli powder
1 teaspoon paprika
1½ teaspoons garlic salt
2 teaspoons Kikkoman or other light soy sauce

Stir the almonds and the oil together in a heavy frying pan until the almonds are coated. (Don't add more oil.) Cook over low heat, stirring often, for 8–10 minutes, until a cut nut is very lightly browned. Meanwhile, mix the icing sugar, chilli powder, paprika and garlic salt together in a dry container.

Turn off the heat, sprinkle the hot nuts in the pan with soy sauce and toss to coat, then sift the mixed dry ingredients over the nuts in the pan and stir to coat well. Cool then store in an airtight container for 1–2 weeks.

Devilled popcorn

A spicy coating for popcorn.

MAKES 4–8 CUPS:

1 tablespoon icing sugar
⅛–¼ teaspoon chilli powder
1 teaspoon paprika (or smoked paprika)
1½ teaspoons garlic salt
¼–½ cup popping corn
oil

Mix together the icing sugar, chilli powder, paprika and garlic salt. Heat the popping corn in 1–2 tablespoons of oil in a large covered saucepan until popped. Drizzle in another 1–2 tablespoons of oil then sift in the seasonings, while tossing with a fork. Eat immediately or store in an airtight jar for up to 2 weeks.

Marinated mushrooms

- -

An irresistible snack with drinks before a meal.

MAKES ABOUT 2 CUPS:

about 300g small, tightly closed button mushrooms
¼ cup wine vinegar
1 teaspoon balsamic vinegar (optional)
1 large clove garlic, crushed, peeled then chopped
1 teaspoon oregano
½ teaspoon salt
1 teaspoon sugar
1 tablespoon tomato paste
½ cup olive oil

Brush the mushrooms clean if necessary. Trim the stem level with the cap of the mushrooms if you like, then put them aside. Halve larger button mushrooms if desired.

Measure the remaining ingredients into a small pot, bring to the boil, stirring to mix everything, then add the mushrooms, stirring until they soften and are covered with the hot liquid. Simmer for about 3 minutes, then transfer to a jar, making sure that the liquid covers them. Cover and leave to cool.

Serve hot, warm or at room temperature. Keep refrigerated in a covered container for up to 3 days.

NOTES: *Olive oil turns cloudy when refrigerated. It will clear again when warmed a little.*

Marinated feta & olives

- -

You can buy both marinated feta and different flavours of marinated olives, but it is cheaper and far more satisfying to make your own.

Marinated feta

MAKES 1½–2 CUPS:

200–250g feta cheese
1–2 cloves garlic
1 small red chilli
½ teaspoon black peppercorns
zest of ½ lemon, finely grated
few sprigs thyme and rosemary, bruised
canola and olive oil* (as required)

Cut the feta into bite-sized (roughly 2cm) cubes or chunks. Peel and slice the garlic cloves, and deseed and slice the chilli. Put a layer of feta cubes in the bottom of a jar. (Don't pack them in too tightly, or the oil won't reach all the surfaces.) Add a slice of garlic, a couple of slices of chilli, a few peppercorns, a pinch of lemon zest and a sprig or two of the herbs. If you want the jar to look its best, poke some of the chilli, garlic and herbs down the side of the jar so you can see them easily.

Continue layering until you have used all the cheese and/or filled the jar. Add any remaining seasonings (unless you are going to start another jar), then two-thirds to three-quarters fill the jar with canola oil, then fill to the top with olive oil, making sure all the cheese is covered. Put the lid on the jar and invert a few times so the oils and flavourings are mixed.

Leave to stand for at least 15 minutes before serving.

* Canola oil is a light flavourless oil that will carry the olive oil flavours. You can use olive oil only, but it is more expensive and can turn cloudy when refrigerated. Use infused olive oil (e.g. garlic, chilli or basil) for added flavour.

Marinated olives

Use the same method as for Marinated feta, replacing the feta with a combination of green and kalamata olives. Alternatively, try the orange and cardamom mixture below.

MAKES ABOUT 1½ CUPS:

200g mixed green and kalamata olives
4–6 whole cardamom pods, crushed
zest of ½ orange, finely grated
1 tablespoon orange juice
canola and olive oil (as required)

Proceed as for Marinated feta, but replace the garlic, chilli, lemon zest and herbs with the orange zest and cardamom, and add the orange juice just before filling the jar with canola and/or olive oil.

Stuffed eggs

These disappear fast whenever we make them. Serve with a small salad for lunch, or with other snacks before a main course.

eggs
½ teaspoon butter per egg
milk to mix
capers, chopped herbs or olives (optional)
salt and freshly ground pepper

To stop the eggshells splitting as you boil them, tap a tiny hole in the rounded end with a metal skewer or an egg-pricker. Cover the eggs in water and simmer for about 12 minutes. Remove from the heat, drain and refill the saucepan with cold water until the eggs are cool enough to handle. Tap gently all over to crack the shells evenly, then peel off the shells.

Halve the eggs lengthwise and gently lift out the yolks. Mash with a fork, adding butter, and enough milk to soften them to a smooth consistency. Add a few capers, chopped herbs or olives if you like, season carefully, then spoon the filling back into the whites.

Marinated feta & olives

Turkish feta pastries

These are based on simple but delicious little Turkish pastries.

Preheat the oven to 180°C. While the oven heats, combine the crumbled feta, parsley and lemon juice in a small bowl.

Trim the filo sheets so they are square, then cut these into quarters to make smaller squares. Place a small square on a board and brush lightly with oil, then cover with a second sheet. Arrange a scant tablespoon of the filling mix diagonally across the square just below the middle (don't be too generous or you may run out and they may burst during cooking). Fold in three corners to cover the filling (so it looks like an open envelope), then roll up towards the open point.

Arrange the pastries on a tray, brush lightly with oil and bake for 8–10 minutes until golden brown. Serve hot or warm.

MAKES 12 PASTRIES:

100g feta cheese, crumbled
¼ cup parsley, chopped
1 tablespoon lemon juice
3–6 sheets filo pastry
1–2 tablespoons olive oil

Thai-style spring rolls

Try these delicious little appetisers once and we're sure you'll make them again . . . and again.

Soak the vermicelli or noodles in warm water for five minutes while you prepare the remaining ingredients.

Drain the noodles well, then mix in a medium bowl with all the other filling ingredients.

Working with a corner pointing towards you (so the wrapper is a 'diamond' shape), arrange about 2 teaspoons of the filling in a line across the wrapper just below halfway. (Don't be too generous with the filling, or you won't be able to fit it in!)

Fold the left- and right-hand corners towards the middle so the ends of the filling are covered, then, working from the corner near you, roll the wrapper up so the filling is completely enclosed. Seal the end by moistening the flap with a little of the cornflour and water mixture.

Repeat this process until you have used all the filling mixture, or all the wrappers.

Heat the oil in a small frying pan or wok and fry the rolls, 5 or 6 at a time, turning occasionally until golden brown. Drain the cooked spring rolls and serve warm, accompanied with bowls of soy and sweet chilli sauce for dipping.

MAKES 20–30 ROLLS:

½ cup lightly packed rice vermicelli (or bean-thread noodles)
1 cup very finely sliced cabbage
1 medium carrot, grated
2–3 tablespoons roasted peanuts, chopped
1 tablespoon each: vegetarian oyster sauce, light soy sauce and Thai sweet chilli sauce
1 tablespoon chopped fresh coriander (optional)
1 teaspoon dark sesame oil
¼ teaspoon each: salt and sugar
20–30 x 10cm square wonton or spring roll wrappers
1 teaspoon cornflour mixed with 2 tablespoons water
1–2 cups oil, for frying
soy sauce and sweet chilli sauce, for dipping

Thai-style spring rolls

Filo samosas

SERVES 4:

2 medium (about 300g) all-purpose or
　floury potatoes
1 tablespoon oil
1 medium onion, finely chopped
1½ teaspoons curry powder
1 teaspoon ground cumin
½ teaspoon garam masala
½ teaspoon ground coriander seeds
¾ cup frozen peas
2 tablespoons water
1 teaspoon salt
½ teaspoon sugar
juice of ½ lemon
2 tablespoons mint or fresh coriander
　leaves, chopped
6 sheets filo pastry
25g butter, melted

This simplified version of the traditional samosa gives an interesting contrast between the light flaky crust and the dense, well seasoned potato filling.

Scrub and cut the potatoes into 1cm cubes. Cook in a covered microwave container (page 35) or in a saucepan in a little water until tender. Drain.

Heat the oil in a large frying pan. Gently cook the onion and all the seasonings until the onion is tender. Add the peas and the water, cover and cook for 2 minutes. Add the drained cooked potatoes, salt, sugar and lemon juice, and mix thoroughly, without breaking up the potato too much. Taste and add extra salt and lemon juice if required. Stir in the chopped herbs.

Preheat the oven to 200°C.

Lightly brush the sheets of filo with melted butter. Stack together 3 sheets of filo. Cut crosswise into 4 even strips. Put a good tablespoon of filling at the end of 1 strip and fold into a triangular parcel (see diagram below).

Repeat this step with the remaining filo sheets and filling mixture. Lightly brush the top of each samosa with melted butter. Place on a baking tray.

Bake the samosas for 10 minutes, then reduce the heat to 180°C and bake for a further 15–20 minutes until golden brown.

Serve warm, as a snack or a light meal, at any time of the day.

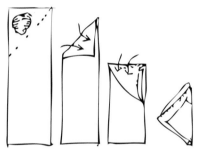

Shaping filo triangles

Angel nests

MAKES 10–12:

200g very thin pasta, vermicelli or
　fine egg noodles
2 large eggs
¼ cup self-raising flour
2 tablespoons grated parmesan
1 tablespoon sundried tomato pesto
　or basil pesto
½ teaspoon salt
freshly ground black pepper to taste
about ¼ cup oil, to fry
additional basil or sundried tomato
　pesto, to garnish

These lovely little fritters are very popular.

Cook the pasta in plenty of boiling water. Drain and allow to cool a little while you mix the batter.

Whisk the eggs, flour, parmesan, pesto, salt and pepper together in a medium-sized bowl. Add the cooled pasta and stir or toss together until the pasta is evenly coated with the batter.

Heat the oil in a large, non-stick frying pan. Make 'nests' of the noodle–batter mixture by sticking a fork into the mixture and turning it against a spoon. Transfer these one by one to the pan (make 2 batches of 5–6 'nests') and cook until golden brown on each side. Drain on paper towels.

Serve warm, accompanied by some additional basil and/or sundried tomato pesto; or try sweet chilli sauce.

Filo samosas (top); Angel nests

As the days shorten and the weather becomes colder, we start to think about soup. Soup is perfect after school, for a Saturday lunch, or as a starter on a cold wintery evening.

As a child, Alison would come home from school during winter to be met by delicious aromas from her mother's kitchen. She would warm her fingers around a mug of soup while she told her mother about all the good and bad things that had happened in her day. By the time her mug was empty, the world seemed a better place!

Soups

Soup stock

Many soups need the addition of flavoured stock to bring out the full flavour of other ingredients. There are a number of ways to prepare stocks; choose the method that best suits your time and inclination.

Instant stock or bouillon

There are a variety of vegetable stock cubes and powders on the shelves of supermarkets and health food shops. Some of these taste good and others can be disappointing. Always read the ingredient list on the container carefully, as some manufacturers add animal fats to their vegetable-flavoured stocks.

When using instant stocks, work out what concentration suits you. In general 1 level teaspoon of powder (or 1 cube) to 1 cup of boiling water should give a strong enough flavour without being too salty.

'Nearly instant' stocks

*As an alternative to using commercial stock preparations you can make stock almost instantly by dissolving **any one** of the following in 1 cup of boiling water:*

1 teaspoon Vegemite or Marmite
1 teaspoon dark (Chinese) soy sauce
1 teaspoon light (Chinese) soy sauce
1 teaspoon Kikkoman soy sauce
1 teaspoon Kikkoman salt-reduced soy sauce
1–2 teaspoons miso
1 teaspoon tomato paste, added to any of the above,
  improves its flavour

It is worth experimenting with different combinations of these ingredients. Our favourite is a combination of 1 teaspoon each of the Chinese light soy sauce and tomato paste per cup of water. It is surprisingly good for something so easy and cheap, and is well worth a try. These quantities should just be multiplied when larger quantities of stock are required.

Vegetable stock from scratch

Making vegetable stock from scratch is often thought of as a time-consuming process. This is because of the long periods of time necessary to allow flavours to 'steep' from vegetables as they boil. Finely chopping the vegetables first (either by hand or, better still, in a blender or food processor) eliminates the need for prolonged boiling. This is the principle employed in this recipe, which makes 1 litre of fresh-tasting stock with an attractive colour in less than 20 minutes.

MAKES 4 CUPS (1L):

1 large onion
2–4 cloves garlic
1 large carrot, scrubbed
2 sticks celery
2 tomatoes or 2 teaspoons tomato paste
1 stalk parsley
¼ teaspoon freshly ground black pepper
4 cups (1L) cold water
½ teaspoon sugar
about 1 teaspoon salt

Quarter but do not peel the onion. Put in the food processor bowl with the unpeeled garlic cloves, the scrubbed but unpeeled carrot cut in chunks, the sticks of celery, broken with their leaves removed, the tomatoes and the parsley leaves and stalks. Process until very finely chopped.

Transfer the chopped vegetables to a large saucepan, add the pepper then the cold water and bring to the boil. Simmer for 10–15 minutes, then press through a sieve, extracting as much liquid as possible. Add sugar and salt to taste.

Asparagus soup

SERVES 6-8:

50g butter
2 cloves garlic, chopped
¼ cup flour
500g tender asparagus
2 cups water
1¼ cups fresh cream
½ teaspoon salt
freshly ground black pepper

Eat this soup as soon as it is made, or, if you have access to a lot of cheap fresh asparagus, make extra for your freezer.

Melt the butter in a saucepan over moderate heat, add the garlic, and cook for 2 minutes without browning. Stir in the flour, then remove from the heat.

Grate the raw asparagus, using the appropriate blade on a food processor. If using a hand grater, hold the bunch of asparagus at right angles to the grater. Place in a saucepan with the water, and boil for 2 minutes. When cooked, the asparagus should be bright green and barely tender.

Drain the asparagus cooking liquid into the butter and flour mixture, and bring to the boil, stirring all the time. Stir in the cream. Bring to the boil, add the cooked asparagus, and return to the boil, then reduce to a gentle simmer.

If serving immediately, thin to desired consistency with milk, vegetable stock, or water, then adjust seasoning.

If you are freezing the soup, do not thin, but cool the thick soup as soon as possible, so that it retains its bright green colour. The fastest way to cool it is to stand the saucepan in a large container of cold or iced water, changing the water as it gets warm. Freeze in covered containers, leaving head space. Use within 6 months. Bring thawed soup to the boil, thin as required, then adjust seasoning.

Serve topped with Croûtons (see page 61), or grated cheese, or with toasted cheese sandwiches.

Broccoli & blue cheese soup

SERVES 4:

2 tablespoons olive oil or butter
1 large onion, finely chopped
1 teaspoon (1-2 cloves) garlic, minced
2 medium to large potatoes (about
    400g), scrubbed
2 cups vegetable stock (page 43) or
    2 teaspoons instant vegetable stock
    and 2 cups water
500g broccoli heads
¼-½ cup cream cheese
½ cup milk
blue cheese to taste, up to 50g
    (½ wedge)
½-1 cup extra milk
salt to taste (probably about
    ½ teaspoon)
freshly ground black pepper, to taste
1-2 tablespoons basil pesto (optional)

Broccoli and blue cheese combine to give a delicious, surprisingly mild flavour.

Heat the oil or butter in a fairly large saucepan. Add the onion and garlic and stir to mix. Cook gently with the lid on, without browning, while you cut the potatoes into 1cm cubes.

Add the potato cubes and the stock, cover again and simmer until the potatoes are tender, about 10 minutes.

While the potatoes are cooking, chop the heads off the broccoli and cut them into 15-20mm pieces. Peel the broccoli stalks starting at the bottom, then cut the peeled stems into 5mm slices. Add the prepared broccoli to the potato mixture, cover and cook 5-10 minutes longer, until the broccoli is tender but still bright green.

Purée this mixture in a food processor. Add the cream cheese (the larger amount makes it richer), then add ½ cup of milk. Add the blue cheese in teaspoon-sized lots, processing and tasting after each addition, until the soup has the strength of flavour that suits you. Add extra milk until the soup is the desired thickness, then season with salt, pepper and pesto for extra flavour if desired.

Refrigerate if the soup is not to be reheated and served immediately. To serve, top with a swirl of cream, sour cream, or cream cheese thinned with milk.

Chunky corn chowder

A large can of creamed corn added to a few basic vegetables will make a substantial soup with interesting texture and flavour, in a short time.

Chop the onions and celery, if using, into small cubes (about 5mm). Heat the butter or olive oil (or a mixture) in a saucepan and cook the onions and celery over moderate heat, without browning.

Cut the unpeeled potatoes into 5mm slices, then into 5mm dice. Add them, all at once, to the onions, add the stock, then cover and simmer over moderate heat for 4–5 minutes, until the potato is tender.

Add the creamed corn, rinse out the can with the ½ cup water and add it, along with the milk and the sour cream or alternative. Stir or whisk everything together. Bring to the boil, simmer for about a minute, then take off the heat and stir in the pesto (if using), and season to taste with salt, pepper and Tabasco.

To reheat, bring to the boil then lower the heat immediately. Add some chopped parsley, fresh herbs or thinly sliced spring onion leaves. Serve with buttered toast or warmed crusty rolls.

NOTE: *Half a red or orange capsicum, diced as finely as the onions and added to the oil before the potatoes, gives the chowder extra flavour and colour. A few green beans or some broccoli, chopped finely and added at the same stage, are good too.*

SERVES 4–5:

2 large onions
1 cup finely chopped celery (optional)
2 tablespoons butter or olive oil
2 medium potatoes, scrubbed
1½ cups vegetable stock (page 43) or
    1½ teaspoons green herb instant
    stock and 1½ cups water
410g can creamed corn
½ cup water
1 cup milk
½ cup sour cream or cream or evaporated milk (unsweetened)
1 tablespoon basil pesto (optional)
salt, pepper and Tabasco sauce to
    taste

Roasted corn & capsicum soup

The ingredients and seasonings give this soup a Tex-Mex flavour.

Preheat the oven to 200°C. Halve the capsicums lengthwise and remove the seeds and stalks. Place cut side down in a large roasting pan sprayed with non-stick oil. Arrange the corn (husks and all) around the capsicums then place in the oven and roast for 30 minutes.

Remove the roasted vegetables from the oven, and as soon as the capsicums are cool enough to handle, place them in a plastic bag and leave to stand for a further 5–10 minutes. (This helps to loosen the skins.)

While the corn and capsicums cool, heat the oil in a large saucepan. Cook the onion and garlic in the oil until soft, stirring frequently to prevent browning. Add the cumin, oregano, chilli powder and paprika (if using), cook for a minute longer, then remove from the heat.

Pull off and discard the capsicum skins (they should lift off quite easily). Place the capsicum flesh, onion mixture and 1 cup of stock in a food processor and process to a smooth purée. Transfer the purée back to the pot.

Peel and discard the husks and silk from the corn, and slice the kernels from the cobs. Place half of the corn and 1 cup of stock in the food processor and process until smooth, before adding to the pot. Repeat this process with the remaining corn before rinsing the processor with the final cup of stock.

Season to taste with salt and pepper, add the coriander or parsley, then simmer for a few minutes.

Serve with crusty bread rolls or cornbread.

SERVES 6:

2 red capsicums
4 whole ears of fresh corn, husks on
1 tablespoon canola or olive oil
1 medium onion, chopped or diced
1 clove garlic, chopped
1 teaspoon cumin
½ teaspoon oregano
¼–½ teaspoon chilli powder, to taste
½ teaspoon paprika (or smoked
    paprika) (optional)
4 cups vegetable stock (page 43) or
    3 teaspoons instant stock powder
    and 4 cups hot water
salt and freshly ground black pepper
    to taste
1–2 tablespoons coriander or parsley,
    chopped

Pasta & bean soup

This soup is not only delicious, it is substantial, and quick to prepare. Use homemade or powdered instant stock, or diluted canned consommé.

SERVES 4–6:

3 tablespoons olive oil
1 clove garlic, peeled and chopped
1 medium onion, quartered and sliced
2 small dried chillis, crushed, or ½ teaspoon chilli powder
2 bay leaves
¼ teaspoon dried thyme
425g can Italian seasoned tomatoes
425g can red kidney beans
440g can four bean mix
4 cups vegetable stock
1 cup (100g) short pasta (e.g. macaroni, spirals, rigatoni)
1 teaspoon salt
black pepper to taste
chopped fresh parsley or pesto and/or grated parmesan, to serve

Heat the oil in a large pot. Add the garlic and onion and cook, without browning, until the onion is soft and clear. Stir in the crushed chillis or chilli powder, bay leaves and thyme. Cook for 1 minute longer.

Add the canned tomatoes, beans and stock. Heat until boiling, then add the pasta. Allow to boil gently until the pasta is cooked (10–15 minutes), then add the salt and black pepper to taste.

Serve topped with chopped fresh parsley, a little pesto and some freshly shaved or grated parmesan.

Carrot soup

A cheerful, bright, creamy soup. Add your own gourmet touches with herbs, cheese, or orange.

SERVES 6–8:

2 cloves garlic, finely chopped
2 large onions, finely chopped
50g butter
500g carrots, finely grated
2 teaspoons sugar
4 cups vegetable stock (page 43)
¼–½ cup cream

Cook the garlic and onion in the butter for 5–10 minutes without browning.

Add the finely grated carrot, sugar and stock, simmer for 10 minutes or until the carrot is tender, then purée. Whisk in as much of the cream as desired, and adjust the seasonings. Reheat without boiling.

VARIATIONS: *Add finely chopped fresh thyme or ¼ teaspoon dried thyme as the carrots cook. Add the grated rind and the juice of an orange when you add the cream. Try replacing the cream with ½–1 cup cheese sauce.*

Curried kumara soup

Kumara has a mild, sweet flavour, and makes a very smooth and satisfying soup.

SERVES 4–6:

500g kumara
75g butter
2 cloves garlic
½–1 teaspoon curry powder
1 cup water
2 teaspoons vegetable bouillon powder or other flavouring (page 43)
3 cups milk, approximately
¼ cup cream (optional))

Peel the kumara with a potato peeler and slice into pieces 1cm thick.

Heat the butter in a large saucepan and add the crushed garlic and curry powder. Add the kumara and cook in the butter for 1–2 minutes without browning. Add the water and bouillon, cover and cook for 10 minutes until tender. Purée, thinning with milk until it reaches the desired thickness. Add the cream (if using) and reheat, but do not boil.

Kumara, pumpkin & peanut soup

A popular and interesting soup with a complex flavour.

Finely chop the onion. Heat the butter or oil in a medium-sized saucepan. Add the onion and garlic and cook over low heat, without browning, until the onion is transparent. Add the curry powder, coriander seed and chilli powder (to your desired level of hotness) to the onion mixture and stir over moderate heat for about a minute longer.

Chop the kumara and pumpkin into 1cm cubes (use more pumpkin if you like, but do not use extra kumara or the soup will be too sweet). Add the vegetables to the pot, add the stock, bring to the boil and simmer for about 15 minutes or until the vegetables are tender. Add the salt, then the peanut butter. Purée in a food processor, blender or mouli or (for a soup with some texture) crush with a potato masher. Adjust the seasoning to taste, and reheat.

Serve topped with yoghurt or coconut cream, finely chopped roasted peanuts and chopped coriander leaves.

VARIATION: *Use less stock or water and thin the soup with coconut cream.*

SERVES 4:

1 large onion
2 tablespoons butter or oil
1 teaspoon (1–2 cloves) minced garlic
½ teaspoon curry powder
½ teaspoon coriander seed (optional)
⅛–¼ teaspoon chilli powder
1 medium (250g) kumara, peeled
250–350g pumpkin, peeled and
 deseeded
4 cups vegetable stock (page 43) or
 3 teaspoons instant stock powder in
 4 cups water
½ teaspoon salt
2 tablespoons peanut butter, smooth
 or crunchy

Pumpkin soup

The wonderful colour and smooth texture of pumpkin soup will brighten the bleakest winter day. Make more than you need and freeze the undiluted purée.

Cut the unpeeled pumpkin into chunks and scrape away and discard the seeds and stringy part with a spoon. Put all the other ingredients except the milk and final seasonings into a saucepan, lay the pieces of pumpkin on top, cover and simmer until the onion and pumpkin are tender. Do not overcook the pumpkin or it will darken and lose some of its appeal. Lift the pieces of pumpkin onto a large plate or board. As soon as they are cool enough to work with, scoop the cooked flesh back into the onion mixture and discard the skin.

Purée the pumpkin mixture, getting it as smooth as possible. Before serving, thin the purée to the desired consistency with milk, adding a little cream if you want extra richness.

Season carefully. Reheat and serve.

SERVES 6–8:

1kg pumpkin
2 onions, chopped
2 cups water
2 cloves garlic, chopped
2 teaspoons vegetable bouillon
 powder
2 teaspoons sugar
½ teaspoon grated nutmeg
2–3 cups milk
salt, freshly ground black pepper and
 sugar

Quick potato soup

A simple, quick and tasty soup with a wonderful smooth texture.

Chop the onion and garlic. Cook in the butter or oil in a large saucepan over medium heat for a few minutes, until the onion begins to brown. Scrub and dice the potatoes and add to the onion and garlic. Pour the stock over the vegetables, add the sugar, pepper, nutmeg and herbs, then stir together and cover. Simmer for 10–15 minutes or until the potato is tender.

Blend the soup until smooth. If you don't have a food processor or blender, force the cooked vegetables through a sieve. Add the cream and reheat (but do not boil) to serve.

Add a swirl of cream and a sprinkling of chopped herbs to each bowl.

SERVES 4:

2 onions
3 cloves garlic
3 tablespoons butter or oil
3 medium-sized potatoes (about 500g)
3 cups of vegetable stock (page 43)
1 teaspoon sugar
generous grind of black pepper
generous pinch grated nutmeg
1 sprig each: parsley and mint
1 pinch each: fresh or dried basil and
 thyme
¼ cup cream (optional)

Kumara, pumpkin & peanut soup (front), Quick potato soup

French onion soup

This classic soup is quick and simple to make, and versatile. Add the Cheesy croûtons for a tasty lunch or light meal.

SERVES 4–6:

1kg (about 5 medium) onions
2 tablespoons olive or canola oil
2 tablespoons balsamic vinegar
½–1 teaspoon dried thyme
4 cups vegetable stock (page 43)
½–1 cup dry white wine
about 1 teaspoon salt
freshly ground black pepper to taste

Halve, peel and thinly slice the onions (a food processor fitted with the slicing blade does this very efficiently). Heat the oil in a large heavy saucepan then add the onions. Cook, stirring frequently, until the onions have softened and are beginning to brown (about 10–15 minutes), then add the balsamic vinegar and the thyme. Continue to cook, stirring frequently and watching that the onions don't burn, until the mixture is well browned (this gives the soup much of its final colour and flavour).

Stir in the stock and wine and season to taste. Bring the mixture to the boil, then reduce the heat and simmer gently for a further 15–20 minutes.

Check the seasonings again, then serve. Add Cheesy croûtons (opposite) and a green salad on the side.

Dot's mysterious beer soup

This soup makes a good conversation piece – it has an interesting flavour not easily identified.

SERVES 6:

2 tablespoons butter
2 large onions, finely chopped
2 large carrots, finely chopped
¼ cup flour
2 cups vegetable stock (page 43) or 2 teaspoons instant
   vegetable stock in 2 cups water
250g cream cheese
about 2 cups lager beer
chopped parsley or chives

Melt the butter in a large saucepan. Add the onion to the melted butter and cook for about 5 minutes over a low heat until quite soft, taking care not to brown it. Add the carrot and cook for a further 5–10 minutes, until the carrot has softened.

Stir the flour into the cooked onion and carrot, then add the vegetable stock. Stir over a gentle heat until thickened. Simmer for 5–10 minutes, then cool slightly before puréeing in a blender or food processor. Pour back into the pot. Process the cream cheese with enough beer to mix it to a thin cream, then combine in the saucepan with the vegetable purée and the remaining beer. Bring to the boil, and adjust seasonings if necessary.

Serve with Bread sticks, Cheesy croûtons or Bread rolls if desired. Garnish with finely chopped parsley or chives.

Cheesy croûtons

The traditional way to prepare these is to ladle the soup into individual bowls, cover the top of each with sliced bread and sprinkle generously with grated cheese. The bowls are then placed under the grill until the cheese is golden brown.

To avoid having to get hot, soup-filled bowls in and out of the oven, make the croûtons separately. Arrange sliced bread on a baking sheet, grill one side until golden, then turn them over, sprinkle with grated cheese and grill them until golden brown. These croûtons can then be floated on top of the individual bowls or served alongside the soup.

Cheese & onion soup

A delicious rich soup that makes a satisfying meal.

SERVES 4–6:

3 medium-sized onions
2 cloves garlic
2 tablespoons oil or butter
1 teaspoon mustard powder
1 teaspoon salt
generous grind of black pepper
2 cups water
2 tablespoons butter
2 tablespoons flour
1½ cups milk
1 cup grated tasty cheese
1 tablespoon sherry
1 teaspoon dark soy sauce
½ teaspoon hot chilli sauce

Slice the onions finely and chop the garlic. Melt the butter in a large saucepan, then sauté the onions with the garlic, mustard powder, salt and pepper until soft, without letting them brown. Add the water, bring to the boil, then cover and simmer over a low heat until the onions are tender.

In another saucepan melt the second measure of butter, then stir in the flour. Continue stirring while the mixture cooks for at least 1 minute. Add the milk and keep stirring until the sauce boils and thickens. Allow to boil for a minute or so, then remove from the heat and stir in the cheese. Add the cheese sauce to the onion mixture then stir in the sherry, soy sauce and chilli sauce. Cook over a very low heat (do not let it boil) for a further 10 minutes. Serve immediately, or reheat if required.

French onion soup

Creamy green pea soup

- -

A bright green, tasty, substantial soup from frozen peas.

Finely chop the garlic. Heat the oil or butter, add the garlic and cook until bubbling but not brown. Add the frozen peas and water, cover and cook for 4–5 minutes until the peas are tender but still bright green.

Put in a food processor with the herb-flavoured salt or stock powder. Stir the cream cheese and add to the mixture. Thin with 1–2 cups of milk to the thickness you like. Adjust the seasoning, adding salt, pepper and Tabasco to taste.

Refrigerate for up to 2 days. Reheat, thinning with water or milk if necessary, and serve with warmed crusty bread. Top with spoonfuls of sour cream and basil pesto, or with tiny croûtons, sour cream and tomato salsa.

VARIATIONS: *Add several chopped lettuce leaves, spring onions and a dozen or so fresh mint leaves to the peas while cooking.*

SERVES 3–4:

3 large cloves garlic
1 tablespoon olive oil or butter
4 cups frozen peas
1 cup water
1 teaspoon herb-flavoured salt or instant stock powder
250g cream cheese (low-fat or regular)
1–2 cups milk
salt and freshly ground black pepper to taste
Tabasco to taste

Pea soup

- -

This soup is particularly smooth, with a good flavour.

Bring the peas, lentils and water to the boil in a large pot. Add the roughly chopped onions, celery, carrots and garlic. If you like, add the bay leaf, along with the other herbs and spices in quantities to suit your taste. Simmer until the peas are mushy, then purée or push through a coarse sieve.

Rinse out the saucepan and melt the butter in it. Stir in the flour, cook gently for 2–3 minutes, then add about 1 cup of the strained purée. Bring this to the boil, stirring constantly, then add another cupful and boil again. Add the remaining mixture and bring to the boil, still stirring all the time. Simmer for 5 minutes.

This mixture will be very thick, and is suitable for refrigerating or freezing.

When the soup is required, thin it with milk, water or vegetable stock to the thickness you want. Bring to the boil, taste, and season carefully. Serve very hot.

SERVES 8:

1 cup yellow split peas
½ cup red lentils
10 cups water
2 large onions, roughly chopped
2–3 sticks celery, roughly chopped
2 carrots, roughly chopped
2 cloves garlic
1 bay leaf (optional)
fresh or dried thyme, oregano and ground allspice (optional)
25g butter
¼ cup flour
milk, water or vegetable stock, to thin
salt and freshly ground black pepper

Spinach soup

- -

This soup has a wonderful bright green colour.

Chop the onions fairly finely and add to the melted butter in a medium-large saucepan. Add the nutmeg, cover and cook gently for 5–10 minutes, being careful not to brown the onions.

Scrub the potatoes and cut into 1cm cubes. Add to the saucepan with the stock. Cover and bring to the boil, then simmer for about 15 minutes, or until the potatoes are tender. Add the spinach and simmer for 3–4 minutes longer, until the spinach is tender but still bright green. Do not overcook at this stage as this will spoil the colour.

Purée everything in a food processor, blender or mouli, in several batches if necessary, then pour back into the pot. Whisk in the cream and milk, adding more milk if you want it thinner. Taste, and adjust the seasoning if necessary, adding extra salt, freshly ground pepper and nutmeg.

Reheat briefly just before serving, either as is, or with a swirl of plain or lightly whipped cream, croûtons or Melba toast.

SERVES 4:

1 large onion
1 tablespoon butter
½ teaspoon freshly grated nutmeg
2 large potatoes
3 cups vegetable stock (page 43) or 2 teaspoons instant stock powder in 3 cups water
250g spinach, well washed and roughly chopped
½ cup cream
½ cup milk
salt and freshly ground black pepper

Creamy green pea soup

Brown mushroom soup

SERVES 4:

2 medium-sized onions
3 tablespoons butter
1 teaspoon (1–2 cloves) minced garlic
4–5 large portobello mushrooms,
    wiped clean
¼ teaspoon dried thyme
3 tablespoons flour
2 cups vegetable stock (page 43) or
    2 teaspoons instant stock and
    2 cups water
½ teaspoon salt
freshly ground black pepper to taste
1 tablespoon sherry (optional)
1 tablespoon wine or balsamic vinegar
2 cups milk

Make this chunky, robust soup from 'wild' field mushrooms – or big flat mushrooms gathered from your nearest supermarket!

Peel and finely chop the onions. Melt the butter in a large pot, add the onions and cook over a medium heat for about 5 minutes until the onions are evenly browned, then add the garlic and cook for 1–2 minutes longer. Chop the mushrooms finely and add to the onions with the thyme. Cook for 5 minutes, stirring often.

Stir in the flour, cook until it has lightly browned, then add the stock, salt and pepper, sherry and vinegar. Stir well to mix, bring to the boil, then simmer for 5–10 minutes.

Stir in the milk and heat until almost boiling. Serve the soup with sliced rolls which have been buttered or brushed with oil (and pesto if you like) then grilled until lightly browned.

Fresh tomato soup

SERVES 4:

1 onion
2 tablespoons butter
2 cloves garlic, chopped
1 tablespoon flour
1 teaspoon sugar
1 teaspoon vegetable stock powder
½ teaspoon paprika
1 cup water
500g ripe red tomatoes
dried herbs (basil, thyme, marjoram,
    cumin), freshly ground black pepper,
    hot chilli sauce, to taste
¼ cup chopped parsley

Make this soup when ripe red tomatoes are plentiful.

Chop the onion finely and cook in the butter without browning for 5 minutes or until tender. Do not hurry this step.

Stir in the chopped garlic and cook a minute longer, then add the flour, sugar, stock powder, paprika and water. Simmer for another 5 minutes. Halve the tomatoes and cut each half into 9 or 16 cubes, depending on their size.

Add the tomatoes and herbs and other flavourings, as you like, and cook gently for 5 minutes more. For a smooth soup, purée at this stage.

Stir in the chopped parsley, adjust the seasoning if necessary, and serve with cheese-topped grilled slices of French bread or Croûtons (page 61) or sour cream.

Quick tomato soup

SERVES 4:

1 tablespoon olive or other oil
1 teaspoon (2 cloves) minced garlic
1 teaspoon ground cumin or curry
    powder
2 level tablespoons flour
425g can tomato purée made up to
    4 cups with hot water
grated rind ½ lemon (optional)
1½ teaspoons sugar
250g (1 cup) sour cream
salt and Tabasco sauce, to taste
1–2 tablespoons basil pesto

The perfect tomato soup, made in 7 minutes flat!

Heat the oil in a medium-sized pot. Add the garlic, cumin or curry powder and the flour and stir until bubbling.

Stir in about a cup of the purée and water mixture, then bring to the boil, stirring all the time. Add the remaining tomato mixture with the grated lemon rind and sugar, and bring to the boil.

Add the sour cream, whisking or beating with a fork to mix, remove from the heat and season to taste. Add 1 tablespoon of basil pesto, taste, and add more if you want a stronger herb flavour.

Just before serving, reheat, without boiling.

Serve with buttered toast, toasted cheese sandwiches, warmed bread rolls, or sliced French bread that has been lightly buttered or oiled, and browned under a grill.

EXTRA OPTIONS: *Top with a little plain, unsweetened yoghurt and a sprinkling of finely chopped fresh herb, spring onions or avocado.*

Brown mushroom soup

Winter soup

- -

This thick, substantial soup tastes as if it has simmered all day, but it can be served an hour after you start making it.

Put the soup mix and water on to simmer in a fairly large covered saucepan, while you prepare the rest of the soup in another saucepan or heavy frying pan.

Chop the onion and garlic and cook over moderate heat in the butter or oil until the onion is evenly browned (but not blackened).

While this is cooking, chop the carrot and the pumpkin or scrubbed kumara or potato into pieces the size of your little fingernail, then add them to the browned onion. Cook for several minutes more, turning frequently, then stir in the chopped capsicums and the herbs.

Tip the vegetables into the boiling soup mix, cover again, and simmer very gently for 45 minutes, until the soup mix is tender.

Mix the yeast extract with enough hot water to dissolve it, then stir in the tomato paste. Add this to the soup, with enough salt to bring out the flavours, then add the chopped parsley.

Serve straight away or, preferably, leave to stand for half an hour or more to blend the flavours. Sprinkle parmesan over each serving, if desired.

SERVES 4–6:

½ cup cereal soup mix*

5 cups hot water

1 large onion

2 cloves garlic

2 tablespoons butter or oil

1 carrot, scrubbed

100g pumpkin or kumara or 1 potato

½ green capsicum, chopped

½ red capsicum, chopped

½ teaspoon each: dried thyme, dried
   basil and dried oregano

2 teaspoons yeast extract

2 tablespoons tomato paste

½ teaspoon salt

¼ cup chopped parsley

*Cereal soup mix is made up of barley, dried peas and beans, pasta, etc.

Minestrone

A substantial soup that is quite simple to make.

SERVES 6–8:

1 tablespoon olive oil
2 cloves garlic, peeled and chopped
1 large onion, finely diced
4 cups vegetable stock (page 43)
2 medium carrots, finely diced
2 medium sticks celery, thinly sliced
1 medium potato, cubed
425g can (2 cups) kidney beans, drained and rinsed
400g can whole tomatoes in juice
¾ cup small pasta shapes
1 cup frozen peas
2 cups finely sliced cabbage
2 tablespoons fresh parsley, chopped
2 tablespoons pesto (or ¼ cup fresh basil, chopped)
   (optional)
½ teaspoon each: dried oregano and dried thyme
1 teaspoon salt
freshly ground black pepper
grated parmesan and pesto, to serve

Heat the oil in a large saucepan over medium heat. Add the garlic and onion. Cook, stirring occasionally, for 5 minutes or until the onion is soft and clear.

Stir in the stock then the fresh vegetables. Add the beans, then the canned tomatoes, breaking them up with a fork. Bring the soup to the boil then reduce the heat, cover and simmer for 30 minutes or until the potato is tender.

Add the pasta, peas, cabbage, herbs and seasonings. Simmer for 10–15 minutes or until the pasta is tender but still firm. Check the seasoning and add some water if you think the soup is too thick.

Ladle into warm soup bowls. Top with a little freshly grated parmesan and/or a spoonful of pesto.

Easy vegetable soup

You can make really easy, surprisingly creamy, soups very quickly when you start with almost any starchy root vegetable.

SERVES 2–3:

1 onion, very finely chopped
1 clove garlic, chopped
pinch of curry powder
2 teaspoons butter or oil
400–500g kumara, or pumpkin, or parsnip or Jerusalem
   artichokes (or a selection of one or more)
¼–½ cup water
about ¼ teaspoon salt or ½ teaspoon instant stock
1–2 cups milk

In the microwave, put the onion, garlic, curry powder and butter or oil in a roasting bag and cook on High (100%) for 2 minutes. Peel the vegetables, cut them into 2cm chunks, and add them to the bag with ¼ cup water. Close the bag loosely with a rubber band, leaving a finger-sized hole for some steam to escape, then microwave for 4–6 minutes or until the vegetables feel soft when pinched through the bag.

On the stovetop, cook the onion, garlic and curry powder in the butter or oil in a medium-sized saucepan on medium heat for 1–2 minutes. Peel and cube the vegetables, add them with ½ cup water, and simmer in the covered saucepan until the vegetables are tender when pierced with a knife.

Purée the mixture in a food processor or blender with the salt or instant stock until smooth, thinning to a creamy soup consistency with milk. Pour through a sieve to remove any lumps, then heat and serve.

Serve in mugs or bowls with toast, Bread rolls (pages 241, 245) or Garlic bread (page 35).

VARIATIONS: *Cook herbs or spices with the vegetables. Purée in a mouli or mash with a potato masher or fork. Add a little cream or cream cheese with the milk. Add a spoonful of smooth peanut butter with the milk. Use coconut cream and water to replace the milk.*

Alphabet soup

A family favourite that is fun for children to make – and eat.

SERVES 4:*

4 cups hot water
4 teaspoons vegetable bouillon or 'Nearly instant' stock
   (page 43)
1 teaspoon sugar
2 teaspoons butter
3 tablespoons alphabet noodles (or up to ½ cup larger
   noodles)
1 small onion, chopped
1 stick celery, chopped
1 small carrot, grated
1 small potato, scrubbed and grated
1 tomato, chopped
1 tablespoon chopped parsley

Put the hot water in a medium-sized saucepan over high heat. Add the stock powder or selected flavourings and the sugar and butter. When this mixture comes to the boil, add the noodles.

Working quickly, prepare and add the vegetables in the given order. The soup should be cooked about 10–12 minutes after the noodles are added. Stir in the chopped parsley and serve, or cool and reheat later.

* Quantities given here may be varied, but the order of additions is important and should be followed.

Corn dahl soup

This main course soup combines an interesting selection of everyday vegetables and takes only half an hour to make.

SERVES 6:

½ cup moong dahl
1 L water
1 large onion
2 cloves garlic
1 tablespoon butter
1 carrot, grated or finely chopped
2 stalks celery, finely chopped
1 cup vegetable stock (page 43) or
    1 teaspoon instant stock in 1 cup water
440g can cream-style corn
2 silverbeet or 4 spinach leaves
2 tablespoons tomato sauce
1 tablespoon cornflour
1 tomato
salt and freshly ground black pepper

Boil the moong dahl and water in a large saucepan for about 20 minutes, until the dahl is tender. Meanwhile, finely chop the onion and garlic. Melt the butter in a heavy-bottomed frying pan, add the onion and garlic and cook gently for several minutes, without browning. Then add the carrot and celery to the partly cooked dahl.

Add the stock to the cooked dahl, with the corn and the silverbeet or spinach leaves, cut into small pieces. Stir in the tomato sauce. Mix the cornflour to a smooth paste with a little water and add, stirring, until the soup thickens. Cut the tomato into small cubes and stir into the soup. Taste, and season as necessary.

Serve immediately, or reheat when required. Sprinkle grated cheddar cheese or parmesan on the soup if desired. Toast or warm crusty bread goes well with this.

Red lentil, carrot & kumara soup

Red lentils cook quickly, without soaking, so you can make this tasty and substantial soup in about half an hour.

SERVES 4:

1 large onion
2 tablespoons olive oil or butter
1–2 teaspoons finely chopped garlic
¼–½ teaspoon chilli powder
2 teaspoons ground cumin
1 teaspoon turmeric (optional)
4 cups vegetable stock (page 43) or 3 teaspoons instant
    stock powder in 4 cups water
¾–1 cup red lentils
2 medium carrots

2 stalks celery
1 large kumara, thinly peeled
¼–½ cup cream or sour cream (optional)
salt and freshly ground black pepper

Chop the onion in 1cm chunks and cook in the oil or butter for about 5 minutes, without browning. During this time, stir in the garlic, chilli powder, cumin and turmeric (if using). The spices should smell fragrant, but should not burn.

Add the stock and the lentils (more makes a thicker soup) and simmer, stirring now and then. Meanwhile cut the carrots and celery in 5mm slices, and the kumara in 1cm cubes. Add them and cook gently, with the lid ajar, for 15–20 minutes, or until everything is tender.

Leave the soup chunky, or purée all or part of it, depending on the texture you like. Thin with extra stock, water or milk if very thick. Add cream or sour cream if you like. Taste and season last of all.

To serve, top with spoonfuls of basil (or other) pesto.

VEGAN OPTION: *Make with oil and without milk or cream.*

Mediterranean bean soup

This is a hearty and nourishing soup with a lovely Mediterranean favour – perfect in cold weather.

SERVES 6–8:

1½ cups haricot or lima beans
10 cups water
2 or 3 cloves garlic, chopped
2 or 3 bay leaves
2 large onions, chopped
2 carrots, chopped
3 stalks celery, chopped
400g can whole tomatoes in juice
1½ teaspoons salt
¼ cup olive oil
freshly ground black pepper
¼ cup chopped parsley
1 teaspoon brown sugar (optional)

Soak the beans in 10 cups of cold water overnight. Add the garlic and bay leaves and simmer for 30 minutes. Add the onions, carrots and celery and simmer for a further 30 minutes, until the beans are very soft and the vegetables are tender. Chop the tomatoes and add them with their juice to the cooked beans. Add the salt, olive oil, plenty of pepper and the chopped parsley.

Allow to stand for a few hours for best flavour, then reheat and adjust the seasonings, adding about a teaspoon of brown sugar if you think it needs it. Remove the bay leaves and serve with crusty bread.

VARIATION: *Purée half or all of the soup to vary the texture.*

Lentil soup with fresh coriander

This soup is made from basic, inexpensive ingredients, but tastes very good

SERVES 6–8:

1½ cups brown or green lentils
2 bay leaves (optional)
2 small dried chillis
10 cups cold water
¼ cup olive oil
2 large onions, finely chopped
4 stalks celery, finely sliced
1 green capsicum, finely chopped
4 cloves garlic, chopped
1 teaspoon each: dried oregano and ground cumin
2 tablespoons chopped coriander leaves
3 tablespoons wine vinegar
1 teaspoon salt
freshly ground black pepper, to taste

Place the lentils, bay leaves (if using) and chillis in a large saucepan with 10 cups of cold water, bring to the boil and simmer for about 45 minutes, or until the lentils are very soft. (Lentils that have been presoaked for 8 hours will be tender in 20 minutes.)

While the lentils cook, heat the oil in a large frying pan. Add the onions, celery and capsicum, and cook, without browning, for about 10 minutes.

Chop the garlic and add half to each mixture. Add the oregano and cumin to the frying pan and cook for a few minutes longer. Remove from the heat.

When the lentils are tender, tip the mixture from the frying pan into the lentils, bring to the boil and simmer for about 15 minutes longer, then remove from the heat. Take out the bay leaves and chillis, add the coriander leaves and vinegar, then add salt and black pepper to taste.

Freeze what is not to be used immediately.

Serve with topped with a spoonful of Easy salsa fresca (page 26).

Lentil soup with fresh coriander

Cream of lentil soup

Cream of lentil soup

Puréed lentils and vegetables are combined with white sauce to give a delicious, creamy soup that is high in protein.

SERVES 4:

2 onions
2 carrots
2 stalks of celery (optional)
2 tablespoons butter
½ cup red lentils
2 cups vegetable stock (page 43)
1 tablespoon butter
1 tablespoon flour
2 cups milk

Chop the onions, carrots and celery. Melt the butter in a medium-sized saucepan, add the chopped vegetables and cook for about 5 minutes, stirring occasionally to prevent browning. Add the lentils and stock, then cover and simmer for 15–20 minutes until the lentils are tender.

While the lentils cook, make a thin white sauce by melting 1 tablespoon of butter in a large saucepan, stirring in the flour and adding ½ cup of milk. Bring this mixture to the boil then add another ½ cup of milk, boil again, then add the remaining cup of milk and return to the boil, then remove from the heat.

Purée the lentil and vegetable mixture in a food processor or blender or by pushing it through a sieve. Add the puréed mixture to the white sauce, taste, and season carefully if required. The flavour of this soup will improve with standing.

Serve topped with Croûtons (page 61), or sour cream and chopped parsley or chives.

Bob's gazpacho

Bob's gazpacho

Enjoy this cool and refreshing chilled soup before a barbecue, on a hot night.

SERVES 6:

2 red capsicums, deseeded and roughly chopped
2 medium carrots, scrubbed
2 stalks celery
1 thin-skinned (telegraph) cucumber, peeled
1 medium red onion, peeled
2 cloves garlic, skin removed
400g can chopped or whole tomatoes in juice
¼ cup tomato paste
¼ cup red wine vinegar
1 teaspoon dried oregano
1 teaspoon salt
1 tablespoon sugar
basil sprigs, to serve

Purée the capsicums in a food processor. Transfer to a large bowl. Chop the carrots and the celery into 4cm lengths and process together until very finely chopped. Put in the bowl. Roughly chop the cucumber, onion and garlic and then process together until finely chopped. Add to the other vegetables.

Process the tomatoes, juice and paste with the vinegar, oregano, salt and sugar. Add to the bowl and mix everything thoroughly.

Refrigerate in a covered container for up to 3 days. Serve chilled, with an ice-block and a basil sprig in each bowl, and pass around a bowl of crisp Croûtons (page 61).

White gazpacho with grapes

This cold soup makes a great dinner party starter or a light main meal on a hot summer's evening.

SERVES 4–6:

4 slices stale, firm-textured white bread (e.g. ciabatta)
2 cloves garlic, peeled
1½ teaspoons salt
1 cup (100g) ground almonds
½ cup olive oil
¼ cup white wine vinegar
4 cups iced water
40–50 green seedless grapes
12 ice-blocks
Croûtons (page 61)

Choose bread with some body and character. Cut off the crusts, then soften the bread by pouring some cold water over it. Leave to stand for a minute or so, then squeeze out and discard most of the liquid.

Put the bread in a food processor with the garlic cloves, salt and ground almonds. Process into a smooth, thick paste. (The garlic gets chopped more efficiently in a thick mixture.) With the motor running, pour in the oil in a thin stream, as if making mayonnaise. Add the vinegar, then add 1 cup of the iced water.

Tip into a large bowl or jug, then stir in the remaining 3 cups of water. Chill for up to 24 hours. Taste and season just before serving.

Serve the soup very cold. Drop about 8 halved grapes and 1 or 2 ice-blocks into each serving, and serve with lots of crisp, freshly made small croûtons.

Smooth & crunchy cream soup

This smooth soup is good hot or cold. Add crisp garden vegetables to the hot or chilled soup just before it is served.

SERVES 4:

250g (2 fairly large) potatoes
2 cups milk
1 clove garlic, finely chopped
¼ teaspoon salt
½ cup cream cheese
¼ cup dry white wine
¼ cup cream
¼ cup each: watercress, lettuce, spinach, cucumber
2 spring onions, finely chopped
¼ cup chopped snowpea sprouts
Croûtons (age 61)

Peel and cube the potatoes and cook gently in the milk with the garlic and salt until tender.

Measure the cream cheese, wine and cream into a food processor. Drain the potatoes, reserving the liquid. Add the hot cooked potato to the food processor, and process until smooth. Add the cooking liquid. Sieve the soup to get it extra smooth, if you like. Taste and adjust the seasonings.

Chill the vegetables you intend to add to the soup. Chop or grate them just before they are to be added, moments before serving.

Serve immediately, or refrigerate until well chilled. Sprinkle with Croûtons before serving.

Yoghurt & cucumber soup

- -

The mixture of cucumber and yoghurt is a useful and versatile one. Depending on its seasoning and concentration, it may be used as a soup, a sauce, a dip or a salad dressing. Although mint, garlic and dill are the herbs usually associated with this, you can please yourself. If possible, allow standing time to allow the flavours to blend well.

SERVES 4:

2–3 telegraph cucumbers
1 teaspoon salt
2–3 spring onions
2 sprigs mint
1–2 cloves garlic
1 sprig parsley
1 sprig dill (optional)
2 cups plain unsweetened yoghurt
2 tablespoons cream (optional)

Peel the cucumbers only if the peel is thick. Halve lengthwise. Scoop out and discard the seeds. Grate the cucumber, sprinkle with salt and leave to stand for 5–10 minutes. Chop the spring onions, mint, garlic, parsley and dill in the food processor with a little of the yoghurt.

Squeeze the cucumber to remove any liquid and combine with the seasonings and remaining yoghurt. Add cream for extra richness, and season. Process again if a smooth mixture is desired. Chill for at least 30 minutes before serving.

Crunchy breads to serve with soup

- -

Interesting, crunchy breads with soup make a satisfying meal. If you can buy firm-textured crusty bread you may not want to read any further. If not, use some of the following ideas to firm up and add interest to softer breads and/or to revitalise stale bread. Also see page 35 for Garlic Bread.

Croûtons

Cut toast-thickness bread into very small cubes (using a sharp serrated knife) and put these in a large bowl. Measure into a small container 1 tablespoon of olive oil for each thick slice of bread you cut up. Drizzle the oil into the bowl of bread while you toss it lightly with a fork or with your other hand. Leave as is, or sprinkle lightly with herb, garlic or onion salt, your favourite seasoning mix or a little curry powder, paprika, etc.

Ways to cook the croûtons:

- Heat in a pan over low heat, turning at intervals, for about 20 minutes or until golden brown.
- Spread the bread on a large shallow dish and bake in a preheated oven at 150°C until golden brown, about 5 minutes.
- Brown under a moderate grill, watching carefully and turning often so they do not brown unevenly.
- Use the croûtons immediately or, as long as they are quite dry, store in an airtight jar.

Crostini

Cut diagonal 1cm thick slices of French bread or bread rolls. Brush lightly on both sides with olive oil or a mixture of olive oil and pesto. Sprinkle with a little parmesan if you like. Grill or bake in one layer until lightly browned, as for Croûtons, but probably for a little longer. Times depend on the moistness of the bread – watch carefully to prevent burning.

Toasted split rolls

Split rolls and brush the cut surface with the same mixture as used for Crostini (above). Grill until the cut surface is golden brown, turn and grill the base slightly. Serve immediately.

Mousetraps

Spread a very thin layer of butter on fresh or stale bread, sliced thick or thin. Cut in strips, place close together, buttered side down, then sprinkle with grated tasty cheddar and bake at 150°C for about 30 minutes until lightly browned. Separate the strips if necessary, cool on wire racks, and eat straight away or store in airtight jars for up to 2 weeks.

After a busy morning, an interesting lunch can brighten up the rest of your day.

We have suggestions for open sandwiches, as well as interesting combinations of fillings for two-slice sandwiches. If you are making sandwiches for your children's lunches, you may find that they like simple fillings best.

Our light meals make particularly good weekend lunches when you have a little more time. Try making roasted red capsicums or your own sushi, you are sure to enjoy the end results!

Lunches & light meals

Open sandwiches

A useful quick snack.

Suggested breads for open sandwich base:

- heavy-textured wholegrain bread
- lighter, softer crumbed brown bread
- fruit bread
- interesting white bread
- English muffins
- crumpets
- pita or pocket bread
- round split rolls or hamburger buns
- long (hot dog) rolls
- lengths of French bread, halved
- crispbread
- any of the above, toasted

Choose several toppings from the list below. Some of these are very substantial!
  Suggested open sandwich toppings:

- Thickly sliced ripe red tomato, on hot toasted rye or mixed grain bread spread with butter, cottage cheese or quark. Top with freshly ground black pepper, basil leaves or alfalfa sprouts.
- Sliced tomato on a split length of French bread, topped with sliced mozzarella or gouda, browned under a grill, or heated in a microwave on High (100%) until the cheese melts. Add lettuce or water-cress if you like.
- Sliced avocado on fresh French bread, with plenty of black pepper or several shakes of a medium chilli sauce. Sprinkle with alfalfa sprouts.
- Mashed avocado on hot toast or a toasted English muffin.
- Drained canned beans mixed with homemade pickle, chopped hard-boiled egg, and chilli mayonnaise, on a fresh crusty roll.
- Canned kidney beans, drained and chopped, mixed with chopped spring onion, sprinkled with Mexican seasoning or cumin, topped with a slice of any cheese and a few thin slices of red capsicum, heated under the grill until the cheese melts.
- Fresh crunchy peanut butter (or a mixture of tahini and peanut butter) and honey on crispbread.
- Peanut butter sprinkled with toasted sunflower seeds, on fruit bread, topped with sliced banana, drizzled with honey or a sprinkling of light brown sugar and a little cinnamon, then grilled.

- Pita bread pockets formed by halving pita bread and spreading the insides of the pocket with a generous spoonful of hummus, finely chopped lettuce, bean sprouts, cucumber and tomato, with whatever dressing is handy.
- Hot refried beans on toast, topped with grated cheese, shredded lettuce and a slice of tomato.
- Hot refried beans, sliced avocado and a little sour cream, sprinkled with hot chilli sauce, on a flour tortilla. Add alfalfa sprouts if available.
- Warm split rolls with one of the dips, spreads, or pâtés in the Finger Foods & Snacks section. Add raw vegetables for extra colour and texture.

Two-slice sandwiches

Try some of our favourite fillings listed below or use your imagination to create your own – remember variety is the spice of life!

Favourite open sandwich fillings:

- cream cheese, chopped nuts and lettuce or alfalfa sprouts
- cream cheese, chopped sultanas and nuts
- chopped dates, walnuts and orange juice, heated together
- cheese, Marmite, and lettuce or sprouts
- Cheese spread (page 64) with lettuce, tomato and sprouts
- peanut butter (or other nut butter) and tahini in equal quantities, mixed with honey or tofu, or chopped sunflower seeds
- coleslaw, raisins and cheese
- peanut butter, cheese and alfalfa sprouts
- tomato and cottage cheese
- Tofu sandwich spread (page 64), lettuce and sprouts
- egg and tomato, with lettuce and sprouts (optional)
- gherkins and cheese
- chocolate spread or chocolate chips with sultanas or raisins
- grated carrot, raisins and lemon juice
- leftover coleslaw and cheese or marinated tempeh or tofu.

Savoury spreads & toppings

Savoury egg topping

On crackers or crostini, in sandwiches, filled rolls or roll-ups, this tastes just the way really good egg filling should. What a treat!

4 hard-boiled eggs, still warm
2 tablespoons milk
1 tablespoon butter, at room temperature
¼ cup finely chopped chives, spring onions or parsley
¼–½ teaspoon salt
freshly ground black pepper, to taste

Shell the eggs and put with the other ingredients into a food processor and process until smooth, adding salt and pepper to taste. Alternatively, mash the eggs with a fork then mix well with the remaining ingredients, adding salt and pepper to taste. Cover and refrigerate until required, up to 3–4 days. Mixture may seem firm when taken straight from the fridge, but will soften as it warms.

Top with a fresh herb sprig, a slice of olive, gherkin, or a tomato wedge.

NOTE: You don't need to butter the bread when using Savoury egg topping for sandwiches.

Cheese spread

This is a 'one-stroke', quick and easy sandwich filling. Try it on toast, too.

100g butter
2 teaspoons flour
1 teaspoon Dijon mustard
½ cup milk
1½–2 cups medium or tasty cheddar cheese, grated
1½ teaspoons wine or cider vinegar
1 lightly beaten egg

Have all the ingredients ready before you start cooking this mixture, as it can overcook or curdle if left too long at any stage. Put some cold water in the sink so that it is ready when you need to cool the pan down quickly.

Melt the butter with the flour and mustard in a frying pan, stirring all the time. Add the milk and stir until the mixture bubbles and is smooth. Without delay, lift it off the heat and add the grated cheese and vinegar, then stir over the heat until the cheese melts.

Take it off the heat again, and stir or whisk in the egg, which has been beaten just enough to combine the white and yolk. Put the mixture back on the heat for 5–10 seconds, until it becomes noticeably thicker. It is important that it is removed from the heat before the fat in it starts to separate, or the egg starts to scramble. Stand the pan in a sink of cold water and stir for about

a minute, until it cools. This should stop any tendency to separate.

Spoon the spread into a jar, cover, and refrigerate or keep in a cool place until you are ready to serve it.

NOTE: You may want to alter the amount of flour or milk in this spread, to make it a little thicker or thinner. The consistency may vary a little, depending on the cheese you use. If you use the filling at room temperature, instead of at fridge temperature, it will be softer; make sure it is soft enough to spread easily.

Potted cheese

Small quantities of this strongly flavoured cheese mixture team well with pears, nuts, grapes, apples, crackers and celery. Matured cheddars 'pot' well.

MAKES ½ CUP:

50g blue and/or matured cheddar cheese
25g unsalted butter
pepper, mace or nutmeg
1–3 tablespoons sherry, brandy or port

Mash, grate or food process the cheese with half its weight of room-temperature, unsalted butter. Add a little pepper, mace or nutmeg. Then add whatever liquid you want to use, about a teaspoon at a time, until you have a soft spreading texture. Store and serve in small, covered pots. Spread on crackers or slices of apples, pears, etc.

Tofu sandwich spread

SERVES 4–6:

250–300g firm tofu
3 tablespoons mayonnaise
1 teaspoon mild prepared mustard
¼ teaspoon turmeric
¼ teaspoon salt
2 tablespoons chopped parsley and chives
juice of ½ lemon (optional)
freshly ground black pepper, to taste

Drain the tofu, then crumble it into a bowl. Add the remaining ingredients and stir gently until everything is well mixed and all the tofu is well coated. Season to taste, then use as you would Savoury Egg Topping.

Avocado topping

Make this topping just before you eat it, as it will turn brown if left standing for long. Roughly mash with a fork 1 medium-sized avocado with 2 teaspoons of lemon juice. Serve on freshly toasted bread without butter. Top with chopped spring onions, chives, basil or coriander leaves, tomato salsa, or thick slices of tomato. Grind black pepper over the lot.

Cottage cheese & tomatoes

Toast a bagel, English muffin, halved roll, or thick slice of wholemeal bread. Spread generously with cottage cheese and top with slices of tomato. This is one of the nicest ways to serve garden-fresh tomatoes. Garnish with basil, snowpea shoots, alfalfa sprouts, etc., if you like.

Basil butter

Cut 100g butter into cubes and soften in the microwave on High (100%) for 20 seconds. Mix in 2 tablespoons of basil pesto.

Serve at room temperature. Spread thinly on hot toast, topped with sliced tomatoes or avocados if you like.

Basil butter will keep in the fridge for up to a week.

Panini

- -

Use panini 'buns' or a flattish bread (5cm thick or less), such as focaccia, ciabatta or Turkish bread.

To fill: Cut the panini (or other bread) in half crosswise, like a hamburger bun.

Spread with your favourite pesto, if you like, then fill with any of the suggestions above, and/or:

- grilled vegetables (asparagus, capsicums, onion, aubergine, mushrooms or zucchini)
- rocket
- baby spinach leaves
- basil leaves
- crushed pineapple (drained)

Other filling combinations that go well together are:

- semi-dried tomatoes, feta and chopped olives or tapenade
- cheese, chargrilled red capsicums and grilled portobello mushrooms
- cheese, semi-dried or fresh tomatoes, basil and/or rocket
- creamy blue cheese, grilled asparagus and grilled mushroom
- grilled aubergine, feta (or other cheese) and grilled capsicum

To cook: Brush the outsides lightly with olive oil, if you like, then place in a sandwich grill preheated to medium-high, until the cheese melts and the bread browns. (For best results the filled panini should be under some pressure as they cook.)

NOTE: *You can use your sandwich grill to pre-grill the vegetables – just brush them with plain or infused (garlic, lemon, etc.) olive oil, then grill until tender.*

Panini

Toasted cheese sandwiches

Toasted cheese sandwiches are versatile, quick and simple to make at a few minutes' notice. What could be more inviting on a cool day?

The essential ingredients are:

bread (toast or sandwich-sliced loaf, or sourdough loaf, etc.)
butter or margarine
sliced cheese (anything from 'plain old' cheddar to brie or camembert, gruyère, raclette, feta, taleggio, etc.)

If you want you can add one or two extras (don't be too generous, or it can get messy), for example:

semi-dried tomatoes (these work better than fresh as they're not as juicy)
thinly sliced avocado
chutney, pesto, mustard or relish

Spread the butter or margarine thinly on two slices of bread. With buttered sides out, make a sandwich of the sliced cheese and any optional extras, with no extra butter on the inside.

Carefully place in a preheated frying pan on medium heat, and cook until golden brown, then turn with a fish-slice and cook the other side. Alternatively, cook the sandwiches in a double-sided sandwich grill, preheated to medium-high. Obviously, this way they don't need to be turned.

Cut into halves or quarters and eat straight away. Perfect with a bowl of soup!

Quesadillas

Quesadillas

The Mexican equivalent of a toasted sandwich or pizza! Quesadillas are flour tortillas topped or filled with a cheesy mixture, then pan-fried or grilled (open or sandwiched) until crisp – all in a very short time.

Flat quesadillas

Brush the outer rim of a flour tortilla lightly with olive or canola oil. Sprinkle the rest of the surface evenly with grated cheese, and a selection of several of the following ingredients, chopped into pea-sized pieces. (Don't use too much filling – less is often better than more!)

- **red onion**
- **canned beans (e.g. kidney, pinto or black beans), drained**
- **olives**
- **tomato**
- **red or green capsicum**
- **mushroom**
- **avocado.**

Sprinkle these on evenly, add a little salsa if you like, then sprinkle a little more cheese on top.

Either heat the tortilla flat in a heavy frying pan; grill it 5–8cm from the heat; or bake it at 180°C for 5–8 minutes. However you cook it, the quesadilla is ready to be cut in wedges and eaten as soon as the tortilla has browned and crisped, the cheese has melted, and any other toppings have heated through. Cut into wedges using a heavy knife while still hot.

'Sandwiched' quesadillas

To make thin, cheese-filled crisp tortilla 'sandwiches', use two flour tortillas, and lightly oil one side of each. Place together with the oiled sides out, and fill with grated cheese and a selection of extra flavourings, as suggested for flat quesadillas. Cut the tortilla sandwich into quarters before cooking, for easier turning and handling. A sandwich press is the perfect way to cook these, but you can also pan-fry or grill them, turning once to brown both sides; or bake (without turning) at 180°C for 5–8 minutes or until lightly browned and crisp.

Cut into smaller wedges soon after cooking, and eat while still warm and fairly crisp.

Eat quesadillas just as they are, or use them as dippers, especially for guacamole and salsa.

VARIATION: *You may find it easier to spread filling on only half of a tortilla which is to be cooked in a pan or under a grill. As soon as the tortilla has been heated enough to become flexible, fold the unfilled side over the filled side.*

Hot asparagus rolls

These simple but delicious rolls are a great way to enjoy asparagus when it is in season in spring.

SERVES 2:

200–250g asparagus
2 teaspoons butter
½ lemon, zest and juice
2–3 tablespoons mayonnaise
½ French stick or two long rolls
salt and freshly ground black pepper, to taste

Trim or break any tough ends from the asparagus. Place it in an oven bag, then roll the bag up loosely. Boil gently or microwave for 1½–2 minutes on High (100%) until tender. Drain, then add the butter and lemon juice.

Put the mayonnaise in a small bowl and stir in the lemon zest. Warm the bread first, if you want. Cut the baguette (if using) into 2 lengths, each about as long as the asparagus, and split along the middle. Spread half the mayonnaise in each roll, then lay in the asparagus spears. Season to taste with salt and pepper, and enjoy!

Aubergine & feta rolls

These delicious rolls are so simple to assemble. Use longer, thinner aubergines to make small starter-sized rolls, or larger aubergines for a scrumptious main course.

SERVES 5–6:

2 small–medium (about 400g total) aubergine
3–4 tablespoons olive oil (plain, or basil- or garlic-infused)
1 medium red capsicum
100–150g feta cheese
1–2 tablespoons balsamic vinegar
about 2 tablespoons chopped basil (or 10–12 basil leaves)
salt and freshly ground black pepper, to taste

Cut the aubergine lengthwise into thin (about 7mm) slices. Lightly brush both sides of each slice with oil. Place slices in a preheated contact grill (you may have to do this in several batches) and cook for 4–5 minutes on a high heat. Alternatively, arrange the slices on a non-stick sprayed baking sheet and place them under a preheated grill (5–7cm from the heat) and cook for about 3–4 minutes before turning and cooking a further 3 minutes. Set the cooked aubergine aside until cool enough to handle.

While the aubergine cools, prepare the remaining ingredients. Cut the capsicum flesh from the core in flattish slices, brush these with any remaining oil and cook like the aubergine, then cut into 10–12 strips (you need the same number as you have of slices of aubergine). Cut the feta into the same number of fingers or slices, too.

Aubergine & feta rolls

To assemble the rolls, lay 1 strip of aubergine on a board, and brush lightly with balsamic vinegar. Lay a strip of capsicum and a piece of feta across one end, add a little chopped basil or a basil leaf, and sprinkle with salt and pepper, then roll up.

Arrange on a serving plate, drizzle with a little extra oil if you like, and serve.

NOTE: *If you're short of time, you can use bottled, chargrilled red capsicum instead.*

Hot crumbed camembert

Serve these delicious cheese wedges warm, with a tart jelly or a sweet-sour pickle.

SERVES 2–3:

1 camembert or brie cheese
flour
1 egg, beaten
about 100g wine biscuits, crushed
canola oil for cooking

Chill a small whole camembert or brie cheese. Cut it into wedges the size that you want, then dip each in flour, then beaten egg, then in fine, dry wine-biscuit crumbs. Repeat the egg and crumb layers to get a thicker coating, if you like. Refrigerate again until required.

About 15 minutes before serving, lower the cheese carefully into very hot (200°C) oil, at least 3cm deep. Remove as soon as the coating is golden brown, and drain on a paper towel. Leave to cool a little before serving.

Roasted red capsicums

SERVES 4 (MAIN) OR 8 (STARTER):

4 red (or yellow) capsicums
8 basil leaves
2 cloves garlic, peeled and thinly
    sliced
about 16 capers
6 medium-sized tomatoes, or canned
    whole tomatoes
8–16 black olives
about ¼ cup extra virgin olive oil
fresh basil leaves for garnish

Make these when capsicums are at their best.

Halve the capsicums lengthwise, cutting through the stems so they remain intact. Remove pith and seeds. Lay the capsicums in one layer in a shallow roasting dish.

Place a basil leaf and several slices of garlic in the bottom of each capsicum, then divide the capers between the capsicums.

If using fresh tomatoes, blanch to remove the skins and cut in halves or quarters. Cut the peeled or canned tomatoes lengthwise, and shake out the seeds and liquid. Place the tomatoes, cut side down, in the capsicums. Top with the olives. Drizzle 1–2 teaspoons of olive oil over each halved capsicum.

Bake uncovered, at 200°C for about 30 minutes, until the capsicums are lightly charred at the edges. Spoon any liquid around the capsicums into them. Refrigerate if necessary.

Garnish with fresh basil leaves and serve at room temperature, with chunks of bread to mop up all the delicious juices.

NOTE: *Do not use green capsicums for this recipe.*

Mushroom & avocado melt

SERVES 4:

6 portobello mushrooms
Parmesan dressing (page 98)
1 flat, focaccia-type round bread,
    about 25cm across (page 241)
2 avocados
1 large red capsicum
grated or sliced cheese

Melts make quick, spectacular and substantial meals. Always make them just before they are to be eaten.

Lightly brush the underside of the mushrooms with Parmesan dressing. Grill until the cheese bubbles, 2–3 minutes. Turn and brush the mushroom tops, then grill again.

Cut the loaf of flat bread through its middle, as you would a hamburger bun. Brush the cut surfaces with more dressing and grill until golden brown and crisp.

Slice the cooked mushrooms and pile onto the toasted bread with slices of avocado and strips of red capsicum. Top with grated or sliced cheese, in quantities to suit. Grill until the cheese melts, then cut into wedges.

Serve at once. As this is a casual meal to be eaten with fingers, follow it with raw fruit, to be eaten the same way.

Stuffed mushrooms

SERVES 4 (MAIN) OR 8 (STARTER):

2 slices wholemeal bread
1 clove garlic, peeled
1 tablespoon olive oil
1 tablespoon basil pesto
1 tablespoon grated parmesan
2–3 tablespoons chopped black olives
¼ teaspoon thyme
¼–½ teaspoon salt
¼ cup pine nuts
8 portobello (10–12cm) or
    12–16 smaller (6–8cm) mushrooms
freshly ground black pepper to taste

Use more, smaller mushrooms to serve as a starter or finger food, or fewer large flat mushrooms for a main. Either way, prepare the filling ahead and bake the mushrooms when required.

Preheat the oven to 225°C.

Tear the bread into smaller pieces and crumb in a food processor. Add the garlic and process briefly. Add all the remaining filling ingredients except the pine nuts and process until just mixed (the mixture should stay as crumbs, not turn to paste). Tip in the pine nuts and whiz again to mix evenly.

Remove and discard the mushroom stems. Arrange the mushrooms (gills up) in a single layer over the bottom of a sponge-roll pan or roasting pan. Spoon the filling into the caps, dividing it evenly between the mushrooms and leaving it sitting 'fluffed-up' rather than packed down.

Bake at 220°C for 12–15 minutes, or until the filling is golden brown. Remove from the oven and leave to stand for about 5 minutes before serving alone or with Vegetarian gravy (page 149).

Roasted red capsicums

Corn fritters

Corn fritters

Keep a can of corn handy to make corn fritters whenever you need a quick meal. The size of the can does not matter – so use a larger can for more fritters.

SERVES 2 (MAIN) OR 6 (STARTER):

1 egg
3–4 tablespoons liquid from corn
1 can whole kernel corn, drained
1 cup self-raising flour

Put the egg into a mixing bowl. Drain the liquid from the can of corn. Put 3 tablespoonfuls of corn liquid in with the egg, and keep the rest aside in case you need to thin the batter later.

Tip the drained corn into the bowl, add the flour, and stir with a fork, just until the mixture is dampened. Do not overmix.

Drop teaspoonfuls of batter into a pan with hot oil, about 1cm deep. (Heat an electric pan to 190°C.) Turn the fritters with tongs as soon as they are brown on the bottom. Lift them from the pan as soon as the second side is cooked, and keep them warm on a plate lined with paper towels.

NOTE: *A large pile of little fritters is much nicer than a small pile of large ones.*

Stuffed grape leaves

These are easy and inexpensive to make.

MAKES 36:

about 40 young grape leaves
1 onion, finely chopped
½ cup olive oil
½ cup uncooked rice
½ cup currants
¼–½ cup pine nuts
¼ cup lemon juice
1–2 tablespoons each: fresh mint, parsley and dill leaves, chopped
1 teaspoon salt
1 cup water

Put the grape leaves into a saucepan of boiling water, and hold them under the surface until they will fold easily without breaking. Refresh in cold water.

Cook the onion gently in half the olive oil for 2–3 minutes. Add the rice, currants and pine nuts, stir for a minute longer, then remove from the heat, and add half the lemon juice, the herbs and the salt.

With the shiny side of the leaves down, put a teaspoon of rice mixture on the centre of each leaf. Fold the stem ends then the sides of the leaf over the filling, and roll up loosely into cylinders.

Arrange the stuffed leaves side by side, in one layer in a baking dish. Drizzle with the remaining oil and lemon juice, then pour the water around them. Cover with flat grape leaves then with a lid or foil. Bake at 150°C for 1–1½ hours, or until the rice is cooked and the stuffed leaves are tender. Drain, cover with cling film and leave to cool. Serve at room temperature.

Sushi

If you are prepared to take the time to prepare sushi, you will be rewarded with a dramatic and inexpensive dish that can be served as a snack or starter at any time of the day.

MAKES 20:

1 cup short grain rice
1¾ cups water
2 tablespoons dry sherry
2 tablespoons wine vinegar
2 tablespoons sugar
1 teaspoon salt
1½ tablespoons flour
¼ cup milk
1 egg
½ teaspoon salt
vegetables (e.g. carrots, celery, capsicum, blanched
    spinach and Japanese pickled vegetables), cut into
    strips
dried nori seaweed sheets, to wrap
wasabi powder mixed to a paste with water (or
    prepared wasabi paste), to serve
Kikkoman (or other Japanese) soy sauce, to serve

Cook the rice and water in a metal bowl standing in a saucepan of hot water, until it is tender. To microwave, place in a microwave-proof dish and cook on High (100%) for about 10 minutes.

Add the sherry, wine vinegar, sugar and salt, and stir together with a fork. Taste, and adjust flavourings if required.

Use a fork to mix together the flour, milk, egg and salt. Pour half the mixture onto a small heated and buttered frypan. Tilt the pan until the bottom is covered. When the mixture is cooked through, loosen the edges and turn the pan upside down and tip the egg mixture onto a square of cling film. Repeat with the rest of the mixture.

Assemble the strips of vegetable that you will roll up in the rice, choosing vegetables of contrasting colours.

Some nori sheets are pretoasted, but if not, hold the seaweed sheet (one at a time) over a hot element until they smell toasted.

Lay 1 sheet of nori on a sheet of cling film. Place a thin, even covering of warm sushi rice all over the wrapper. Place 1 of the egg mixtures over the layer of sushi rice. Then, on the end which will be rolled first, arrange lines of vegetable strips. Lie blanched spinach leaves flat so that you will see a spiral of dark green when the roll is cut, later on.

Using the sheet of cling film to help you, roll the wrapper up firmly to form a compact cylinder, with the vegetables in the centre. Wrap in cling film, refrigerate until required (up to 2 days), then cut into short lengths with a sharp or serrated knife.

Serve with a dish of soy sauce for dipping, and a dab of wasabi paste.

Sushi

In the following pages you will find an interesting and varied collection of salad recipes.

A home-prepared salad will add colour and crunch, as well as flavour, to a main course, but salads don't have to be complicated – in fact, simple salads are sometimes better than one with too many ingredients.

Don't limit yourself to raw ingredients – use warm or cold cooked vegetables and raw fruit on occasion. You can also add cooked rice, pasta and croûtons to your salad.

Salads

Salad basics

Research has shown that fruit and vegetables have important health-protecting qualities. Many of us, however, do not eat the recommended minimum five daily servings. The best way to increase your fruit and vegetable intake is to make a point of eating more salads.

A good salad will add variety and interest to any meal and it's not difficult to find a salad that's right for any season and situation. A salad can be quickly made from one vegetable, a tub of mesclun or a bag of sprouts or undressed coleslaw from the supermarket, tossed in a made-ahead dressing from the fridge. Try including different ingredients and experiment with textures and flavours until you find the ideal combination.

Here are some suggestions for salad ingredients.
- raw apple cubes (toss in dressing before they brown)
- avocado halves or cubes, drizzled with lemon juice
- lightly cooked asparagus spears
- lightly cooked green beans, chopped
- beansprouts, pea sprouts, sunflower sprouts
- beetroot, especially baby beets, canned
- shredded cabbage
- cauliflower florets
- celery, thinly sliced or lightly cooked, sliced
- shredded raw carrots or sliced cooked carrots
- coleslaw mixes (undressed)
- corn kernels, roasted, boiled, canned or frozen
- kiwifruit slices or cubes
- cooked kumara, sliced
- lettuce, in chunky pieces, torn or sliced
- mesclun (baby salad leaves)
- raw button mushrooms, sliced or marinated
- raw pears, sliced (toss in dressing to stop browning)
- cooked green peas
- raw sugarsnap peas or snowpeas in pods
- capsicums, raw or roasted, all colours
- cooked waxy potatoes
- radishes, sliced
- spinach leaves
- swede, shredded, raw
- tomatoes, small or large
- watercress sprigs or leaves
- zucchini, lightly cooked or raw

Memorable coleslaws

It's worth learning how to make a good coleslaw for a number of reasons. Coleslaw doesn't call for anything exotic or expensive, and its ingredients will keep in the fridge for days, will be available right through the year, and won't cost very much. You can make coleslaw ahead of time and take it to potluck meals or picnics. It need never be boring, because you can make so many variations.

For basic coleslaw, shred a quarter of a cabbage very finely (with a sharp knife or a food processor slicing blade), coarsely grate a scrubbed carrot or two, and toss the 2 together with any of the dressings on pages 97–99.

Other suitable vegetable additions are thinly sliced celery, capsicums, cauliflower and spring onions. Look for packets of sprouts of chickpeas, lentils, adzuki, mung beans and peas; these give coleslaw a lovely, slightly nutty flavour. For sweetness, add cubes of unpeeled apple tossed in lemon juice, sultanas, currants or raisins.

Add grated cheese, or a sprinkling of toasted seeds and nuts for a change. 2-Minute Noodle Coleslaw is always a good talking point (see instructions below)!

Toasted seeds & nuts

½ cup each: sunflower seeds, pumpkin seeds and chopped raw almonds (skin on)

Toss all in ½ teaspoon of sesame oil and cook in a heavy frying pan, shaking the pan at intervals, for 5–10 minutes, until the pumpkin seeds look plump. Cool, then store in a screw-top jar. Sprinkle a few tablespoons into coleslaw when serving.

2-Minute Noodle coleslaw

Partially break up the noodles from a packet of 2-Minute Noodles. Place on foil and heat under a moderate grill until the noodles turn golden brown (1–2 minutes). Break into smaller pieces, store in an airtight container and toss through coleslaw which has been tossed with sesame dressing, just moments before it is to be eaten.

Kumara salad

SERVES 3–4:

3 kumara (750g in total), scrubbed
¼ cup sultanas
1 firm banana
¼–½ cup flaked coconut
1 can mandarin segments (optional)
1 green capsicum, chopped
2 spring onions, finely chopped

DRESSING
½ cup olive oil or other oil
¼ cup white wine vinegar
1 teaspoon mixed mustard
1–2 teaspoons grated ginger root
½ teaspoon salt
1 teaspoon honey or brown sugar

Try this salad as an interesting alternative to potato salad.

Cook the kumara in a covered container in the microwave on High (100%) (or oven bake) until tender. When they are cool enough to handle, peel and chop into bite-sized pieces.

Put the sultanas into a sieve and pour boiling water over them to plump them up a little, then drain well. Mix through the kumara.

Slice the banana and add to the kumara and sultanas. Add the coconut, drained mandarin segments (if using), capsicum and spring onions.

Combine all the dressing ingredients in a screw-top jar and shake well.

Toss all the salad ingredients gently with about half of the dressing, adding the remainder just before serving.

Serve with freshly made Bread Rolls (page 245).

Curried kumara salad

SERVES 2–3:

500g kumara
2–3 sticks celery, sliced
½ cup roasted cashews or peanuts,
    roughly chopped
¼–½ cup chopped dates
¼ cup chopped fresh coriander

DRESSING
½ cup plain unsweetened yoghurt
1–2 tablespoons sweet mango
    chutney
1 clove garlic, minced
1 teaspoon curry powder
½–1 teaspoon salt

This substantial salad involves several different stages, but all of them are easy, and the result is worth the effort.

Peel the kumara and cut into 2–3cm cubes. Cook until tender either by microwaving on High (100%) in a covered container for 7–10 minutes, or by boiling gently, then drain and leave to cool to room temperature.

While the kumara cooks, stir the dressing ingredients together and prepare the remaining salad ingredients.

Place the cooled kumara in a large bowl with the celery, nuts, dates and coriander, reserving a little of the coriander and a few of the nuts to garnish. Drizzle with dressing, then toss gently to combine.

Garnish with the reserved coriander and nuts, and serve immediately or refrigerate until required.

Sweet-sour carrot salad

SERVES 4:

1 tablespoon Dijon mustard
1 tablespoon honey
1 tablespoon lemon juice
1 teaspoon grated ginger root
1½ cups shredded raw carrot
watercress leaves or chopped parsley,
    to garnish

This salad has a zesty character that will 'lift' other bland foods.

Measure the mustard and honey into a shallow serving bowl. Mix in the lemon juice. Squeeze the ginger root so the juice runs into the mustard mixture. Discard the fibres.

Turn the shredded carrot in the dressing until it is evenly coated. Taste and season only if necessary.

Garnish with a few watercress leaves, or with chopped parsley.

VARIATION: *Mix ½–1 cup of chopped roasted peanuts through the salad a few minutes before serving.*

Avocado with Mediterranean dressing

Give avocados star status with this dressing!

Warm a little of the olive oil in a frying pan, add the pine nuts and heat until golden brown. Add the rest of the oil and the remaining dressing ingredients, then put aside until required.

Just before serving, halve two ripe avocados by cutting around them and twisting the halves gently. Remove the stones by chopping a sharp knife into the stone and twisting the knife. Spoon dressing into the avocado cavities and serve promptly.

SERVES 4:

DRESSING
2 tablespoons olive oil
¼ cup pine nuts
4 sundried tomatoes, chopped
2 teaspoons balsamic or wine vinegar
1 clove garlic, very finely chopped
¼ teaspoon salt
freshly ground black pepper, to taste
2 ripe avocados

Avocado with Mediterranean dressing

Wilted cucumber salad

SERVES 4–6:

1 telegraph cucumber
1 teaspoon salt in 1 cup water
2 spring onions, chopped
1 small clove garlic, finely chopped
    (optional)
2 tablespoons wine vinegar
pinch chilli powder
1 tablespoon each: toasted sesame
    seeds and sugar

A good side dish for a curry or for grilled lamb with a peanutty sauce.

Halve the cucumber lengthwise. Scoop out the seeds using a teaspoon. Cut the cucumber in thin slices and soak these in the salted water for 10 minutes or longer.

When you are ready to serve, drain the cucumber well, and place in a serving dish with the spring onion, garlic (if using), vinegar and chilli powder. Crush the toasted sesame seeds with the sugar in a pestle and mortar or blender, add to the salad and mix well.

Elizabeth's favourite salad

SERVES 4:

1 tablespoon lemon juice
1 teaspoon sugar
¼ teaspoon salt
1 large avocado
2–3 firm, red tomatoes
10cm length telegraph cucumber,
    unpeeled
about 2 cups chopped crisp-leaf
    (iceberg or romaine) lettuce
1 or 2 spring onions
1 tablespoon olive oil
freshly ground black pepper, to taste

This is an ever-popular salad, made by Alison's granddaughters at the drop of a hat!

Mix the lemon juice, sugar and salt in the bottom of a fairly large salad bowl. Remove the skin and stone from the avocado, cut the flesh into 1cm cubes and turn gently in the lemon juice without breaking up.

Cut the tomatoes into slices 1cm thick, then into 1cm cubes. Discard any excess juice and place the tomato pieces on the avocado, without tossing. Cut the cucumber in 1cm cubes and sprinkle over the tomato.

Cut a firm hearty (iceberg) lettuce into 1–2cm squares, without separating the leaves; or romaine lettuce hearts into 1cm slices. Thinly slice spring onion stems and some leaves and add to the bowl, without mixing.

Cover with cling film and refrigerate up 1 hour if not serving immediately. When serving, sprinkle with the olive oil, freshly ground pepper, add a little extra salt if necessary, and toss gently to coat the ingredients without bruising or breaking them.

Good with almost any main course, or for lunch.

'Brocauli' salad

SERVES 4:

200–250g prepared broccoli
250–300g prepared cauliflower

DRESSING

½ cup olive oil
¼ cup white wine vinegar
1 clove garlic, very finely chopped
1 teaspoon dried oregano
1–2 teaspoons Dijon mustard
    (optional)
salt and freshly ground black pepper,
    to taste

A tasty salad can be made almost year-round from a mixture of lightly cooked broccoli and cauliflower. You can eat it as soon as you coat the cooked vegetables with dressing, or leave it to stand for up to 24 hours.

Cut the broccoli and cauliflower into bite-sized pieces, peeling off and discarding any tough outer skin, then boil in a little lightly salted water in a covered saucepan until tender-crisp. Drain, cool to room temperature by immersing in very cold water, then drain again and refrigerate in a plastic bag if not using immediately.

To make the dressing, combine the oil and vinegar in a screw-top jar, and add the garlic, crumbled dried oregano and mustard. Shake well, then add salt and pepper to taste.

To keep the broccoli bright green, toss the cooled broccoli and cauliflower in the dressing just before serving. For more flavour, add the dressing to the vegetables as soon as both are prepared and leave to stand; the broccoli will turn olive green.

American-style potato salad

- -

This ever-popular salad travels well (although it should be kept cool) and makes a great lunch. It can also be 'dressed-up' by the addition of some optional extras.

Scrub the potatoes, then boil them gently until just cooked. Drain, then return the potatoes to the saucepan and add the first measure of vinegar and the oil. Toss gently to coat, then leave to stand until room temperature.

Thin the mayonnaise with the milk or lemon juice and 2 teaspoons vinegar. Slice or cube the cooled potatoes into a large bowl, then add the celery, parsley, spring onions and the mayonnaise mixture (and one or two of the optional extras, if you like). Mix gently, without breaking up the potato too much. Season to taste with salt and pepper.

Serve this salad at about room temperature; but if you're making it in advance, it should be refrigerated until shortly before it is required. Serve as is or garnished with some more parsley and/or chives.

SERVES 3–4:

1kg waxy or new potatoes
2 tablespoons white wine vinegar
2 tablespoons olive oil
½ cup mayonnaise
about 2 tablespoons milk or lemon juice
2 teaspoons white wine vinegar
2 sticks celery, sliced
¼ cup chopped parsley
2 spring onions, sliced
salt and freshly ground black pepper, to taste

OPTIONAL EXTRAS
chopped hard-boiled egg
sliced or chopped gherkins
roasted pumpkin seeds

Marinated mushroom salad

- -

Serve these tender button mushrooms marinated in tangy lemon and oil dressing as a salad, or try them piled on warm, crispy bruschetta for a delicious pre-dinner aperitif, starter or even a light lunch.

Wipe the mushrooms if necessary, trim off the stems and slice the mushrooms thinly (about 3mm). Place the sliced mushrooms in a wide (about 30cm across) flat-bottomed bowl or casserole dish.

Place all the marinade ingredients except the black pepper in a bowl. Whisk to combine, then season to taste with black pepper.

Pour the marinade mixture over the mushrooms and stir gently, then cover and leave to stand in the fridge for 3–12 hours, stirring gently once or twice. Remove from the fridge and allow to stand at room temperature for 30 minutes before serving.

SERVES 4–6:

250g button mushrooms

MARINADE
2 small or 1 large clove garlic, finely chopped
¼ cup lemon juice
1 tablespoon balsamic vinegar
1 teaspoon Dijon mustard
½ teaspoon salt
about 6 basil leaves, finely chopped
2 sprigs marjoram, finely chopped
½ cup virgin olive oil
freshly ground black pepper to taste

Roasted capsicum salad

- -

Capsicums prepared like this have a wonderful flavour and an interesting texture, quite different from raw capsicums.

Use fresh, firm and fleshy capsicums. Heat whole capsicums under a grill, over a barbecue rack, or on a gas burner, keeping them close to the heat, and turning them as their skin blisters and blackens, or roast in an oven preheated to 220°C for about 30 minutes. When they have blackened in patches and have blistered fairly evenly, put the capsicums in a paper or plastic bag and leave to stand for 5–10 minutes, then hold them, one at a time, under a cold tap and peel or cut off the skin. The flesh underneath should be brightly coloured and partly cooked.

Quarter the capsicums, and trim away the seeds and pith. Cut into even shapes, put them in a shallow dish, and coat with the lemon juice and oil, using less or more as needed. Refrigerate for up to 2 days.

Serve at room temperature, sprinkled with freshly ground black pepper.

4–6 plump, fleshy, red, green, yellow or orange capsicums
¼ cup lemon juice
¼ cup olive oil
freshly ground black pepper

American-style potato salad

Crunchy spinach salad with blue cheese dressing

- -

SERVES 3–4:

300–400g young spinach leaves

DRESSING

50g blue cheese, crumbled

1 tablespoon wine vinegar

3 tablespoons olive oil

1 tablespoon finely chopped fresh
   chives

2–4 tablespoons milk

salt and freshly ground black pepper,
   to taste

CROÛTONS

4 slices toast-sliced bread

2 tablespoons olive or canola oil

garlic salt (optional)

When we've asked friends and family about salads they like, one that keeps coming up as most popular is also one of the simplest – good old spinach salad; so here it is.

To make the dressing, combine the blue cheese, vinegar, olive oil and chives in a blender or food processor. Process until smooth, stopping once or twice to scrape down the sides. Add enough milk to thin the dressing to a pouring consistency, then season to taste with salt and pepper.

To make the croûtons, cut the bread into very small cubes (you should have about 2 cups) and put these in a large bowl. Drizzle the oil into the bowl while you toss the bread with a fork or your hand. Sprinkle lightly with the garlic salt, if you like.

Heat the bread cubes in a frying pan over low heat, turning at intervals, for about 10–15 minutes or until golden brown. Or spread on a large shallow dish and bake in a preheated oven at 150°C until golden brown, about 5 minutes. Or brown under a moderate grill, watching carefully and turning often so they do not brown unevenly. Set aside while you prepare the remaining ingredients.

To prepare the salad, soak the spinach in a sink full of cold water to remove any grit, then shake or spin dry. Remove and discard the stalks and any large tough-looking leaves and place the rest in a large salad bowl.

Just before serving, sprinkle in most of the croûtons and toss gently to combine. Sprinkle the remaining croûtons over the top then drizzle the salad with about half of the dressing.

Serve immediately, accompanied with crusty garlic bread and a jug of the remaining dressing.

Caesar salad

- -

SERVES 4–6:

1 cos (romaine) lettuce

½–1 cup croûtons (above)

½ cup freshly grated parmesan

DRESSING

1 egg

1 clove garlic

juice of one lime or lemon

1 teaspoon Dijon mustard

½ teaspoon Worcestershire sauce

about ½ teaspoon salt

freshly ground black pepper

½ cup extra virgin olive oil

Here is our version of this popular dish. It is important that it is made with crisp lettuce leaves.

Separate and wash the lettuce leaves, then dry well. Chill for several hours, or overnight. The leaves should be cold and dry when the salad is made.

To assemble the salad, arrange the leaves in a large salad bowl, sprinkling the croûtons through them. Just before serving, drizzle the dressing through and around the leaves, toss carefully to coat the leaves with dressing, then sprinkle with freshly grated parmesan.

To make the dressing, combine all ingredients except the oil in a food processor bowl. Blend until smooth, then, while the motor is still running, pour the olive oil in a slow, steady stream until the dressing is the consistency of thick pouring cream. Taste and adjust the seasonings.

A salad as good as this may be served as a course by itself.

VARIATION: *Make the dressing exactly as above but without the egg.*

Crunchy spinach salad with blue cheese dressing

Roasted red onion salad (back); Roasted capsicum salad (page 79)

Marinated tomato salad

It's hard to beat a tomato salad, especially with ripe red tomatoes from your own garden.

SERVES 4:

5–6 medium-sized tomatoes
1 teaspoon sugar
¼–½ teaspoon salt
freshly ground black pepper, to taste
few drops hot pepper sauce
1 tablespoon wine vinegar
1 tablespoon chopped fresh basil, marjoram or parsley
1–2 tablespoons oil (optional)

Slice, quarter or cube the tomatoes and place in the serving dish.

About 10–15 minutes before serving, sprinkle the remaining ingredients, in the order given, over the tomatoes. Toss lightly and leave to stand at room temperature.

Spiced tomato & cucumber salad

This salad needs no dressing. With or without the cucumber it is delicious, but is especially good as an accompaniment for curries and Mexican foods that do not contain tomatoes.

SERVES 4–6:

3–4 red, firm, flavourful tomatoes
½ telegraph cucumber, unpeeled (optional)
2 spring onions or ¼ red onion
1 tablespoon sugar
1–2 teaspoons ground cumin
½ teaspoon salt
chopped coriander leaves (optional)

Cut the tomatoes into neat 1cm cubes. Cut the cucumber (if using) into cubes the same size. Slice the spring onions thinly or finely chop the red onion. Place the prepared vegetables in a serving dish, sprinkle with the sugar, cumin and salt and toss gently. (Use only 1 teaspoon of cumin if not using the cucumber.) Sprinkle with coriander leaves if you like, and serve chilled or at room temperature.

Roasted red onion salad

Red onions are milder than other onions. Roasted, they make an interesting and different salad.

SERVES 4:

4 red onions, quartered, leaving the roots on
1 tablespoon olive oil
2 teaspoons wine vinegar
1 teaspoon balsamic vinegar
1 teaspoon sugar
½ teaspoon finely chopped fresh sage or thyme leaves (optional)

Roast the quartered red onions at 180°C for 25–30 minutes, or until tender.

While the onions are still hot, transfer to a serving dish, sprinkle with remaining ingredients and turn lightly to coat, without breaking up the onions.

Serve warm or at room temperature (but not chilled).

Tomato & bread salad

Made with firm, red, flavourful tomatoes, this is an outstanding salad, served for lunch or to liven up a light main course. A firm-textured bread like a French stick or ciabatta works best, but you can use whatever you have.

SERVES 4:

20cm-length French bread
about ¼ cup olive oil
2 teaspoons pesto (basil is good)
4 ripe red tomatoes
¼ red onion or 2 spring onions
about 20 basil leaves
sprinkling of salt, sugar and freshly ground black
    pepper

Cut the French bread in quarters lengthwise. Mix the olive oil with the pesto, then brush the surfaces of the bread lightly with some of the oil, reserving some for later.

Ten minutes before serving, toast the bread under a moderate grill, turning so that all the edges are golden but no surfaces burn.

Chop the tomatoes into 1cm cubes and put in a large salad bowl with the finely chopped onion and the basil leaves, whole or broken up by hand.

Just before serving, cut the warm, browned bread into 15mm lengths. Sprinkle the tomatoes with a little salt, sugar and pepper, toss gently, and when the juices start to run, add the bread cubes, toss to mix, drizzle with the remainder of the oil and pesto mix, and serve immediately.

Greek salad

This makes a good hot-weather meal when served with crusty bread rolls. Use quantities to suit yourself.

Arrange in individual dishes:

- chunks of telegraph or other tender-skinned cucumber
- chunks or thick slices of tomato
- chopped onion, or sliced spring onion or thinly sliced red onion
- whole black olives
- fresh oregano, or crumbled dried oregano
- cubed feta cheese

Drizzle olive oil over, and serve with lemon wedges if you like.

Mediterranean salad

This is like a Greek salad with extra 'goodies'.

SERVES 4:

100g assorted lettuce leaves, washed
1 red capsicum, diced
1 green capsicum, diced
6–8 small tomatoes, quartered
½–1 cup cucumber, cubed
50–70g feta cheese, cubed
20 black olives

DRESSING
2 tablespoons olive oil
2 tablespoons lemon juice
1 teaspoon prepared mustard
1–2 tablespoons chopped fresh herbs (e.g. basil, parsley,
    oregano, thyme)
salt and freshly ground black pepper

Arrange the lettuce leaves in the bottom of 4 individual dishes. Prepare then toss together the rest of the salad ingredients, and arrange over the lettuce.

Combine all the dressing ingredients in a screw-top jar, and shake until opaque.

Drizzle the dressing evenly over the salad just before serving.

Fruit salad

This salad makes a fresh-tasting curry accompaniment and is useful when salad vegetables are expensive or in short supply. It is a cross between a salad and a fruit salsa.

SERVES 4:

2 apples, pears, or an equivalent amount of fresh
    pineapple, kiwifruit, bananas, etc.
2 tablespoons unsweetened lime juice
¼ cup olive oil
1 clove garlic, finely chopped
¼ teaspoon chilli paste
¼ teaspoon salt
¼ cup chopped fresh coriander
1 cup sunflower, rocket or other crunchy sprouts
about 2 tablespoons chopped walnuts or toasted
    almonds

A short time before serving, remove the cores of the apples or pears and slice the fruit into the salad bowl. (Or peel and cut other fruit into bite-sized pieces.)

Mix together lime juice, oil, garlic, chilli paste and salt.

Turn the fruit gently in the dressing, sprinkle the coriander leaves, sprouts and chopped nuts through the fruit or over the top, and serve immediately.

'Greek-style' pasta salad

SERVES 3-4:

300g short pasta shapes (shells,
  spirals, crests, penne, rigatoni, etc.)
200g feta cheese, cubed
1 large green capsicum
250–300g cherry tomatoes
¼–½ cup kalamata olives (black or
  mixed)
2–3 tablespoons capers (optional)

DRESSING

¼ cup extra virgin olive oil
3 tablespoons lemon juice
1–2 tablespoons chopped fresh
  oregano
1 clove garlic, minced
½ teaspoon salt
½ teaspoon sugar
freshly ground black pepper, to taste

This is another salad that is great as a side dish, or that can easily form the basis of a quick and delicious summer meal.

Put the pasta on to cook in plenty of boiling water. While the pasta cooks, prepare the remaining ingredients.

To make the dressing, combine the olive oil, lemon juice, oregano, garlic, salt, sugar and pepper in a screw-top jar and shake until well mixed.

Put the cubed feta in a bowl, add 2 tablespoons of the prepared dressing and leave to marinate for a few minutes.

Quarter and deseed the green capsicum then cut into 1cm chunks. Halve any larger tomatoes.

Drain the barely cooked pasta (slightly underdone pasta has a firmer, more pleasant texture), and rinse it with plenty of cold running water. Drain well, then transfer to a large bowl. Add the feta, olives, tomatoes, capsicums, capers (if using), and dressing. Stir or toss gently until well combined.

Garnish with some additional sprigs of herbs and/or capers and serve.

Chargrilled vegetable & feta salad

SERVES 4-6:

1 medium aubergine
2–3 zucchini, green or yellow
1–2 red or yellow capsicums
1–2 bunches asparagus (optional)
10–12 spring onions
2–3 portobello mushrooms
2 cloves garlic, crushed, peeled and
  chopped
2 tablespoons olive oil
2 tablespoons balsamic vinegar
pinch salt
freshly ground black pepper, to taste
4–6 cups mesclun mix
100–150g feta cheese, crumbled

DRESSING

2 tablespoons olive oil
1 tablespoon balsamic vinegar
1 teaspoon wholegrain prepared
  mustard
¼–½ teaspoon salt

This salad was inspired by one made by Mike, Simon's friend. He chargrilled a selection of vegetables, then used them as the basis for an impressive-looking and delicious salad. Exact quantities and proportions are not critical – use these as a rough guide only and let your imagination be your guide.

Begin by preparing the vegetables. Cut the aubergine into crosswise slices 1.5–2cm thick and the zucchini lengthwise into slices about 1cm thick. Core, deseed and quarter the capsicums. Trim any tough ends from the asparagus, and trim the root ends and floppy green tops from the spring onions. Remove any protruding stems from the mushrooms.

To save brushing the vegetables individually with the dressing, place them in a large plastic bag. Add the garlic, oil, balsamic vinegar, salt and pepper, then gently turn the vegetables in the mixture until they are evenly coated. Set aside to marinate while you preheat the barbecue or ridged hotplate.

Place the aubergine, zucchini and capsicums on the barbecue grill first, as they cook more slowly. Then add the asparagus, onions and mush-rooms. Cook, turning once or twice, until softened and lightly browned (about 10–15 minutes). Remove the vegetables as they are done and set aside to stand until just warm.

Meanwhile, measure the dressing ingredients into a small screw-top jar and shake to combine.

Cut the warm vegetables into bite-sized pieces. Spread the mesclun leaves over a large platter then, just before serving, scatter the cooked vegetable pieces evenly over the top and sprinkle with the crumbled feta. Drizzle with the dressing and serve with plenty of crusty bread.

Bird's nest salad

- -

This salad is a talking point – different, interesting and very popular. Rice vermicelli noodles are worth keeping in your store cupboard.

Pull the rice noodles away from the block and cut them into shorter lengths for easier handling, if you like. Heat oil about 1cm deep in a wok or medium-sized saucepan or frying pan until one or two noodles dropped into it puff up. Keeping the oil at this heat, fry the noodles in small handfuls, turning them with tongs when the underside is puffed. They should be very lightly coloured (but not brown), rather than white. Drain and cool on paper towels. (Make ahead and store, once cooled, for up to an hour in an airtight plastic bag, if you like.)

To make the dressing, measure all the ingredients into a screw-top jar and shake together until well combined.

Wash the salad greens and dry well. Chop the spring onions, coriander and peanuts.

Assemble the salad 30 seconds before serving. Toss together the noodles, salad greens, other salad additions, chopped coriander and most of the peanuts. Add half the dressing, toss, then taste, adding more dressing if needed.

SERVES 4–6:

about 50g dry rice vermicelli noodles
oil for frying
about 4 cups mesclun, lettuce or other salad greens, beansprouts, chopped spring onions, etc.
¼ cup chopped coriander leaves
½ cup roughly chopped or halved roasted peanuts

DRESSING

1 clove garlic, very finely chopped
½ teaspoon chilli paste
1 tablespoon each: sugar and sesame oil
1 tablespoon rice vinegar or wine vinegar
2 tablespoons each: water and Kikkoman soy sauce

Pasta salad

- -

Pasta salads are very popular, but don't always taste as good as they look! The trick is in the dressing. Here we've added a particularly flavourful dressing that makes a delicious salad.

Cook the pasta until just tender, in plenty of boiling, lightly salted water with the tablespoon of oil, then drain thoroughly. Take care not to undercook or overcook the pasta, if you want a good salad.

Mix together the ingredients for the dressing. Stir the dressing gently into the hot, drained pasta, and allow to stand for at least 15 minutes. During this time the pasta will absorb a lot of the dressing. Refrigerate the salad until you want to serve it.

Just before serving, add any optional extras, such as tomatoes or spring onions, and stir into the salad.

SERVES 4–6:

250g curls, spirals, or other pasta shapes
1 tablespoon oil

DRESSING

½ cup tomato purée
2 tablespoons sour cream
¼–½ cup olive oil
1 tablespoon wine vinegar
1 teaspoon sugar
½ teaspoon salt
1 teaspoon cumin
½ teaspoon oregano, crumbled

OPTIONAL EXTRAS

1 or 2 firm tomatoes, diced
2 spring onions, sliced thinly
2 tablespoons finely chopped parsley
1 stalk celery, sliced thinly
¼–½ cup small cubes unpeeled telegraph cucumber

Bird's nest salad

Peanutty noodle salad

SERVES 4-6:

250g fine or ribbon egg noodles
oil to toss
1 large carrot
½ cup round green beans
½ small cucumber
1-2 spring onions
2 tablespoons lime or lemon juice
fresh red chilli, chopped (optional)

DRESSING
3 tablespoons peanut butter
2 teaspoons sesame oil
1 tablespoon sherry
1 tablespoon brown sugar
2 tablespoons light soy sauce
1 tablespoon canola oil
1 clove garlic, minced
2 tablespoons grated ginger root
¼ cup hot water
2-3 tablespoons chopped fresh coriander leaf
½ -1 teaspoon minced red chilli
salt, to taste

Serve this either as an interesting side salad, or as a delicious main meal on its own.

Prepare the dressing by measuring all the ingredients except the salt into a screw-top jar and shaking until they are well combined. Add the salt to taste, then leave to stand while you prepare the remaining ingredients.

Cook the noodles until they are just done (overcooked noodles will be soggy and weak). Drain, then rinse well with cold water. Toss the noodles with a little oil and set aside. Cut the carrot into fine strips or matchsticks, then combine these with the beans in a shallow pan, cover with water and boil for about 1 minute. Drain and set aside with the noodles.

Halve the cucumber lengthwise and scoop out and discard the seeds. Cut into thin strips or matchsticks. Cut the white part of the spring onion lengthwise into fine strips (keep some of the green part for garnish), and add these to the other vegetables.

Toss the noodles, vegetables and dressing together in a large bowl. Leave to stand for 15-30 minutes, then sprinkle with the lime or lemon juice and toss again. Garnish with some chopped spring onion greens and/or fresh red chilli and serve.

Orzo & feta salad

SERVES 3-4:

250g orzo
2 medium tomatoes
½ red capsicum, deseeded
½ green capsicum, deseeded
100g feta
2 spring onions
about 12 kalamata olives, pitted

DRESSING
3 tablespoons olive oil
1 lemon, zest and juice
1 tablespoon wholegrain mustard
1 clove garlic, minced
½ teaspoon salt
freshly ground black pepper, to taste

Orzo (sometimes also called risoni) is small rice-shaped pasta. It is relatively solid and travels well, making this a great salad for a picnic!

Put the orzo on to cook in a large saucepan of rapidly boiling, lightly salted water. While the orzo cooks (usually about 12-15 minutes), prepare the remaining ingredients.

Cut the tomatoes and deseeded capsicums into 7-10mm cubes. Crumble the feta into roughly similar-sized pieces. Thinly slice the green parts of the spring onions (don't add the white parts unless you want a strong onion flavour), and roughly chop the pitted olives.

To make the dressing, measure the olive oil into a small bowl, finely grate the zest from the lemon and add it to the oil, then squeeze the lemon and add the juice. Add the remaining ingredients, then whisk until thoroughly combined.

When the orzo is cooked, drain it, then rinse with cold water until it is cool and drain again. Tip the drained orzo back into the pot, add the vegetables, feta and dressing and stir gently until evenly mixed.

Transfer to serving bowls and serve immediately, or refrigerate until required (for up to 2 days).

Gado gado salad (vegetables with peanut sauce)

Assemble a platter of vegetables, top with the sauce and wait for the compliments!

To make the sauce, measure the tamarind paste into a small bowl, then add the boiling water. Break up the tamarind and leave to stand for 2–3 minutes.

Place the remaining sauce ingredients into a food processor or blender. Process briefly, then strain in the tamarind water, discarding the tamarind pulp. (If using lemon juice, add to the food processor with 1 cup of water.) Process again to make a fairly smooth paste.

Transfer the sauce to a microwave-proof bowl or a saucepan and cook on High (100%) or boil for 2–3 minutes, or until the sauce has thickened to the desired consistency. Set aside to cool (a little) while preparing the vegetables.

To assemble the salad, cover a platter (or individual plates) with a layer of lettuce or spinach leaves. Add a layer of sliced potatoes, then any of your other selected foods, finishing with the bean sprouts or eggs.

Cover generously with the peanut sauce, garnish with some chopped fresh basil or coriander, and serve.

MAKES ABOUT 1½ CUPS

PEANUT SAUCE
½ teaspoon tamarind paste (or 1–2 tablespoons lemon juice)
1 cup boiling water
100g roasted peanuts
1 clove garlic
1–2 teaspoons grated ginger root
1 teaspoon minced chilli (or 1 small red chilli)
1 tablespoon brown sugar
1 tablespoon dark soy sauce

VEGETABLE PLATTER
lettuce leaves or spinach, washed, stalks removed
a selection of 3 (or more) of:
- cooked potatoes, sliced
- green beans (or snake beans), lightly cooked
- cucumber, halved lengthwise, deseeded and sliced
- tofu, cubed or sliced
- bean sprouts
- hard-boiled eggs, quartered or sliced
- chopped fresh basil or coriander

Oriental noodle salad

This simple salad 'is greater than the sum of its parts'! 2-Minute Noodles may sound like an unusual addition, but we're sure once you've tried it you'll agree it really is good!

Boil the water in a saucepan. Add the noodles. Boil for 2 minutes, then drain.

While the noodles cook, mix the noodle flavour sachet contents together with the vinegar and oil and prepare the vegetables.

When the noodles are cooked, drain then place them in a bowl. Stir in the prepared vegetables and the oil and vinegar mixture. Serve immediately, or pack into an airtight container and refrigerate until required.

VARIATIONS: *Add ¼–½ cup chopped peanuts. For a more pronounced Asian flavour add a sprinkling of sesame oil and soy sauce.*

SERVES 2–3:

2 cups water
1 packet 2-Minute Noodles, broken into pieces
1 tablespoon wine vinegar
2 tablespoons oil
1 cup finely shredded cabbage
1 carrot, cut in thin strips
2 celery stalks, sliced thinly
1–2 spring onions, sliced

Gado gado salad

Mee grob (fried rice noodles in sweet & sour sauce)

SERVES 4:

200g rice vermicelli

oil to fry

2 eggs, lightly beaten

2 tablespoons each: white vinegar, water, fish sauce and tomato sauce

¼ cup sugar

100g bean sprouts

2 spring onions, thinly sliced

1 small red chilli, finely chopped (optional)

2–3 tablespoons chopped roasted peanuts

Somewhere between a salad and an appetiser, these tasty little noodles make a great way to start a meal. Presented on a serving platter they look really good, but are very light and not too filling.

Place the noodles in a large plastic bag and tear them into smaller pieces (doing this in the bag helps stop them spreading around your kitchen!).

Heat about 5cm of oil in a large saucepan or wok (a wok is very good for this). Test that the oil is hot enough by adding a few noodles: they will puff up in 5–10 seconds. Add the noodles one handful at a time, and cook until they are puffed and white. Remove the cooked noodles and drain them on paper towels. Carefully remove the oil from the wok. (The noodles can be cooked up to 1 hour in advance.)

Heat another, preferably non-stick, frying pan and cook the lightly beaten eggs to make a very thin omelet. Remove the omelet from the pan, then roll it up and cut it into narrow slices.

Heat the wok over a low heat, add the vinegar, water, fish sauce and tomato sauce, then the sugar. Stir until the sugar dissolves, then add the cooked noodles and the bean sprouts. Add most of the spring onion, chilli and peanuts, reserving some of each for garnish.

Stir until the noodles have soaked up all the liquid, then transfer to a serving dish. Garnish with the remaining chopped spring onion, chilli and peanuts, then serve.

Chilled soba noodle salad

SERVES 2-3:

250g soba noodles

½ small cucumber, deseeded

1 medium carrot

¼ small daikon* (optional)

1 tablespoon canola oil

2 teaspoons dark sesame oil

1–2 tablespoons toasted sesame seeds

DRESSING

2 tablespoons lime or lemon juice

2 tablespoons light soy sauce

3–4 tablespoons peanut oil

1–2 teaspoons finely grated ginger root

Japanese soba noodles are made from buckwheat rather than conventional flour, which gives them an interesting, slightly nutty flavour.

Put the noodles on to cook in plenty of boiling water. While they cook, prepare the vegetables. Cut the cucumber, carrot and daikon into long, thin (5mm wide) matchsticks. Soften the carrot sticks by plunging them briefly into boiling water.

Prepare the dressing by combining the lime or lemon juice with the soy sauce, oil and grated ginger.

Drain the cooked noodles then rinse them with plenty of cold water. Toss the cooked noodles with the canola and sesame oils. Tip the noodles and vegetables into a large bowl. Add the dressing and half of the sesame seeds and toss together.

Sprinkle with the remaining sesame seeds and serve immediately or refrigerate until required.

* Daikon is a large, mild, white radish.

Nutty brown rice salad

The brown rice, sesame oil and peanuts give this salad a lovely nutty flavour. It's delicious just made and still warm, but is equally good made ahead and served cool from the fridge.

Place the rice, boiling water and salt in a large microwave-proof bowl, then cover and microwave on Medium–high (70%) for 25 minutes, or until the water is absorbed and the rice is tender. If using the stovetop, see the cooking instructions on page 202.

While the rice cooks, grate or finely dice the carrot and dice the red capsicum. Thinly slice the green part of the spring onions. (If you want a stronger onion flavour, slice the white parts too.)

Make the dressing by measuring all the ingredients in a small bowl (or screw-top jar) and whisking (or shaking) until combined.

As soon as the rice is cooked, stir in the frozen peas (this 'cooks' the peas, and cools the rice). Add the peanuts, prepared vegetables, chopped coriander and the dressing, then stir gently to combine.

Serve immediately, or allow to cool then refrigerate until required. (Will keep for up to 2 days.)

SERVES 2–3:

1 cup brown rice
1¾ cups boiling water
½ teaspoon salt
1 medium carrot
½ red capsicum
2 spring onions
½ cup frozen peas
½–¾ cup roasted peanuts
1–2 tablespoons chopped coriander

DRESSING

1 tablespoon sesame oil
1 tablespoon canola oil
1 tablespoon Kikkoman soy sauce
1 tablespoon white wine vinegar
1 clove garlic, minced (optional)
1–2 teaspoons grated ginger root
1 teaspoon brown sugar
¼ teaspoon minced red chilli (optional)

Nutty brown rice salad

Rice salad

SERVES 4–6:

2–3 cups cooked brown or white rice
1–2 carrots, shredded
1–2 sticks celery, thinly sliced
about 6 radishes, thinly sliced
2–3 spring onions, thinly sliced
¼ cup chopped parsley

DRESSING

½ cup oil
¼ cup wine or cider vinegar
1 tablespoon mixed mustard
2 teaspoons sugar
1 teaspoon salt

Rice makes substantial salads, to which small amounts of vegetables may be added for flavour and texture contrast. It's amazing how often we are asked for this recipe by people who have tried it somewhere, then want to make it themselves!

Make this salad with leftover or freshly cooked rice. (Leave freshly cooked rice to stand for at least 10 minutes, then toss lightly with a fork to separate the grains.)

Place the rice in a bowl and fold in the carrot, celery, radishes and spring onions. Add the chopped parsley and any other fresh herbs you like.

Shake the dressing ingredients together in a screw-top jar. Toss about half the dressing through the salad, and taste for flavour. As the rice absorbs much of the dressing on standing, add more dressing just before serving.

Serve as part of a buffet or a picnic meal.

VARIATIONS: *For Peanutty rice salad add chopped sultanas and chopped roasted peanuts with the carrot. Mix enough sesame oil into the dressing to give it a nutty flavour. Add sweet chilli sauce for hotness and extra sweetness.*

Tabbouleh

SERVES 4:

1 cup bulgar or kibbled wheat*
2–3 cups water
¼ cup chopped spring onions or
    chopped red onion
¼ cup lemon juice
¼ cup olive or salad oil
½–1 cup chopped parsley
½ cup chopped mint
1–2 cups finely cubed tomato
salt and freshly ground black pepper,
    to taste

Make this salad when fresh, ripe tomatoes and fresh mint and parsley are plentiful.

Bring the bulgar or kibbled wheat to the boil with the water. Simmer for 2–3 minutes, then remove from the heat and leave to stand for about an hour.

Squeeze the water out of it by lining a sieve with a clean teatowel, then squeezing the teatowel. Put the drained wheat mixture in a bowl with the remaining ingredients, toss to mix, and season carefully, using enough salt to bring out the flavours. Serve in a bowl lined with lettuce leaves.

NOTE: *If you are making this salad several hours before it is to be eaten, stir the tomato into it in the last ½ hour so the tomato does not make the wheat soggy. You can also make the salad with precooked brown rice. Alter the proportions to suit your taste, or make additions such as chopped red or green capsicums, olives, celery, cucumber, radishes, garlic, etc.*

*For extra speed and convenience, we often make this salad with couscous instead of bulgar. Simply place 1 cup of instant couscous in a large bowl, add 1 teaspoon instant vegetable stock powder, then add 1–1½ cups boiling water. Stir briefly, then cover with cling film and leave to stand for 5 minutes. Fluff the couscous with a fork, then proceed as described above.

Couscous & chickpea salad with orange-balsamic dressing

- -

Couscous is a wonderful food for summer – all it needs is a quick soak in boiling water and it's ready to go. Use it in place of rice or pasta as a side dish or accompaniment; or with a few embellishments it can form the basis of a meal. The orange-balsamic dressing and currants used here give this salad an interesting, slightly sweet flavour.

Measure the couscous, currants and instant stock powder (if using) into a large bowl. Add the boiling water, then cover and leave to stand for about 5 minutes while you prepare the remaining ingredients.

Fluff the soaked couscous with a fork, then add the chickpeas, diced capsicum, spring onions, olives and most of the chopped herbs to the bowl.

Prepare the dressing by putting all the ingredients in a screw-top jar, then shaking to combine.

Pour the dressing over the salad and toss to combine. Garnish with the remaining chopped herbs.

SERVES 2–3:

1 cup couscous

¼ cup currants

1 teaspoon instant vegetable stock powder (optional)

1¼ cups boiling water

300g can chickpeas, rinsed and drained

1 red capsicum, deseeded and cubed

2 spring onions, finely sliced

½ cup kalamata olives

2–3 tablespoons chopped fresh parsley, coriander and mint

ORANGE-BALSAMIC DRESSING

¼ cup orange juice

2 tablespoons balsamic vinegar

2 tablespoons extra virgin olive oil

2 teaspoons ground cumin

½ teaspoon salt

1 clove garlic, peeled and finely chopped

Confetti salad

- -

This is a very pretty salad! It's perfect to serve as part of a buffet meal, or even as an interesting filling for pita bread.

Cook the lentils in the water until very tender, then drain. Add the rice and the prepared vegetables to the hot lentils.

Mix together the vinegar, oil, salt and sugar, sprinkle over the salad, and mix again. Stir in the parsley and as much black pepper as you like. Cover the salad and leave it to stand for 30–60 minutes before tasting it again, adjusting seasonings if necessary, and serving.

VARIATIONS: *Add cooked corn, barely cooked carrots or peas, firm tomatoes or cucumber cut into cubes, sunflower seeds or pinenuts, currants, chopped mint or other herbs, bean sprouts. Do not include too great a mixture, as this can spoil the flavour.*

SERVES 4:

½ cup uncooked brown lentils

1½ cups hot water

about 1 cup cooked rice

1 cup chopped celery

about ½ cup chopped red capsicum

¼–½ cup chopped spring onions

2 tablespoons wine vinegar

¼ cup oil

½ teaspoon salt

½ teaspoon sugar

¼ cup chopped parsley

freshly ground black pepper

Bean salad

Bean salad

- -

Alison keeps modifying this useful do-ahead salad which she has made for years! It keeps for 2 or 3 days. It is a good companion to plain tomatoes or avocados, and a tasty addition to filled rolls.

SERVES 3–4:

310–400g can mixed beans or kidney beans
¼ red onion, chopped
3 tablespoons olive oil
2 tablespoons wine vinegar
1 tablespoon sugar
½ teaspoon ground cumin
½ teaspoon salt
1 cup chopped capsicums (any colour)
¼ cup chopped celery (optional)

Tip the beans into a sieve, saving about 2 tablespoons of liquid from the can if possible. Rinse the beans under a tap.

Put the beans into a bowl and add the red onion, oil, vinegar, sugar, cumin and salt. Add the reserved bean liquid or 1 tablespoon of water and mix gently until the sugar dissolves.

Cut the capsicums and celery into 5mm cubes, stir into the bean mixture and leave at least 15 minutes before serving. Serve with a slotted spoon, so the re-maining salad is covered with dressing. Add chopped parsley when serving, if you like.

May be kept in the fridge for up to 3 days.

Cumin bean salad

- -

Use canned or freshly cooked dried beans for this salad. A combination of white haricot, pink pinto, black tiger beans and red kidney beans with the addition of some lightly cooked fresh green beans makes a most attractive, quick and easy salad.

SERVES 6:

4 cups cooked, drained dried beans or canned beans
1 cup chopped cooked green beans
½–1 cup diced green capsicum
1 cup diced celery
Cumin dressing (page 98)
about 1 cup diced tomato

Put the drained beans, capsicum and celery in a large, covered container. Add the dressing and mix to coat. Cover and refrigerate for at least 2 hours before serving. When required, bring to room temperature, add the tomato, and toss to mix.

NOTE: *Cook the beans following the guidelines on page 201.*

Salad dressings

Be adventurous with the salad dressings that follow. Use them to add zing and zest to a variety of plainly cooked hot or cold vegetables. Try dressings with all sorts of salad vegetables and with ripe fruit in season. Many of our salad dressings are made with olive oil, which though it adds delicious flavour, is not essential and can be replaced with other salad oils. If you do use olive oil, make sure you bring dressings to room temperature before serving, as olive oil solidifies on refrigeration.

French dressing

This is a good basic all-purpose dressing which you can put together in a few minutes and keep in the fridge. The mustard in it is important, since it stops the dressing from separating.

Use French dressing as is or add other flavourings, following the suggestions in the recipes below. Use on leafy salads and warm or cold cooked vegetable salads.

¼ cup olive oil or other oil
2 teaspoons wine vinegar
½ teaspoon balsamic vinegar or extra wine vinegar
1 teaspoon prepared mustard
¼ teaspoon salt
1 teaspoon sugar
1 tablespoon water

Refrigerate for up to 1 week.

Italian dressing

Especially good on leafy salad vegetables, warm potatoes, cold cooked beans and baby carrots, lightly cooked asparagus, raw mushrooms, tomatoes, raw or cooked capsicums, cold roasted capsicums, shredded carrot, or as a dressing for avocados.

2 teaspoons cornflour
½ cup water
2–3 teaspoons onion pulp
1 small clove garlic, finely chopped
1 teaspoon dried oregano, crumbled
1 teaspoon mixed mustard
½ teaspoon paprika
1 teaspoon salt
1 tablespoon sugar
1 tablespoon tomato paste
¼ cup wine vinegar
½ cup olive oil or other oil

Mix together the cornflour and water in a small saucepan and bring to the boil, stirring until thick.

Cool slightly and put into a screw-top jar with the remaining ingredients. Shake until well combined.

Refrigerate for up to 1 month. Shake well before use.

Herbed dressing

Shake the ingredients for French Dressing with 1–2 tablespoons very finely chopped fresh herbs, such as parsley, chives, dill, tarragon, thyme, and rosemary. Use one or more herbs, depending on your taste and what is available. Replace the salt with ½ teaspoon of seasoned salt, if you like.

Herbed creamy vinaigrette

There are times when you want a dressing that is sharper than mayonnaise but thicker and more substantial than an oil and vinegar dressing. This dressing provides the answer. It is particularly good on vegetables that have been lightly cooked, cooled and well drained, e.g. carrots, beans and cauliflower. It makes a good potato salad dressing, too.

1 egg yolk
1 tablespoon Dijon mustard
¼ cup wine vinegar
1–1½ cups oil
2 spring onions, finely chopped
2 tablespoons finely chopped parsley
2 teaspoons finely chopped tarragon (optional)
salt and freshly ground black pepper

Beat the egg yolk, mustard and vinegar together with a wire whisk, then add the oil in a thin stream, beating all the time. Stop adding the oil when it gets to the thickness you want. Stir in the very finely chopped herbs, and add extra seasonings if you think they are needed. If you have a blender or food processor, use it to make the dressing, following the same order.

Refrigerate in a covered container for up to 1 week.

Pesto dressing

Add 1–2 tablespoons basil pesto or any other pesto to the French dressing above, then shake well. Use within 24 hours.

OR: Shake or stir together ¼ cup of olive oil with 1–2 tablespoons pesto, 1 teaspoon wine vinegar or lemon juice, and add salt to taste. Use immediately.

Stir these dressings into cooked vegetable salads, rice or pasta salads, and leafy salads. Alter proportions to suit your taste, taking into consideration the different flavour strengths of different pestos.

Cumin dressing

The addition of some cumin to this delicious dressing gives it a distinctive, almost earthy flavour. It works really well with beans or potatoes.

½ cup corn oil or soybean oil
¼ cup wine or cider vinegar
2 teaspoons ground cumin
1–2 teaspoons onion powder
¾ teaspoon salt
2 teaspoons dried oregano
½–1 teaspoon garlic powder
freshly ground black pepper and hot pepper sauce, to taste

Place all the ingredients in a screw-top jar. Shake well.

NOTE: *It is very important that the cumin is fresh and has a pungent, definite flavour.*

Tomato dressing

This dressing is especially good with sliced or halved avocado, or with pasta salad.

1 tablespoon onion pulp
¼ cup tomato purée
3 tablespoons wine vinegar
1 tablespoon sugar
½ teaspoon salt
½ teaspoon celery salt
1 teaspoon Dijon mustard
¾ cup corn oil or soybean oil

Combine all ingredients in a blender, food processor or screw-top jar. (For onion pulp, scrape a halved onion, cut crosswise, with the tip of a teaspoon.) Refrigerate in a screw-top jar for up to 1 week.

Peanutty dressing

3 tablespoons crunchy peanut butter
2 cloves garlic
2 tablespoons light soy sauce
2 tablespoons wine vinegar
1 tablespoon brown sugar or runny honey
1 tablespoon sesame oil
1 tablespoon Tabasco sauce
about ¼ cup very hot water

Put all the ingredients except the hot water into a food processor or blender. Process until well combined. Thin down to pouring cream consistency with very hot water.

Refrigerate for up to 2 weeks, warming before use if necessary.

Especially good over hot or cold kumara or potatoes. Toss through warm pasta or noodles, or cooked julienned vegetables. Add to cooked rice.

Parmesan dressing

¼ cup olive oil or other oil
1 tablespoon wine vinegar or herb vinegar
1 teaspoon mixed mustard
1 clove garlic, finely chopped
¼ teaspoon salt
2 tablespoons grated parmesan

Put all the ingredients in a screw-top jar and shake.

Brush on bread or vegetables, especially flat mushrooms, zucchini or aubergine before grilling. Toss through sautéed potatoes, use on salad greens, diced raw apples or pears, pour over plainly cooked carrots or green vegetables before serving.

Lemon honey dressing

¼ cup lemon juice
2 tablespoons light soy sauce
2 tablespoons salad oil
2 tablespoons honey
1 tablespoon Dijon mustard
1 tablespoon sesame oil
1 teaspoon finely grated lemon zest
1 clove garlic, finely chopped

Combine all ingredients and either process until smooth using a food processor, or shake well in a screw-top jar.

Very good over diced fresh fruit, such as apples, pears, peaches or nectarines. Use over finely shredded raw vegetables, or lightly cooked stirfried asparagus, green beans or other vegetables.

Sesame dressing

This strongly flavoured dressing is addictive! It turns bought packages of coleslaw or the simplest coleslaw vegetables into something exciting. It also dresses tomato, sprout, mesclun, cooked vegetable and pasta salads well. It keeps well and may be refrigerated for weeks.

2 cloves garlic, finely chopped
1 teaspoon grated ginger root
1 tablespoon dark soy sauce
1 tablespoon light soy sauce
1 teaspoon sesame oil
2 teaspoons sugar
2 teaspoons rice vinegar
2 tablespoons finely chopped fresh coriander leaves

Combine all ingredients in a screw-top jar and shake well to combine.

Serve over stirfried vegetables, or with grilled vegetables such as aubergine, zucchini or red capsicums.

Tex-Mex dressing

We use this assertive dressing to liven up many gently flavoured foods. We spoon it into avocado halves, use it to top baked potatoes, drop spoonfuls onto poached eggs, stir it into drained beans to make spicy bean salad, and spread it on bread rolls before we add cheese and salad vegetables.

MAKES ¾ CUP:

½ cup olive oil
1 teaspoon ground cumin
1 teaspoon salt
1 teaspoon sugar
½ teaspoon dried oregano
½ teaspoon paprika
¼–½ teaspoon chilli paste
1–2 cloves garlic, very finely chopped
2 teaspoons Dijon mustard
1 tablespoon tomato paste
1 tablespoon wine vinegar
2 tablespoons boiling water

Measure the first seven ingredients in a jar with a screw-top lid and shake well to mix.

Mix the very finely chopped garlic, the mustard, tomato paste and wine vinegar in a cup or small bowl. Stir in the boiling water to make a smooth paste, then transfer to the jar holding the other ingredients and stir well, then shake thoroughly until smooth and thick.

Leave to stand for at least 30 minutes before using. Refrigerate for up to 1 week.

Spicy yoghurt dressing

Stir this versatile dressing through chopped celery, chopped or sliced cucumber, sliced firm bananas or cold, cooked new potatoes. With any of these it makes a good curry accompaniment. Spoon over bean and lentil mixtures, or use as a dip.

MAKES 1 CUP:

1 clove fresh garlic, finely chopped
1–2 teaspoons chopped pickled Jalapeno peppers
¼ cup chopped fresh coriander leaves
2 spring onions, finely chopped
1 teaspoon ground cumin
½ teaspoon sugar
½ teaspoon salt
1 cup plain unsweetened yoghurt

Stir all the ingredients together in a bowl, or combine in a blender or food processor. Stand for 30 minutes before use if possible. Refrigerate for up to 24 hours.

Mayonnaise

This is an extremely useful and delicious dressing which is easy and quick to make in a food processor or blender.

MAKES 1½ CUPS:

1 egg
½ teaspoon salt
½ teaspoon sugar
1 teaspoon Dijon mustard
2 tablespoons wine vinegar
about 1 cup corn oil or olive oil

Measure the egg, salt, sugar, mustard and vinegar into a blender or food processor. Turn on, and pour in the oil in a thin stream until the mayonnaise is as thick as you like.

Store in a covered container in the fridge for up to 2–3 weeks.

Garlic mayonnaise

Add 1–2 cloves of garlic before adding the oil. Leave to stand for 1 hour to soften the flavour before using.

Chilli mayonnaise

This is a particularly delicious variation. Add ½–1 teaspoon chilli powder, 1 teaspoon dried oregano, 1–2 teaspoons ground cumin and 1 clove of garlic before adding the oil. The flavour improves and becomes hotter after it stands for several hours.

Tofu 'mayonnaise'

MAKES 1 CUP:

2 small cloves garlic
2 tablespoons roughly chopped parsley
1 tablespoon roughly chopped chives
1 cup (300g) crumbled firm tofu
¼ cup vegetable oil
1 tablespoon white wine vinegar
½ teaspoon mustard powder or 1 teaspoon Dijon
    mustard
½ teaspoon salt
¼ teaspoon sugar
juice of ½ lemon
freshly ground black pepper, to taste

Chop the garlic and herbs in a blender or food processor. Don't be overgenerous with the garlic, or the dressing will taste of little else. Add the remaining ingredients and blend until the mixture is smooth and creamy.

Refrigerate in a screw-top jar for several weeks, if desired.

We were taught that when we sit down for the main meal of the day, at least half the food on our plates should be vegetables, of a variety of colours and flavours.

Aren't we lucky to live in a country where so many vegetables thrive? We have a wonderful selection available, of many different colours, shapes and sizes. If you grow vegetables in your own garden you are even luckier, because vegetables picked, prepared and put promptly on the table have an even better flavour.

Vegetables

Making the most of vegetables

When vegetables are an important part of your meal it is particularly important to serve them in a way that retains their maximum flavour, colour, texture and food value.

There are so many inviting vegetables available that it is a pity to limit your choice to only a few varieties. Use different cooking and serving methods, remembering that many vegetables make good salads, when raw or when cooked and cooled. Mix and match, or alternate simple and more complex recipes. A squeeze of lemon juice and a pinch of herbs can add as much interest as a rich sauce.

The suggested cooking times are a guideline only — these will vary depending on the size of pieces and the maturity of the vegetables used.

Artichoke, globe: Look like giant thistle buds. Spectacular, interesting and sometimes addictive! Require long, slow cooking in well seasoned water to cover (30–45 minutes), until an outer leaf pulls off easily. The bottom of each leaf is the edible part. Pull out the upper part of each leaf and bite so the bottom part of the leaf stays in your mouth. When you have removed all the outer leaves, take the stamens off the base, cut it into pieces (the base is the most tender and tasty part of the artichoke). We have not microwaved these successfully. Serve hot, warm or cold, with melted butter or mayonnaise.

Artichoke, Jerusalem: Easily-grown lumpy tubers, from plants related to the sunflower. Scrub or peel, boil or steam to serve with sauce, purée for soup, or slice raw into salads for water chestnut-like texture. Distinctive flavour, not popular with everyone.

Asparagus: Should be enjoyed during its short season. Early in the season try peeling the skin from the lower part of the stalk for more even cooking. Lie asparagus flat in a covered pan, add a little butter and water, and cook over a high heat until tender-crisp, for 3–5 minutes. Alternatively, slice diagonally and stirfry-steam. Fairly thick stalks of asparagus microwave well. Serve hot with butter or other sauce, or cold with French dressing or mayonnaise. Raw, tastes like young peas, good for dipping.

Aubergine (eggplant): During season, valued for dense, solid flesh, and attractive colour. Many different varieties, sizes, and colours grown in other countries. Sauté then simmer (about 15 minutes), bake, grill, barbecue, fry, microwave, purée for dips. Serve hot, warm, cold.

Avocado: Usually eaten raw, in halves or wedges, or mashed or puréed in dips. The cut surface will brown if not coated with lemon juice or vinegar, etc. Unripe avocados are horrible, so wait until flesh 'gives' when pressed gently. If overripe, delicate green flesh turns brown.

Beetroot: Choose young, smallish beetroots. Naturally sweet. May be shredded raw for salad, but usually boiled (for 15–60 minutes depending on size and maturity), then peeled, sliced or cubed, and served hot or cold in a sweet-sour sauce.

Broad beans: If you grow your own, start eating sliced baby pods early, so that you don't get bogged down by overabundance of mature beans. Pod and stirfry-steam bigger beans using a little oil or butter, for 1–3 minutes, taking care not to overcook. Remove the outer skin of each bean if cooking overmature beans. Young beans microwave well; serve hot. Young beans are good raw.

Green beans: Buy or pick when young and tender. Remove tips and strings if necessary. Slice or cook whole, for 3–10 minutes depending on size and age. Stirfry-steam until slightly crunchy. Beans do not microwave as well as peas. Serve hot, or cold after marinating. Really young beans are good raw.

Broccoli: The stalks are as tender as the heads if you peel them first, by pulling skin from bottom end. Slice the stem and cook with the head (for about 5 minutes). Stirfry-steam or microwave for 1 minute per serving. Good with cheese sauce.

Brussels sprouts: Like miniature cabbages. Heads should be tight. Halve, or cut deep crosses in stem ends for faster, more even cooking (from 3–8 minutes). Marinate when cold and cooked, for salads.

Cabbage: Don't throw away all the dark green outer leaves, just shred them more finely than quicker-cooking inner leaves. Stirfry-steam for 3–5 minutes, stirfry or microwave for 1 minute per serving. Do not overcook. Stuff leaves, or finely slice inner leaves for coleslaw.

Capsicums: Very high in vitamin C. Slice and stirfry until tender-crisp. Use in vegetable mixtures like ratatouille or caponata, add to stews and casseroles, or stuff them. Brown under grill to char the skin, peel, then serve with French dressing. Cut into strips or slices for dipping or salads. Green capsicums are immature capsicums and have a strong flavour. They're best when stirfried or lightly sautéed.

Carrots: Inexpensive, always in season. Very versatile, raw or cooked. Shred, slice, cube, cut in sticks, serve whole, purée, juice. Naturally sweet. Good dipping sticks. Flavour and texture much nicer if not overcooked. Boil 3–10 minutes depending on age and size. Microwave best in small pieces, about 1 minute per serving.

Cauliflower: Break or cut into florets. Excellent dipping food when raw. Stirfry, steam, microwave for about 1 minute per serving, coat in batter and deep fry; cook only until tender-crisp in each case. Good just boiled (for 5–10 minutes), with sauce.

Celery: Pull the fibres from larger outer ribs, starting from the base. Slice stems diagonally or cut into julienne strips. Stirfry, braise (for 15–20 minutes) or microwave. Use to flavour soups, cereals, etc. Good raw in salads or as dipping sticks.

Choko: Use when young if possible. Rub off outer prickles, peel only if mature. Halve lengthwise and slice. Simmer for 10–15 minutes. Seed is edible, too. Add to stirfries, or stirfry-steam or microwave. Add garlic and herbs for extra flavour. Serve hot. Treatment and texture is that of firm zucchini.

Corn: Enjoy on the cob during fairly short season. Good processed corn available at all times, and small whole cobs available canned. Corn on cob is best when not overmature. Look for new varieties. Don't choose largest. Best microwaved (allowing 3 minutes per cob, husk on) when on cob. Can be boiled, barbecued, etc.

Cucumber: Usually eaten raw but can be cooked like zucchini. Peel only if skin is tough. Salt, then rinse to remove excess water for some recipes. Makes excellent pickles.

Florence fennel: Halve or quarter lengthwise, depending on size. Simmer (10–15 minutes) or braise until tender. Alternatively, slice crosswise and stirfry-steam. Serve hot with butter, or cold with French dressing. Serve sliced, raw in salads, too.

Leek: Pick or buy when young before the base bulges. Remove the outer skin, it is tougher than the inner stalks. Wash carefully, then halve lengthwise to braise. Slice 5–10mm thick to stirfry-steam or simmer (5–10 minutes) and serve with sauce, or cold in dressing.

Kumara (sweet potato): Sweet-fleshed tubers, texture and flavour between potatoes and pumpkin, but more distinct flavour. Good baked in jackets, roasted, steamed or microwaved. Cooking times similar to potatoes.

Lettuce & salad greens: Wide range of colours, textures and flavours available, to grow and buy. Store and prepare carefully to ensure crispness. Add dressing just before serving, or let people add their own, so leaves do not wilt. Use different combinations and dressings.

Marrow: Use while young enough to have tender skins and edible seeds. Slice or shred coarsely and stirfry-steam (about 5 minutes) or microwave. Stuff halves or slices. Add herbs or garlic for flavour.

Mushrooms: Young, fleshy mushrooms are good raw, marinated or with dips. Cook older mushrooms briefly (3–5 minutes) with a little butter or oil, garlic and herbs. Add to other vegetable mixtures for extra body and flavour. Also good stuffed and baked, or battered and fried. Look for other new types of edible fungi also.

Onion: Widely used to intensify flavours of other foods. Flavours of browned onions, sautéed but not browned onions, and raw onions are all different. Red onions have a milder flavour. Spring (young) onions are used raw or briefly cooked, for colour as well as flavour.

Parsnip: Creamish-coloured root vegetables, more distinctive flavour than carrots. Nice glazed with sugar mixture after cooking. Boil (15–20 minutes) or steam and mash, roast or deep-fry. Sweeter when harvested after frosts.

Peas: Unless you grow your own and pick them young, use frozen peas. Cook for a short time (2 minutes after coming to the boil) in just enough water to stop them sticking; or stirfry-steam or microwave.

Pea pods: Flat pea pods, sugarsnap peas or snowpeas need very little or no cooking (about 1 minute). Remove ends and strings. Blanch, stirfry or stirfry- steam for 1–2 minutes. Try coating with tempura batter.

Sugarsnap peas: Look like ordinary peas in pods, but the pods are edible and even sweeter than the peas inside. Eat raw or stirfry-steam for 1–4 minutes, depending on age.

Pumpkin: Available in a variety of shapes, sizes and colours. Mealy, sweet, bright orange flesh with a smooth texture. Steam (10–20 minutes), purée, microwave, roast, batter and deep-fry, or stuff and bake.

Radish: Vary in size, colour and strength of flavour; small red to large long white. Best when young. Nearly always served raw for colour and texture. Crisp in water if necessary. Slice and add to lettuce salads.

Scallopini & summer squash: These belong to the marrow family. Cube or slice and stirfry-steam for about 10 minutes, with herbs, garlic and tomatoes for best flavour.

Silverbeet & spinach beet (Swiss chard): Use while young if possible; use leaves as you would spinach. Very young leaves may be added to salads. Slice older leaves, putting stems at the bottom of the pot, since these take longer to cook than leaves. Cook for 5–10 minutes depending on age, until the whites are just tender. Thicken cooking liquid by adding butter, milk or cream.

Spinach: Wash very carefully, dunking in a large container of water to get rid of grit. Blanch, stirfry or stirfry-steam, without adding any extra water, for 3–5 minutes. Do not overcook. Drain well, pressing out water, before combining with sauce for soufflés, flans, etc. Microwaves well. Use raw in salads.

Tomatoes: Enormously versatile. Best flavour in late summer, early autumn. Different varieties, shapes, sweetness, etc. Pear-shaped varieties tend to be more fleshy with fewer seeds. Small tomatoes are extra sweet. Use raw or cooked as sauces, purées, concentrates. Good commercially prepared cooked tomato products may be as good as you can make at home.

Yams: Usually small pink shiny tubers. Scrub and simmer (for about 10 minutes), stirfry-steam or roast. In some countries, larger sweet potatoes (not as sweet as kumara) may also be called yams.

Zucchini (courgette): Do not peel. Slice, shred or cut in strips, stirfry or stirfry-steam with garlic and herbs for 3–5 minutes. Coat with batter and deep-fry. Use in breads, etc. Yellow varieties available.

Cooking methods

Here are some of the different ways you can cook vegetables. Don't drown them! You are throwing away a lot of flavour and vitamins when you boil vegetables in water to cover, or leave them to soak before cooking, or boil them until they discolour, or throw out lots of cooking liquid! Try to vary your cooking techniques, giving emphasis to methods using very little liquid.

Blanching: Vegetables are immersed for a short time in a large pan of boiling water. They are usually then dipped into cold water to halt the cooking process. This produces a very bright colour and is one of the steps in freezing vegetables.

Boiling: Add vegetables to boiling water in a saucepan, then cover to keep the steam in. With this method it is best to use only a small amount of water.

Steaming: Place vegetables in steamer basket with perforated bottom, resting above the water level in a saucepan. The vegetables cook in steam instead of water, and lose fewer nutrients. Neither their flavour nor their food value is as good as that of stirfried vegetables, however.

Sautéeing: This method is good for conserving flavour and nutrients. Cook sliced or chopped vegetables in a little oil, butter, margarine, etc., in a pan over a high heat, stirring at intervals. With a non-stick pan very little oil, etc., is required. Many vegetables can be sautéed before being cooked by another method.

Stirfrying: Single vegetables or a mixture may be cooked this way. Vegetables are usually sliced in varying sizes so they all take the same time to cook. Heat a little oil, sometimes with garlic and/or ginger, in a large pan or wok. Add the vegetables and toss and stir them to keep them moving, and to coat them. Pour in a little liquid and cover, so the steam formed cooks the vegetables until tender-crisp. Evaporate remaining liquid, or add extra flavourings mixed with cornflour to thicken juices. Toss to coat the vegetables. Excellent for conserving flavour, texture and nutrients.

Stirfry-steam: This very good way of cooking vegetables falls into none of the foregoing categories, but is best described as the 'stirfry-steam' method. Fry the prepared vegetable in a non-stick pan containing a little butter, and sometimes garlic. Soon afterwards add a small amount of water, cover the pan tightly and cook over a fairly high heat, turning or stirring occasionally. By the time the vegetables are cooked tender-crisp, the water should have disappeared completely. The vegetables are lightly glazed with the butter, and usually need no other seasoning. The heat used is lower than that required for a real stirfry, but hotter than that used in braising.

Braising: Fry the vegetables in hot butter or oil, then add flavoured liquid and cook slowly in a saucepan or in

a covered ovenproof dish. Cooking liquid is often eaten with vegetables.

Pressure cooking: Vegetables are cooked in superheated steam, resulting in a considerably shortened cooking time, saving nutrients. Take care not to overcook green vegetables with this method, or colour and texture will suffer.

Barbecuing & grilling: Food is turned above hot embers or under a hot element. Pieces of capsicum, aubergine, onion, tomato, mushrooms, zucchini, etc. may be threaded on skewers with other food. Brush with oil, butter, mayonnaise, French dressing, etc., to prevent them burning before they cook.

Deep-frying: Coat tender vegetables in light batter, then cook briefly in hot oil, as in Japanese tempura.

Microwaving: The microwave cooks many vegetables very well in a short time, conserving colour, flavour and food value. In most cases green vegetables need very little or no added liquid. They should be cooked in a covered container which they nearly fill, and seasoned very lightly after cooking, if necessary.

NOTES:

EASY ON THE SALT! *It is easy to add salt by habit rather than by taste. We now season most vegetables very lightly – after cooking. Vegetables cooked so that no liquid remains (e.g. in frying pan or microwave) require little or no salt. If a little butter is added at any stage, it is probable that no salt will be needed at all.*

KEEP COOKING LIQUID: *Keep any vegetable cooking liquid that remains when vegetables are served. Refrigerate for up to 2 days. Use this as liquid for sauces, soups and stocks.*

Asparagus with poached eggs & easy orange hollandaise sauce

- -

SERVES 3-4:

500–600g asparagus
1–2 tablespoons butter
3–4 eggs
3–4 slices thick toast

EASY ORANGE HOLLANDAISE

2 egg yolks (preferably at room
    temperature)
1 tablespoon each: lemon and orange
    juice
1–2 teaspoons finely grated orange
    zest
100g butter, cubed
salt, to taste (optional)

Who can refuse a meal of poached eggs on top of steaming fresh asparagus, drizzled with hollandaise sauce – any time of the day.

To make the hollandaise, place the egg yolks, lemon juice, orange juice and rind in a food processor (fitted with a metal chopping blade) or blender.

Put the butter in a microwave-safe container, cover to prevent spattering (a saucer works well if your container doesn't have a lid) and microwave on High (100%) for 2–3 minutes until bubbling vigorously.

Turn the processor on and add the very hot butter in thin stream while the motor is running. Season with salt to taste.

The hot butter should thicken the mixture, but if you think the sauce is too runny, transfer it back to the microwave container and heat on Medium (50%) for 15 seconds then whisk briefly. Repeat if necessary. Warm the same way just before serving.

To cook the asparagus, bring 5–10mm water to a rapid boil in a large (lidded) frying pan. Add the asparagus and cook covered for 3–4 minutes, shaking it occasionally. When tender, drain off the water, return it to the hot pan, add the butter and toss to coat evenly. Cover and set aside while you poach the eggs.

Heat about 5cm water in a large pan until it just boils. Add a tablespoon of white wine or cider vinegar and about ½ teaspoon salt and stir. Break the eggs gently into the water. Cook, just at boiling point or slightly below, for about 4–5 minutes or until the yolks are as set as you like.

Place a piece of toast on each plate, divide the asparagus between the plates, arranging it on top of the toast, then, using a fish-slice or perforated spoon, gently lift an egg onto each pile of asparagus. Pour a little of the warmed sauce over each, serve immediately and enjoy!

Marinated artichokes

- -

1 globe artichoke per person
juice of 1–2 lemons
garlic cloves
peppercorns
1 bay leaf
basil and oregano
oil
mayonnaise

Serve 1 artichoke per person as a starter, or as a light lunch.

Place artichokes in a large saucepan and cover with lightly salted water. Add lemon juice, several crushed garlic cloves, a few peppercorns, a bay leaf, some basil and oregano, and a few tablespoons of oil.

Cover the saucepan and simmer the artichokes for 30 minutes or more, until the outer petals pull away from the base easily. Leave to cool in the cooking liquid.

Serve each drained artichoke on a flat plate big enough to hold mayonnaise for dipping and a pile of discarded petals. To eat, pull off a petal at a time. Dip the stem end into the mayonnaise, then bite off the fleshy part of the petal and discard the fibrous core. You will find the inner petals are more fleshy and less fibrous. Eventually only the fleshy base, holding immature seeds, remains. Discard these if they are stringy, cut the base into quarters, and eat each piece with mayonnaise.

Asparagus with poached eggs & easy orange hollandaise sauce

Aubergine casserole

SERVES 4:

1 large aubergine (about 750g)
1 egg
1 tablespoon water
½ cup dried breadcrumbs
2 tablespoons oil
2 onions, quartered and sliced
1 tablespoon oil
8 large tomatoes, sliced
fresh basil or 1 teaspoon dried basil
½ cup water
1 teaspoon salt
2 teaspoons sugar
freshly ground black pepper
1 cup grated tasty cheese

Kirsten sent this recipe with the note 'Absolutely delicious – even the most suspicious people ask for more.' Aubergine has a very meaty texture and colour, and is often used in casseroles. This is a casserole which can be served as part of a buffet meal for a group that includes vegetarians.

In this recipe you prepare two mixtures. For speed, brown the aubergine slices while the tomato mixture simmers. Cut the aubergine into slices about 1cm thick. In a shallow dish big enough to hold the slices, beat the egg with the water, just enough to combine. Dip the aubergine slices first in the egg, then in the breadcrumbs, coating both sides. Fry slices in a little hot oil until brown on both sides. Leave to drain on paper towels.

In another pan, sauté the sliced onions in 1 tablespoon of oil until lightly browned. Add the tomatoes, basil, water, salt, sugar and pepper, and simmer until the onion is tender.

Coat a large, shallow casserole dish (about 23 x 30 cm) with non-stick spray or butter, then put half the browned aubergine slices into the dish, cutting them to fit, if necessary. Pour half the tomato mixture over this layer, top with remaining aubergine, then spread the remaining tomato mixture on top. Top with the grated cheese. Bake, uncovered, at 180°C for 45 minutes, or until the top browns and the aubergine is very tender. Do not hurry the cooking. Leave to stand for at least 10 minutes before serving, or reheat later, preferably in a microwave oven.

VARIATIONS: *Put a layer of grated cheese between the two layers of aubergine, as well as above the top layer.*

Aubergine & mushroom casserole

SERVES 4:

2 medium or 1 large aubergine
2–3 tablespoons olive or canola oil
1 medium onion
1 tablespoon olive oil
1 teaspoon (1–2 cloves) minced garlic
250g mushrooms, sliced
1–2 tablespoons basil pesto
½–1 teaspoon salt
freshly ground black pepper, to taste
1 cup sour cream or plain unsweet-
    ened yoghurt
1 large egg
½ teaspoon salt
½–1 cup grated tasty cheese

This dish does require several different steps during its preparation; however, individually they are all very simple – and the results are delicious.

Preheat the oven to 200°C. Cut the aubergine/s into 1cm thick slices, brush both sides lightly with oil and arrange the slices in a single layer on 1 or 2 baking sheets. Place these in the oven and bake for 15–20 minutes, until the aubergine is soft and beginning to brown at the edges. (If you have to use 2 trays, swap their position in the oven after 10 minutes so the aubergine cooks evenly).

While the aubergine bakes, peel and slice the onion, then heat the oil in a large (non-stick) pan. Add the garlic and onion and sauté, stirring frequently, until the onion has softened. Stir in the sliced mushrooms and cook gently until the mushrooms have wilted. Add the pesto, salt, and pepper to taste, and cook for 1–2 minutes longer, then remove from the heat.

Lightly oil or non-stick spray a 25 x 30cm casserole dish. Arrange half the baked aubergine slices in a layer over the bottom of the casserole dish, cover this with the mushroom mixture, then another layer of the aubergine slices.

Mix the sour cream or yoghurt, egg and salt together in a small bowl. Pour and spread this mixture over the layered mixture, then sprinkle the top with the grated cheese.

Bake at 200°C for 20 minutes or until the top is bubbly and turning brown. Remove from the oven and leave to stand for 5–10 minutes. Serve with a salad or lightly cooked vegetables and some crusty bread.

Aubergine stacks

Aubergine stacks

An interesting and delicious recipe. We have given quantities for two adults, but it is easy to multiply for larger numbers.

Turn the oven on to preheat to 200°C. Cut the aubergine lengthwise into 6 even slices. Lay these on a baking tray, and drizzle lightly with olive oil, then turn them over and do the same to the other side. Sprinkle lightly with salt and pepper, then bake for 12–15 minutes, until soft and beginning to brown.

Sprinkle each of the slices with the some of the chopped basil, or brush with pesto, then cover the four larger slices with sliced tomato. Sprinkle the chopped olives, if using, over the tomato, then put the sliced or grated cheese over these. Sprinkle lightly with salt and pepper.

Re-assemble the aubergine halves by stacking the slices (smallest pieces on top!), more or less as they were cut. Sprinkle each half with any remaining cheese then bake at 200°C for another 10–15 minutes until the cheese has melted and the tomato looks cooked.

Serve with a green salad and crusty bread.

SERVES 2:

1 medium aubergine
2–3 tablespoons olive oil
salt and freshly ground black pepper
2–3 tablespoons chopped fresh basil
   (or 2 tablespoons basil pesto)
2–3 medium tomatoes, thinly sliced
6–8 black olives, chopped (optional)
100g thinly sliced (or 1 cup grated)
   mozzarella cheese

Aubergine kebabs

Aubergine that is marinated and grilled makes a good accompaniment for food from any part of the world.

Combine all the marinade ingredients by shaking in a jar, or using a food processor or blender. Pour the marinade over the aubergine cubes and leave to marinate for about 30 minutes. Thread aubergine pieces onto medium-length skewers that have been soaked in cold water.

Grill or barbecue until cut flesh is evenly golden, turning frequently, about 10 minutes. Brush with extra marinade during cooking.

Serve hot or at room temperature.

SERVES 4:

200g aubergine, cut into cubes

MARINADE
2 cloves garlic, finely chopped
¼ cup olive oil
2 tablespoons sesame oil
2 tablespoons wine vinegar
1 tablespoon light soy sauce
1 teaspoon honey
1 teaspoon grated ginger root
½ teaspoon salt

Carrot & mushroom loaf

SERVES 4:

1 medium-sized onion

1–2 cloves garlic

2 tablespoons oil or butter

200g mushrooms

1 teaspoon basil

¼ teaspoon thyme

½ teaspoon salt

freshly ground black pepper

3 cups grated carrot (400g)

½ cup dried breadcrumbs

½ cup grated cheese

½ cup milk

2 eggs

2 tablespoons dried breadcrumbs

2 tablespoons grated cheese

paprika

Everybody likes this loaf! Team it with mashed potatoes, green beans or broccoli, and cubed pumpkin or baked tomatoes.

Finely chop the onion and garlic, then cook in the oil or butter until the onion is soft. Add the sliced mushrooms and continue to cook until these have softened.

Transfer the cooked onion and mushroom mixture to a medium-sized bowl and then add the next 9 ingredients. Mix together well, then pour into a thoroughly non-stick sprayed loaf tin. (Line the long sides and bottom with a strip of baking paper, if you think it might stick.)

Sprinkle with the remaining measures of breadcrumbs and cheese, and dust lightly with paprika.

Cover the pan with foil, and bake at 180°C for 30 minutes, then uncover and cook for a further 30 minutes or until the centre is firm when pressed.

Stuffed capsicums

SERVES 4:

4 large or 8 small capsicums

3 onions

2 cloves garlic

3 tablespoons oil

1 cup brown or white long grain rice

2 cups water

½ cup pine nuts or chopped almonds

½ cup currants

¼ cup chopped mint

¼ cup chopped parsley

½ teaspoon ground allspice

½ teaspoon grated nutmeg

½ teaspoon cinnamon

1 teaspoon salt

425g can savoury tomatoes or tomatoes in juice

We like all the Middle Eastern flavourings that are added to stuffed vegetables, so we put them all in, without restraint! Use only fleshy, plump red, yellow or orange capsicums for this recipe.

First prepare the capsicums. Cut across the tops, removing the stem portion; or cut large capsicums in half lengthwise. Remove and discard seeds and pith, and chop any trimmings from around the stem.

Finely chop 2 of the onions and the garlic. Heat in 1 tablespoon of the oil in a large frying pan with a lid, until transparent. Add any chopped capsicum trimmings, then the rice, and cook for 1–2 minutes longer. Then add 2 cups water, cover, and simmer until the rice is tender – about 30 minutes for brown rice, or about 15 for white rice.

Soften the prepared capsicums by putting them in a bowl, pouring boiling water over them, and leaving them to stand for 5 minutes. Drain, and discard the water.

Put the second tablespoon of oil in another frying pan and lightly brown the pine nuts or chopped almonds in it. Watch carefully so they do not darken. When evenly coloured, add the currants, and cook a little longer, until they have plumped up. Turn off the heat and remove the nuts and currants from pan. Mix with the chopped mint and parsley.

Stir the allspice, nutmeg, cinnamon and salt into the almost-cooked rice. Watch the rice carefully as it cooks, adding extra water if necessary. It should be tender and dry by the time it finishes. Stir most of the currant mixture into the cooked rice.

Lightly brown the last onion in the last tablespoon of oil, in the saucepan or frying pan in which the capsicums will cook. Add the can of tomatoes, chopping them into smaller pieces.

Pack the rice into the capsicums, so that the tops are rounded, and all or most of the filling is used. Arrange the capsicums on the tomato mixture, then cover the pan and simmer very gently for 20–30 minutes, until the capsicums are tender and the tomato mixture has thickened.

Serve 2 capsicums or half-capsicums per serving, standing each on a spoonful of tomato mixture. Top with the reserved currant mixture. Add a green salad and bread to complete the main course. Cooked green beans go well with these capsicums, too.

Carrot & mushroom loaf

Crunchy curried cauliflower

SERVES 6:

2 tablespoons each: sesame and
    cumin seeds
2 cloves garlic, finely chopped
1½ teaspoons grated ginger root
2 tablespoons roasted peanuts, finely
    chopped
½ teaspoon each: turmeric, chilli
    powder, ground cloves
1 teaspoon salt
2–3 tablespoons oil
2 medium-sized onions, chopped
1 large cauliflower, cut into walnut-
    sized florets
juice of ½ lemon
¼ cup water

The seasonings are interesting, but not too hot.

Toast the sesame seeds, then the cumin seeds in a dry frying pan. Grind these seeds, then add the garlic, ginger, peanuts turmeric, chilli powder, cloves and salt and set aside.

Heat the oil in a large frying pan, then add the onions and cook until transparent and lightly coloured. Stir in the spice mixture, stirfry for about 1 minute, then add the cauliflower florets, lemon juice and ¼ cup water. Cover and cook over a moderate heat, stirring occasionally, until the cauliflower is tender crisp. Taste and season with extra salt if required.

Serve with cooked rice, tomato or cucumber salad and/or other curry accompaniments.

Curried cauliflower & eggs

SERVES 3–4:

4 eggs
1 medium onion
2 medium-small potatoes (200g total)
1 tablespoon canola oil
1 teaspoon each: minced garlic and
    ginger
1 tablespoon curry powder
1 teaspoon garum masala
2 whole cardamoms, crushed (optional)
4–5 whole cloves (optional)
400g can whole tomatoes in juice
¾ cup coconut cream
250g cauliflower
½ cup frozen peas (optional)
½ teaspoon salt
1–2 tablespoons chopped fresh or
    bottled coriander

This is much more interesting and delicious than it sounds!

Put the eggs in a small saucepan and cover with hot water, bring to the boil and simmer for 12 minutes. (Making a small whole in the blunt end of each egg will help prevent them cracking or splitting). Cover with cold water to cool, then peel and set them aside.

Peel and slice the onion and cut the potatoes into 1cm cubes. Heat the oil in a large pan, then add the onion, potatoes, garlic and ginger. Cook (preferably covered) without browning, for 5 minutes stirring occasion-ally, then add the curry powder, garam masala and the whole spices (if using). Continue to cook, stirring frequently, for 1 minute longer, then add the tomatoes in their juice. Break up the tomatoes with a spoon, stir, then cover the mixture and simmer gently until the potatoes are tender, about 5–10 minutes.

Add the coconut cream and cauliflower and simmer uncovered for another 5 minutes, or until the cauliflower is tender. Stir in the peas (if using) and the coriander, cook for 1–2 minutes longer, before adding the quartered or roughly chopped hard-boiled eggs.

Cauliflower in curried tomato sauce

SERVES 4–6:

500g prepared cauliflower
½–1 cup grated tasty cheese
SAUCE
2 tablespoons butter
1 teaspoon curry powder
2 tablespoons flour
425g can tomato and onion or diced
    tomatoes in juice

Similar to cauliflower cheese, but the sauce makes it really special.

Preheat the oven to 180°C. Break the cauliflower into 3cm-diameter florets and simmer in lightly salted water until barely tender, then drain and arrange in a baking dish in one layer.

While the cauliflower cooks, make the sauce. Heat the butter and curry powder in a saucepan until bubbling, stir in the flour, then the tomato mixture, and bring to the boil, stirring constantly. Thin with a little water if necessary, then pour evenly over the cauliflower in the baking dish. Sprinkle with as much cheese as you like.

Bake uncovered at 180°C, just until the cheese melts and the cauli-flower heats through. Do not overcook.

Serve as part of a main meal, or with rice as a meal in itself.

Crunchy curried cauliflower (top); Curried cauliflower & eggs

Fresh corn cakes (or fritters)

SERVES 3-4:

SALSA

2 firm ripe tomatoes, deseeded and
    diced
1 medium avocado, peeled and diced
½ red onion, diced
2 tablespoons chopped fresh
    coriander
1–2 tablespoons lemon (or lime) juice
1–2 tablespoons sweet chilli sauce
salt and freshly ground black pepper,
    to taste

CAKES OR FRITTERS

1 cup self-raising flour
2 large eggs
½ cup beer (or soda water, milk, etc.)
2 tablespoons sweet chilli sauce
1 teaspoon cumin
1 teaspoon paprika
½ teaspoon salt
1½–2 cups fresh corn kernels (2–3 cobs)
2 spring onions, finely sliced
2–3 tablespoons chopped coriander
1 medium red (or green) capsicum,
    deseeded and diced
oil to fry

Serve these delicious corn cakes or fritters topped with salsa. Or for something even easier, serve them accompanied with sweet chilli sauce. Use fresh corn if it is in season.

To make the salsa, toss the tomatoes, avocado, onion and coriander together in a small bowl. Add enough lemon (or lime) juice and chilli sauce to moisten thoroughly, then stir. Season to taste with salt and pepper, then leave to stand while you cook the fritters.

To make the fritters, measure the flour into a medium-sized bowl. Add the eggs, beer (or other liquid), chilli sauce, spices and salt, then stir together to make a smooth batter.

Remove the husk and silk from the corn cobs, then slice off the kernels using a sharp knife. Separate then measure the kernels, and add to the batter along with the remaining 3 ingredients.

Heat the oil in a large non-stick pan – for 'traditional' fritters you will need oil 5–10mm deep, or for corn cakes, rather than fritters use 1–2 tablespoons. Cook batches of fritters for 3–5 minutes per side until golden brown, or cakes until they are lightly browned on both sides and firm when pressed in the centre.

Drain cooked fritters on several layers of paper towels. Keep cooked fritters or cakes warm in the oven until all the mixture is cooked, then serve immediately topped with the salsa above, or bowls of sweet chilli sauce.

Fresh corn cakes

Kumara & corn cakes

- -

To vary the Asian, lightly curried flavour, with an equally delicious but quite different alternative, replace the curry and coriander with basil or sundried tomato pesto.

Trim the ends off the kumara, and microwave it on High (100%), turning once, for 6 minutes, or until flesh feels soft all over when pressed. When it's cool enough to handle, peel off the outer skin, then mash the kumara with a fork. (You should have about 3 cupfuls.)

Add the chopped spring onions, drained corn, curry paste, salt and fresh coriander. Stir in the unbeaten eggs with a fork, then add enough flour to hold the mixture together.

Heat a non-stick frying pan, and add enough oil to barely cover the bottom of the pan. Using a dessertspoon, drop 4–6 rough-surfaced patties onto the pan. Cook, uncovered, over moderate heat for 3–5 minutes until nicely browned, then turn and cook the other side. Keep warm while you cook the remaining patties, then serve immediately.

VARIATIONS: *Use more (or less) kumara, corn and spring onions, and add more (or less) flour to hold the cakes together.*

Leave out the curry paste and coriander and add 2 tablespoons basil pesto or sundried tomato pesto for cakes with quite a different flavour.

SERVES 3–4:

500g (2 large) kumara
3–4 spring onions
1 cup whole kernel corn, drained
1–2 teaspoons green curry paste
about 1 teaspoon salt
2–3 tablespoons chopped fresh or
   bottled coriander
2 large eggs
about ¼ cup self-raising flour

Kumara & potato cakes with mango salsa

- -

These crisp little kumara and potato cakes really come to life when served with this delicious mango salsa!

Scrub the potatoes and kumara, then grate with the skins on. Place the grated mixture in a bowl and cover with water. Leave to stand for 1–2 minutes, then drain in a sieve, squeezing out as much water as you can. Transfer back to the dried bowl.

Thinly slice the spring onions and add these to the grated mixture along with the egg, salt and a generous grind of black pepper, then stir lightly with a fork to combine. Leave the mixture to stand while you prepare the salsa.

Drain the mango slices and cut the flesh into 5mm cubes. Thinly slice the spring onion, then mix this together with the cubed mango, lemon or lime juice, chilli, salt and chopped coriander in a small bowl.

Heat the oil in a large non-stick pan, gently drop generous dessert spoons of the kumara-potato mixture into the pan, flattening them into cakes about 1cm thick. Cook over a medium-high heat for 3–4 minutes per side, or until crisp and golden brown. Drain briefly on paper towels, then arrange on plates and serve with a generous dollop of the salsa, and a green salad.

SERVES 2–3:

150–200g kumara
150–200g potatoes
2 spring onions
1 large egg
½ teaspoon salt
freshly ground black pepper
about ¼ cup oil for cooking

MANGO SALSA

400g can mango slices in light syrup,
   or 1 cup finely chopped fresh mango
1 spring onion
1 tablespoon lemon (or lime) juice
½ teaspoon minced red chilli
½ teaspoon salt
1–2 tablespoons chopped coriander
   leaf

Corn cobs

- -

For barbecued corn cobs, use small cobs of tender young corn. Soak the cobs in a bucket of water for 10 minutes, then barbecue over low heat, turning frequently, until the husks are charred. Cut the base from each cob, and peel off the husks and silk.

To cook corn cobs in the microwave, place 1 or 2 cobs, as picked, in a microwave oven, without further coverings, allowing 3 minutes on High (100%) per cob. Cut off base, peel off husk and silk. Serve with Chilli mayonnaise (see page 99).

Pumpkin, spinach & feta cakes

SERVES 3–4 (12 LARGE CAKES):

250g peeled and cubed pumpkin

2 large eggs

¼ cup milk

125g frozen spinach, thawed

100–125g feta cheese, crumbled

½ cup self-raising flour

½ teaspoon cumin

½ teaspoon curry powder

½ teaspoon salt

freshly ground black pepper, to taste

2–3 tablespoons canola oil, for frying

The salty tang of feta in these delicious cakes goes well with the sweetness of pumpkin. The flavours are interesting enough that no sauce is required, but if you want you could serve them with raita, sweet chilli sauce, or even tomato sauce on the side.

Place the pumpkin in a small bowl or roasting bag and microwave for 4–5 minutes on High (100%), stirring after 2 minutes, or until tender. Mash roughly then set aside.

Break the eggs into a medium-sized bowl, then add the milk, spinach and feta. Add the mashed pumpkin and stir until well mixed. Sprinkle in the flour, cumin, curry powder, salt, and pepper, to taste and gently fold together, until all ingredients are just combined.

Heat 1 tablespoon of the oil in a large non-stick pan. Drop serving spoon-sized blobs of the batter into the pan, leaving several centimetres between each to allow easier turning. Cook over a medium heat for 2–3 minutes per side, or until golden brown. Arrange cooked cakes on a double layer of paper towels and keep warm while you cook the remaining batter in batches that fit comfortably in the pan.

Serve with one or two interesting salads, and sweet chilli or tomato sauce for dipping if desired.

Kumara purée with coriander

Freshly crushed coriander seeds add a lovely aromatic flavour.

Scrub the kumara thoroughly. Microwave on High (100%) for 6–8 minutes per 250g kumara; or bake in a conventional oven, in an oven bag, for 45–60 minutes. Kumara is cooked when the flesh 'gives' when squeezed.

Peel the cooked kumara without removing the coloured flesh under the skin. Chop the flesh roughly and mash with a potato masher or purée in a food processor, adding a little butter and milk in equal quantities. Add pepper and salt to taste, then add freshly crushed coriander seeds to taste.

Creamy mushroom stroganoff

SERVES 3–4:

300–400g long pasta (fettuccine, spaghetti, etc.)

2 tablespoons olive oil

1 medium onion, quartered and sliced

500g button mushrooms, halved

½ teaspoon tarragon

¼ teaspoon thyme

¼ cup sherry (or dry red or white wine)

1 tablespoon tomato paste

1 tablespoon dark soy sauce

250g regular or lite sour cream

2–3 tablespoons chopped parsley

½–1 teaspoon salt

freshly ground black pepper, to taste

chopped parsley and paprika to garnish

This delicious creamy sauce, served over pasta or rice, makes a wonderful quick meal.

Put the pasta on to cook in plenty of rapidly boiling water. While the pasta cooks, prepare the sauce.

Heat the olive oil in a large saucepan, add the sliced onion and cook, stirring frequently, until the onion begins to brown. Add the halved mushrooms and continue to cook, stirring occasionally, until the mushrooms have softened and wilted.

Gently stir in the tarragon, thyme, sherry (or wine), tomato paste and soy sauce. Leave the sauce to simmer for 3–5 minutes, then stir in the sour cream. Reheat without boiling, then add the chopped parsley, and season to taste with salt and pepper.

Spoon stroganoff over the drained and lightly oiled pasta, garnish with some additional chopped parsley and a dash of paprika. Serve immediately, accompanied with steamed vegetables or a salad.

Five-minute mushrooms

SERVES 2:

400g portobello or cup-shaped brown
  mushrooms
2–3 teaspoons olive oil
2– 3 teaspoons butter
1tsp minced garlic
½ cup vegetable stock (page 43) or
  ½ teaspoon vegetable stock powder
  in ½ cup water
¼ teaspoon minced red chilli or chilli
  paste
¼ teaspoon dried thyme, crumbled
freshly ground black pepper
1 teaspoon flour
1 tomato (optional)
pinch salt
1–2 tablespoons fresh or sour cream
  (optional)

This recipe must be made with brown, portobello or cup-shaped mushrooms (or mature meadow mushrooms) which are 'meaty' and satisfying, with an excellent flavour. Cook them on high heat for a great 5-minute meal.

Trim the mushroom stalks to level with the edge of the caps. (This makes it easier to brown the undersides.)

Heat the oil and butter in a heavy frying pan. Add the garlic and mushrooms, rounded sides down, and brown over high heat. Turn the mushrooms over, add about half the stock, cover, then shake the pan so the mushrooms wilt in the steam and brown on their undersides, too. Keep the heat high enough to evaporate the stock.

Remove the lid, lower the heat a little, then add the chilli or chilli paste, thyme, and a good grinding of black pepper. Sprinkle the flour over the mushrooms, turn them over, then add the finely cubed tomato, and the remaining stock.

Add more liquid if necessary, to finish up with mushrooms glazed in lightly thickened liquid. Add a little fresh or sour cream if you like. Heat again, adjust the seasonings, and sprinkle with chopped herbs.

Serve on toast, a toasted split roll, pasta or rice.

Mushroom burgers

SERVES 2:

1 medium-sized onion
1 clove garlic
1 tablespoon oil
150g mushrooms
1 cup fresh wholemeal breadcrumbs
1 teaspoon cornflour
1 tablespoon fresh chopped parsley (or
  1 teaspoon dried parsley)
1 teaspoon nutritional yeast
1 egg
1 tablespoon lemon juice (juice of
  ½ lemon)
1 teaspoon dark soy sauce

These burgers are very popular with mushroom lovers. The recipe is especially good made with older mushrooms with dark gills, as these have a stronger flavour.

Chop the onion and garlic, then sauté in the oil until the onion begins to soften. Add the mushrooms and continue cooking until they turn soft and dark.

Tip the onion-and-mushroom mixture into a medium-sized bowl, and add the remaining ingredients. Mix well, using your hands if necessary. Add a few more breadcrumbs if the mixture seems too wet.

Divide into four equal portions and then shape each quarter into a 10cm pattie. Cook in a little oil or butter, using a non-stick pan if you have one, until lightly browned on each side and firm when pressed in the middle.

NOTE: *A little fresh thyme is a nice addition to these burgers.*

Sweet & sour onions

SERVES 4–6:

500g small onions
2 tablespoons tomato paste
2 tablespoons wine vinegar
1 tablespoon olive oil or other oil
1 tablespoon sugar
1 teaspoon salt
1 cup water
¼ cup sultanas
1 bay leaf

These small onions are a treat.

Pour boiling water over the onions and leave to stand for 1 minute. Drain and cut off the root and top sections of the onions, then lift off the skins.

Combine the tomato paste, wine vinegar, oil, sugar and salt in a microwave-proof dish or saucepan big enough to hold the onions in one layer. Add the water, sultanas and bay leaf, then the onions.

Cover and microwave on High (100%) for 6 minutes or until the onions are tender; or simmer on the stovetop for 20–30 minutes. Serve immediately, or leave to stand and serve at room temperature.

Savoury beans & tomatoes

An interesting sauce like this gives new life to yet more beans from your garden!

Trim the beans and cut each diagonally into 2 or 3 pieces. Cook in a small amount of water in a covered saucepan. Drain.

Make the sauce in another saucepan or frying pan. Chop the garlic and onion, cover and cook in the oil until the onion is tender, then add the sugar, wine vinegar and mustard. Add the tomatoes and salt and boil rapidly for 2–3 minutes, breaking the tomatoes into smaller pieces as the mixture boils down. Either add the beans to the sauce, or serve the sauce over the beans.

SERVES 4:

250g green beans
1 large clove garlic
1 onion
2 tablespoons olive oil
1 tablespoon sugar
2 tablespoons wine vinegar
1 tablespoon grainy mustard
400g can whole tomatoes or 2 cups
    ripe tomatoes, cubed
½ teaspoon salt
basil and/or sliced black olives
    (optional)

Shredded beetroot

Beetroot does not have to be boiled whole or pickled before it is used. Try this for a truly colourful side dish.

Thinly peel then shred or coarsely grate the raw beetroot. Cook the garlic in the butter, without browning. Add the beetroot, water, and orange or lemon juice, cover and cook over moderate heat for 5–15 minutes, until the beetroot is tender. Try to have all the liquid evaporated by this time.

Taste and add seasoning as required. Add a little sugar if the flavour is too bland. Add any fresh herbs you like, finely chopped. Serve hot.

SERVES 4:

300–400g beetroot
1 garlic clove, chopped
2 teaspoons butter
¼ cup water
1 tablespoon orange or lemon juice
freshly ground black pepper, salt and
    sugar (as required)
fresh herbs (optional)

Braised red cabbage

This recipe is surprisingly good!

Chop the onion and garlic finely. Melt the butter in a large saucepan and add the onion and garlic. Cook over medium heat while you slice the cabbage thinly. Add it to the saucepan, with the grated apples and water. Pour ½ cup vinegar over the vegetables in the pot, cover and simmer for 30 minutes, removing the lid for the last 5 minutes, to evaporate most of the liquid.

Add the salt and brown sugar, and mix well. Mix the cornflour with 1 tablespoon of vinegar, and add just before serving. Taste – you may need to add more salt.

Serve hot or reheated. This mixture refrigerates and freezes well.

SERVES 8:

1 large onion
2 cloves garlic
2 tablespoons butter
1 small red cabbage
2 apples, grated
1 cup water
½ cup vinegar
1 teaspoon salt
1 tablespoon brown sugar
1 teaspoon cornflour
1 tablespoon vinegar

Joanna's cabbage

This is an interesting alternative to 'plain' cabbage. It's particularly good if you're a gardener and you have got lots of cabbages to deal with.

Heat the butter or oil in a medium-large frying pan. Add the onion and cabbage, toss to coat, then add the remaining ingredients. Mix well, cover the pan and cook over fairly high heat for 5–10 minutes, then remove the lid. Cook, turning the mixture frequently, for 5 minutes more, or until the cooking liquid has evaporated and the cabbage is tender but still crisp.

SERVES 4:

2 tablespoons butter or oil
1 medium-sized onion, sliced thinly
½ medium-sized cabbage, shredded
2 tablespoons wine vinegar
1 tablespoon sugar
1 teaspoon salt
freshly ground black pepper, to taste
1 cup tomatoes, skinned and chopped

Potatoes

Potatoes are an all-round basic ingredient that may be used in many ways — as part of a main course dish, in salads (especially on a warm day) and as side dishes, especially when baked.

Choose waxy, firm potatoes for salads and for slicing into quiches, frittata, vegetable squares, etc. Use floury potatoes for roasting, mashing and baking.

How to cook potatoes

Here are the basic instructions for cooking potatoes absolutely plainly. You may like to refer to these outlines when making a recipe which tells you to start with cooked potatoes.

All-purpose, floury potatoes and 'main crop' waxy varieties:

Wash or scrub the potatoes you are going to cook. Peel them thinly, using a sharp vegetable knife or a potato peeler, or rub them all over with a 'green scratchy' pot-scrub. Scrubbing them like this is quick, and there's much less wastage than when peeling potatoes. Cut out and discard any damaged parts of the potato.

Cut the peeled potatoes into even-sized pieces.

Bring a saucepan of lightly salted water to the boil. Drop the potatoes into the boiling water, and check that the water covers the potatoes. Cover with a lid.

When the water returns to the boil, lower the heat so the water is simmering.

Cooking time will vary – anything from 15–30 minutes – and will depend on the variety of potato used, their size, and the heat source. Check by piercing a large piece of potato with the sharp point of a knife. The potatoes are cooked when there is little resistance.

Drain the cooked potatoes, saving the cooking water for use in gravy, sauce or to add to a pot of soup.

Early season waxy or new potatoes:

Using a vegetable knife or a pot-scrub (see above), scrape off the thin, delicate skin of new potatoes. Cut out any imperfections, leaving the potatoes whole if they are small, or cutting them in pieces of similar size.

Bring a saucepan of lightly salted water to the boil. Add a little sugar, salt, garlic, some mint sprigs or herbs of your choice to the water. Drop the potatoes into the water and check that the water covers the potatoes. Cover with a lid so the potatoes are surrounded by water or steam.

Bring back to the boil and cook the potatoes at a gentle simmer until tender when pierced. Cooking time will probably be a little shorter than the time required for main crop potatoes.

Drain the cooked potatoes, then turn them in a little melted butter. If you have cooked them with mint, you can serve the edible leaves with the potatoes.

Mashed potatoes

Stovetop mashed potatoes

Mashed potatoes are comfort food with a capital M! A pile of light, fluffy, creamy mashed potatoes can be the highlight of a meal, whether you are cooking for yourself, your family, or guests.

It's worth taking a little time and trouble over their preparation, so they finish up absolutely perfect.

Start with all-purpose or floury potatoes; new or waxy potatoes will not turn out to be fluffy. Wash or scrub the potatoes you are going to cook. Cut them into even-sized pieces.

Bring a saucepan of lightly salted water to the boil. Drop the potatoes into the water, and cover with a lid. Bring back to the boil, then lower the heat and simmer until cooked.

Drain the potatoes when they are tender right through. Pour off the cooking liquid, saving it for later use in a gravy or sauce. If you have time, allow the drained potatoes to stand in the dry saucepan for 2–3 minutes.

Mash with a potato masher, or push the potatoes through a potato ricer. Add 1 teaspoon of butter per serving. Lastly, beat the mashed potatoes with a fork, adding milk until they are light, smooth and creamy. Season as needed.

Serve immediately, or leave to stand in a warm place for a few minutes before serving.

Microwaved mashed potatoes

It is hard to give accurate timing for cooking potatoes in the microwave because of the difference in cooking time between potato varieties and the varying levels of power in microwave ovens. Keep a note of how long it takes to cook a certain weight of potatoes, especially if you buy in bulk. After a little experimenting and accurate timing, you should be able to produce consistently good results.

Peel all-purpose or floury potatoes, and cut into 1–2cm cubes, and put in a microwave-proof bowl with a lid. Add 1 teaspoon butter and 1 tablespoon water per serving.

Cover and cook on High (100%) in a microwave oven for 2–3 minutes per serving, shaking to reposition the potato cubes about halfway through the cooking time.

Leave to stand for 5 minutes after cooking, then test to make sure all the cubes are cooked through completely.

Mash without draining, adding milk, salt and pepper to taste. Then beat with a fork until they are light, smooth and creamy.

NOTE: *If the potato cubes appear to be slightly shrunken when you check them after cooking, you have cooked them too long. Next time you cook the same variety, allow half a minute less per serving.*

Baked potatoes

Baked potatoes

Baked potatoes are easy to prepare and cook. Serve them plain, as part of a meal; or stuff with a variety of fillings and serve as a main dish.

In the oven

Scrub medium to large potatoes, then brush or rub with oil (this will keep the skins soft). Bake on a rack, rather than on a solid surface, in a preheated 200°C oven for 50–60 minutes, or at 180°C for 60–75 minutes, until the potato flesh gives when pressed.

In the microwave

Scrub medium to large potatoes (try to choose potatoes roughly the same size for even cooking), then prick each one several times before cooking. Cook in the micro-wave on High (100%). Turn the potatoes over halfway through the cooking time.

The following are approximate cooking times for dif-ferent amounts of potatoes.

NOTE *Cooking times will vary with different microwave ovens, depending on their wattage. Use less time if you have a high-powered oven.*

100g	3 minutes
200g	5½ minutes
300g	7½–8 minutes
400g	10 minutes

NOTE: *A small number of potatoes will microwave faster than boiled potatoes. However, it is easy to*

overcook them, in which case they will be slightly shrivelled. Avoid this next time by cooking for a shorter period.

In a slow-cooker

It is very handy to be able to fill up your slow-cooker with foil-wrapped potatoes in the morning, then return to the kitchen hours later to find them ready and waiting! It's so easy, too – all you need are potatoes, some foil and, of course, a slow-cooker.

Choose potatoes that are labelled 'suitable for baking'. Larger potatoes will take longer to cook all the way through, so for best results select potatoes of similar size.

Wrap potatoes individually in foil (to stop them drying out) and arrange them in the cooker. Cover, turn the slow cooker to low, and in 6–8 hours you should have delicious baked potatoes!

Sometimes potatoes that have been pressed against the sides of the cooker bowl can brown a bit. To prevent this happening, turn or rearrange them after 4–5 hours.

To serve

Once the potatoes are baked (in oven or microwave), leave them to stand for 3–5 minutes, then cut a cross in the top of each one. Press down gently between the cuts to open out the cross. Put a little butter, sour cream or cheese in the opening.

Serve the baked potatoes with butter and/or sour cream as a side dish. Or they can be stuffed, e.g. with baked beans and grated cheese, leftover mince mix-tures, etc., and served as a main dish, in which case it is best to reheat them, either in a microwave or regular oven, until the filling is heated through.

Checkerboard potatoes

Sometimes it's good to cook potatoes in a way that is just a little different. Checkerboard potatoes are worth trying – they cook more quickly than regular baked potatoes, they look more colourful and they don't require any last-minute attention.

Scrub some fairly large, oval potatoes – as many as are required – and cut in each one in half lengthwise. Using a sharp vegetable knife make a series of parallel cuts lengthwise, 5mm apart, cutting down as deeply as you can without cutting through the skin. Then cut similar lines crosswise so you finish up with a checkerboard design.

Blot the cut surface with a paper towel, pressing down firmly, then lightly brush the same surface with melted butter or oil. Sprinkle evenly with paprika. (You will get a nice even result if you shake the paprika through a fine sieve.)

Bake the potatoes, cut side up, in a preheated 200°C oven for 35–40 minutes or until the potatoes feel soft when squeezed. The cuts should open slightly during the cooking process. Serve immediately.

Stuffed baked potatoes

Everybody likes potatoes that have been baked, emptied of their cooked insides, filled again with mashed potato and exciting additions, and reheated.

Scrub large potatoes, bake at 200°C for about an hour, or microwave on High (100%) for 4–6 minutes per potato. Potatoes are cooked when they 'give' when pressed. Halve the cooked potatoes, or remove a slice from the long side of each one. Scoop out the flesh with a small spoon, and mash it with one or more of the following:

- **butter or quark**
- **grated cheese**
- **cubed cheese**
- **tofu**
- **mayonnaise**
- **milk**
- **sour cream**
- **cream cheese**
- **yoghurt**
- **cottage cheese.**

Season with:
- **chopped spring onion or chives**
- **chopped parsley**
- **finely chopped thyme, basil, marjoram, dill, mini, etc.**
- **freshly ground black pepper**
- **chutney, pickle, or relish**
- **garlic or garlic spreads**
- **mustard**
- **chilli sauce**
- **chopped gherkins**
- **chopped red or green capsicums.**

Stir in:
- **sautéed mushrooms**
- **corn**
- **sautéed onions**
- **asparagus**
- **chopped avocado**
- **baked beans**
- **chopped nuts**
- **Mexican beans.**

Taste, and season if necessary. Pile the filling back into the potato shells. Reheat at 200°C until heated through and browned, for about 15 minutes; or microwave on High (100%) until heated through, for about 2–3 minutes per potato. Brown under a grill if desired.

Easy oven-baked chips

Instead of deep-frying chips, we bake them: it uses much less oil and makes very little mess – and the chips always disappear very quickly!

SERVES 2–3:

Preheat the oven to 230°C, positioning the tray in the centre.

Peel or scrub 2–3 large all-purpose or floury potatoes and thinly slice into 5–7mm thick chips. Drop the chips into a bowl of cold water as you go and leave them to stand in the water for 5 minutes after you have finished, to avoid browning.

Rinse the chips under cold running water, then thoroughly pat or blot them dry, using a clean teatowel or paper towels. Dry the bowl, too, and return the chips to the dry bowl. Pour 2–3 tablespoons of canola or other flavourless oil over the chips and mix with your fingers until they are completely coated with a thin film of oil.

Line a roasting pan or sponge-roll pan with baking paper. Place the chips in the dish in one layer. Bake in the oven for 20 minutes until the chips are tender, turning once. If they do not brown enough in this time, slide out the baking paper and brown the chips under the grill.

Just before serving, sprinkle the chips with a little plain or seasoned salt. Serve immediately.

Roast potatoes

Roast potatoes that cook in a roasting pan need very little attention. They will brown better and crisp up more if they are not packed too tightly in the pan: choose a large shallow roasting pan rather than a small deep one and cover the potatoes in 2–3mm of oil.

Although large potatoes can be cut in half or in quarters for roasting, oval-shaped whole smallish potatoes look particularly good when roasted. The heat seems to circulate round them better, too.

'Main crop' potatoes (page 118) take about 60–75 minutes at 180°C, depending on their size. It is a good idea to turn potatoes over occasionally, so they become golden brown and crisp on as many surfaces as possible.

NOTE: *New potatoes do not roast well.*

Crusty roast potatoes

Peel the required number of potatoes – 'main crop' potatoes are best – and cut into even-sized pieces. Parboil (partly cook) in boiling water for 15 minutes.

Drain and pat the potatoes dry. Coat them lightly with flour, then roast as above. Some people like to roughen the surface of the parboiled potatoes with a fork so they brown better, but it's not really necessary.

Garlic roast potatoes

Peel the required number of potatoes — ideally oval-shaped, smallish and whole. Preheat the oven to 200°C.

Bring a saucepan of lightly salted water to the boil. Drop the potatoes in, and check that the water covers them. Cover and cook for 15 minutes.

Drain the potatoes, pat dry, then put them on a board until they are cool enough to handle.

While the potatoes are cooking, mash 2 cloves of garlic in ¼ cup oil using a pestle and mortar or a small grinder or blender.

When the potatoes are cool enough to handle, make deep crosswise cuts, 5mm apart, on each potato, taking care not to cut them right through. Thoroughly brush each potato with the garlic oil, ensuring that the oil gets into the cuts.

Put the potatoes in a shallow baking dish and cook in the oven for about 1 hour, brushing with more garlic oil at intervals.

Potatoes to die for!

This is delicious, if sinful, since it contains rather a lot of sour cream. Serve it as an occasional treat.

SERVES 4:

1.5kg potatoes, preferably waxy
3 large cloves garlic
¼ cup flour
½ teaspoon salt
2 cups sour cream
½ cup milk
200g gruyère cheese, grated

Scrub the potatoes, cut in 5mm slices, and drop into a large container of cold water. Drain and transfer to a microwave dish or oven bag, cover the bowl or tie the bag loosely, and microwave 12–15 minutes on High (100%) until the potatoes are tender.

Make the sauce while the potatoes cook. Using a food processor if available, finely chop the garlic, then add the flour, salt, sour cream and milk. Process until smooth.

Butter or spray a large shallow oval or rectangular baking dish, about 23 x 30cm. Overlap half the potatoes in it, drizzle almost half the sauce mixture over them, then sprinkle over almost half of the cheese. Repeat with the remaining potatoes and cream sauce, and then sprinkle the rest of the cheese evenly over the top.

Bake uncovered at 180°C for about 30 minutes, until the potatoes have heated through and the topping is golden brown. Allow to stand in a warm place for 5–10 minutes before serving.

Serve with a mixed green salad or a spinach salad.

Sinfully good potato wedges

These rich and sinful but delicious potatoes should be served only as an occasional treat. Coated with a heavily herbed and spiced mixture and baked until crisp, they are wonderful!

SERVES 3–4:

4 large (about 1kg) all-purpose or floury potatoes
25g butter, melted
½ teaspoon salt
3 tablespoons olive oil
2 teaspoons finely chopped garlic
2 teaspoons ground cumin
1 teaspoon dried oregano
¼–½ teaspoon chilli powder

Scrub the potatoes, then microwave on High (100%) or boil them whole until they are barely tender. Cool them if you have time, then cut each one lengthwise into 8 wedges.

Preheat the oven to 180°C.

Warm the butter in a large roasting pan until it is liquid but not hot. Add the salt, olive oil, garlic, cumin, oregano and chilli, and mix well.

Using your hands, turn the potato wedges in the pan, mixing gently but thoroughly until all surfaces are well coated. Spread them out in a single layer, then bake for 1–1½ hours until crispy, turning once.

Serve warm, as a snack, with your favourite tomato-based salsa.

Minted green pea & potato frittata

SERVES 4-6:

500-600g new potatoes or white
    waxy potatoes, washed
2 cups minted frozen peas
2-3 spring onions, finely sliced
4 medium firm tomatoes, deseeded
    and chopped into 1cm cubes
2 cups grated tasty cheese
4 large eggs
1 cup evaporated milk
1 teaspoon salt
freshly ground black pepper, to taste

This easy-to-make frittata makes wonderful picnic food, is excellent for packed lunches, and is a good informal weekend meal, with a salad.

Line a rectangular metal baking pan, about 20 x 30cm, with sides about 5-6cm tall, with a sheet of baking paper. The paper should fit neatly in the base of the pan and up the sides, with the corners folded (but not cut). Coat the baking paper with non-stick spray.

Preheat the oven to 220°C with the rack positioned in or just below the middle.

Scrape the new potatoes, or rub them if they are the white variety, then cut in half lengthwise, then in quarters crosswise. Cook in about 2cm of lightly salted water in a medium-sized saucepan, covered, for about 20 minutes or until the potatoes are almost tender. Add the peas and cook for 5-10 minutes longer. Drain the vegetables and spread them out on a shallow tray or dish to cool. When the potatoes are cool enough to handle, cut the quarters into small chunks.

Mix together the spring onion, tomato, peas and potatoes, then spread half over the paper-lined base of the pan. Sprinkle half the cheese over the vegetables, then top with the remaining vegetable mixture.

In a bowl, beat together the eggs, milk, salt, and pepper to taste. Pour evenly over the vegetable layers, and sprinkle the remaining cheese over the top. Evaporated milk gives body and extra richness to the frittata.

Bake for 40-45 minutes, until the egg mixture is set and the cheese topping has browned attractively. Leave to cool for at least half an hour before cutting with a serrated knife into about 12 slices: 3 portions crosswise and 4 lengthwise.

Eat immediately, or cover and refrigerate for up to 2 days until required.

VARIATIONS: *Replace the peas with mixed frozen vegetables, adding any suitable chopped fresh herbs to replace the mint flavour of the peas.*

Replace the chopped tomatoes with 1-2 chopped red capsicums, and add them, with the peas, to the partly cooked potatoes.

Potato frittata

SERVES 4-6:

50g butter
3 onions, sliced
3-4 medium-sized potatoes
    (500-600g), unpeeled, sliced
2 zucchini, sliced (or other vegetables)
4 eggs
2 tablespoons water
½ cup grated parmesan

Make this recipe at weekends when you want something quick and easy; when you haven't bought any special ingredients, but want to use up leftovers; or for a picnic.

Melt the butter in a large heavy frying pan. Cook the sliced onions in the butter over moderate heat, until they are evenly browned. Add the sliced potatoes, stir well, cover the pan and cook for 15-20 minutes, stirring occasionally. After 10-15 minutes, add the zucchini or other vegetables, so they will be cooked at the same time as the potatoes.

Beat the eggs with the water and half the cheese. Pour this mixture over the pressed-down vegetable mixture, and cook over gentle heat for 10 minutes or until the sides and bottom are cooked.

Sprinkle the remaining parmesan over the top, then place under a grill until the top puffs up and browns lightly. Serve hot, warm or at room temperature, with a salad if desired.

VARIATIONS: *Add chopped garlic with the potatoes; and fresh or dried herbs with the egg mixture.*

Minted green pea & potato frittata

Potato pancakes

SERVES 6:

2 eggs, unbeaten

2 tablespoons milk

1 onion, very finely chopped

1 teaspoon curry powder

1 teaspoon salt

½ teaspoon celery salt

500g raw potatoes, scrubbed or thinly peeled

¼ cup flour *

corn or soy oil

* If the mixture seems a little wet, add 2–3 tablespoons of extra flour. This will depend on the potatoes.

Potato pancakes are especially popular with children – they enjoy their texture and mild flavour.

Because potatoes brown on prolonged standing, do not mix the batter before you plan to cook it; if you like, mix the first 6 ingredients in a bowl and add the potato and flour just before cooking. In this recipe the potato is grated straight into the bowl, and is not squeezed first.

In a bowl, place the eggs, milk, onion, curry powder, salt and celery salt. Stir with a fork until mixed.

Just before cooking, grate the potatoes into the mixture and add the flour. If wholemeal flour is used, increase the quantity slightly.

Fry spoonfuls of the mixture in hot oil, about 5mm deep, for 3 minutes per side, until golden brown. If the cooking time is too short, the potato will not be cooked in the centre.

Serve alone, or with tomatoes or mushrooms.

Potato cakes

SERVES 4:

2 cups cold grated cooked potato or 2 cups mashed potato

1 cup self-raising flour

1 teaspoon celery salt

1 teaspoon garlic salt or onion salt

½ teaspoon curry powder

4 spring onions, chopped

½ cup chopped parsley

up to 1 cup cooked cold carrots, peas or mixed vegetables (optional)

oil or butter, to cook

Enormously popular, the seasonings can be varied using what is available. Do not mix the flour and potatoes until you are ready to cook, as the mixture may turn sticky with prolonged standing.

Mix the grated or mashed potato with the remaining ingredients, adding other fresh or dried herbs and spices, if you like. Shape the potato dough into a 10cm-wide cyclinder. If the dough is too dry to shape, add a little milk. If it is too moist, add a little extra flour.

Cut the cylinder into 1cm-thick slices with a sharp serrated knife. Turn each disc in a little extra flour, and cook in a preheated, preferably non-stick frying pan in a small amount of oil or butter. Allow about 3 minutes per side.

Serve with a salad or cooked vegetables.

Jacket wedges

SERVES 3–4:

4 large potatoes (about 1kg)

3 tablespoons olive oil

1 tablespoon Kikkoman (or other) light soy sauce

1 teaspoon (1–2 cloves) minced garlic

1 teaspoon ground cumin

1 tablespoon grated parmesan

1 tablespoon flour

These easy-to-cook, tasty and filling snacks are popular with all age groups. Add different spices for flavour and serve with dips.

Preheat the oven to 200–220°C.

Scrub but do not peel the potatoes. Cut each potato lengthwise into halves, quarters, then eighths. Put the prepared wedges into a bowl of cold water and leave to stand. Mix together the olive oil, soy sauce, garlic, cumin, parmesan and flour in another bowl.

Drain the potato wedges and pat completely dry between several layers of paper towels. Drop the dried wedges into the seasoning mixture, then, using your fingers, gently turn them to coat thoroughly.

Line a large shallow roasting pan with baking paper or a non-stick Teflon liner, or drizzle a little oil into the pan. Lie the wedges in one layer in the pan.

Bake for 35–40 minutes, or until tender and golden brown, turning after 20 minutes. If you like, sprinkle the wedges with a little salt, seasoned salt and/or grated cheddar cheese before lifting off the baking pan. (Wedges that are salted before cooking are not as crisp.)

Serve straight away, with dips such as guacamole, salsa, satay sauce or sour cream, as snacks or appetisers.

Raclette

Raclette

A variation on a Swiss tradition, where an easily melted type of cheese is heated and served on boiled potatoes, with pickled gherkins and beer or white wine. Use a New Zealand-made raclette cheese or, for a milder flavour, use a mild cheddar; or try Pyrenees or St Paulin cheese.

To microwave new or 'main crop' potatoes, cut 500g of scrubbed potatoes into even-sized pieces (smaller pieces cook more quickly).

Microwave on High (100%) in a covered dish or an oven bag with ½ cup water for new potatoes, or ¼ cup water for main crop potatoes, for 6–8 minutes. Leave to stand for 2–3 minutes.

Heat slices of cheese in shallow dishes until soft and bubbly around the edges. Use the microwave, or place them under the grill.

NOTE: *Mixed salad and bread rolls make fine accompaniments for this meal.*

Sautéed potatoes

Skillet potatoes

These potatoes are especially good served in warm weather, with cold meat and a tomato salad or a mixed salad. The recipe is particularly easy to make in an electric frypan. Don't forget to keep an eye on the potatoes as they cook.

SERVES 3–4:

4–5 medium-sized potatoes (about 600g)
2 sliced onions
3–4 tablespoons butter (or
  1 tablespoon each butter and oil)
salt and freshly ground black pepper, to taste
2 tablespoons finely chopped fresh herbs

Scrub or peel the potatoes and cut into 5mm thick slices, dropping them into a bowl of cold water as you go.

Cook the onions the butter or butter and oil mix in a large electric frypan with a lid.

Drain the raw potato slices, pat them dry and add them to the onion in the pan. Turn to coat with butter, then cover and cook on low heat for 15 minutes, turning occasionally.

Remove the lid, then turn up the heat a little and allow the vegetables to brown slightly, cooking for a further 10–15 minutes.

Just before serving, drain off any excess butter or oil, season the potatoes with salt and pepper or any other seasonings you think would be good, and sprinkle with chopped fresh herbs.

Sautéed potatoes

Simple though they may be, sautéed potatoes are always really popular with everybody. Because of this, in our house we often cook more potatoes than we need for a meal – so there will be leftovers to sauté later on! Perfect baby new potatoes are not suitable: choose potatoes that have matured a bit and are not so waxy when cooked.

SERVES 2:

3–4 cold cooked medium potatoes
3–4 tablespoons butter (or
  1 tablespoon each butter and oil)
chopped parsley

Slice the potatoes into chunky pieces. Heat the butter or oil or butter and oil mix in a non-stick frying pan that is large enough for the potatoes to be easily turned. When the pan is hot, add the potatoes and cook, uncovered, turning every few minutes for 20–30 minutes until they are evenly crisp and golden. Sprinkle with chopped parsley before serving.

VARIATION: *Bring to the boil in a small saucepan: 2 tablespoons wine vinegar, 1 chopped garlic clove, 1 teaspoon finely grated lemon zest and 2 tablespoons olive oil. Drizzle over the potatoes just before serving.*

Spicy potatoes

These potatoes make a great accompaniment for any Indian-style meal. Curry leaves make an interesting addition.

SERVES 4:

600–800g waxy or all-purpose potatoes
1 teaspoon turmeric
1 teaspoon salt
2 tablespoons canola oil
1 teaspoon mustard seed
1 teaspoon cumin seeds
1 teaspoon: each paprika, ground coriander and garam masala
handful of curry leaves (optional)
½–1 teaspoon minced red chilli (optional)
2 tablespoons lemon juice
salt, to taste

Scrub the potatoes, cut into 2cm cubes and place in a large saucepan. Add just enough hot water to cover, then add the turmeric and salt. Bring to the boil and cook for 8–10 minutes, until tender. Drain well and set aside.

Heat the oil in a large non-stick frying pan. Add the mustard and cumin seeds and cook until the seeds begin to pop. Add the cooked potato, ground spices, curry leaves and chilli if using, and the lemon juice. Cook for 4–5 minutes, stirring frequently.

Remove from the heat, season to taste and serve immediately.

Curried new potatoes

This recipe offers several options on the curried potato theme, one of which makes a complete vegetarian main course.

SERVES 4:

2 tablespoons butter
1–2 teaspoons curry powder, or to taste
1 onion, chopped
6 medium (about 600g) new or waxy potatoes
1 teaspoon instant vegetable stock powder
1 teaspoon sugar
½ cup hot water
½ cup coconut cream or ¼ cup sour cream (but not both)
extra water, if needed
½ cup frozen peas, thawed (optional)
¼ cup sour cream (optional)
4–6 hard-boiled eggs (optional)
freshly chopped coriander leaves (optional)

Melt the butter in a medium frying pan. Add the curry powder and onion and cook gently for a few minutes.

Scrape or thoroughly scrub the potatoes, then cut lengthwise into halves or quarters for quicker cooking. Add to the curry mixture, along with the instant stock and sugar dissolved in the hot water, and the coconut cream.

Cover tightly and gently simmer for 15 minutes or until the potatoes are tender and the liquid is thick. Add ½ cup peas when the potatoes are nearly done, and cook until the peas are tender.

Add extra water or raise the heat so you finish up with sauce thick enough to coat the potatoes.

VARIATION: *To make a main course for 2–3 people, make the sauce using the coconut cream. Add 4–6 hard-boiled eggs, sliced lengthwise, cut side up. Heat them through, covered, over very low heat. Serve the curried potatoes, peas and eggs on rice. Sprinkle with the coriander leaves if using.*

NOTES:

If using sour cream rather than coconut cream, the sauce will be thinner.

Cook uncovered until the sauce thickens to the desired consistency.

Cheesy potato bake

This layered potato-and-cheese bake can be made from any cream soup you like – select a flavour that goes well with potatoes and cheese. The bake firms up on standing after cooking, and is just as nice reheated a day or two later, cut in wedges and served like a pie.

SERVES 4–6:

5–6 (1 kg) large all-purpose or floury potatoes
440g can cream of vegetable soup
¼–½ cup milk, cream or sherry (or any combination)
2 cups (200g) grated tasty or raclette cheese
paprika

Cook the potatoes, then cut them into slices 1cm thick.

Pour the contents of the can of soup into a small bowl, and add enough milk, cream or sherry (or a mix of these) to make the soup up to 2 cups.

Non-stick spray a large shallow ovenware dish, then cover the bottom with half of the potato slices. Sprinkle half of the cheese over the potatoes, then pour half of the soup over this. Repeat this process using the rest of the potato, cheese and soup mixture.

Sprinkle the top with paprika, and bake, uncovered, at 200°C for 45 minutes. Leave to stand for half an hour or so prior to serving. This will allow the flavours to blend and the potatoes to absorb all the remaining liquid.

Serve with a green or tomato salad, and crusty bread rolls.

Bird's nest potatoes

Spiced potatoes & peas

When you use several spices to flavour a cococonut cream-flavoured sauce, you can turn potatoes and peas into a whole meal – and an interesting one at that. The mixture will not be 'hot' unless you add the chilli powder.

SERVES 4:

1 large onion, chopped
2 cloves garlic, chopped
2 tablespoons oil or butter
½ teaspoon each: ground cumin, cardamom and
    coriander
¼ teaspoon each: ground celery seed and cloves
⅛ teaspoon chilli powder (optional)
¾–1 teaspoon turmeric
410g can coconut cream
600–700g small potatoes, preferably new
3 cups frozen peas
1 tablespoon sugar
½ teaspoon salt

Put the chopped onion and garlic into a large frying pan with the oil or butter. Cook gently for 4–5 minutes, until transparent. Add the cumin, cardamom, corian-der, celery seed, cloves, chilli powder (if using) and tur-meric. Stir over low heat for 2–3 minutes longer. Add the coconut cream and bring to the boil.

Scrub, scrape or peel the potatoes, and halve or quarter if large. Add to the pan, cover and simmer, turning the potatoes occasionally, until they are just tender – around 15–20 minutes.

Add the peas, sugar and salt and cook for a few minutes longer until the peas are tender. Adjust the thickness of the sauce by boiling briskly for a few minutes, if too thin, or adding a little water if it is too thick. Taste, adjust the seasonings if necessary, and serve.

Bird's nest potatoes

This recipe has been popular with Alison's family for more than 40 years. A food processor makes light work of grating the raw potatoes, and a large electric frypan will do a great job of cooking them (you need a large pan unless you are just cooking for one or two people).

Scrub then grate 1 large all-purpose or floury potato per person. Pile the shredded potato in the centre of a clean teatowel. Squeeze the teatowel to remove most of the liquid from the shredded potato.

Heat a little canola or olive oil in a very hot frying pan, then drop handfuls of grated potato into the pan. Flatten each 'cake' lightly, but do not pack the shreds too tightly. Turn the cakes over when they are golden brown, adding more oil when cooking the second side if necessary.

NOTE: *Work quickly, putting the grated potato into the pan soon after grating it, or the raw potato will turn brown on standing.*

Scalloped potatoes

Although we often use the microwave to make scalloped potatoes for two, we tend to cook a family-sized dish in the oven. If you aren't in the habit of making scalloped potatoes, do try this recipe – we think it will win you over.

SERVES 4:

600g medium all-purpose or floury potatoes
25g butter
1–2 cloves garlic or 2 small onions, finely chopped
1 teaspoon salt
freshly ground black pepper, to taste
1 cup milk

Preheat the oven to 200°C, positioning the rack just above the centre.

Choose even-shaped potatoes that will look attrac-tive when layered. Thinly peel or scrub them with a pot-scrub. Cut the potatoes crosswise into thin slices, and put them in a bowl of cold water.

Heat the butter in a small pot, but don't let it brown. Add the garlic or onion, stirring until it heats through, then add the salt, pepper and milk.

Drain the potatoes and arrange them in an oven dish that has been lightly coated with non-stick spray. Flatten the potatoes with your hand or a fish-slice, then evenly pour the hot milk mixture over the potatoes.

Cover with a lid, a sheet of foil or baking paper folded over loosely at the edges, and bake for 20–30 minutes. Uncover, and bake for a further 15–30 minutes until the top is golden brown, and the potatoes feel tender when pierced with a sharp knife.

Greek-style garlic & lemon potatoes

It's amazing how the flavours and aromas of food can bring the memories flooding back. The smell of these always evokes for Simon vivid memories of the Greek beach where he first tried them.

SERVES 3–4:

1kg all-purpose or floury potatoes
2 cloves garlic, crushed
½ cup vegetable stock (page 43)
1–2 tablespoons lemon juice
2–3 tablespoons olive oil
salt and freshly ground black pepper, to taste

Preheat the oven to 225°C.

Scrub the potatoes and cut in 2cm cubes. Coat the inside of a shallow 20 x 30cm casserole dish with non-stick spray. Add the potatoes, garlic, stock, lemon juice and oil, then toss gently to combine. Season with the salt and pepper.

Place the dish in the middle of the oven and cook for 20–25 minutes until golden brown, turning the potatoes gently once after about 10 minutes.

Potato & egg casserole

This is probably our most popular potato recipe – 'comfort food' at its best! It does take some time and effort to prepare, but it can be organised ahead.

SERVES 4–6:

4 (800g) cooked potatoes
4 hard-boiled eggs
50g butter
2 large onions
¼ cup flour
1 teaspoon dry mustard
½ teaspoon salt
freshly ground black pepper, to taste
2½ cups milk
1 cup grated cheese

TOPPING
1 tablespoon butter
1 cup fresh breadcrumbs

Slice the cooked potatoes into a large buttered casserole dish, then add the quartered, sliced or chopped hard-boiled eggs.

Melt the butter in a saucepan and cook the chopped onions until they are tender, but not browned. Stir in the flour, mustard, salt and pepper. Add 1 cup of milk and bring to the boil, stirring constantly. Stir in the remaining milk and bring back to the boil. Remove from the heat and add the grated cheese, stirring until smooth. Pour the cheese sauce over the potato and egg mixture, and stir to combine. Cover with the topping made by tossing the melted butter and breadcrumbs together. If making ahead of time, refrigerate at this stage until needed.

Bake, uncovered, at 180°C for 30–45 minutes, until the crumbs are golden brown and the filling has heated through completely.

Curried potatoes

This potato curry is an easy microwave recipe. For a quick meal for one person, quarter the recipe and reduce the microwaving times to about one-third.

SERVES 4:

1 onion, finely chopped
8 small waxy potatoes (800–900g)
425ml can coconut cream
2 teaspoons curry powder
½–1 teaspoon salt
½ teaspoon sugar
1–2 cups frozen peas
about 300g cauliflower florets (optional)
1–2 cups chopped cabbage (optional)

Put the onion and the unpeeled, halved or quartered potatoes into a microwave dish with the coconut cream and seasonings, adding ½ teaspoon salt. Stir to mix, cover, and microwave on High (100%) for 12 minutes, turning the potatoes once or twice, until they are barely tender.

Add the frozen peas, and microwave on High (100%) for about 4 minutes. Alternatively, add the peas, cauliflower and cabbage, stir to coat the vegetables, then microwave for 6–8 minutes, stirring at least once during the cooking time. Check that the cauliflower and cabbage are cooked to the tender-crisp stage, and taste the sauce, adjusting the seasonings if necessary.

Serve immediately, or allow to stand, then reheat when required. Pile in bowls, and serve with bread rolls.

Joginder Kaur Basi's dry potato curry

This delicious curried potato recipe was given to Alison for use in this book by an experienced Indian cook who, with her daughters, set up Aashiayana, one of New Zealand's first Indian restaurants, in the late 1970s.

Peel or scrub the potatoes and cut into 1.5cm cubes. Set aside.

Heat the oil in a large frying pan with a lid. Add the asafoetida, if using, and brown for about 30 seconds over moderate heat.

Stir in the seeds and cover the pan until you hear the seeds begin to pop. Remove the lid and add the garlic, ginger, chilli if using, and the potato, sugar, salt and turmeric. Stir well. Reduce the heat to low, cover and cook for 10 minutes. Add the lemon juice, cover again, and cook for a further 10–20 minutes until the potatoes are tender. Stir in the garam masala and sprinkle with the coriander.

Serve with another curry, a salad if desired, and with naan or other Indian bread.

* Asafoetida is a spice with a rather strong odour, mainly used in Indian cooking. You may need to look in a speciality store for it.

SERVES 4:

- 6 medium (about 600g) all-purpose or floury potatoes
- 2 tablespoons vegetable oil or ghee
- ½ teaspoon asafoetida (optional)*
- 1 tablespoon sesame seeds
- 1 tablespoon coriander seeds
- 1 tablespoon cumin seeds
- 4 garlic cloves, peeled but left whole
- 2–3cm piece ginger root, finely chopped or grated
- 2 green chillis, deseeded and finely chopped (optional)
- 1 teaspoon sugar
- 1 teaspoon salt
- 1 tablespoon turmeric
- 1 teaspoon lemon juice
- 1 teaspoon garam masala
- 2 tablespoons fresh coriander leaves, chopped

Peppery chickpea & potato curry

Black pepper gives this easy curry an interesting 'kick', quite different from chilli and not too hot. Use a mild curry powder with this recipe: it gives flavour without masking the pepper effect.

Measure the peppercorns into a blender or mortar and pestle. Add the garlic and the whole coriander plant and blend or pound to a paste. Add the oil and mix well.

Transfer the paste to a medium non-stick frying pan and cook over a medium heat, stirring frequently, for 2–3 minutes or until fragrant. Stir in the curry powder and cook for 1–2 minutes longer.

Add the potatoes, chickpeas and the tomatoes. Stir so that the potatoes are coated with the spice mixture, then add the coconut cream, hot water, soy sauce and sugar. Bring to the boil, then reduce the heat to a gentle simmer and cook, stirring occasionally, for 10–15 minutes or until the potato cubes are cooked through.

Season to taste with salt, garnish with the chopped coriander and serve. Wilted cucumber salad (see recipe page 76) and naan or roti make great accompaniments.

SERVES 2–3:

- 1 teaspoon black peppercorns
- 2 large cloves garlic, peeled
- 1 whole coriander plant (root and all), well washed
- 2 tablespoons canola oil
- 1 tablespoon curry powder
- 2 medium potatoes, scrubbed and diced
- 300g can chickpeas, rinsed and drained
- 2 medium tomatoes, diced
- ¾ cup coconut cream
- ½ cup hot water
- 1 tablespoon soy sauce
- ½ teaspoon sugar
- salt, to taste
- 1–2 tablespoons chopped fresh coriander

Peppery chickpea & potato curry

Egmont potatoes

SERVES 4:

800g potatoes
¼ cup water
2 tablespoons butter
4 onions
1 cup (250g) sour cream
milk, to thin
herbs, chopped
2 cups grated tasty cheese

We have eaten casseroles like this for years. Everybody loves them. Whenever one is served as part of a buffet meal, people seem to bypass exotic and expensive foods to take second helpings!

If using the microwave, scrub or thinly peel the potatoes and slice them 5mm thick. Put them in an oven bag with the water and half the butter, and close the bag with a rubber band, leaving a finger-sized hole. Or place the potatoes, water and half the butter in a small covered microwave-proof casserole dish. Microwave on High (100%) for 10 minutes or until tender, shaking the container once after about 4 minutes. If using the stovetop, boil the potatoes until they are cooked, then slice thinly.

While the potatoes cook, slice the onions and cook them in the butter, in a covered frying pan, with the heat high enough to brown them lightly. Stir them several times as they cook.

Thin the sour cream with enough milk to make it pourable, then pour this over the cooked potato and mix well. Add chopped herbs to this, then spoon half the creamy potatoes into a buttered dish, about 20 x 20cm. Sprinkle with half the cheese and half the onions, then arrange the remaining potato on top. Cover with the rest of the onions and cheese.

Grill for about 5 minutes, until the top is brown. For even browning, have the dish 18–20cm from the heat. If potatoes on the bottom have not heated through completely, microwave on High (100%) until bubbling. This is nicest if left to stand for 5 minutes before serving.

Nelson potatoes

SERVES 2–3:

2 medium onions (red if possible)
2 tablespoons butter or oil
3 medium apples
3 large potatoes, sliced (600g)
½ cup liquid (apple juice, white wine or
  ½ teaspoon instant stock and ½ cup
  of water)
thyme or sage (optional)
freshly ground black pepper and salt
2 or 3 poached eggs (optional)
chopped parsley (optional)

Apples and onions, browned together, have a wonderful flavour. Add potatoes for substance, and top the lot with an egg if you have one on hand, since the yolk makes a perfect sauce.

Peel and halve the onions from top to bottom, then cut each half in 4–6 wedges. Cook in a large non-stick frying pan in the butter or oil until transparent and browned on the edges. Raise the heat, add the peeled, sliced apples and cook uncovered, stirring often, until the apples are lightly browned, too.

Mix in the sliced potatoes, then add the liquid. Add a sprinkling of fresh or dried thyme or sage if you have them. Cover pan tightly and cook for about 20 minutes until potatoes are tender. Turn occasionally, adding extra liquid if the mixture becomes too dry before potatoes are cooked, or taking off the lid for a few minutes if mixture is too wet. Tast and adjust the seasonings.

If you would like a poached egg on top of each serving, cook these in another pan or pot when the potatoes are nearly cooked.

Pile the vegetable mixture on the plates, sit the poached eggs on top, add freshly ground pepper and chopped parsley, and serve immediately.

Friggione

- -

This is a great vegetable mixture which you can make in the morning and bring out to serve with barbecued meat on a warm summer evening. For this to be at its best, do not scrimp on the cooking time. It tastes better as the liquid disappears and the mixture darkens in colour.

Heat the oil in a large, preferably non-stick frying pan. Cut the scrubbed potatoes in 1cm cubes and slice the onion and capsicums.

Add the prepared potato, onion and pepper combination to the hot oil. Cover and cook over a moderate heat for 20 minutes, stirring several times, until the vegetables are tender and lightly browned.

Add the tomatoes and juice. Cook, uncovered, over a medium heat for 15–30 minutes until the mixture darkens in colour and the liquid has reduced to just a small amount around the vegetables. Season to taste with the salt, sugar and pepper, and sprinkle with the chopped parsley, if using, before serving.

Serve warm or hot, or reheat later in the frying pan or in a microwave. Serve with crusty rolls and a leafy green salad.

SERVES 4–6:

¼ cup olive oil

5 medium (about 750g) all-purpose or floury potatoes, scrubbed

2 large red onions

2 red or yellow capsicums

425g can Italian seasoned tomatoes

1–1½ teaspoons salt

1 teaspoon sugar

freshly ground black pepper

chopped parsley (optional)

Duchesse potatoes

- -

These potatoes always look impressive, and are great for special occasions. They are made by adding egg to firm mashed potatoes,* which can then be piped into any shape you like — e.g. large rosettes or circular nests – then filled with a colourful vegetable mixture. For best results use floury potatoes. Duchesse potatoes can be prepared ahead, browned in the oven, and reheated in a low oven just before serving.

Preheat the oven to 200°C.

Peel the potatoes and chop into even-sized pieces. Boil until tender, but not mushy. Press the drained, cooked potato through a sieve or potato ricer, then mash with the butter and the beaten egg and extra yolk. Keep the mixture firm. Season to taste, then transfer the mashed potatoes into a forcer bag with a star-shaped nozzle. Pipe out the mixture onto a sheet of baking paper on a baking tray, into shapes of your choice - e.g. rosettes or circles - that can later be filled with a vegetable mixture.

Bake the piped shapes in the oven for 20 minutes or until the edges turn brown.

* It is really important to ensure that the mashed potato mixture is completely smooth — any lumps can block the piping bag. To make lump-free mashed potato, use a potato ricer (a metal cylinder with holey sides — a bit like a giant garlic crusher), available from most speciality kitchen shops. Fill it with boiled, floury potatoes, then put the presser in place and push down until all the potato has been squeezed out the small holes. If you do not want to invest in a potato ricer, simply press the cooked potatoes through a sieve to get rid of any lumps — it takes a bit longer, but it works!

SERVES 4:

5 small floury potatoes

25g butter

1 large egg plus 1 extra yolk, beaten

Potato gnocchi

SERVES 4-6:

3 medium (750g) all-purpose or floury
 potatoes
1 egg
½ teaspoon salt
¼ teaspoon freshly ground nutmeg
freshly ground black pepper
1–1½ cups flour
flour for dusting
knob of butter
freshly grated parmesan
freshly chopped herbs to garnish

These little potato gnocchi (Italian-style dumplings) are moist and delicious, with just a hint of nutmeg. Serve them tossed in melted butter and topped with freshly grated parmesan.

Microwave on High (100%) or boil the whole unpeeled potatoes until cooked but still firm. Drain and set aside until cool enough to handle. Halve the potatoes and scoop out the flesh from the skins. Place the flesh in a large bowl or food processor. Mash or briefly process until lump-free.

Add the egg, salt, nutmeg and pepper to taste. Measure in 1 cup of flour, then, with clean hands, mix all together to form a smooth non-sticky dough. If it seems too wet, add ¼ cup more flour and mix again, adding more flour if necessary.

Working on a lightly floured surface, knead the dough for about 1 minute, then divide it into 4 roughly equal balls. Roll the balls, one at a time, into a 35–40cm long and 1.5cm thick cylinder. Using a sharp knife, cut the dough into a number of smaller lengths measuring about 2.5–3cm. Shape by rolling each small piece lightly under your fingers, then rolling it under the tines of a lightly floured fork. This will give the gnocchi a better surface to hold sauce. Arrange the prepared gnocchi on a floured baking sheet or tray.

Bring a large saucepan of water to the boil. Tip 20 or so gnocchi into the boiling water and boil for 2–3 minutes until they rise to the surface. They know when they're cooked! Leave in the water for a further 30 seconds, then remove with a slotted spoon. Transfer the cooked gnocci to a pre-warmed dish and place the butter on top. Cook the remaining gnocchi in several batches, adding them to the warmed dish and tossing them in the melted butter as they are done.

Serve on warmed plates and top with parmesan and the herbs, if using.

Pumpkin gnocchi

SERVES 4-6:

750g pumpkin (seeds removed)
½ cup cornflour
¼–½ teaspoon freshly grated nutmeg
½ teaspoon salt
freshly ground black pepper, to taste
1½–2 cups standard flour

Pumpkin gives these gnocchi a beautiful golden orange colour. They look (and taste) great served tossed with melted butter and some chopped fresh herbs, or in more elaborate sauces.

Cut the pumpkin into pieces about 5cm by 5cm, leaving the skin on. Arrange the pieces in one layer in a roasting pan and bake at 180°C for 40–50 minutes until soft. When the pumpkin has cooled enough to handle, remove the skin and mash the flesh. Forcing the pumpkin through a large sieve works well and gets rid of lumps.

Place the mashed or puréed pumpkin in a large bowl and add the corn-flour, nutmeg, salt, and pepper to taste, and 1 cup of flour, then stir to form a dough. Keep adding flour ¼ cup at a time, until the dough will hold a smooth ball shape and is not too sticky. Tip the dough out onto a lightly floured surface, knead for a minute, then divide into 4 pieces and shape and cook as for potato gnocchi.

NOTE: *If you are short of time, arrange the pieces of pumpkin on a microwave dish and microwave uncovered on High (100%) for 10–12 minutes, until soft; but baking is better as it dries the pumpkin out more.*

Pumpkin bake

- -

Here is an easy, good, substantial recipe that uses pumpkin as one of the main parts of a meal.

SERVES 6:

800g pumpkin
2 eggs
½ cup cream
½ cup milk
½ teaspoon ground cardamom (or cinnamon)
½ teaspoon salt
freshly ground black pepper, to taste
2 cups grated tasty cheese

Weigh the pumpkin before cooking, after removing seeds, etc., then cook. Using a tablespoon, scoop pieces of pumpkin into a lightly sprayed or buttered casserole dish that is large enough to hold it in one layer. Do not smooth the surface completely.

Beat the eggs, cream and milk together with a fork. Add the cardamom or cinnamon, salt and pepper. Pour this evenly over the pumpkin and top with grated cheese.

Bake at 220°C for 20–25 minutes, or until the custard is set, the mixture has puffed up, and the top is brown.

Serve as soon as possible (it deflates on standing), with a cooked green vegetable or with Brown rice salad (page 93).

Cheese & pumpkin balls

- -

The combination of a crisp coating and soft smooth inside is very appealing in these balls. If you want to prepare them ahead, reheat under a grill so they do not lose their crispness.

SERVES 4–6:

500g peeled and seeded pumpkin (about ½ a small
  pumpkin)
7 cloves garlic
1 medium onion
1 tablespoon oil
1 teaspoon dried parsley
½ teaspoon salt
½ cup grated cheese
½ cup dried breadcrumbs
freshly ground black pepper

COATING
flour
1 lightly beaten egg
breadcrumbs
sesame seeds, toasted (optional)

Peel the pumpkin, scoop out the seeds with a spoon, cut the pumpkin into 6–8 pieces and cook until barely tender. It is best steamed, or microwaved (5–6 minutes on High [100%]), to get it as dry as possible.

Crush and chop the garlic, then sauté with the diced onion in the oil. When the onion is soft and clear, remove from the heat and transfer to a bowl or food processor, with the cooked pumpkin. Mash or process until smooth and well mixed, and then add the remaining ingredients. The mixture should be thick enough to hold its shape when formed into balls. If not, add extra breadcrumbs.

With wet hands, form the mixture into golfball-sized balls, and coat with flour. Next, coat each ball with the beaten egg and then with fine dried breadcrumbs, or a mixture of equal parts breadcrumbs and toasted sesame seeds. Refrigerate for 15 minutes, or longer if possible.

Deep-fry, 3 or 4 balls at a time, for about 5 minutes in oil heated to 180°C.

Delicious served with a peanut sauce, your favourite cooked vegetables or a mixed salad, and rice.

Tomatoes

- -

Tomatoes are called for in many recipes because of their flavour, colour and acidity. There are plenty of good ready-prepared tomato products available, including tomato juice, purée, paste or concentrate, whole peeled tomatoes in juice, diced tomatoes and savoury tomatoes.

If you grow or have access to a good supply of ripe red tomatoes, you may want to preserve some to use during the winter. Try these recipes if you want to put aside a few kilograms at a time.

For the following recipes you will need carefully prepared, completely clean jars. Thoroughly wash preserving jars or empty jars with metal screw-top lids (with composition inserts), then place them in a large saucepan, cover with water and bring to the boil. Boil gently for at least 5 minutes, with the preserving seals, or the screw-top metal lids.

The lids should be concave when the jars are cold and sealed. If any gas forms during storage, or if any off flavours or odours develop, do not taste or eat the contents.

Any of the bottled recipes may be frozen in plastic bags or covered containers, if preferred.

'Overflow' bottled tomatoes

Quarter or cube firm ripe red tomatoes, cutting off the white core at the stem end, and squeezing and shaking the tomatoes to remove extra juice and seeds. When you feel you have enough to fill the jars, bring to the boil, stirring often, pressing the tomatoes until liquid forms.

Add about ¼ teaspoon of salt, ¼ teaspoon sugar and 1 tablespoon lemon juice for each cupful of tomato mixture.

Remove the jars from the saucepan. When the tomato mixture has been boiling fast for 3–4 minutes, quickly spoon or ladle the very hot tomato pieces into the hot jars. Remove any pockets of air in the jars by inserting a clean knife or metal skewer down the side. Fill to the top of the jar, wipe around the rim with a clean paper towel, top with the hot seal, then screw on the band; or top with the clean metal lid, screwing it on tightly.

Tomato purée & paste

Chop ripe tomatoes into a microwave dish or saucepan. Add some finely chopped onion and red pepper, and fresh or dried oregano and basil if you like. Microwave on High (100%), or boil until everything is soft, then push through a coarse sieve, discarding seeds and skin, etc.

Microwave on High (100%) or cook the pulp uncovered until boiled down to half or less of its original volume. Stir occasionally in the microwave, or frequently on the stovetop, until the mixture is as thick as you want it. Season with salt and sugar to taste, at this stage. Spoon into smaller jars which have been cleaned and boiled as above, and seal as above.

Thick tomato savoury

Prepare Tomato Purée as above, using tomatoes only, and boil down to about half its original volume. Measure the mixture and put it aside. For 2 cups of purée, cut in small cubes: 1 medium onion, 1 red capsicum, and 1 green capsicum. Sauté these in 2 tablespoons oil (not butter) without browning, until the onion is transparent, then add the tomato purée, ½ teaspoon each of dried basil, oregano, and mustard seed and ¼ teaspoon celery seed. Cook over moderate heat for 5–10 minutes, until thick enough to spread on pizza, etc., add salt to taste, then spoon into small jars with metal screw-tops, heated as above. Fill the jars to overflowing and seal as above.

Dehydrated tomatoes

The easiest way to preserve tomatoes is to dry slices or 1cm cubes, using a dehydrator. Spread the prepared tomatoes on the dehydrator trays and dry according to the instructions until they are crisp. Store in screw-top jars, or chop to powder in the food processor, alone or mixed with dehydrated chopped capsicums, onions and herbs, to use for salad and pizza toppings.

Use dried tomato cubes and slices as snacks (they are remarkably sweet), or add them to simmered mixtures, or microwave on High (100%) them with water for 5–15 minutes.

Tomato leather

Make tomato purée as above, and pour it onto the solid dehydrator trays to make tomato leather. When you want it, rip pieces off the discs of dried tomato and reconstitute to instant juice, purée or paste in a food processor according to the amount of hot water you add. The discs of tomato leather are also good eaten dry, as snacks! They are very light to carry, and ideal for a tramping trip.

Stuffed marrow (or zucchini)

SERVES 6–8:

1 large marrow, or 8 x 15cm zucchini

2 medium onions, diced

2 cloves garlic

2 tablespoons butter

200g mushrooms, sliced

1 large tomato, peeled and chopped

1 egg

¼ cup white wine

¾ cup dried breadcrumbs

¼ teaspoon dried thyme

2 tablespoons chopped fresh parsley
  (or 1 tablespoon dried parsley)

2 tablespoons pesto (or 1 tablespoon
  dried basil)

1 teaspoon salt

1 teaspoon sugar

½ cup grated cheese

freshly ground black pepper, to taste

TOPPING

¼ cup dried breadcrumbs

¼ cup grated cheese

paprika

This recipe provides a good way to use large zucchini or marrows that are so plentiful and cheap towards the end of summer.

Halve the marrow or zucchini lengthwise, and scoop out the seeds and some of the flesh with a spoon, leaving a 'shell' about 1cm thick. Chop up the edible flesh that you scooped out and set it aside.

Sauté the onion and minced garlic in the butter until beginning to soften and then add the mushrooms and tomato. When the mushrooms are soft, add the chopped marrow or zucchini pith and cook for a few minutes longer, until this softens also. Remove from the heat and stir in the egg, wine, breadcrumbs, herbs, pesto, salt and sugar. Add the cheese, and black pepper to taste.

Preheat the oven to 180°C. While it heats, arrange the marrow shells in a shallow baking dish. If they will not sit flat, take a thin slice off the bottom of each, forming a flat base to stand on. Fill the shells, heaping the filling up well in each. Sprinkle each with breadcrumbs and a little cheese, then dust lightly with paprika. Cover with foil. Bake for 30–60 minutes, until the cases are soft and the filling is set. The time will depend on the age and size of the marrows. Test flesh with a skewer to see if it is soft.

VARIATIONS:

Cut fairly large marrows into slices and fill the central round holes with the stuffing. Take care to butter the dish well, or stand the slices on non-stick Teflon liners.

Cook the stuffed marrows in a savoury tomato mixture, as for Stuffed capsicums (page 108).

Layered zucchini & mushroom casserole

SERVES 4:

1–2 tablespoons oil or butter

1 onion, chopped

2 cloves garlic, finely chopped

200g mushrooms, sliced

500g zucchini, finely sliced or coarsely
  grated

1 cup grated cheese

2 eggs

½ cup (125g) sour cream

1 tablespoon pesto or 2 tablespoons
  chopped fresh basil

½ teaspoon salt

¼ cup milk

paprika

grated parmesan

This dish can stand alone as part of a meal, but it is also a popular addition to a buffet meal.

Heat the oil or butter in a frying pan and cook the onion and garlic until the onion is soft and translucent. Add the mushrooms, and cook until wilted.

Mix the zucchini with the grated cheese. Spread half of this mixture over the bottom of a well buttered or sprayed 18 x 25cm baking dish. Cover with the onion and mushroom mixture, then with the other half of the zucchini and cheese.

Beat together the eggs, sour cream, pesto or basil, and salt. This should make an easily pourable mixture, but if it is very thick, add the milk. Pour this mixture over the layered zucchini and mushrooms, then top with a sprinkling of paprika and grated parmesan.

Bake, uncovered, at 175°C for 30–40 minutes, until the top is brown and the centre is firm. Serve with buttered new potatoes or rice, and a salad.

Zucchini & mushroom loaf

- -

This loaf has an excellent texture and an interesting flavour. It is also a great way to disguise zucchini, if you are cooking for those who would not otherwise enjoy such a treat!

Dice the onion and garlic, then sauté until soft in the oil. Add the sliced mushrooms and cook until soft and beginning to darken.

Grate the zucchini coarsely, and squeeze to remove as much liquid as possible. Put the zucchini in a large bowl, and add the onion and mushroom mixture then add the remaining ingredients, except ¼ cup of grated cheese and the dried breadcrumbs.

Transfer the mixture to a thoroughly non-stick sprayed loaf pan, and top with the remaining cheese and the dried breadcrumbs.

Bake at 180°C for 1 hour, or until the middle feels firm to touch, covering with foil during the first half of the cooking. Unmould and leave for 5 minutes before slicing.

SERVES 4–6:

1 medium-sized onion, diced
2 cloves garlic, crushed
2 tablespoons oil
200g mushrooms, sliced
500g zucchini, grated
2 cups fresh wholemeal breadcrumbs
2 eggs
1 cup grated cheese
1 teaspoon salt
1 teaspoon basil
¼ teaspoon thyme
freshly ground black pepper
2 tablespoons dried breadcrumbs

Easy zucchini pie

- -

If you like this sort of easy, crustless pie, invest in some heavy non-stick dark-coloured metal pie plates or flan pans. You can make this recipe in a heavy non-stick 23 x 25cm roasting pan, but it looks more elegant when made in two 23cm flan pans.

Grate the zucchini and onion, and place in a fairly large mixing bowl with the eggs, cheese and salt. Mix well with a fork. Add the flour, and pepper to taste, and chop in any fresh herbs you like.

Pour the mixture into a pan or pans that have been well sprayed or buttered. Because the mixture rises quite a lot as it cooks, do not fill any pan more than two thirds-full – even though it may look skimpy.

If you like, top the pies with sliced tomatoes, and sprinkle herbs and extra grated cheese or grated parmesan.

Bake at 200°C for 25–40 minutes, until the centre feels firm, and the top has browned slightly. Leave to stand for at least 5 minutes before cutting and serving.

SERVES 6–8

3 cups (500g) grated zucchini
1 onion, grated
4 eggs
1½ cups grated cheese
½ teaspoon salt
¾ cup self-raising flour
freshly ground black pepper, to taste
herbs
tomato slices (optional)

Zucchini & red onion fritters

- -

These popular little fritters are made with high-protein pea flour. They are particularly good as finger food for an informal meal.

Beat together the egg, pea flour, water and spices to form a smooth batter. Allow to stand for 15 minutes (the mixture will thicken on standing).

Shred unpeeled zucchini in a food processor, using a blade that cuts long matchstick strips, if possible (see note). Cut the onions into rings about the same thickness as the zucchini. Stir the zucchini and onion into the batter. Heat oil about 5mm deep in a frying pan. Drop tablespoons of the mixture into the hot oil and cook for 2–3 minutes, then turn and cook for a further 1–2 minutes. If patties are not golden brown in this time, adjust the heat until they cook nicely. Lift from the pan onto paper towel. Cook the remaining fritters in batches.

Serve immediately while crisp.

SERVES 4:

1 egg, beaten
1 cup pea flour
¾ cup water
2 teaspoons garam masala
2 teaspoons ground cumin
2 teaspoons coriander
300g (1½ cups) shredded zucchini
1 large red onion
oil

Zucchini cakes with red capsicum purée

Zucchini cakes with red capsicum purée

SERVES 4:

2 eggs
1 large garlic clove
½ teaspoon salt
3 cups shredded zucchini, unpeeled
¼ cup grated parmesan
about ½ cup self-raising flour
oil

These little cakes, served in a luminous red capsicum sauce, are likely to convert those who are not excited about zucchini.

In a medium-sized bowl beat the eggs to combine white and yolks. Crush the garlic clove into the salt, and add the paste to the eggs. Mix again. Add the firmly packed shredded zucchini and the parmesan, then stir in enough self-raising flour to make a batter of fritter consistency.

Drop batter into hot oil, 5mm deep, a tablespoon at a time to make small cakes. Turn when golden brown. Lower heat if necessary and cook until centres are firm. Serve with the following sauce.

Red capsicum purée

1 onion, finely chopped
1 clove garlic, chopped
1 large red capsicum
1 tablespoon butter or oil
1 cup water

Finely chop the onion, garlic and capsicum. Sauté in the butter or oil until transparent. Add water, cover, and cook for 10 minutes until tender. Purée, then press through a sieve. Boil down to thicken, if necessary, then season carefully and serve hot.

Cubed roast vegetables

A platter of seasoned roasted vegetables makes an interesting addition to almost any dinner. A good combination of vegetables includes some all-purpose potatoes, orange kumara, pumpkin, carrots, parsnip, beetroot, red onions, red, green and/or orange capsicums, mushrooms, etc.

Combine all the ingredients for the seasoning mix into a screw-top jar. Shake to mix.

Preheat the oven to 220°C.

Prepare the vegetables. Remove the skin from the pumpkin and onions and wash the other vegetables. Cut everything except the onions and mushrooms into 2–3cm cubes. Cut the onions into quarters through the root. Leave the mushrooms whole.

Put all the vegetables except the mushrooms in a large plastic bag (supermarket bags are good for this). Drizzle three-quarters of the oil over them, then toss to coat. Sprinkle into the bag about 3–4 teaspoons of the seasoning mix (save the rest for future use) and toss the vegetables again. Lastly, add the rosemary leaves and toss again. Brush the mushrooms with the rest of the oil.

Place a Teflon liner or some non-stick baking paper into each of two large roasting pans Tip in the vegetables and spread them out so they are no more than two deep.

Bake for about 1 hour.

VARIATION: *Toss some chopped fresh herbs or toasted pine nuts, black olives or grilled cherry tomatoes after the veges have been roasted.*

SERVES 8:

8–10 cups prepared vegetables

4 teaspoons garlic-infused or plain olive oil

handful of fresh rosemary leaves

SEASONING MIX

1 tablespoon ground cumin

1 teaspoon each: curry powder, plain or smoked paprika, celery salt and garlic salt

½–1 teaspoon chilli powder (optional)

Cubed roast vegetables

Spinach & cheese crêpes

Savoury crêpes

These thin, delicate, tender pancakes are made in a small pan. They may be made ahead and refrigerated or frozen until required. Crêpes make wonderful wrappers for many vegetable mixtures. Don't be discouraged if the first crêpes you make are not perfect. Once you get the hang of it, you will find you can turn out a pile of crêpes remarkably quickly and easily!

MAKES 12–20:

2 eggs
¾ cup milk
½ cup flour
½ teaspoon salt

Combine the ingredients, in the order given, in a food processor or blender. If mixing in a bowl, add the egg then the milk to the dry ingredients and beat until smooth.

Preheat a small, smooth-surfaced frying pan that has been well buttered or sprayed with non-stick oil. Pour a measured quantity (around 2 tablespoons) into the hot pan. Immediately tilt the pan so the batter covers the bottom in a thin film. If the batter does not spread thinly, add more milk to thin it before making the next crêpe. Do not worry if crêpes are not evenly shaped circles.

When the batter no longer looks wet in the centre, ease the edges of the crêpe from the pan. Lift and turn carefully. Cook the second side until it is dry, without browning it. Remove from the pan. Stack the crêpes until required.

Use the following suggestions as a guide to make your own 'creative crêpes'.

NOTE: *If freezing or refrigerating crêpes, place a piece of plastic between each, for easy removal later, and wrap the crêpes well in an airtight plastic bag, so they don't dry out.*

Asparagus crêpes

Roll cooked asparagus spears in crêpes that have been spread with cream cheese, or cheese sauce. Top with more cheese sauce and/or grated parmesan. Heat in the microwave, or brown under a grill.

Savoury apple crêpes

Sauté sliced onions in butter until tender, then add sliced apple, and brown lightly. Add a little white wine and chopped sage. Cook until tender. Taste and season. Spread this mixture on crêpes. Fold or roll the filled crêpes, sprinkle with parmesan if you like, and reheat if necessary. Serve with maple syrup.

Oriental crêpes

Fill crêpes with lightly sautéed bean sprouts, sliced tofu (if desired), mushrooms and spring onions. Season with sweet chilli sauce. Roll or fold in parcels.

Cheesy mushroom crêpes

Fill crêpes with sautéed mushrooms in cheese and white wine sauce, with or without herbs. Roll. Sprinkle with grated parmesan and brown under a grill.

Creamy vegetable crêpes

Mix lightly cooked vegetables, such as broccoli, corn, capsicum and mushrooms. Bind lightly with cheese or curry-flavoured sauce, or sour cream and cottage cheese. Add herbs. Sprinkle the crêpes with grated parmesan, or top with extra cheese sauce. Brown under a grill or in a hot oven.

Chilli bean crêpes

Spread crêpes with refried beans. Roll up around several strips of sautéed red and green capsicum, or a wedge of avocado. Brush the surface with Chilli mayonnaise (page 99) and heat in the microwave, or brown under a grill. Serve with more chilli mayonnaise or tomato salsa.

Spinach & cheese crêpes

- -

For really successful spinach crêpes, thicken the spinach and season it carefully.

SERVES 4–6:

1 recipe crêpe batter
1–2 cups cooked, drained, chopped spinach
3 tablespoons butter
3 tablespoons flour
½ teaspoon salt
1 teaspoon grated nutmeg
1½ cups milk
1½ cups grated cheese
paprika or grated parmesan

Prepare the batter and make the crêpes according to the Savoury Crêpe recipe, using a small pan.

Cook, drain, squeeze and chop the spinach.

To make the cheese sauce, melt the butter and add the flour, salt and nutmeg. Add the milk, ½ cup at a time, boiling and stirring between additions. After the last boiling, add the cheese. Mix a third of the cheese sauce with the spinach.

Spread the spinach mixture over the crêpes and roll up. Place the filled crêpes in an ovenware pan that has been well sprayed with non-stick oil. Pour the remaining sauce (thinned a little if necessary) over the crêpes. Sprinkle with paprika or parmesan.

Bake at 200°C for 20 minutes or until bubbly. Brown the surface under the grill before serving, if you like.

Stirfried vegetables

- -

SERVES 2:

400g of quick-cooking vegetables such as cabbage, celery, cauliflower, broccoli, green beans, bean sprouts, mushrooms, pea pods, capsicums and zucchini
1 tablespoon oil
1 clove garlic, finely chopped
2 tablespoons water
1 teaspoon cornflour
1 teaspoon brown sugar
1 teaspoon light soy sauce
¼ teaspoon salt
1 tablespoon sherry
½ teaspoon sesame oil (optional)

Prepare the vegetables, cutting them into slices. Heat the oil in a large pan or wok. Add the garlic clove, then the prepared vegetables. Toss over high heat, then add the water, cover and leave to steam for 1–2 minutes, or until tender-crisp.

Add the rest of the ingredients together in a small container. Stir the mixture into the vegetables to coat them, and serve immediately over rice or noodles.

MICROWAVE VARIATION: *Toss prepared vegetables in the preheated garlic and oil in a microwave dish, then cover and microwave on High (100%) for about 3 minutes, or until tender-crisp. Stir in the mixed liquid, then cook for about 30 seconds longer, or until the glaze thickens.*

Barbecued fresh vegetables

- -

Choose a colourful mixture of seasonal vegetables, such as red onions, aubergines, zucchini, red and yellow capsicums, etc. Cut them into chunky pieces. Quarter the onions so the pieces are held together by the base.

Brush with Seasoned Oil (see box) and barbecue or grill, about 12cm from the heat, turning frequently so vegetables cook but don't burn. Allow vegetables to brown but not burn on their edges.

Seasoned oil

½ cup olive oil
2 cloves garlic, peeled
6 basil leaves, chopped
2 tablespoons each: fresh thyme and rosemary

Process all ingredients in a food processor until finely chopped. Allow to stand for at least 10 minutes then strain, discarding the flavourings.

Vegetables à la Grecque

SERVES 2–4:

¼ cup olive oil or other oil

2 cloves garlic, chopped

2 tablespoons wine vinegar

1½ teaspoons coriander seeds, crushed

1 teaspoon sugar

½ teaspoon salt

425g can diced or Italian tomatoes

400–500g prepared vegetables,
   such as carrots, beans, cauliflower,
   celery, zucchini

1 tablespoon lemon juice

¼ cup chopped parsley

This is a lovely way to serve vegetables in the summer.

Cut one or several types of vegetables into long strips or neat pieces.

   Heat the oil in a frying pan. Cook the garlic in the oil without browning it. Stir in the vinegar, crushed coriander seeds, seasonings and the tomato mixture, then add the vegetables. Cover and simmer for 10–15 minutes or until tender-crisp, turning the vegetables after 5 minutes. Sprinkle with lemon juice.

   The vegetables are best served at room temperature, in their sauce, on a shallow dish, generously sprinkled with parsley. Accompany with plenty of crusty bread to mop up the delicious sauce.

Vegetable kebabs

Thread 2cm cubes of aubergine, red and green capsicums and zucchini with squares of onion, blanched button mushrooms and quartered or whole small tomatoes. Brush liberally with Tomato or Cumin dressing (page 98), or Chilli mayonnaise (page 99), before and during cooking, and cook on a barbecue or under a grill, about 12cm from the heat, turning frequently until tender. Thread only one type of vegetable on each skewer for more even cooking, if desired.

VARIATIONS: *Thread Marinated tofu (page 219) or pan-browned cubes of polenta (page 197) between the vegetables.*

Vegetable combo

SERVES 4:

1 small–medium (about 200g)
   aubergine

¼ cup oil

1 medium onion

2 cloves garlic

1 green capsicum

1 red capsicum

1 cup chopped marrow or zucchini or
   butternut pumpkin

1 cup cauliflower pieces or green
   beans

1 cup water

freshly ground black pepper

1–2 teaspoons sugar

salt, to taste

fresh herbs, chopped (optional)

2 teaspoons cornflour

¼–½ cup chopped parsley

This recipe makes a very pretty vegetable mixture. It may be served on rice or on flat egg noodles, topped with grated cheese, as a complete meal. You need a large frying pan and a high heat. If you have a non-stick pan, use it!

Cut the aubergine into 1cm (fingertip-sized) cubes. Heat the frying pan, add the oil and, when hot, drop in the aubergine pieces. Cook on high heat, turning frequently, until golden brown on some surfaces. While the aubergine cooks, add the chopped onion and garlic.

   Meanwhile, cut the remaining vegetables into 1cm cubes. When the aubergine is evenly coloured, add the remaining vegetables, and stir to coat with oil. Keep the heat high, and put the lid on the pan. Cook for 3–4 minutes until all the vegetables are wilted and brightly coloured, then add the water, cover, and cook on high heat for 3–4 minutes longer.

   By this stage the vegetables should be tender-crisp, and quite a lot of the added water should have evaporated. Remove the lid and add the pepper, sugar and salt in the order given. Keep tasting. After adding the sugar, add enough salt to bring out all the other flavours. Add fresh herbs at this stage, too. Mix the cornflour to a paste with cold water. Add enough of this to thicken the mixture.

   Sprinkle generously with parsley, stir it through briefly, then serve immediately.

Easy ratatouille

Every autumn, we get the urge to make a big, strongly flavoured vegetable stew which we enjoy for several meals, each better than the last. This shortcut version is excellent.

Make this in the largest, heaviest (lidded) pot, frying pan or flame-proof casserole dish that you have. Heat the first measure of olive oil in it and add the unpeeled aubergine, sliced capsicums, and zucchini, all cut in 2cm chunky pieces. Cook over a medium to high heat for 15 minutes, so that the vegetables brown lightly but do not steam in large amounts of watery juices. Add the onions chopped into similar sized pieces, the garlic, and enough extra oil to stop the mixture sticking or burning. Raise the heat slightly, and cook for 15 minutes longer, until the onions are transparent and lightly browned, too. (Cook the vegetables in batches if you find this easier.)

Stir in the tomatoes (and juice), add the sugar, salt and pesto, and bring to the boil with the lid ajar.

Cook on medium heat so the liquid bubbles and thickens, but the vegetables do not burn. We like the stew at the stage where the liquid is quite thick but the vegetables still have some firmness, after about 15 minutes simmering. Taste and adjust seasoning.

Serve in bowls, with chunks of firm, crusty bread, as a complete meal OR serve on pasta or rice, topped with parmesan or ladle generous amounts into a saucepan of cooked, drained, firm potatoes, heat through, and serve in bowls.

VARIATION: *To reduce cooking time, use less oil and maximise flavour, brush the thickly sliced egg plant with olive oil and brown in a contact grill (on medium setting). Repeat with the halved capsicums and zucchini and thickly sliced onions. When browned, cut in cubes and simmer with the remaining ingredients, as above.*

SERVES 6–8:

¼ cup olive oil
2 medium-sized aubergines
4 red, orange and yellow capsicums
4 green and/or yellow zucchini
4 large onions
1½ teaspoons (2 cloves) minced garlic
up to ¼ cup extra olive oil
2 x 400g cans of whole tomatoes
2 teaspoons sugar
1 teaspoon salt
2 tablespoons basil pesto
2–3 tablespoons chopped fresh herbs

Pea flour patties

- -

Pea flour is high in protein and makes a good fritter batter without using eggs or milk. In this easy recipe the raw vegetables are surrounded by batter flavoured with Indian spices. Make the patties small – they cook quickly, with a crisp coating.

Try making them with different vegetables, but don't leave out the onion. To shorten their cooking time you can partly cook dense vegetables before coating them with batter, if you like.

Mix the pea flour with water and the spices to make a fairly stiff paste. Leave to stand for 5 minutes or longer.

Scrub the potatoes. Cut the potatoes and the onion (and any other vegetables) into pea-sized cubes.

Mix all the vegetables into the batter just before you intend to start cooking. They will thin down the mixture. Add extra pea flour or water to make a batter thick enough to hold spoonfuls of the vegetables together.

Heat oil 2cm deep in a frying pan. Drop teaspoons of mixture carefully into it. Adjust the heat so the patties brown nicely in about 4 minutes, then turn them and cook the other side for the same time. Faster cooking will leave the vegetables raw. Drain, and serve as soon as possible, with yoghurt sauce (page 216).

SERVES 4:

1 cup pea flour
about ½ cup water
1 teaspoon turmeric
2 teaspoons ground cumin
2 teaspoons ground coriander
2 teaspoons garam masala
2 medium potatoes
1 onion
1 cup frozen peas, or cauliflower
    florets, etc.
oil for frying

Tempura vegetables

- -

For this dish, guests prepare and cook their own food in a communal cooking vessel such an electric wok or a deep-frier. Best eaten as soon as they are cooked.

Prepare the vegetables, cut them into pieces about 5mm thick, and arrange attractively on plates.

Using a fork, lightly beat the egg and the cold water. Sift the dry ingredients into this mixture while you stir. Mix enough to combine everything. Thin the batter with extra water, so that it lightly coats each piece of vegetable.

Heat the oil to about 200°C. Dip the vegetables in the batter, and fry, a few pieces at a time, until golden brown and puffed up. Raise the heat if necessary. Serve with brown or white rice and tempura sauce, or make the following sauce for dipping.

SERVES 4–6:

500g assorted vegetable pieces, such
    as cauliflower florets, thinly sliced
    potato, kumara and/or pumpkin,
    broccoli, small whole mushrooms,
    strips of capsicums, zucchini, etc.
1 cup cold water
1 cup plain white flour
¼ teaspoon baking soda
¼ teaspoon salt
oil for deep frying

Dipping sauce

¼ cup water
¼ cup Kikkoman light soy sauce
1 tablespoon dry sherry
2 teaspoons brown sugar
2 teaspoons grated ginger root
juice of ½ lemon
1 clove garlic, crushed and chopped
1 teaspoon dark sesame oil

Mix together all the ingredients and allow to stand for about 10 minutes.

NOTE: *Use leftover sauce as a marinade for tofu or other vegetables.*

Thai curried vegetable-noodle stew

This tasty vegetable curry is somewhere between a soup and a 'traditional' curry. Despite a long-looking list of ingredients, it is simple as the vegetables and noodles are simmered and served together in a spicy peanut and coconut cream sauce.

SERVES 2–3:

100g rice sticks or noodles, or other pasta
1 medium onion
1 tablespoon canola oil
2 cloves garlic, minced
1 tablespoon grated ginger root
2 tablespoons red curry paste*
2–3 small potatoes
400g can coconut cream
1 cup vegetable stock (page 43)
3–4 tablespoons peanut butter
1 teaspoon each: salt and sugar
1 small aubergine
½ each: red and green capsicum (or one of either)
2 medium zucchini
100g brown button mushrooms
1–2 tablespoons Kikkoman soy sauce
2–3 tablespoons chopped fresh coriander
100g soybean or mung bean sprouts

Cut or break the noodles into 10cm lengths, put them in a large bowl and cover them with boiling water. Leave to stand while you prepare the curry.

Peel, halve and slice the onion. Heat the oil in a large saucepan or wok, add the onion, garlic, ginger and red curry paste and stirfry for 1–2 minutes. Cut the potatoes into 1cm cubes and add these with the coconut cream, stock, peanut butter, salt and sugar. Bring the mixture to the boil, then reduce the heat to a gentle simmer and cook for 10 minutes, stirring occasionally.

While the potatoes simmer, cube the aubergine, deseed and slice the capsicums, cut the zucchini into 1cm slices and halve the mushrooms. Add these vegetables and the drained rice noodles to the pot, then simmer until the potatoes and vegetables are just tender (about 10 minutes).

Add soy sauce to taste, then the coriander and the bean sprouts (reserve a few to use as a garnish). Serve ladled into large bowls and topped with a few bean sprouts. Bowls of chopped roasted peanuts, minced chillis and chopped coriander also make good accompaniments.

* Check that the curry paste does not contain shrimp paste.

Thai curried vegetable-noodle stew

Sauces

- -

Vegetarian gravy

2 medium-sized onions
2–3 cloves garlic
2 tablespoons oil or butter
1 teaspoon sugar
2 tablespoons flour
2 cups water
2 tablespoons dark soy sauce
freshly ground black pepper, to taste
¼–½ teaspoon salt

Finely chop or mince the onions and garlic. Heat the oil or butter in a large frying pan or saucepan. Add the onions and garlic, and cook, stirring occasionally, until they brown. Stir in the sugar and flour and cook for about a minute longer.

Add half the water, stirring to remove any lumps. Bring to the boil and allow to thicken before adding the remaining water and soy sauce. Bring to the boil again, season with black pepper and salt to taste, then serve!

Cheese sauce

2 tablespoons butter
2 tablespoons flour
½ cup milk
½ cup milk, vegetable cooking liquid or other stock
1 teaspoon Dijon mustard (optional)
about ½ cup grated, well-flavoured cheese
salt and freshly ground black pepper, to taste

Melt the butter, then stir in the flour and cook over low heat, or microwave until it bubbles. Add the first measure of liquid and bring to the boil, stirring constantly, or bring to the boil in the microwave. Stir again. Add the remaining liquid and heat again, stirring until smooth and quite thick. Thin down with extra liquid and bring back to the boil if you like.

Stir in the grated cheese and heat only until the cheese melts. Taste, and adjust seasoning if necessary.

Pesto

3–4 cups lightly packed basil leaves
1 cup parsley
4 cloves garlic
¼– ½ cup parmesan
¼ cup pine nuts, almonds or walnuts
½–1 cup olive and/or corn oil
about 1 teaspoon salt

Put the basil and parsley leaves into a food processor with the peeled garlic cloves, the parmesan and the nuts.

Using olive oil for preference, or some olive and some corn oil, process the leaves, adding up to ½ cup of oil until they are finely chopped. Keep adding oil until you have a dark green paste, just liquid enough to pour. Add salt to taste. Store in the fridge, in a lidded glass or plastic container, for use within 3 months. Freeze pesto for longer storage.

NOTE: *Pesto may darken at the top of jars where it is exposed to the air. Make sure there is a layer of oil at the top of each jar.*

Green sauce

1 egg yolk
1 tablespoon Dijon or other mild mustard
1 teaspoon sugar
¼ teaspoon salt
2 cloves garlic
2 spring onions
3 tablespoons wine vinegar
½–1 cup mixed fresh herb leaves (e.g. parsley, chives, dill, tarragon)
½–¾ cup corn or soya oil
2 hard-boiled eggs, chopped

Measure the first 7 ingredients into a food processor and process to combine. Add the herbs. (Use small amounts of strongly flavoured tarragon.)

Process while adding oil gradually, stopping when thick. Add 1 hard-boiled egg and process until chopped through the sauce. Chop the remaining egg fairly finely and sprinkle it over the sauce when serving. Spoon the sauce over cooked cauliflower, asparagus, beans, new potatoes, avocado halves, tomatoes, etc., just before serving.

Hollandaise sauce

2 egg yolks
2–3 tablespoons lemon juice
100g butter

Break the egg yolks into a food processor bowl. Add the lemon and process to combine.

Cut the butter into cubes and put in a microwave-proof jug. Cover to avoid splattering. Heat in the microwave on High (100%) for 2–3 minutes until very hot and bubbling vigorously.

With the food processor running, add the bubbling hot butter in a thin stream onto the egg yolks. If the sauce is not thick, heat it gently in the microwave for 1 minutes on Defrost (30%), stirring after 30 seconds.

If making the sauce ahead, reheat by standing in a bowl of bath-temperature (not boiling) water, stirring occasionally. Do not overheat, as the sauce will curdle.

Peanut sauce

See Gado gado salad page 91.

Good old eggs and cheese – what would we do without them? The recipes in this chapter are particularly useful staples, as they do not call for exotic or expensive ingredients, and are not complicated to assemble and cook. Many of them can be prepared quickly and easily after work. You will probably find – as we do – that they make good lunch dishes, too.

Eggs & cheese

Crispy (coin purse) eggs

These eggs are purse-shaped, with a soft 'gold coin' inside, and a crispy brown coating, well worth a little practice to perfect.

SERVES 1:

2 teaspoons canola or olive oil
1 large, fresh egg
pepper and salt or Spicy salt (below)
about 1 cup hot cooked rice
sweet chilli sauce
spring onion curls or chopped spring onions

Preheat a wok or a small rounded frying pan over a fairly high heat. Add the oil, and tilt the wok (or pan) to coat a saucer-sized area. When the oil is hot and almost smoking, carefully slide in the egg (previously broken into a small bowl or saucer). Take care doing this, because the egg and hot oil splutter and sizzle. Sprinkle the egg with a little pepper and salt, or with spicy salt (below) as it cooks.

When the bottom and the edges of the egg white are browned and crusty, slide a spatula under half of the egg and flip it over to make a half-moon shape. Gently press the edges together until the 2 sides set and hold the egg in a purse shape.

Lower the heat and cook 10–20 seconds longer, until the white round the yolk has just set, the yolk is still runny, and the outside surfaces are crispy and brown.

Place a cupful of hot rice on a plate and top with the hot egg. Drizzle with sweet chilli sauce. Garnish with spring onion curls, or with chopped spring onions.

NOTES: *To make spring onion curls, shred spring onions lengthwise. Soak pieces in iced water until they curl.*

Spicy salt

2 tablespoons Szechuan peppercorns
2 tablespoons salt
1 teaspoon black peppercorns

Heat Szechuan peppercorns (from stores selling Asian foods) on foil under a grill until they smoke slightly. Using a coffee grinder or a mortar and pestle, grind them with the salt and black peppercorns. Keep in an airtight jar.

Swiss eggs

This is an interesting omelette variation.

SERVES 1:

2 thick slices bread
2 tablespoons butter
2 eggs
2 tablespoons milk
½ teaspoon salt
25g cubed cheese

Cut the bread into small cubes. Heat half the butter in a small frying pan and toss the bread in it. Cook over moderate heat until the croûtons are crisp and golden brown. Remove from pan.

Beat the eggs, milk and salt together with a fork. Heat the pan again. Heat the remaining butter in it until straw-coloured. Pour in the egg mixture. Cook, tilting pan and lifting the edge of the omelette to let the uncooked mixture run underneath.

Sprinkle the croûtons and the cheese over half the omelette when it is barely set. Flip the other half of the omelette over the croûtons and cheese. Serve immediately. The cheese should be warm but not melted, and the croûtons still crunchy.

Crispy (coin purse) eggs

French omelette

SERVES 1:

2 eggs
2 tablespoons water, milk or cream
¼ teaspoon salt
fresh herbs, finely chopped (optional)
1 teaspoon butter, for cooking

A French omelette for 1 person cooks in less than a minute. The mixture must be mixed, heated and cooked carefully for good results.

For a small omelette you need an 18–20cm pan, preferably with a non-stick finish. In a bowl, place eggs, water, milk, or cream, salt, and herbs if desired.

Stir the ingredients together with a fork, only until the whites and yolks are combined. Do not overmix.

Melt the butter in a hot pan until it is straw-coloured, and pour in the egg mixture.

Stir mixture for the first 5 seconds only. Tilt pan and lift the set edges to let uncooked egg run underneath.

When egg is set but surface is still moist, omelette is ready to fold, or to fill with a precooked mixture.

Spoon hot filling onto half the omelette. Fold the other half over the filling. Slide or flip onto plate.

Spanish omelette

SERVES 2:

3 large waxy or all-purpose potatoes
  (about 600g)
3 tablespoons oil
2 large eggs
½ teaspoon salt

Known in Spain as a tortilla, this can be found throughout Spain, but with slight variations. Feel free to modify this recipe yourself.

Scrub and cut the potatoes into cubes.

Heat the oil in a smallish non-stick frying pan, then put the potatoes in. Cover and cook until tender, about 5–10 minutes (the potatoes need not brown).

Beat the eggs and salt with a fork. Tip the cooked potatoes into the beaten egg, then the mixture back into the hot pan, after adding a dribble of extra oil to the pan.

Cook, uncovered, tilting the pan occasionally, until the omelette is nearly set. Slide it from the pan onto a plate, then flip it back into the pan to brown the uncooked side.

Serve the omelette alone, or with salad vegetables.

VARIATIONS: *Add a chopped onion to the frying pan with the potatoes. Mix a chopped red and/or green capsicum or chopped cooked vegetables into the potato and uncooked egg mixture.*

It's good to eat cold, too, so add leftovers to packed lunches.

NOTE: *The omelette works best when the mixture almost fills the pan it is made in.*

Cottage cheese omelette

SERVES 2:

1 egg
2 tablespoons small-curd cottage
  cheese
1 spring onion, chopped (or other
  herbs)
1 teaspoon butter

Always use small-curd cottage cheese for omelettes, and do not add salt.

Stir together with a fork the egg, cottage cheese and spring onion (or other herbs) until barely mixed.

Heat the butter in a small frying pan until it bubbles and turns straw-coloured. Swirl to coat the pan, then pour in the egg mixture. Lift the edge to let the unset mixture run underneath, then fold in half and serve immediately.

French omelette (front); Spanish omelette (back)

Cheese & onion 'sausages'

Cheese & onion 'sausages'

SERVES 3:

1 small–medium onion
1½ cups grated cheese
3 cups (150g) soft breadcrumbs
½ teaspoon salt
¼ teaspoon each: sage and thyme
freshly ground black pepper, to taste
2 large eggs
about ¼ cup dried breadcrumbs to
   coat

These sausages are quick and surprisingly like the 'real thing'. Once cooked they are quite firm, but they are fairly soft until cooked. If you want to barbecue them, use a well oiled hotplate or grill, and handle very gently.

Chop the onion very finely (a food processor does this well), then mix together with the grated cheese, breadcrumbs, salt, herbs and pepper. Add one of the eggs, then separate the other, adding the yolk to the crumb mixture and reserving the white. Stir until well combined.

Using wet hands, shape the mixture into 6 even-sized sausages (if the mixture is too wet and sticky, add 1–2 tablespoons of the dried breadcrumbs and mix again). As each one is completed, roll it first in the egg white, then in the dry breadcrumbs. Leave to stand for at least 5 minutes, then cook in a well oiled pan until golden brown on all sides (6–8 minutes in total). Serve with salad or vegetables.

Bean-sprout eggs (egg foo young)

SERVES 4:

SAUCE
1 tablespoon cornflour
2 teaspoons soy sauce
1 teaspoon vegetable stock powder
1 teaspoon sugar
1 cup water

OMELETTE
2 cups mung or soy bean sprouts
1–2 cups sliced mushrooms
3–4 spring onions, chopped
cooking oil
3 or 4 eggs
2 tablespoons water
½ teaspoon salt

Crunchy, lightly cooked, tender bean sprouts, smooth egg and flavourful sauce make a remarkably satisfying combination.

Make the sauce by mixing the ingredients, in the order given, in a saucepan. Simmer 2–3 minutes, then remove from the heat and put aside.

Sauté first the bean sprouts, then the mushrooms and spring onions in about 1 tablespoon of oil in a hot frying pan. Cook just enough to wilt the vegetables. Remove to a flattish dish, mix, then divide into 4 piles.

Beat together the eggs, water and salt to combine. Pour into a measuring cup. Heat a medium-sized frying pan, add 1 teaspoon oil, then a quarter of the egg mixture. Before this sets, sprinkle one-quarter of the vegetables over it. Lift the edges and let uncooked egg from surface run under the edges to cook. Roll loosely, or fold in quarters, as soon as the egg in the centre is no longer liquid.

Serve with some of the sauce. Repeat the method for the other 3 servings.

Spinach & mushroom frittata

What could be more convenient than grabbing some eggs and assorted bits and pieces from the fridge and having a meal ready in minutes

Peel and slice the onion, then heat 1 tablespoon of the oil in a large non-stick pan. Add the onion and garlic (if using) and sauté until the onion begins to softens and browns slightly, then add the mushrooms. Continue to cook until these have wilted. Remove from the pan and set aside, wipe the pan out with a paper towel.

Combine the eggs, cottage cheese, spinach, parmesan and seasonings together in a small bowl. Add the onion-mushroom mixture and stir gently to combine. Heat the remaining oil in the pan then add the egg mixture. Cook over a moderate heat for about 5 minutes, or until the bottom is golden brown. Sprinkle with a little extra parmesan (if desired) and place the pan under a hot grill (leave the handle protruding so it doesn't burn) until the top looks dry and the centre is firm when pressed.

Serve hot or warm, cutting wedges from the pan, or turning out onto a large flat board or plate.

SERVES 2-3:

1 medium onion

3 tablespoons olive oil or canola oil

1 teaspoon (1–2 cloves) minced garlic (optional)

about 250g mushrooms, thickly sliced

4 large eggs

½ cup cottage cheese

250g frozen spinach, thawed and squeezed

2 tablespoons grated parmesan

1–2 tablespoons basil or sundried tomato pesto

½ teaspoon salt

freshly ground black pepper, to taste

Spinach & mushroom frittata

Spaghetti scramble

SERVES 4:

1 large onion
1 green capsicum
1–2 tablespoons oil or butter
450g can spaghetti
herbs, chopped (optional)
3 eggs
2 tablespoons milk
¼ teaspoon salt
freshly ground black pepper

For a quick, satisfying meal, cook eggs in a pan with vegetables and spaghetti.

Chop the onion and green capsicum, and cook in the butter or oil in a large frying pan until tender but not browned. Add the spaghetti and any herbs you like, and heat until bubbling.

Beat the eggs, milk and seasonings with a fork, and pour over the hot spaghetti. Without stirring, lift the spaghetti with a fish slice so the egg can run underneath.

Serve, garnished with chopped parsley or spring onions, as soon as the egg has set. This is nice in split toasted buns.

Easy vegetable square

SERVES 4:

2–3 cups cooked drained vegetables*
4 large eggs
¾ cup low-fat or regular sour cream
6 tablespoons parmesan
3 tablespoons basil pesto
3 tablespoons couscous or dried
   breadcrumbs
2 tomatoes (optional)
about ½ cup grated cheddar

* Suitable vegetables are asparagus, cabbage, cauliflower, young green beans, broccoli, whole kernel corn, kumara, squeezed spinach, well drained silverbeet, young carrots, pumpkin, new potatoes, peas, frozen mixed vegetables, zucchini and mushrooms. (Tomatoes and aubergine are too juicy.)

Make this useful recipe with cooked or canned vegetables, or leftovers. The pesto and parmesan add an interesting flavour.

Turn the oven on to 180°C to preheat.

Cook vegetables in a small amount of salted water until just tender, then drain thoroughly, in a sieve. Alternatively, use leftover cooked vegetables, or canned vegetables. (If vegetables are cooked without salt, add ½ teaspoon salt to the egg mixture.) Cut the cooked vegetables into pieces no bigger than 1cm cubes.

Put the eggs, sour cream, parmesan cheese and pesto in a bowl. Stir with a fork or whisk until well mixed.

Lightly butter or spray a baking pan about 20cm square. Sprinkle the base with couscous or breadcrumbs, so any liquid that comes from the vegetables during baking will be soaked up. (Couscous works well and makes the base firmer, almost like a thin pastry crust.)

Sprinkle the well-drained cooked vegetables evenly over the base of the prepared pan, then pour the egg mixture over them. Shake gently so the mixture surrounds the vegetables.

Cover the surface with slices of tomato (if using), then sprinkle with grated cheese. Bake at 180°C for 30 minutes or until the top is golden brown and nicely risen, the sides are golden brown, and the centre feels firm. Leave for a few minutes before cutting and serving.

Cheddar cheese fondue

SERVES 2 (STARTER) OR 4 (MAIN):

2 cups grated cheddar cheese*
2 tablespoons flour
1 teaspoon butter (for stovetop only)
1 clove garlic, chopped finely
½ teaspoon nutmeg
1 cup flat or fresh beer

* For special occasions, replace half (or all) of the cheddar with other cheeses such as raclette, emmentaler or gruyère.

A cheese fondue is a companionable meal for a cold night: everybody enjoys dipping bread into the communal pot.

If using a microwave, mix the grated cheese and flour in a bowl or flat-bottomed casserole dish. Add the garlic, nutmeg and beer. Stir to mix. Microwave on High (100%) for 2 minutes, stir with a whisk, then heat until the whole surface bubbles, stirring each 1 minute.

If cooking on the stovetop, mix grated cheese and flour. Melt a teaspoon of butter in a small saucepan or frying pan, then add the garlic and nutmeg and cook gently for about a minute, without browning. Add the beer and heat until hot but not boiling. Stir in the floured cheese gradually, while stirring or whisking the mixture over low heat. Remove from the heat when the cheese has all melted, and the mixture is smooth.

Serve very hot with chunks of crusty bread to dip. Keep the fondue warm over a candle or low alcohol burner.

Cheese soufflé

Soufflés are not as complicated or temperamental as they are made out to be – but you would be wise to make one or two first before serving them to impress guests!

Melt the butter in a medium-sized saucepan. Add the salt and mustard, then the flour. Stir over a low heat until the mixture bubbles. Add the milk, half a cup at a time, stirring continuously and boiling between additions. Add the grated cheese, then remove from the heat and stir until smooth.

Separate the eggs. Put the whites in a medium-sized bowl, and add the yolks to the cheese sauce. (Prepare to this stage in advance if desired.)

Beat the egg whites until the peaks turn over at the tips when the beater is removed. Fold the whites into the sauce. Butter the bottom only of a 6-cup soufflé dish and pour the mixture in. Run a knife through the mixture in a circle 2cm inside the edge of the dish (this helps to give even rising).

Bake at 190°C for 40–45 minutes, or until a knife inserted in the middle comes out clean. Serve immediately, since soufflés shrink on standing.

VARIATIONS: *For vegetable soufflés, add 1–2 cups of very well drained, finely chopped cooked broccoli, spinach, asparagus, or mushrooms to the cheese sauce after stirring in the egg yolks.*

SERVES 3–4:

3 tablespoons butter
½ teaspoon salt
1 teaspoon Dijon mustard
¼ cup flour
1½ cups milk
1½ cups grated cheese
3 eggs, separated

Asparagus, egg & cheese casserole

This casserole is always popular, and is good when you are entertaining, since it can be made ahead, and heated through when you want it.

Make a cheese sauce by melting the butter, adding the flour, mustard and salt, and stirring until blended. Add the milk, half a cup at a time, bringing to the boil between each addition, stirring constantly. Stir in the cheese, and remove from the heat.

In a buttered 20cm casserole, layer the sauce, well drained chopped asparagus and hard-boiled eggs, starting and finishing with sauce. Top with the crushed potato crisps.

Bake in the oven at 180°C until the sauce bubbles around the edges and the centre is hot.

Serve as is, or on noodles or brown rice if you are cooking for particularly hungry people. A salad is a nice accompaniment.

SERVES 4:

2 tablespoons butter
3 tablespoons flour
1 teaspoon Dijon mustard
½ teaspoon salt
1½ cups milk
½–1 cup grated cheese
1 bunch cooked fresh asparagus
    (or 340g can asparagus spears),
    drained
3 or 4 hard-boiled eggs, chopped
½ cup crushed potato crisps

Cheese strata

The bread in this dish puffs up and browns slightly so that it resembles a soufflé, but has more body.

Make cheese sandwiches using thick slices of cheese, mustard to taste, and no butter. Cut in quarters and stand, crusts down, in a buttered casserole dish.

Beat the eggs, milk and garlic salt together and pour over the sandwiches. Leave to stand for 30 minutes or longer, spooning the egg over the exposed bread at intervals.

Bake, uncovered, at 190°C for 30–45 minutes, or until the bread is puffed and golden brown, and the centre is firm.

SERVES 4–6:

6 slices of sandwich bread
sliced cheese
Dijon mustard, to taste
3 eggs
2 cups milk
1 teaspoon garlic salt

Asparagus roulade

- -

SERVES 4:

50g butter
¼ cup flour
¾ cup milk
3 tablespoons tomato paste
½ cup grated tasty cheese
3 large (size 7) eggs

FILLING

400g can asparagus spears
1 clove garlic, finely chopped
¼ cup cream cheese
¼ cup finely chopped parsley (or other herbs)
salt and freshly ground black pepper

Make ahead, then slice and serve hot or cold as a starter or main.

Preheat the oven to 200°C. Melt the butter in a saucepan. Stir in the flour until it bubbles, for about 30 seconds. Add the milk gradually, stirring continuously, until the sauce boils and thickens. Stir in the tomato paste, and bring to the boil again. Remove from the heat.

Separate the egg yolks and whites. Add the yolks to the hot sauce and quickly stir to combine. Stir in the grated cheese.

Beat the egg whites until soft peaks form. Fold into the cheese mixture. Pour the mixture into a sponge-roll pan (about 20 x 30cm), lined with baking paper or a Teflon liner.

Bake at 200°C for 12–15 minutes or until puffed and golden brown. The roulade is cooked as soon as the centre springs back when lightly pressed with a finger. Remove from the oven and turn out onto a rack covered with a teatowel, or another Teflon sheet. Carefully remove the baking paper or liner.

Make the filling while the roulade cooks. Drain the asparagus liquid into a saucepan. Chop the asparagus and press gently to remove more liquid, and add the liquid to the pan. Boil the asparagus liquid with the chopped garlic down to 1 tablespoon, then stir into the chopped asparagus in a bowl. Fold together the asparagus, cream cheese and parsley. Taste, and adjust the seasoning.

Spread the filling evenly over the room-temperature roulade, leaving one long side uncovered. Holding the teatowel or Teflon sheet with both hands, gently roll the roulade, starting with the side nearest you, and finishing with the uncovered side.

Wrap the roll in cling film and refrigerate until needed, up to 24 hours. A short time before serving cold, cut carefully in 1cm straight or diagonal slices, using a sharp, serrated knife.

If serving warm, microwave carefully on Low. Alternatively, cover in foil and reheat at 180°C until warm (but not very hot) right through, before or after slicing. Serve with a salad, or salad leaves as garnish.

Paneer cheese

- -

SERVES 2–3 (300G):

2 litres milk
50–60ml lemon juice

This Indian-style cheese tastes rather like cottage cheese, but has a firm texture. It is fairly bland alone but is a good protein 'base'.

Pour the milk into a large saucepan and heat slowly, stirring occasionally, until boiling. Remove the saucepan from the heat and gradually add the lemon juice, while stirring continuously. The milk should separate, producing thick, whiteish curd and clear whey. Leave to cool for a few minutes, stirring every now and then.

Line a large sieve or colander with cheesecloth or a teatowel, then strain the milk mixture, discarding the whey. Stand the sieve over a saucepan or bowl, and place a small plate on top of the curds, and a weight on top of this (a milk container full of water works well). Allow to stand for several hours or, better still, overnight.

Paneer will keep quite well in the fridge for several days, until required.

Asparagus roulade

Paneer cheese in spicy tomato curry

- -

Heat the oil in a large frying pan over a moderate heat, then add the onion and garlic. Cook for about 10 minutes, stirring frequently to prevent burning. When the mixture is very soft and beginning to brown, add all the spices (except the garam masala) and cook, stirring continuously, for about 1 minute longer. Stir in the tomatoes, salt, sugar and garam masala.

Take off the heat and remove the bay leaves and cinnamon stick, then process until smooth. Return the sauce to the pan, add the cubed paneer, and heat over a medium heat until warmed through.

Serve on rice with your favourite curry accompaniments (page 186).

SERVES 2–3:

2 large onions, finely chopped

2–3 cloves garlic, finely chopped

3 tablespoons oil

2.5cm cinnamon stick

2 bays leaves

10 black peppercorns

4 whole cloves

3 cardamon pods

1 teaspoon ground cumin

½ teaspoon each: coriander, chilli powder, fenugreek seeds, turmeric, and mustard seeds

425g can whole or diced tomatoes in juice

½ teaspoon salt

1 teaspoon sugar

1 teaspoon garam masala

300–400g Paneer cheese (see opposite), cubed

Pasta comes in a remarkable range of sizes and shapes. It cooks quickly and can be served in many interesting ways.

There is now a wide variety of fresh and dried pasta available in most supermarkets. When choosing, look for pasta made from 100% durum wheat, as it has a firmer texture when cooked.

The following recipes are for main meal pasta and noodle dishes, but almost any of these could be served in smaller quantities as side dishes; after all, 'plain' lightly oiled or buttered pasta and noodles make great 'sides'!

Pasta

Making fresh pasta

- -

You don't need special flour to make your own fresh pasta. Everyday, standard plain flour is fine.

Mixing, rolling and cutting pasta entirely by hand really is a 'labour of love'; a food processor and a pasta machine really help!

Mixing by hand

Measure or weigh out the flour. If using a measuring cup, pour the flour out of the bag into the cup rather than scooping it out as this may pack in too much.

Mound the flour in a large bowl. Make a well in the centre and add the salt then the eggs.

Using clean hands or a mixing spoon, work the eggs through the flour until evenly combined. The dough should first be crumbly, then form a smooth but firm ball. If it is too sticky, add a little more flour; or if it is too dry, carefully add a little more water (a teaspoon of water can make a big difference!).

Turn the dough onto a lightly floured board or bench and knead for at least 5 minutes.

Cover the dough with plastic and leave to stand for 10–15 minutes before rolling.

Mixing in a food processor

Measure the flour and salt into the food processor fitted with the metal chopping blade.

With the machine running, add the eggs one at a time. After the last egg is added the dough should look like crumbs for a few seconds, then form a ball. If the dough has not formed a ball, gradually add a little more water (teaspoon by teaspoon) until it does; or if it looks too sticky, add 1–2 tablespoons additional flour.

Tip the dough out onto a lightly floured board or bench and knead for a couple of minutes.

Cover the dough with cling film and leave to stand for 10–15 minutes before rolling.

Rolling & cutting by hand

Cut the dough into 2 or 3 pieces. Leave 1 out to work with and cover the others.

Working on a lightly floured surface (use only just enough flour to prevent sticking at all stages), begin to roll the dough into a thin sheet, turning it over and rotating it frequently.

When it seems the sheet won't stretch any more, set it aside and move on to the next piece, then return to it later. Working the dough in cycles gives the sheets time to 'relax', making them easier to roll out.

When the sheets are as thin as you want (remember they will swell quite a lot during cooking), set them aside for a few minutes before cutting. If you are going to make filled pasta (page 162), roll them very thinly so they are nice and flexible. For lasagne, simply trim the sheet to size.

To cut long pasta, loosely roll up each sheet (square up the edges first if you like) and, working with a sharp knife, cut the roll crosswise into slices of the desired width. Each slice should then unroll to make a long ribbon.

Rolling & cutting with a pasta machine

Divide the dough into two or three pieces, leave one out to work with and cover the others.

Flatten the dough piece with your hands. Set the rollers to the widest gap and crank the dough through several times. Fold the dough in half, then pass it through several times again. Repeat this process 5–6 times (alternate the direction of the folds, or the sheet will become very long and thin) until the dough feels smooth and satiny – this should be a noticeable change.

Reducing the gap one step at a time, pass the sheet through once or twice at each level, until it reaches the desired thickness. Trim sheets up for use as lasagne or for making filled pasta (page 162).

If you are going to cut the dough into long shapes using the machine, hang the sheets over the back of a chair or a broomstick (a clothes-rack works brilliantly!), and leave them to dry out for about 10 minutes. This helps stop the noodles sticking together as they come out of the cutter.

If they do stick, or won't separate into individual noodles cleanly, leave the next sheets to dry for a little longer. If the sheets crack during cutting, they are too dry.

Hang the cut noodles back over the rack, and gently run your fingers down through them to ensure they are all separated. Hanging freshly cut pasta to dry for a few minutes before cooking helps to stop them sticking as they cook, or during storage.

Cooking or storing fresh pasta

Fresh pasta is best cooked almost immediately, or coiled loosely in plastic bags and frozen.

Basic egg pasta

FOR 3-4 SERVINGS:

300g (2-2½ cups) standard plain flour*
¼-½ teaspoon salt
3 large (60-65g each) eggs
additional flour or water if required

* Because the weight of flour in a measuring cup can vary so much depending on how it is packed in, weight really is the best measure for flour when making pasta.

Spinach pasta

Spinach doesn't really add too much to the flavour of the finished pasta, but it does give it an amazing colour. Try mixing spinach and 'plain' pasta for a real colour contrast.

125g (½ cup) well squeezed cooked (or frozen) spinach
300g (2-2½ cups) plain flour
1 large egg
½ teaspoon salt

Finely chop the spinach (a food processor does this very well) before mixing and processing the dough as described above.

NOTE: *As the moisture content of the dough depends on how hard you squeeze the spinach, you may have to add a little more flour (or liquid) than for plain egg pasta.*

Making filled pasta

Making ravioli (or any of its other close relatives) by hand can be a very rewarding process. Like all pasta making you do, however, have to be prepared to commit some time – even more than for regular pasta.

If you're going to the trouble of making filled pasta, you want to be sure you will be able to taste the results in the end. For this reason most of the fillings given below have strong, bold flavours.

Aside from some no doubt very old traditions, there is no reason why you cannot mix and match pasta fillings and shapes to suit yourself. See the possibilities given below and have a go!

Preparing the sheets

Basic dough preparation is as given above (you can use plain or spinach pasta).

Take extra care to ensure the dough sheets do not dry out and become brittle; and during the final stage, roll the dough out as thinly as possible. If using a pasta machine use the smallest setting, or if rolling the dough by hand try to get the dough 1-2mm thick. Remember, the final product is two sheets joined together and these will double in thickness as they are cooked.

Making ravioli

There is a variety of devices on the market designed to help make ravioli, but we think the most successful method requires none of these!

Take 1 sheet of thinly rolled dough and place it on a lightly floured board or bench. Starting about 3cm in from one edge, place teaspoonfuls of filling at 5-6cm intervals down the length. Repeat this process, spacing rows of filling 5-6cm apart, until the sheet is covered.

Brush the lines between the blobs of filling with lightly beaten egg. Place another, preferably slightly larger, sheet over the top. Working from the centre out, run a finger gently down the lines between the mounds of filling. Using a sharp knife, or better still a pastry wheel, cut between the little parcels.

Arrange cut ravioli in a single layer on a lightly floured surface and cover lightly until ready to cook. (Ravioli can be frozen for longer-term storage.)

Making agnolotti

Agnolotti are little half-moon-shaped packages. Roll the dough very thinly and lay it on a lightly floured surface. Using a wineglass rim or a fluted cookie cutter 5-6cm across, cut as many rounds as you can from the sheet.

Place a teaspoonful of filling in the centre of each round, then brush the exposed edges lightly with beaten egg. Fold in half and press the edges together to form little half-moon-shaped pillows.

Arrange in a single layer on a lightly floured surface and cover lightly until ready to cook.

Making tortellini

Lay the thinly rolled dough on a lightly floured surface and cut into 6cm squares.

Place a teaspoonful of filling in the centre of each square, then brush the exposed edges lightly with beaten egg. Fold diagonally (so 2 pointed corners meet) and lightly seal the edges. Bend the 2 very pointed corners around the filling and pinch them firmly together to create the characteristic 'navel-like' appearance.

NOTE: *If you don't have the time, energy or inclination to start from scratch and make your own dough, use wonton wrappers instead. Sandwich filling between 2 wrappers to make 1 large (or 4 very small) ravioli, or cut rounds from individual wrappers to make agnolotti.*

Spinach & ricotta filling

MAKES 40–50:

2–3 bunches fresh spinach (125g cooked)

¾ cup ricotta cheese

¼ cup grated parmesan

1 lightly beaten egg (reserve half for sealing pasta edges)

freshly grated nutmeg

salt and freshly ground black pepper, to taste

1 recipe fresh pasta (in sheets)

Rinse the spinach well in plenty of cold water. Drain and shake the leaves, removing any tough stalks. Heat a covered saucepan and steam the leaves without adding any extra water, stirring occasionally until well wilted.

Chop the spinach finely and squeeze out any excess water. Mix the spinach with the remaining filling ingredients in a small bowl.

Proceed with shaping as described above.

Roast pumpkin ravioli

Use wonton wrappers to make quick ravioli. Serve a few in a bowl as a starter course, or a pile in a bigger bowl for a main course for two, with crusty bread and side salads.

MAKES 12:

24 wonton wrappers or ½ recipe Basic egg pasta (page 162)

1 medium onion

400g pumpkin, peeled

1 tablespoon olive oil

2 teaspoons wine vinegar or balsamic vinegar

2 teaspoons sugar

100g feta cheese

sprigs of fresh herbs (optional)

2 cups vegetable stock

Thaw the wonton wrappers if necessary.

Cut the peeled onion in half from top to bottom, then into 8 wedges. Cut the prepared pumpkin into 2cm cubes.

Coat the onion and pumpkin with the olive oil. Roast the pumpkin and onion at 200°C for about 30 minutes, until both are tender and lightly browned. Stir the vinegar and sugar through the vegetables after they have roasted for 20 minutes.

Mash the pumpkin and onion with the feta cheese. Taste and season if necessary, adding any fresh herbs you like, and moistening with a little stock, milk or cream if necessary.

Place the filling in the centre of 12 of the wonton wrappers. Place a sprig of fresh herb on the filling if desired. Brush around the filling with water to dampen, then top each filled wonton wrapper with a plain wrapper, pressing the tops and bottoms together carefully, without leaving any air bubbles. Leave the prepared ravioli square, or cut into rounds with a suitable cutter.

Simmer in a pan of vegetable stock for 5–6 minutes, until the ravioli are cooked. Serve immediately, in a little stock, with basil pesto.

Sundried tomato & olive filling

MAKES 40–50:

8 sundried tomato halves

12 black olives, pitted

1 cup cream cheese, softened

1 tablespoon basil pesto (optional)

salt and freshly ground black pepper, to taste

1 recipe fresh pasta (in sheets)

Finely chop the sundried tomatoes and black olives. Stir these into the cream cheese with the pesto (if using) and salt and pepper to taste.

Proceed with shaping as described above.

Pasta al' Alfredo

Pasta al' Alfredo

SERVES 2–3:

250–300g fresh or dried pasta
(fettuccine is the 'traditional' choice
but any shape will do)
2–3 tablespoons butter
¼ cup cream
¼ cup grated parmesan
freshly ground black pepper
extra parmesan to serve

OPTIONAL EXTRAS
pesto or chopped fresh herbs
strips of sundried tomato or halved
cherry tomatoes
a little crumbled blue cheese

This simple and delicious pasta sauce can easily be dressed up to make the basis for an elegant and substantial meal.

Put the pasta on to cook in plenty of boiling water. While the pasta cooks, assemble the sauce ingredients.

Drain the pasta, then add the butter and toss through. Pour in the cream and sprinkle the parmesan over, then stir together. Allow to stand for a minute or so, then stir again and serve.

Served with salad and bread this makes an easy meal in about 10 minutes!

NOTE: *For Pasta Primavera, add 1–2 cups of lightly cooked, preferably spring vegetables such as asparagus, baby carrots, zucchini, sugarsnap peas or broccoli florets – the fresher the better. (You may also need to add a little extra cream so everything is lightly coated.)*

Spaghetti carbonara

SERVES 4–6:

400g fresh or dried spaghetti
2 eggs
½ cup cream
½ cup freshly grated parmesan
½ teaspoon salt
25g (2–3 tablespoons) butter, cubed
freshly ground black pepper, to taste

OPTIONAL EXTRAS
¼ cup chopped fresh basil, parsley,
chives, oregano, etc.
¼ cup thinly sliced sundried tomatoes
½–1 cup lightly cooked baby peas
½–1 cup sautéed button mushrooms

This is a simple but quite delicious pasta sauce.

Put the pasta on to cook in plenty of boiling water. While the pasta cooks, combine the eggs, cream, grated parmesan and salt.

When the pasta is cooked, drain then return to the saucepan and add the butter. As soon as the butter has melted, add the egg mixture and stir to thoroughly combine. The heat of the pasta and the saucepan should thicken the sauce, making it thick and creamy. If the sauce is not thickening, return the saucepan to a very low heat for a minute or two, stirring frequently.

Add a generous grind of black pepper and any one or two of the optional extras, then stir again and leave to stand for 1 minute. Serve immediately, with extra grated parmesan and black pepper on hand.

Pasta with 'instant' sauce

- -

This is a sauce which can be prepared while the pasta cooks. Choose a pasta shape with lots of convolutions and crevices, since these hold more of the sauce, which is stirred in so that it coats and flavours each individual piece.

Cook the pasta, following packet instructions.

Melt the butter, and add all the remaining ingredients except the parmesan, stirring to make sure there are no lumps. Pour this mixture over the hot, cooked pasta. Add the grated parmesan and any of the optional additions, if desired. Stir together, reheating over a low heat if necessary, and serve.

SERVES 4–6:

350–500g uncooked pasta

75g butter

¼ cup hot water

1 tablespoon instant vegetable stock

1 tablespoon basil pesto (or chopped fresh basil or 1 teaspoon dried basil)

1 teaspoon sugar

½ teaspoon salt, to taste

½ teaspoon garlic powder

freshly ground black pepper, to taste

dash of hot chilli sauce

¼ cup grated parmesan

OPTIONAL ADDITIONS

½ cup grated tasty cheese

3–4 tomatoes, diced

1–2 tablespoons chopped fresh herbs, such as basil, parsley or chives

Pasta with summer sauce

- -

This cold, uncooked sauce stirred through hot pasta makes an easy, delicious and nutritious meal on a hot day.

Cook the pasta in plenty of boiling, lightly salted water with about 1 tablespoon of oil or butter added. Drain when cooked.

While the pasta is cooking, cut the avocado and tomatoes into 1cm cubes and put in a bowl. Add the onion, garlic, basil and capers.

Mix the remaining ingredients thoroughly, and toss through the vegetable mixture.

When ready to serve, put the hot drained pasta into a shallow bowl, toss half the sauce through it, and spoon the rest over the top. Serve at once.

VARIATIONS: *Add any of the following: 6–8 black olives, 4 chopped sundried tomatoes, 50g cubed feta, ¼ cup toasted pinenuts, chopped parsley.*

SERVES 2–3:

150–200g large spiral pasta

1 large avocado

4 medium (about 400g) ripe red tomatoes

¼–½ red onion, finely chopped

1 clove garlic, minced

8 large basil leaves, roughly chopped

2 teaspoons capers

3–4 tablespoons extra virgin olive oil

2 teaspoons balsamic vinegar

2 teaspoons lime juice

½ teaspoon sugar

½–1 teaspoon salt

¼ teaspoon chilli paste

½ teaspoon dried oregano, crumbled

freshly ground black pepper to taste

2–3 tablespoons grated parmesan

Pasta with tomato & olive pesto

- -

What could be easier to prepare (or more delicious!) than pasta with this simple raw tomato and olive sauce.

Bring a large saucepan of water to the boil, then add the pasta. While the pasta cooks, prepare the pesto.

Halve the tomatoes, then scoop out and discard the seeds and roughly chop the flesh. Put the tomato flesh, garlic, almonds, basil and oil in a food processor, and blend until smooth. Add the olives and salt and pepper to taste, then process briefly so some chunks of olive remain.

Drain the cooked pasta, toss in the sauce, serve and enjoy!

SERVES 2–3:

200g pasta, long or short

3 medium tomatoes

2 cloves garlic

½ cup blanched almonds

½ cup lightly packed basil leaves

3 tablespoons olive oil

¼ cup black olives, pitted

salt and freshly ground black pepper, to taste

Pasta with pistachio & parsley pesto

SERVES 4:

1 cup (100g) unshelled pistachios
400g fresh pasta
1 cup (60g) parsley
2 cloves garlic
½ cup avocado oil
½ teaspoon salt
extra avocado oil and pistachios
shavings of parmesan

Pistachios, parsley and avocado oil give this a vibrant green colour and a nutty flavour.

Shell the pistachios (this yields about ½ cup). Cook the pasta in plenty of boiling water. While it cooks, put the parsley, garlic and oil in a food processor and blend until finely chopped. Add the nuts and salt and process until the nuts are finely chopped. Add more oil if mixture seems too dry.

Toss the pesto through the drained pasta, adding a little extra oil if you like. Serve topped with shavings of parmesan and a few extra chopped pistachios.

NOTE: *This is also delicious mixed with oil and brushed over bread to make crostini.*

Pasta with roasted red capsicum pesto

SERVES 4-6:

3 medium red capsicums
2 large cloves garlic
¼ cup lightly packed fresh parsley
¼ cup olive oil
1 tablespoon balsamic vinegar
1 teaspoon salt
500g rigatoni-type pasta

This brilliant red sauce has an amazing flavour – a delicious combination of sweet concentrated red capsicum aromas and garlic.

Turn on the grill to preheat, then halve the capsicums and remove the seeds. Arrange the cut capsicums so they lie as flat as possible on a baking tray or sponge-roll pan (cut lengthwise into quarters if necessary). Place the tray 5–10cm under the grill and cook until the capsicum skins are well blistered and beginning to char. Remove from the grill and cover, leaving the capsicums to sweat and cool for 5–10 minutes.

Remove the skins from the cooled capsicums (don't worry if you can't get all the skin off), and place the flesh in a food processor. Add the garlic, parsley, olive oil, balsamic vinegar and salt, and process until finely chopped (or smooth if you prefer).

Use immediately, or store in an airtight container in the fridge for up to a week.

To serve with pasta, stir the pesto into freshly cooked, drained and lightly oiled pasta.

Pasta with basil & walnut pesto

SERVES 4-6:

400–500g fresh or dried pasta, short
   or long
¼ cup shelled walnuts, preferably
   fresh
¼ cup lightly packed fresh basil leaves
1 clove garlic
2 tablespoons dried breadcrumbs
¼ cup cottage cheese
2 tablespoons grated parmesan
   cheese
3–4 tablespoons walnut oil or olive oil
salt and freshly ground black pepper,
   to taste

This is really a variation on traditional basil pesto, but the freshly shelled walnuts and the cottage cheese give it an unusual twist. Toss it through cooked pasta, or over cooked vegetables.

Put the pasta on to cook in plenty of boiling water, and while the pasta cooks, prepare the sauce.

Place the walnuts, basil, garlic and breadcrumbs in a food processor, and process until finely chopped. Add the cheeses and oil and process to make a smooth sauce, then season to taste.

Serve with a loaf of crusty bread or rolls, and a fresh tomato salad.

Pasta with pistachio & parsley pesto

'Country-style' tomato & mushroom sauce

SERVES 4:

400g long pasta (spaghetti,
　fettuccine etc.)
¼ cup olive oil
2 onions, peeled and chopped
3 cloves garlic, peeled and chopped
500g mushrooms (see above), sliced
400g can whole tomatoes in juice
1 tablespoon tomato paste
½ teaspoon each: basil, oregano, thyme
½–1 teaspoon salt
freshly ground black pepper, to taste
chopped fresh parsley and grated
　parmesan, to serve

If you can find wild mushrooms, use them — otherwise, portobellos are the best for this recipe.

Put the pasta on to cook in plenty of boiling water. While the pasta cooks, heat the oil in a large pan. Add the onion and garlic and sauté until the garlic is a pale gold colour.

Stir in the sliced mushrooms and cook for 2–3 minutes, stirring frequently. When the mushrooms have wilted, add the canned tomatoes in their juice, the tomato paste and the herbs. Break up the whole tomatoes with the back of a spoon.

Taste the sauce and add salt and pepper to taste. Reduce the heat and leave the sauce to simmer gently until the pasta is cooked.

Drain the cooked pasta and toss it with a little extra olive oil. Arrange the pasta on plates or a platter and top it with the sauce. Garnish with the chopped parsley and some freshly grated parmesan.

Peanut & sesame pasta sauce

SERVES 4:

1 large onion
1 tablespoon oil
¼ cup peanut butter
1 tablespoon tahini (optional)
2 tablespoons sweet chilli sauce
1½ cups water
light soy sauce or salt
2 tablespoons toasted sesame seeds
350g of your favourite pasta

This sauce has a nice nutty flavour.

Cut the onion in half from top to bottom, then cut in thin slices to form half-rings. Cook these in the oil in a covered saucepan for about 5 minutes, stirring and turning several times until evenly and lightly browned.

Add the peanut butter, tahini, sweet chilli sauce and water, and stir over moderate heat until the lumps have dissolved. Add extra water, or cook for a little longer until the sauce is of thin coating consistency.

Season carefully, adding more chilli sauce for more sweetness or hotness, and enough light soy sauce or salt to bring out the flavour.

Stir the sauce into the freshly cooked, drained pasta, sprinkle with toasted sesame seeds, and serve hot or warm with a cucumber salad, marinated green beans or a crisp green salad.

VARIATION: *For extra richness, add cream cheese or sour cream to taste.*

Tofu & tomato pasta sauce

SERVES 4–6:

2–3 cloves garlic, crushed and
　chopped
1 large onion, finely chopped
2 tablespoons oil
1 small green capsicum, diced
300–500g tofu
¼ cup red or white wine
425g can tomato purée
2 teaspoons sugar
½ teaspoon salt
1 teaspoon each: dried basil, dried
　marjoram
dash hot chilli sauce
freshly ground black pepper
2 tablespoons chopped parsley
400–500g spaghetti or fettuccine

The protein content of this pasta meal is boosted by the addition of the tofu.

Heat the oil in a large frying pan and sauté the garlic and onion. When the onion is soft, add the green capsicum and cook for a few minutes longer.

Crumble the tofu into 5mm pieces, draining off any liquid, and add to the mixture in the frying pan. Cook for 5 minutes, stirring occasionally. Allow any liquid that appears to boil away, or if there is a lot, drain it off instead. Add the wine, tomato purée and seasonings, except the parsley, then reduce the heat and simmer for 5 minutes.

Cook the pasta in plenty of boiling salted water.

Drain the cooked pasta and toss with butter or oil. Divide it between plates and top with the sauce. Sprinkle with chopped parsley and serve.

VARIATION: *Top with sliced green or black olives.*

Chunky vegetable & tomato sauce on pasta

Creamy tomato ravioli sauce

Grated onion gives a smooth sauce that still has body and flavour.

Grate the onion and mince the garlic. Melt the butter in a large saucepan, and sauté the onion and garlic for 3–5 minutes, stirring frequently to prevent browning. Stir in the tomato purée and let the mixture come to the boil, then simmer gently for 5 minutes.

Pour in the cream and add the seasonings. (For an extra-smooth sauce, sieve the tomato mixture before adding the cream.) Mix thoroughly and leave over a very gentle heat while you cook the ravioli. When cooked, drain and then stir very gently through the sauce. Serve, topped with a little freshly shredded or grated parmesan. Alternatively, toss the ravioli in a little butter, arrange on plates and spoon the sauce over.

SERVES 2–3:

1 small onion
1 clove garlic
25g butter
300g can tomato purée
½ cup cream
1 tablespoon basil pesto
½ teaspoon salt
½ teaspoon sugar
freshly ground black pepper
400–500g ravioli
shredded or grated parmesan, to serve

Ravioli with lemon & saffron cream

Saffron gives this sauce a beautiful golden colour, with a delicate but distinctive flavour.

Heat a dry frypan over moderate heat. Add the saffron threads and toast them, stirring frequently, for about 1 minute. Transfer the saffron to a mortar and pestle, add the salt and grind to a fine powder.

Melt the butter in the pan, then add the finely chopped or diced onion or spring onion. Cook, stirring occasionally, until the onion is soft and clear, then add the cream, lemon zest and juice.

Allow the sauce to come to the boil and reduce slightly, then turn down the heat to a gentle simmer and add the saffron-salt powder. Stir until the salt has dissolved and the sauce turns yellow. Remove the sauce from the heat and season to taste with salt and pepper, then leave to stand, stirring occasionally (the colour will continue to brighten), while you cook the pasta. (Sieve the sauce to make it extra smooth, if you like.)

When the pasta is cooked, drain it and transfer to a warmed serving dish. Pour the sauce over the pasta and serve topped with a little freshly grated parmesan and /or some finely chopped fresh parsley.

SERVES 2–3:

¼ teaspoon saffron threads
½ teaspoon salt
25g butter
1 small onion or spring onion, finely diced
¾ cup cream
zest of 1 lemon (2–3 teaspoons), finely chopped or grated
2 tablespoons lemon juice
salt and freshly ground black pepper, to taste
300–400g ravioli
freshly grated parmesan and finely chopped parsley, to garnish

Lentil & tomato pasta sauce

This lentil sauce for pasta is well flavoured, cheap, with an interesting texture, and very versatile.

Rinse the lentils, then cover with plenty of water, add the bay leaf, and boil until tender (page 201). Alternatively, drain and rinse the canned lentils.

While the lentils are cooking, finely chop the onions and sauté with the crushed, chopped garlic in the oil until tender. Add the sliced mushrooms and diced green capsicum (if you like) and continue to cook until the onion is soft and clear.

Pour in the tomato purée, then add the herbs, sugar, salt and pepper. Simmer for a few minutes over a low heat to allow the flavours to blend. Drain the cooked (or canned) lentils and stir in.

This mixture may be eaten immediately, but its flavour improves if it is allowed to stand for a while, then reheated. Serve over spaghetti or rice, or as filling for lasagne or cannelloni (page 172).

SERVES 4–6:

1 cup brown lentils (or 2 x 400g cans lentils)
1 bay leaf
3 medium-sized onions
3 cloves garlic
2 tablespoons oil
100g mushrooms (optional)
1 green capsicum (optional)
425g can tomato purée
1 teaspoon each: dried basil, marjoram and oregano
¼ teaspoon dried thyme
½ teaspoon sugar
½ teaspoon salt
freshly ground black pepper
350–500g spaghetti or other long pasta

Creamy tomato ravioli sauce

Spinach & cottage cheese cannelloni

SERVES 4-6:

1 packet (about 16) cannelloni tubes
('instant' cannelloni are easiest)

SAUCE

2 medium-sized onions

4 cloves garlic

2 tablespoons oil

1 small green capsicum

1 teaspoon dried basil

½ teaspoon dried thyme

½ teaspoon sugar

½ teaspoon salt

300g can tomato purée

1 tablespoon wine vinegar

¼ cup water

FILLING

about 1kg of fresh spinach (2 cups
when lightly cooked)

1 cup cottage cheese

1 teaspoon dried oregano

½ teaspoon salt

½ teaspoon sugar

¼ teaspoon grated nutmeg

freshly ground black pepper, to taste

TOPPING

1 cup cream cheese

1 cup grated cheese

This is an exceedingly popular and delicious mixture. Cook the whole casserole ahead and reheat it, or prepare the sauce and the filling ahead, but once the filling is put into the cannelloni tubes the casserole should be cooked promptly.

Chop the onions finely and peel and chop the garlic. Heat the oil in a saucepan, add the onions and garlic and sauté, stirring occasionally. Stir in the chopped capsicum and continue to cook until everything has softened and the onion turns clear.

Add the seasonings, then the tomato purée, vinegar and water. Bring to the boil, then reduce the heat and leave to simmer while you prepare the filling. (The sauce should be no thicker than tomato sauce – if it is, add a little more water to thin it down.)

Bring a large saucepan of water to the boil, then add the fresh spinach. Cook for 1–2 minutes, just until the spinach has softened and wilted, then remove from the heat and drain well. Coarsely chop the spinach, then return it to the saucepan or to a medium-sized bowl. Add the cottage cheese and remaining filling ingredients to the spinach, and mix everything together until evenly combined.

Select a shallow casserole dish that will hold all the cannelloni tubes comfortably, then butter or oil it lightly.

Fill each cannelloni tube, then place in the casserole dish. There is no neat and tidy way to do this — just use your hands. Don't stuff the tubes too full or they may break, or you might run out of filling. 'Instant' cannelloni tubes make life much easier as you don't have to cook them first.

Once all the tubes are full and arranged in the casserole, pour the sauce over. Shake the casserole gently to ensure the sauce is evenly distributed and has reached all the nooks and crannies.

Soften the cream cheese by microwaving on High (100%) for about 30 seconds, or stand the unopened container in hot water for a few minutes, and spread over the sauce-covered tubes. Sprinkle the grated cheese evenly over this, then bake at 180°C for 40 minutes, or until the top is nicely browned and the pasta is tender.

Serve with your favourite vegetables or a salad.

Fusilli alla fagioli (spirals with beans)

SERVES 4-6:

250–300g pasta spirals (or macaroni,
orecchiette, etc.)

3 tablespoons olive oil

3–4 cloves garlic

2 small dried chillis, crushed

410g can kidney beans

300g can chickpeas

400g can Italian-seasoned tomatoes

2 tablespoons tomato paste

1 teaspoon dried basil

½ teaspoon dried thyme

1 teaspoon each: salt and sugar

¼ cup chopped fresh parsley

This combination of pasta with a 'dry sauce' of tomato and beans makes a delicious vegetarian meal.

Put the pasta on to cook in plenty of boiling water. While the pasta cooks, prepare the sauce.

Heat the oil in a large pan. Crush, peel and chop the garlic, add this to the pan with the crushed chillis, and cook until the garlic turns golden.

Drain and rinse the beans and chickpeas. Add these to the pan along with the canned tomatoes, tomato paste, basil, thyme, salt and sugar. Stir well to combine, then allow the sauce to simmer, bubbling quite vigorously, until the pasta is cooked. Remember to stir frequently to prevent burning. By the time the pasta is cooked the sauce should be quite thick and 'dry' – that is, the tomato mixture should barely flow, sticking to and coating the beans.

Drain the cooked pasta and add the sauce and the chopped parsley, stirring to combine. Serve as is, or accompanied by some freshly grated parmesan and some additional chopped parsley.

Pappardelle with rich mushroom sauce

Pappardelle with rich mushroom sauce

Pappardelle is a really wide long pasta (like fettuccine, but 2–3 times as wide). Make your own pasta and cut it into strips about 2cm wide, or buy fresh lasagne sheets and cut them the same way.

Heat the oil in a large frying pan. Add the finely chopped onion and garlic and cook, stirring frequently, over a medium heat until the onion has softened.

While the onion cooks, cut the mushrooms into slices about 5mm thick, then gently stir them into the pan. Continue to cook, stirring occasionally, until the mushrooms soften, then add the sherry and herbs. Toss to mix, then when the sherry has mostly evaporated, stir in the cream.

Allow the sauce to boil, then reduce to a gentle simmer and cook for 3–5 minutes longer before seasoning to taste with salt and pepper and adding the infused oil (if using). Keep the sauce warm while you cook the pasta.

Bring a large saucepan of lightly salted water to a rapid boil. Add the pasta and cook uncovered for 3–5 minutes (depending on how thin you rolled the pasta). Drain the cooked pasta, then return it to the saucepan. Sprinkle it with a little extra olive oil, then add the sauce and stir gently until it is evenly distributed through the pasta.

Serve immediately garnished with a little extra basil, and with crusty bread and a green salad on the side.

SERVES 3–4:

2 tablespoons olive oil

1 small onion, finely diced

2 cloves garlic, crushed and chopped

200g portobello mushrooms

200g button mushrooms

¼ cup medium or dry sherry

1 tablespoon chopped fresh basil, plus extra to garnish

1 teaspoon chopped fresh thyme

½ cup cream

½–1 teaspoon salt

freshly ground black pepper, to taste

2 teaspoons truffle- or porcini-infused oil (optional)

400g pappardelle

Penne with broccoli, mushroom & almonds

SERVES 2–3:

200–300g penne or other short pasta
½ cup slivered almonds
2 tablespoons olive oil
2 cloves garlic
100g mushrooms, sliced
1 head broccoli (350–400g), cut into small florets
½ cup cream
1 tablespoon pesto
50g creamy blue cheese, cubed
salt and freshly ground black pepper, to taste

This is a simple, but nonetheless very good sauce. Blue cheese is available in different strengths – vary the type and the quantity you use to suit your own taste.

Put the penne on to cook in plenty of boiling water. While the pasta cooks, prepare the sauce.

Heat a large frying pan and toast the slivered almonds until they are golden. Remove the almonds and set aside. Heat the oil in the same pan, then add the garlic and cook for about 1 minute. Stir in the mushrooms and broccoli, florets and stirfry until the mushrooms are soft and the broccoli is tender.

Add the cream, pesto, and the cubed blue cheese. Stir until well combined and the blue cheese has melted. Taste, add salt and pepper as required, then remove the sauce from the heat.

Drain the cooked pasta, and toss it with a little extra olive oil or butter. Add the sauce and the toasted slivered almonds, stir gently until well combined, and serve.

Farfalle with aubergine, tomato & garlic sauce

SERVES 4:

1 medium (500–600g) aubergine
3 tablespoons olive oil plus 1 tablespoon olive oil
3 cloves garlic, peeled and chopped
1 medium onion, diced
1 medium green capsicum
425g can Italian-seasoned tomatoes
1 tablespoon tomato paste
2 tablespoons basil pesto
1 teaspoon salt
freshly ground black pepper, to taste
400g dried farfalle (bow-tie) pasta
shaved or freshly grated parmesan

Make this sauce in summer when vegetables like aubergine are plentiful and can be picked up for a song. This recipe is a quick and substantial meal for four hungry adults.

Cut the aubergine in half lengthwise, then cut each half into cubes 1.5–2cm square.

Heat 3 tablespoons of olive oil in a large non-stick frying pan, and add the cubed aubergine. Turn the cubes frequently until they are lightly browned on all sides, then transfer to a bowl and set aside.

Using the same pan, heat 1 tablespoon of olive oil. Add the garlic and onion, and cook without browning until the onion has softened. Quarter the capsicum lengthwise, discarding the seeds and stem, then slice crosswise. Add the capsicum slices to the garlic and onion mixture. Cook for a couple of minutes longer, then stir in the can of tomatoes, tomato paste and pesto.

Let the tomato mixture come to the boil, then add the browned aubergine cubes, the salt, and pepper to taste. Stir to mix everything well, then reduce the heat. Leave to simmer gently, stirring occasionally while you cook the pasta according to the manufacturer's instructions. Drain the cooked pasta and toss it with a little extra olive oil.

Arrange the pasta in a large serving dish or on individual plates and top with the sauce, then some shaved or grated parmesan. Serve immediately.

Pasta with feta & roasted vegetables

The slight tang of feta with the sweetness of roasted pumpkin and the earthy mushrooms works really well. It's particularly inviting on a cool winter's day.

Heat the oven to 225°C. While the oven heats, peel and deseed the pumpkin and cut the flesh into 2cm cubes. Cut the onion into about 12 thin wedges, leaving the root end on (this helps to hold it together). Halve the capsicum, remove the seeds and pith, then cut into 1cm strips.

Place the prepared vegetables in a large bowl. Add the garlic and 2 tablespoons of oil, and toss gently until the vegetables are coated with oil (add extra oil if required). Line a roasting dish or sponge-roll pan with baking paper (or use a non-stick liner), spread the vegetables in a single layer in the dish, then place in the preheated oven. After 10 minutes, gently turn the vegetables, add the mushrooms, then return them to the oven for a further 10 minutes.

While the vegetables roast, cook the pasta in plenty of lightly salted, rapidly boiling water. Drain the cooked pasta and return it to the saucepan. Add the evaporated milk, pesto and salt, and stir to combine.

Remove the roasted vegetables from the oven and cut the mushrooms into strips about 1cm wide. Gently stir the vegetables (plus any oil and/or juices) and about two-thirds of the crumbled feta into the pasta. Season with pepper to taste, garnish with the remaining feta, then serve with a simple mesclun salad.

SERVES 3–4:

400g pumpkin
1 medium red onion
1 medium red capsicum
2 cloves garlic, chopped
2–3 tablespoons olive oil
2–3 (about 150g) large portobello
  mushrooms
300g penne, rigatoni or other short
  pasta
¼ cup evaporated milk
2–3 teaspoons basil pesto
½ teaspoon salt
about 100g feta, crumbled
freshly ground black pepper, to taste

Pasta with feta & roasted vegetables

Penne with spinach & blue cheese sauce

SERVES 2–3:

250g short pasta (penne, macaroni, spirals, curls, etc.)
250g fresh spinach
125g creamy blue cheese
¼ cup milk
¼ teaspoon grated nutmeg
½ teaspoon salt
freshly ground black pepper
2–3 tablespoons butter
½–1 cup grated cheese (optional)

Pasta sauces don't get much simpler than this. The delicious creamy blue cheeses now available have a quite mild flavour and are excellent for sauces like this.

Put the pasta on to cook in plenty of boiling water. While the pasta cooks, wash the spinach in plenty of cold water. Remove any tough stems, then transfer the spinach to a large lidded saucepan or frying pan. Cook the spinach (using only the water clinging to the leaves) until the leaves and stems are wilted.

Crumble the blue cheese and combine it with the milk, nutmeg, salt and pepper in a microwave-proof dish or a small saucepan. Microwave (about 2 minutes on High [100%]) or heat gently, stirring frequently, until the cheese has melted. Set aside until the pasta is cooked.

Drain the cooked pasta, then return it to the saucepan and toss with the butter. Squeeze excess water from the cooked spinach, then add this and the sauce to the pasta. Stir gently to combine, leave to stand for 2–3 minutes before serving, or transfer to a 20 x 25cm casserole dish that has been lightly oiled or sprayed with non-stick oil. Sprinkle with the grated cheese and brown the top under the grill.

Egg & cheese pasta bake

SERVES 2–3:

250g dried pasta (curls, spirals, etc.)
1 tablespoon olive oil
1 medium onion, peeled and diced
1 clove garlic
2 large eggs
1 cup cream
1½–2 cups (150–200g) grated cheese (cheddar, gruyère, emmentaler or raclette)

This is even easier than conventional macaroni cheese!

Turn the oven on to preheat to 200°C, then put the pasta on to cook in plenty of boiling water. While the pasta cooks, heat the oil in a frying pan, then add the onion and garlic and sauté until the onion has softened and turned clear. Remove the pan from the heat and set aside.

Whisk together the eggs and cream.

Drain the cooked pasta well, then transfer it back to the saucepan. Stir in the onion and garlic mixture, the egg mixture and about half of the grated cheese. Tip the pasta mixture into a lightly oiled 20 x 25cm casserole dish and sprinkle with the remaining grated cheese.

Bake at 200°C for 20–25 minutes until the edges are bubbling and the top has browned (if the top has not browned after this time, turn the oven to grill for a few minutes).

Pasta & tomato bake

SERVES 4–6:

500g short pasta shapes, eg curls, macaroni, spirals or shells
2 medium onions
2 cloves garlic
2 tablespoons canola oil
2 x 400g cans whole or diced tomatoes in juice
2–3 tablespoons tomato paste
1 teaspoon salt
1 teaspoon basil
1 teaspoon thyme
freshly ground black pepper, to taste
1–2 cups grated cheese

Most of the ingredients for this easy meal are 'staples' that can be kept on hand in the pantry, and they are economical.

Turn the oven on to preheat to 180°C. Cook the pasta in a large saucepan of lightly salted water.

While the pasta cooks, dice and sauté the onions and garlic in the oil. When the onion is soft, reduce the heat and add all the remaining ingredients except for the cheese (break up whole tomatoes with the back of a spoon). Simmer gently over a low heat for a few minutes, until the pasta has finished cooking.

Drain the pasta, then combine with the tomato mixture in a large shallow casserole or soufflé dish. Sprinkle the cheese evenly over the top.

Bake uncovered at 180°C for about 25 minutes or until the top is lightly browned. (If you are in a hurry, just brown the top by placing under the grill for a few minutes.)

Artichoke heart & sundried tomato pasta

- -

The artichoke hearts and sundried tomatoes used in this pasta dish make a delicious treat.

Quarter then peel the onion, and cut into 5mm slices.

Heat the oil in a large frying pan, add the onion and garlic and cook until the onion has softened but not browned. Add the capsicum and cook for a few minutes longer.

Add the roughly chopped tomatoes and juice and cook for about 5 minutes, stirring occasionally, until the sauce has thickened. Stir in the chilli powder, salt, vinegar, pesto and capers.

Turn off the heat, but leave the pan on the element. Stir the artichoke and sundried tomato pieces gently through the sauce mixture.

Meanwhile, cook the pasta until barely tender in plenty of boiling salted water. Drain well, and toss with a little butter.

Serve in a large bowl or on individual plates, with the sauce spooned over the pasta. Sprinkle with parmesan.

SERVES 4:

1 large onion
2 tablespoons oil
2 cloves garlic, finely chopped
1 green capsicum, sliced
425g can whole tomatoes, roughly chopped
½ teaspoon chilli powder
½ teaspoon salt
1 teaspoon balsamic vinegar (optional)
1 tablespoon pesto
1 tablespoon capers
4 marinated artichoke hearts, quartered
¼ cup sundried tomatoes, cut into 1cm strips
400g fresh pasta
butter
parmesan

Zucchini & yoghurt pasta

- -

This is a lovely light, summery pasta dish – although it tastes so good you may find yourself making variations all year round.

Cut the zucchini into slices not more than 1cm thick.

Put the pasta on to cook, using the instructions on the packet.

Sauté the zucchini with the garlic, until it has softened and is beginning to turn golden. Remove from the heat and add the rest of the ingredients. Stir gently until everything is well combined. Stir into the cooked pasta and serve while hot.

Sprinkle individual servings with grated parmesan if desired, and serve by itself or with a mixed green salad.

SERVES 4:

500g zucchini
250g fresh or dried pasta ribbons
3 cloves garlic, crushed and chopped
1 tablespoon butter
1½ cups plain unsweetened yoghurt
½ cup sour cream
½–1 teaspoon salt
freshly ground black pepper
½ teaspoon sugar
1 teaspoon paprika
2–3 tablespoons freshly chopped parsley
1 tablespoon lemon juice
grated parmesan (optional)

Layered macaroni bake

- -

Preheat the oven to 180°C. Cook the macaroni in plenty of lightly salted boiling water until tender, then drain, and stir through the butter, flour and tomatoes, and additional vegetables if you like. Spread in a 20–24cm ovenware dish, smoothing the top so it is reasonably compacted and level. Sprinkle evenly with grated cheese.

Beat the eggs and milk to blend, then pour this mixture over the pasta and cheese mixture.

Bake uncovered for 30–40 minutes or until the cheesy topping is firm in the centre. Allow to stand for 5–10 minutes before serving.

Serve with broccoli, beans, a green salad or coleslaw.

SERVES 4:

300g large macaroni shapes
1 tablespoon butter
1 tablespoon flour
425g can Italian tomatoes
cooked mushrooms, corn or other vegetables (optional)
1 cup grated cheese
2 eggs
1 cup milk

Spicy rice noodles

SERVES 2-3:

150g rice sticks or noodles

150g firm tofu, finely cubed

2 tablespoons dark soy sauce

1 tablespoon rice wine or sherry

1 teaspoon each: minced ginger and
   sesame oil

1 large clove garlic or 1 teaspoon
   minced garlic

½ teaspoon minced chilli (optional)

2 tablespoons canola oil

1 tablespoon red curry paste*

1 medium onion, peeled, quartered
   and sliced

1 large carrot, cut into matchsticks

150–200g broccoli florets

½ red capsicum, sliced

½ green or yellow capsicum, sliced

2 spring onions, cut into 2cm lengths

1–2 tablespoons extra oil and
   1–2 tablespoons water, if required

1 cup mung or soy bean sprouts

2 tablespoons chopped coriander leaf

salt (or extra soy sauce), to taste

**Check that the curry paste is fully
vegetarian and does not contain
shrimp paste.*

We love fried noodle dishes. This one combines some of our favourite flavours with the convenience of rice noodles (sometimes called rice sticks), which only require soaking, not cooking.

Place the rice sticks or noodles in a large saucepan or bowl and cover with boiling water. Leave to stand for 5–10 minutes or until tender (different brands take different times), then drain and toss with about 2 teaspoons of oil.

Place the cubed tofu in a small bowl, add the soy sauce, rice wine or sherry, ginger, sesame oil, garlic and the chilli (if using), and stir to combine. Leave to stand while you prepare the remaining ingredients.

Heat the oil in a very large pan or wok, then add the red curry paste and the onion. Stirfry until the onion begins to soften, then add the carrot and broccoli. Continue to stirfry for about 1 minute, then add the capsicums and the tofu mixture and cook for another 2–3 minutes.

Add the drained noodles and the spring onions and stirfry for 3–4 minutes, adding a little extra oil and/or water if the noodles are sticking. Toss in the bean sprouts, chopped coriander, and salt or additional soy sauce to taste, and stir to combine.

Serve immediately.

Super special macaroni cheese

Turn macaroni cheese into something special! The sauce is very carefully seasoned, and tastes 'extra cheesy'.

Cook the macaroni in a large saucepan of boiling, lightly salted water. Rinse with cold water and leave to drain in a sieve.

Melt the butter in a saucepan, add the curry powder then the flour and heat until it bubbles. Add the milk 1 cup at a time, bringing to the boil and stirring constantly between additions. Remove from the heat and stir in the remaining ingredients to combine.

Carefully stir the macaroni and sauce together, and turn into a well-buttered or oiled 12-cup-capacity ovenware dish.

For the topping, melt the butter and remove from heat. Stir in the breadcrumbs and cheese, and sprinkle over the surface of the macaroni cheese.

Bake at 180°C for 30 minutes or until the sauce bubbles and the top browns.

This is particularly good served with Crunchy spinach salad (page 80).

SERVES 4–6:

400g macaroni or other pasta
50g butter
1 teaspoon curry powder
¼ cup flour
3 cups milk
1 tablespoon Dijon mustard
1 teaspoon salt
¼ teaspoon freshly ground black pepper
½ teaspoon grated nutmeg
2 cups grated tasty cheese

TOPPING
1–2 tablespoons butter
1 cup fresh breadcrumbs
½ cup grated tasty cheese

Spinach & mushroom lasagne

This is a popular dish, and is relatively straightforward to make.

Heat the olive oil in a large frying pan. Add the garlic and onion and cook until the onion is soft and turning clear, then add the sliced mushrooms and herbs. Continue to cook for 2–3 minutes longer, or until the mushrooms have wilted. Remove the pan from the heat and set aside.

Melt the butter in a medium-sized saucepan. Add the flour and stir well so there are no lumps. Cook, stirring continuously, for about a minute. Pour in a third of the milk and bring to the boil, stir vigorously, ensuring there are no lumps. Allow the sauce to thicken and boil for a minute, then add half the remaining milk and bring to the boil again, stirring frequently. Add the remaining milk and bring to the boil once again, then remove the sauce from the heat. Add the seasonings and 1 cup of grated cheese. Stir until the cheese melts.

Combine the spinach, cottage cheese and salt in another bowl.

Lightly oil (or non-stick spray) a 20 x 30cm casserole or lasagne dish. Cover the bottom with a single layer of lasagne. Spread half of the spinach mixture evenly over the lasagne. Arrange another layer of lasagne over the spinach, then cover this with the mushroom mixture. Add another layer of lasagne, then the remaining spinach mixture and a final layer of lasagne. Pour the cheese sauce over the top and sprinkle this with the grated parmesan.

Dust the top lightly with paprika and bake at 175°C for 40–45 minutes. Serve with bread and a side salad.

SERVES 4–6:

2 tablespoons olive oil
2 cloves garlic, chopped
1 medium onion, diced
250g mushrooms, sliced
½ teaspoon each: dried thyme and marjoram
2–3 tablespoons (25g) butter
¼ cup flour
2 cups milk
salt and freshly ground black pepper to taste
¼ teaspoon freshly grated nutmeg
1 cup grated cheese
500g frozen spinach, thawed (or 2 cups cooked fresh spinach)
1 cup cottage cheese
½ teaspoon salt
250–300g curly lasagne noodles or sheets
¼ cup grated parmesan
paprika

Vegetable lasagne

SERVES 6:

FIRST LAYER
1 onion, finely chopped
1 clove garlic, finely chopped
1 tablespoon olive oil
300g mushrooms, sliced
1 teaspoon fresh thyme, finely
  chopped
1 cup vegetable stock (page 43)
1 tablespoon cornflour
¼ cup water
salt and freshly ground black pepper

SECOND LAYER
300g broccoli or spinach, chopped
1 cup (250g) cottage cheese
2 eggs
1 cup grated tasty cheese
salt and freshly ground black pepper
250g fresh lasagne sheets (spinach or
  plain)
425g can Italian-seasoned tomatoes
½ cup grated tasty cheese

Mixtures of savoury foods layered between lasagne noodles have become so popular in recent years that they are now considered part of our basic cuisine.

For the first layer, cook the onion and garlic in the oil until soft but not browned. Add the mushrooms and thyme, and cook for 5 minutes more. Add the vegetable stock, then thicken with the cornflour mixed with ¼ cup water. Season to taste.

For the second layer, cook the broccoli or spinach until barely tender. Drain. Mix together the cottage cheese, eggs, grated cheese, and salt and pepper to taste. Stir in the drained broccoli or spinach.

To assemble the lasagne, butter or spray with non-stick oil a 20 x 30cm casserole dish. Cover with a layer of lasagne sheets. Spread with the mushroom mixture then top with a second layer of lasagne. Spoon the cottage cheese mixture over this, and cover with more lasagne. Pour the tomatoes evenly over the top, covering it completely. Sprinkle with the grated cheese.

Cover and bake at 180°C for about 40–45 minutes. Remove the cover and bake for about 15 minutes longer, until the top is lightly browned.

Lentil lasagne

SERVES 4–6:

1 quantity Lentil & tomato pasta
  sauce (page 171)

TOPPING
3 tablespoons butter
3 tablespoons flour
2 cups milk
½ teaspoon salt
grated nutmeg
freshly ground black pepper
2 cups (200g) grated cheese – tasty
  cheddar, gruyère or emmentaler
2 eggs
200–350g lasagne noodles
paprika

Pasta is alternated with a flavoursome lentil and tomato mixture and a rich cheese sauce.

The lentil and tomato mixture needs to be fairly sloppy, as the pasta absorbs any surplus liquid from this layer as it cooks. You may wish to cook the lasagne ahead and reheat it when needed, but it should be cooked as soon as you have assembled the layers, so the pasta doesn't disintegrate.

Prepare the Lentil and tomato pasta ssauce according to the recipe given on page 171, then prepare the cheese sauce as follows.

Melt the butter in a medium-sized saucepan, then stir in the flour. Cook for 30 seconds, stirring continuously.

Add about a third of the milk and bring to the boil, allowing the mixture to thicken. Add another third of the milk and bring to the boil again, stirring vigorously to ensure the sauce is smooth. Stir in the last of the milk, then bring to the boil again, remove from the heat, then stir in the seasonings and grated cheese. Reheat to melt the cheese if necessary, but do not boil as the cheese will turn stringy. Remove from the heat and beat in the eggs.

Spread a thin layer of the lentil sauce (about a quarter) over the bottom of a large, shallow casserole dish. Arrange half of the lasagne in a layer over this, then spread half of the remaining lentil and tomato mixture on top. Pour half of the cheese sauce over, then arrange the remaining lasagne in a layer over this. Spread the remaining lentil mixture over, then top with the remaining cheese sauce and sprinkle with paprika.

Bake at 150°C for 45 minutes, or until the top is firm when pressed in the centre.

Mushroom lasagne

If you like mushrooms, you'll love this easy lasagne. It makes a great everyday meal, but it's also ideal for entertaining.

Heat the oil in a large, lidded, non-stick frying pan. Add the onion and garlic and cook, stirring frequently, until the onion is soft and clear. Gently stir in the mushrooms, then cover the pan and cook, stirring occasionally, until they have softened and wilted. Remove from the heat and add the pesto and salt, and pepper to taste.

Melt the butter in a medium-sized saucepan. Stir in the flour and cook, stirring continuously, for 1 minute. Add the nutmeg and salt, then 1 cup of the milk. Stir well to ensure there are no lumps and allow the sauce to thicken and boil, then add the remaining milk and bring to the boil again, stirring frequently. Remove from the heat and stir in the grated cheese.

Preheat the oven to 200°C. Lightly oil or non-stick spray a 20 x 25cm casserole dish. Spread ½ cup of the cheese sauce over the bottom of the dish, then cover this with a sheet of lasagne. Cover this with half of the mushroom mixture, ½ cup cheese sauce, then another sheet of lasagne. Repeat with the layering process, finishing with another sheet of lasagne.

Spread the remaining cheese sauce over the top, then bake the lasagne for 30–40 minutes, until the top is golden brown. Remove from the oven and leave to stand for 5 minutes before serving.

SERVES 4–6:

2 tablespoons olive oil

1 large onion, quartered and sliced

2 cloves garlic, crushed, peeled and chopped

500g mushrooms, cut into 1cm slices

1 tablespoon basil pesto

½ teaspoon salt

freshly ground black pepper, to taste

2–3 tablespoons (25g) butter

3 tablespoons flour

about ¼ teaspoon freshly grated nutmeg

½ teaspoon salt

2½ cups milk

1 cup grated tasty cheese

150–200g fresh lasagne sheets

Mushroom lasagne

Grains, the seeds of grasses, are the most important staple foods in the world. Rice, wheat and corn are the most commonly used grains, but many others are grown in different countries, according to climate.

Grains are processed in many ways: left whole, flaked, chopped (kibbled), ground coarsely or to fine powders. The outer layer of the grain is often removed during processing, but this layer contains valuable nutrients and dietary fibre, so it is important to include unprocessed whole grains in your diet.

Rice & grains

Grains & rice

BARLEY

Flaked barley: Made from steamed, rolled barley grains. Use as you would other flaked grains.

Pearl barley: Polished to remove the outside layers. Use in soups, as rice, or in salads etc.

BUCKWHEAT

Buckwheat: Often toasted before sale, to improve flavour. Cook in place of rice and in porridge mixtures. Ground for use in pancakes.

CORN

Coarse and fine cornmeal: Corn kernels ground to different particle sizes. The finer types are usually used in baking, while the coarser types may be boiled with water to make a porridge-like mixture (polenta).

Popping corn: Whole kernels of a special variety of corn. When heated with a little oil, the grains expand and pop violently. Without additions, pop-corn is a low-calorie, low-fat snack.

MILLET

Flaked millet: Flaked for quicker cooking in porridge mixtures. Millet is gluten-free.

Millet: Small, round grain (also sold for birdseed) which will grow in very hot and dry places.

OATS

Oat bran: Made from outer layers of oat grain; cooks with water to a much softer mixture than bran. Acclaimed as soluble fibre. If used to replace flour in baking, texture becomes drier.

Whole grain rolled oats: Oat grains which are steamed then flattened. Widely used in muesli, etc. Cook, without stirring, in mixtures to replace rice.

QUINOA

Quinoa: An ancient food of Andean origin, cultivated for 3–4000 years. Not a true cereal (it is in the spinach family), but the seeds can be cooked much like rice and have a slightly nutty flavour. A relatively high protein content (12–18%) and a complete set of essential amino acids make quinoa highly regarded for its nutritional properties.

RICE

Basmati rice: Aromatic rice, with appearance and nutritive value of long grain white rice. Cooking smells are startling, and unusual. Flavour outstanding, stronger in some brands than others. More highly priced, understandably, than white rice.

Black glutinous rice: Novelty value. Cooking water is dark red, and cooked grains reddish-brown. When mixed with plain cooked rice, it looks interesting. Available in Asian food stores.

Brown rice: long grain and short grain: Retains its bran layers and germ, thus more vitamins, minerals and protein. Needs longer cooking, and often more water than white rice. It has firmer, more chewy texture and nutty flavour. Microwave or pressure cook to reduce cooking time. Little difference in behaviour of long and short grains. Serve in same way as cooked long grain white rice. Pressure cooks in less than 10 minutes.

Heat-treated rice: Easily recognisable by its yellowish colour. Is heat-treated before outer layers are removed, and is said to contain more nutrients than white rice because of this. Costs more than plain long grain rice, but cooks more easily and produces greater volume. Microwaves very well. When cooked, loses most of its yellowish colour. Usually sold under brand names.

Mixed rice: Mixed long grain rices, mainly brown and glutinous rices. Need long cooking time, as for brown rice. Looks attractive, and may be used to replace other cooked rice, in recipes.

Wild rice: Formerly expensive and rare because it was not cultivated, but is now grown commercially, so price has decreased, and availability increased. Nutty flavour; cooking time similar to that of brown rice. Sold in rice mixtures. A luxury item.

White rice: long grain: Grain shape and length vary slightly, but cooking and nutritional qualities are similar. The usual choice for plainly cooked rice to accompany other foods. Many different cooking methods are used. Methods where all water is absorbed give slightly more flavour. Overcooking causes stickiness. Microwaves well.

White rice: short grain: The short, plump grains tend to break down during cooking, becoming sticky and thickening surrounding liquid. This is desirable in rice puddings, soups, and in sushi.

RYE

Flaked rye: If stirred during cooking, forms a chewy porridge-like mixture. If lightly browned in butter or oil, before cooking without stirring, the grains stay separate.

Kibbled rye: Chopped rye grains. Boil or microwave, and serve instead of rice.

Wholegrain rye: Requires long cooking. Serve like brown rice. Sauté in butter or oil before cooking.

WHEAT

Bulgar: Heat-treated, precooked chopped wheat which needs soaking or brief cooking in water, before being used in salads and savoury mixtures. Soaks up flavours of accompanying foods.

Flaked wheat: Steamed and crushed wheat. If stirred as cooked, the flakes produce a porridge mixture. If cooked without stirring, with a little oil or butter, they keep their shape. Use in place of rice, or in muesli mixtures.

Kibbled wheat: Chopped wheat grains. Not cooked during manufacture, it needs more cooking than bulgar. Cook and serve as rice, include in porridge mixtures, or use in coarse-textured bread, after heating to boiling point in water, then draining.

Semolina: The coarsely ground heart of wheat kernels. In Indian cookery it is lightly browned before cooking, with interesting results.

Wheat bran: Made from the outer layers of wheat grains. Does not contain the wheat germ. High in fibre. Sometimes sold as baking bran. May be added to baking, porridge, etc.

Wheatgerm: A small part of the wheat grain, from which the new wheat plant grows. A concentrated food, especially high in protein, vitamins and minerals. Add it to baking, porridge, and other foods, to enrich them. Excellent value for money, nutritionally.

Wheat grains (wheat berries): Use as rice, etc. Requires longer cooking than kibbled or flaked wheat.

Wholemeal flour: Made by milling the whole wheat grain. It contains the outer bran layer and the germ, which are high in fibre, vitamins and minerals, as well as the inner white part (or endosperm) of the grain. It gives a more solid texture to baked products. To include more in your diet, try replacing half, rather than all the flour in an existing recipe with wholemeal flour, and be prepared to add a slightly different amount of liquid to reach the usual consistency.

Cooking rice & grains

Foolproof white rice

If you coat rice grains with oil or butter before you cook them, there is much less chance that they will stick together. Heat 1 tablespoon oil or butter in a heavy-bottomed saucepan with a tight-fitting lid. Add ½ teaspoon salt. Stir in 1 cup long grain white rice. Add 2 cups boiling water. Put on a tight-fitting lid and cook gently, without lifting the lid or stirring, for about 15 minutes. Lift out a few grams of rice and test by squeezing them. (See Butterless White Rice below.) If it is not cooked, check if there is any water left in the pan. If not, add about ¼ cup more, cover again and cook for 3–4 minutes longer. Transfer to serving dish, forking it lightly to get a fluffy appearance.

Foolproof heat-treated rice

Cook as above, adding 2½ cups water of any temperature to 1 cup of rice. Allow a little longer cooking time.

NOTE: *For softer-textured rice, add ¼–½ cup more water, and cook for about 5 minutes longer.*

Butterless white rice

This is a good way to cook rice when you don't have a heavy saucepan with a tight-fitting lid, or when you don't want to add oil or butter.

Bring 8 cups water and 1 tablespoon salt to the boil in a large saucepan. Slowly shake 1 cup long grain rice into the bubbling water, making sure water doesn't stop boiling. Boil gently with the saucepan lid ajar, or without a lid, for about 15 minutes.

Squeeze a grain of rice between your finger and thumb. If you can squeeze it completely in half, without having a hard core left, it is cooked.

Drain, using a large sieve. If serving within an hour, rinsing is not necessary. If serving later, rinse with hot (or cold) water, leave to drain again, then store in a container in which the rice will not dry out.

Butterless heat-treated rice

Proceed as above for quantities, adding the rice to hot or cold water, but stirring until the water boils again, if necessary. Rice may be removed from heat, then heated again, if necessary, before cooking is completed. Cooking time is unlikely to be shorter than that of plain long grain rice.

Microwaved white rice

The microwave oven cooks rice very well. Use heat-treated or plain long grain rice. You do not need to attend to it at all during or after cooking, so you can put in the rice, turn on the oven, and go away. When you come back later (any time after the cooking time plus the standing time), all you need to do is reheat the rice on High (100%), allowing 1–2 minutes per cup. It needs no draining, no stirring. It will not have stuck to the container, and will have a good flavour.

In a large microwave bowl, turn 1 cup long grain or heat-treated rice in 1–2 teaspoons oil (or melted butter). Add 2¼ cups (preferably hot) water, and cover, folding back the edge 5mm if you use plastic cling wrap. For 1 cup, cook on High (100%) for 12–15 minutes. Allow 10 minutes standing time. For 2 cups allow 20–25 minutes, with 15 minutes standing time.

If rice boils over, use a larger container, keep lid ajar, or lower power level (to 50%) and increase cooking time by 5 minutes.

Brown rice

Brown rice has a nutty flavour, an interesting, slightly chewy texture, and is nutritionally better than white rice. It is available in long- and short-grained varieties. Both may be cooked and served as long grain white rice is served. All types of brown rice take longer to cook than white rice. Some brown rices absorb more liquid than others, and take longer to cook. You should always be prepared to add some extra water, and cook for longer, if the grains seem dry and hard.

Undercooked brown rice may put your friends and family off it forever! Brown rice is, in fact, easier to cook than white rice, because the outer coating on the grains stops them sticking together as they cook. Make sure that you allow plenty of cooking time, though.

Simmered brown rice

Turn 1 cup brown rice in 1 teaspoon oil or melted butter.

Add 2½ cups water and ½ teaspoon salt. Cover tightly and simmer for about 45 minutes, adding extra water if rice dries out before it is tender.

Microwaved brown rice

Microwave for 25 minutes, using same proportions as for simmered brown rice and general method as for white rice. Allow 15 minutes standing time.

Pressure-cooked brown rice

A pressure cooker revolutionises the cooking of brown rice. Our modern German pressure cooker cooks 1 cup of brown rice in 3 cups of water, with ½ teaspoon salt, at high pressure, in 9 minutes. We leave it to stand for 3–5 minutes after the pressure is lowered, before draining off any remaining water and serving it.

Allow a little longer if pressure cooker is old, or is not working efficiently.

Adding flavour to rice

Add butter, or chopped fresh herbs, or parmesan, or soy sauce, or sesame oil, or chopped, sautéed sesame or sunflower seeds or nuts (or a combination of several of these) to cooked rice.

Replace salt with vegetable stock powder when cooking. Use 1–2 level teaspoons to 1 cup rice. When using little butter, use the larger quantity. Sauté onion, celery, capsicums, or mushrooms in extra butter before stirring in uncooked rice. Add curry powder, paprika, etc., before water. Add raisins, sultanas, currants, orange or lemon rind to rice when it is about half-cooked.

It is important to season rice carefully. Add extra salt with herbs, butter, etc., after cooking, if rice tastes too bland.

Storing & reheating rice

Cooked rice should be covered to prevent drying out, and refrigerated to prevent spoilage. Tough, heatproof plastic oven bags (without holes) make excellent containers for refrigerating and reheating rice. Stir with fork or toss in bag once or twice during reheating. Sprinkle with extra water if rice looks dry before or during heating.

NOTE: *It is important for food safety that cooked rice is reheated thoroughly (ensure it is heated to over 60°C) before it is eaten.*

- Reheat rice in microwave oven on High (100%) for 1–2 minutes per cup, in its serving dish or in an oven bag (without a metal twist tie).

- In conventional oven, spread oven bag flat on a flat, shallow dish, e.g. a sponge-roll pan. Tie loosely. Reheat at whatever temperature oven is already heated to. Flip bag over once during reheating, so both sides heat.

- Reheat in a sieve or colander over a saucepan of boiling water. Cover with a lid so that the steam from the boiling water is prevented from escaping.

- For fastest reheating (without a microwave oven) but with some flavour loss, pour boiling water through cooked rice in colander or sieve, or add boiling water to rice in saucepan, then strain.

- Add rice to hot oil, or melted butter, or sautéed, finely chopped ingredients, in a preheated, preferably non-stick pan. Stir to heat evenly.

- Flavour and store other cooked grains in the same way as you would rice.

Cooking bulgar

This is a quickly prepared grain made from chopped wheat which has been precooked and dried. It may be used in place of rice, by itself, or in mixtures.

1 cup of bulgar absorbs 1–1½ cups of liquid. Either pour boiling vegetable stock over it and leave to stand for 10–15 minutes, or bring the bulgar and stock to the boil, remove form the heat and leave to stand for 5–10 minutes, until the liquid is absorbed. Add herbs, or other seasonings if desired. Serve in place of plain cooked rice, or leave to get cold and add vegetables and dressing to make a salad.

Cooking kibbled wheat & kibbled mixed grains

Kibbled grains are chopped but not precooked. They cook much more quickly than the whole, unchopped grains, but take longer than bulgar.

Heat 1 cup of kibbled wheat or mixed grains in 1 tablespoon of oil over moderate heat, for 4–5 minutes. Add 2 cups vegetable stock or 2 cups water with 2 teaspoons of vegetable stock powder and cook gently, with the lid ajar for 20–30 minutes. If the liquid is absorbed before the grains are as tender as you like, add more water and simmer for longer.

Curry accompaniments

Poppadoms

Spray poppadoms with non-stick spray and microwave on High (100%), one at a time on a folded paper towel for 40–70 seconds, until puffed over the whole surface.

Toasted sesame seeds

Toast sesame seeds by tipping them into a large frying pan and heating over low to moderate heat, shaking often, until lightly and evenly browned. Use immediately or store in an airtight jar.

Toasted coconut

Spread fine or medium desiccated coconut or shredded in a sponge-roll pan. Heat under a low grill or in a moderate oven until the coconut is lightly browned. Watch carefully as coconut browns and burns quickly.

Chopped roasted peanuts

Buy good quality roasted peanuts, chop coarsely, and serve alone, with Banana Raita (below), or with sliced cooked kumara in plain yoghurt or Cucumber in Yoghurt (below).

Banana raita

Slice fairly firm bananas and sprinkle with lemon or orange juice to stop them from browning. Fold plain yoghurt (using quantities to suit your own taste) through the banana. Add cinnamon, chopped mint, chopped coriander leaves, chopped peanuts or toasted sesame seeds, if you like.

Cucumber in yoghurt

Thinly slice or coarsely grate an unpeeled telegraph cucumber. Sprinkle with a teaspoon of salt, mix gently, allow to stand for 10 minutes, then rinse with cold water and drain. Make a dressing by mixing ½ cup plain un-sweetened yoghurt, the juice of ½ lemon, a small crushed garlic clove, and about ¼ teaspoon finely grated ginger root. Mix the cucumber and dressing about 10 minutes before serving.

Basic pilaf

Try this recipe with kibbled or flaked wheat, quinoa, rye, oats or barley. You will wonder why we so often ignore these grains in favour of rice!

SERVES 4:

2 tablespoons butter or oil
1 medium-sized onion

2 cloves garlic
¾ cup kibbled grain or long grain white rice (or 1 cup flaked grain or quinoa)
1 cup finely chopped celery
3 cups water
½ teaspoon salt
¼ cup chopped parsley
freshly ground black pepper, to taste

Melt the butter in a large non-stick frying pan with a close-fitting lid. Add the chopped onion and garlic and cook gently for 3–4 minutes without browning. Stir in the flaked or kibbled grain, or long grain rice. Continue to stir until all the grains are evenly coated with the butter and have browned lightly.

Add the celery, water and salt. Cover and cook for 20–30 minutes, or until the water is absorbed and the grains are tender. Add a little more water (½ cup) if you think the mixture looks too dry and the grains are not cooked right through. Stir in the parsley and pepper, and add a little more salt if desired, then serve.

Spicy rice pilaf

A very tasty alternative to plainly cooked rice.

SERVES 4:

2 tablespoons oil
1 medium onion, finely chopped
2 cloves garlic, finely chopped
¼ cup whole or slivered almonds
1 cup long grain rice
1 medium carrot, finely diced
¼ cup dried currants or sultanas
½ teaspoon each: ground cumin, coriander, cinnamon and chilli powder
¼ teaspoon ground cloves
zest of 1 lemon or orange
3 cups (boiling) vegetable stock (or 3 cups water plus 3 teaspoons instant stock)

Heat the oil in a large frying pan (or flameproof casserole dish), and cook the onions and garlic over moderate heat for about 2 minutes. Add the almonds and cook until lightly browned.

Stir in the rice, diced carrot, currants and spices, and cook for a few minutes longer, stirring frequently. Add the citrus zest and the boiling stock.

Bring the mixture to the boil, cover and simmer gently for about 15 minutes until the rice is cooked and the liquid is absorbed. Or bake, covered with a close-fitting lid or foil, at 170°C for 1 hour. Or microwave in a covered dish on Medium High (70%) for about 15 minutes.

Serve with any Middle Eastern-type foods.

Spicy mushroom pilau

It may sound unlikely, but this combination of flavours really is delicious!

SERVES 3–4:

1½ cups basmati rice
2 tablespoons canola oil
1 medium onion, diced
1–2 cloves garlic, chopped
2 teaspoons grated ginger root
6 whole cloves
2 cardamom pods, crushed
2 bay leaves
½ teaspoon mustard seeds
½–1 teaspoon minced red chilli
250g mushrooms, sliced
½ red capsicum, diced (optional)
2 cups hot water plus 2 teaspoons instant
　mushroom stock
2–3 tablespoons chopped coriander

Measure the rice into a large bowl and cover with cold water. Let it stand for 5–10 minutes.

Heat the oil in a large non-stick frying pan. Add the onion, garlic, ginger, spices and chilli. Cook, stirring frequently, until the onion is soft and turning clear. Add the mushrooms and capsicum (if using). Drain the rice, then add it to the pan along with the stock and stir until evenly mixed.

Allow the mixture to come to the boil, then reduce the heat to a very gentle simmer. Cover the pan with a close-fitting lid and cook for 10–15 minutes, until the rice is tender. Stir every few minutes to prevent sticking.

Season to taste with salt, then stir in the chopped coriander and serve.

Spicy mushroom pilau

Asparagus risotto

SERVES 2–3:

10 medium stalks (about 250g)
   asparagus
2 cups vegetable stock (page 43) (or
   2 cups water and 2 teaspoons
   vegetable stock powder)
2 tablespoons butter
1 medium onion, finely chopped
1 teaspoon (1–2 cloves) minced garlic
1 cup calrose or arborio rice
¼ cup dry white wine or extra stock
salt and freshly ground black pepper
½ cup grated tasty cheese
grated parmesan, to serve

Celebrate the start of spring with this tasty risotto.

Cut the asparagus stalks diagonally into 4cm pieces. Put them (with any trimmings and stalk bottoms, etc.) into a medium-sized saucepan with the vegetable stock, cover, and boil for 3–4 minutes until barely tender. Drain, reserving the cooking liquid in another container, discard the trimmings, and put the asparagus aside.

In the same saucepan or a medium-sized non-stick frying pan, melt the butter, add the finely chopped onion and the garlic, and cook over moderate heat for 3–4 minutes until onion is transparent but not brown. Add the rice, mix thoroughly, and cook for about a minute, stirring frequently.

Add the ¼ cup wine or extra stock to the vegetable stock. Add ¼ cup of the stock to the rice, and continue to add in ¼ cup lots each few minutes, or as the rice soaks it up and seems dry. Stir at regular intervals, since stirring helps to make the mixture creamy. Between stirrings, cover with a lid.

The rice should be tender after 20 minutes, with no uncooked core in the middle of each grain. If not, add ¼ cup of water and cook longer. Stir in the asparagus and stand over very low heat for about 5 minutes.

At the end of this time — half an hour after you started cooking the onion — the rice grains should be soft and clumping together, with no liquid left. Add enough salt and pepper to bring out the asparagus flavour, then fold the grated tasty cheese through the risotto. Sprinkle with parmesan cheese and serve straight away, alone or with a salad and warmed bread rolls.

Crusty rice cakes

SERVES 2–3:

1½ cups cooked short or long grain
   brown rice (page 185)
1 large egg
2–3 tablespoons grated parmesan
2 tablespoons basil pesto
canola or other oil

These delicious little cakes are particularly good made with brown rice, but may be made with any cooked rice.

Put the cooked rice, egg, parmesan and pesto in a bowl, and mix with a fork until combined. Heat the oil in a non-stick frying pan, then drop spoonfuls of the rice mixture into the hot pan.

Cook over moderate heat for about 10 minutes each side until golden brown and crunchy.

Curried rice & tomato casserole

SERVES 4–6:

1 cup long grain rice (preferably
   heat-treated)
2 medium onions, finely chopped
1 teaspoon salt
1 teaspoon curry powder
1 cup tomato purée
1½ cups water
25–50g butter, cubed (or 3 tablespoons oil)
2 firm tomatoes, cubed
1 each: green and red capsicum, cubed
chopped parsley, to garnish

Any leftovers from this casserole are good piled on toast, sprinkled with grated cheese, and browned under a grill.

Preheat the oven to 180°C. Put the rice, onion, salt, curry powder, tomato purée, water and butter or oil in a medium-sized casserole dish. Bake, tightly covered, for 45 minutes, or until the rice is tender and all the liquid is absorbed, stirring once after about 20 minutes.

Add the tomato and capsicums and fold through the hot rice. Bake for 5 minutes longer, then leave to stand for 10 minutes. Sprinkle with parsley and serve with a selection of vegetable and/or salad dishes.

VARIATION: *Replace the white rice with brown rice, add an extra ½ cup of water, and cook for 1½ hours, or until rice is tender, making sure mixture does not dry out.*

Pumpkin & mushroom risotto

SERVES 3–4:

1 medium onion
2 tablespoons olive oil or canola oil
1 clove garlic, chopped
250g piece pumpkin, deseeded and peeled
250g Swiss brown mushrooms
1 tablespoon olive or canola oil
1 cup arborio rice
2½–3 cups hot water or mushroom stock
1 tablespoon basil pesto
2–3 tablespoons grated parmesan
½–1 cup fresh or frozen peas
½–1 teaspoon salt
freshly ground black pepper, to taste

The sweetness of pumpkin and the earthiness of mushrooms combine perfectly to give this risotto a wonderful flavour.

Peel, quarter and slice the onion while the oil heats in a large (preferably non-stick) frying pan. Add the onion and garlic and cook for 2–3 minutes until the onion is softening. Grate the pumpkin and halve the mushrooms, then add these and continue to cook, stirring frequently to avoid browning, for about 5 minutes. Remove the vegetable mixture from the pan and set aside.

Heat the second measure of oil in the pan, then stir in the rice and cook for 1–2 minutes. Add the vegetable mixture and stir gently, then pour in 1 cup of the water or stock. Bring to the boil, then reduce the heat and leave the uncovered pan to simmer gently, stirring occasionally, until most of the liquid has disappeared (this should take 3–4 minutes). Add another 1 cup of liquid and when this liquid too has been absorbed (in another 4–5 minutes), add another ½ cup of liquid and leave to simmer again.

When this liquid has almost gone, test the rice to see if it is done. If the liquid has all gone before the rice is cooked, gradually add an extra ½ cup or so of hot water. Test the rice frequently, taking care not to overcook it or it will turn mushy – but do not serve undercooked either, as hard-centred rice is very unpleasant!

As soon as the rice grains are tender right through, add the pesto, parmesan and peas. Stir frequently for another 3–4 minutes until the peas are cooked. Season to taste (you may not need any salt if you have used instant stock). Serve immediately.

Pumpkin & mushroom risotto

Rich mushroom risotto

A few slices of dried porcini give this a really intense flavour.

Place the dried mushrooms in a shallow container and cover with the hot water. Leave to soak for 15–20 minutes while you prepare the remaining ingredients.

Heat the oil in a large (preferably non-stick) frying pan then add the diced onion. Cook, stirring frequently, until the onion has softened and is turning clear. While the onion cooks, drain the soaked mushrooms, reserving the soaking liquid, and chop them into smaller pieces. Add the soaked mushrooms and the fresh mushrooms to the pan and cook, stirring occasionally, until the fresh mushrooms have wilted. Add the rice, thyme and a generous grind of black pepper and stir until the rice is coated with oil.

Reduce the heat a little and pour in the reserved mushroom-soaking liquid and the sherry, vermouth or wine and stir continuously until the liquid has almost disappeared. Stir in 1–1½ cups of hot water plus the instant stock powder and simmer, stirring frequently, until this has almost disappeared, then stir in another 1 cup of water. Continue to cook, stirring frequently, until this too has almost been absorbed.

When the rice has cooked for about 20 minutes, try a few grains to see if they are tender right through. If they are still hard in the middle, add another ½ cup of water and cook for another 3–4 minutes; repeat if required. When the risotto is cooked, the rice should be coated with a creamy, but not soupy, mixture. If you think it looks too dry, add a little extra water.

Stir in the grated parmesan (if using) and season with salt and pepper if required. Spoon on to plates or bowls, and garnish with a few sprigs of thyme, some shaved parmesan and/or strips of grilled mushroom (see below), then serve immediately accompanied with a simple green salad and crusty bread.

SERVES 3–4:

15–20g dried mushrooms (preferably porcini), sliced
½ cup hot water
3 tablespoons olive oil
1 medium onion, finely diced
250g Swiss brown mushrooms, sliced
1 cup arborio rice
1 teaspoon dried thyme
freshly ground black pepper, to taste
¼ cup dry sherry, vermouth or white wine
2½–3 cups hot water plus 2 teaspoons instant mushroom stock
3–4 tablespoons freshly grated parmesan (optional)
Grilled portobello mushrooms (see box) (optional)
salt and freshly ground black pepper, to taste

Grilled portobello mushrooms

If you want an extra mushroom 'fix', try serving these with your risotto or as an interesting side dish for any meal.

SERVES 4:

2 tablespoons olive oil
2 tablespoons balsamic vinegar
1 tablespoon pesto
1–2 cloves finely chopped garlic
4 large portobello mushrooms

Combine the oil, vinegar, pesto and garlic in a small bowl.

Preheat the grill. Brush the top and bottom of the mushrooms with the oil mixture, then arrange them stem side up on a baking tray. Place under the grill 5–10cm below the heat and cook for 4–5 minutes. Slice the grilled mushrooms into 1–2cm strips and pile on top of the risotto; or serve the risotto piled into the whole mushrooms.

Baked green rice with tomatoes

FOR 6–8 SERVINGS:

1½ cups basmati rice

3 cups boiling water

500g spinach

2 cups grated tasty cheese

1 teaspoon grated nutmeg

4 eggs

1 cup milk

2 cloves garlic, finely chopped

2 tablespoons chopped fresh herbs or
    1 tablespoon pesto

425 g can Mexican tomatoes or
    tomato and onion

1 cup grated tasty cheese

Served with one or more salads, this is an interesting family meal or addition to a summer buffet.

Preheat the oven to 200°C.

Cook the rice in a saucepan of lightly salted boiling water on the stove, then drain well. Alternatively, cook for about 12 minutes on High (100%) in the microwave. Allow to stand for 5 minutes if microwaved, then drain if necessary.

In a separate saucepan, cook the spinach until barely tender, then drain well, squeezing out all the water. Chop the spinach finely and add to the cooked rice with the 2 cups grated cheese, nutmeg, eggs, milk, garlic and chopped herbs or pesto.

Put the rice mixture into a roasting dish and bake, uncovered, at 200°C for about 15 minutes or until it feels firm. Spread the tomatoes evenly over the hot rice, sprinkle with 1 cup of grated cheese, and bake for 10 minutes longer, until the cheese melts.

Serve hot, warm, or reheated, cut into squares, with a leafy salad.

VARIATION: *Replace the basmati rice with the same amount of brown rice. Cook longer, until completely tender, before mixing with the other ingredients.*

Spiced rice scramble

SERVES 4:

1½ cups basmati rice

1 cup seedless raisins or sultanas

3 tablespoons balsamic or wine vinegar

3 tablespoons water

1 each: red and yellow capsicums
    (optional)

4 eggs

3 tablespoons water or milk

¼ teaspoon salt

1 tablespoon butter or oil for frying

¼–½ cup pine nuts

1 tablespoon oil

4 spring onions, finely chopped

SAUCE

2 tablespoons each: tomato paste,
    water and sherry

1 tablespoon each: sesame oil and
    Thai sweet chilli sauce

Put together this delicious and slightly out of the ordinary rice recipe for a main meal, and serve any leftovers cold as a salad.

Prepare the rice, raisins, capsicums and sauce before you need them, up to several hours ahead.

Microwave the rice on High (100%) in a large, covered bowl with 3½ cups of boiling water and 1 teaspoon salt for about 20 minutes. Leave to stand for at least 10 minutes until all the water is absorbed.

Boil the raisins in the vinegar and water in a small saucepan for 5–10 minutes, until all the liquid has disappeared.

If using the capsicums, turn them under a grill for 5 minutes or until their skins have charred on all sides. Cool in a plastic bag, peel off the skin and chop the flesh into small pieces.

To make the sauce, shake all the ingredients together in a screw-top jar.

About 10 minutes before serving, assemble the dish.

With a fork, beat the eggs with 3 tablespoons of water or milk and ¼ teaspoon of salt. Heat a large non-stick frying pan and scramble the eggs in 1 tablespoon of butter or oil until they are set, then remove from the pan.

Return the pan to the heat and add 1 tablespoon oil. Lightly brown the pine nuts in the hot oil, then add the raisins and heat through. Add the rice and toss over fairly high heat until hot, then gently fold in the prepared capsicums, scrambled eggs and spring onions and heat through. Add the sauce, toss everything together, and serve alone or with sliced fresh tomatoes.

Special spiced rice

When you cook rice with these spices, you raise it to 'special treat' status. With two additions this recipe may be transformed into an interesting dessert.

Soak the saffron strands in ½ cup boiling water.

Melt the butter or oil in the microwave on High (100%), or in a saucepan. Add the cardamom pods, cloves, and the cinnamon stick broken into pieces. Heat for 2 minutes. Stir in the rice and heat for 1 minute longer, then add the bay leaf, orange and lemon peel, salt, 2 cups boiling water and the soaked saffron and liquid. Cover and microwave on Medium (50%) for 15 minutes, or simmer in the pan for 20 minutes. Leave to stand for 10 minutes.

Meanwhile, heat 1 tablespoon butter or oil in a small saucepan, add the currants and pine nuts, and stir until the pine nuts turn golden brown. Sprinkle the currants and pine nuts over the cooked rice, and serve.

SERVES 4–6:

¼ teaspoon saffron strands
½ cup boiling water
1 tablespoon butter or oil
4 cardamom pods, crushed
4 whole cloves
1 small cinnamon stick
1 cup basmati rice
1 bay leaf
20 cm strip orange peel
10 cm strip lime or lemon peel
1 teaspoon salt
2 cups boiling water
1 tablespoon butter or oil
¼ cup currants
¼ cup pine nuts

Takefumi rice

Spiced rice and eggs make an interesting quick meal.

In a saucepan with a tight lid, heat the water, salt, cinnamon, cloves and chilli sauce until boiling. Add the rice and simmer gently for 15 minutes, or until the rice is tender and the water is absorbed.

Melt the butter in a large frying pan. Sauté the onion, celery and garlic until tender but not browned. Add the beaten eggs, stir for 30 seconds, then add the hot spiced rice. Mix carefully but thoroughly, then serve with a salad.

SERVES 4:

3 cups water
1½ teaspoons salt
½ teaspoon cinnamon
8 whole cloves
3–4 drops hot chilli sauce
1½ cups long grain rice
50g butter
1 onion, sliced
¼ cup chopped celery
1–2 cloves garlic, chopped
3–4 eggs, lightly beaten

Egg fried rice

This is a useful and delicious way to use up small quantities of leftover vegetables.

Put the cooked rice in a large bowl, break in the eggs and add the salt. Add the chopped spring onions and stir until the rice is evenly coated in egg.

Heat a large, non-stick frying pan or wok. Heat the oil or butter and lightly cook the mushrooms and vegetables (but not the lettuce). Add the rice, then lift the mixture with a fish slice as it heats. The grains should separate as the mixture cooks.

When it is thoroughly heated through, add the shredded lettuce, stir briefly, and remove from the heat. (The lettuce should still be slightly crisp when the rice is served.) Taste, and add a little soy sauce if desired. Sprinkle with extra soy sauce and sesame oil just before eating.

SERVES 4:

4 cups cooked long grain white rice or
  brown rice*
2–3 eggs
½ teaspoon salt
6 spring onions
3–4 tablespoons oil or butter
1 cup sliced mushrooms
1–2 cups beansprouts, chopped capsicums, celery, etc.
½–1 cup shredded lettuce
soy sauce
sesame oil

* Use rice that has been cooked and left to cool for several hours. Freshly cooked, overcooked or soggy rice is not suitable for this dish.

Brown rice & lentil loaf

This grain-based loaf is surprisingly solid, satisfying and well flavoured.

SERVES 4–6:

½ cup brown rice
½ cup brown lentils
1 large onion
2 cloves garlic
2 tablespoons oil
½ cup sunflower seeds
1 teaspoon each: basil and marjoram
½ teaspoon thyme
1 teaspoon sugar
½ teaspoon salt
1 tablespoon dark soy sauce
freshly ground black pepper
¼ cup wheatgerm
2 eggs
1 cup grated cheese
¼ cup extra sunflower seeds
paprika

Cook the rice and lentils separately (pages 184 and 201), or use 1–1½ cups each of precooked rice and lentils if you have them on hand.

Preheat the oven to 180°C. Chop the onion and garlic and sauté in the oil until lightly browned. Add the sunflower seeds and herbs, and continue to cook for a few minutes.

Combine the sugar, salt, soy sauce, pepper, wheatgerm, eggs and half of the cheese in a large bowl. Stir in the cooked rice, lentils and the onion mixture, and mix until well combined.

Transfer the mixture to a carefully oiled or lined loaf pan. Sprinkle with the remaining cheese, sunflower seeds, and a little paprika.

Bake uncovered for about 45 minutes, until the centre feels firm when pressed. Remove from the oven and leave to stand for 5–10 minutes before turning the loaf out. Serve with a selection of cooked vegetables, or salad of your choice.

NOTE: *Leftovers taste good cold.*

Barley loaf

Pearl barley gives this loaf a wonderful texture.

SERVES 4:

1 cup pearl barley
3 cups boiling water
2 tablespoons oil
2 medium onions, sliced
2 cloves garlic, peeled and chopped
100g mushrooms, sliced
1 teaspoon each: basil and oregano
½ teaspoon each: thyme and salt
1 teaspoon sesame oil
1 tablespoon light soy sauce
3 eggs, lightly beaten
1 cup cooked spinach
1 cup grated cheese
paprika (optional)

Place the barley in a large saucepan or microwave bowl, and cover with the boiling water. Simmer gently on the stove for about 30 minutes, or cook in the microwave on Medium (50%) , until the grains are swollen and tender. Drain off any excess water and allow to stand.

Heat the oil in a large frying pan. Cook the onions and garlic until the onions are soft, then add the mushrooms and cook until soft.

Combine the onion mixture with the cooked barley and all the remaining ingredients, reserving half of the grated cheese. Mix thoroughly, then transfer the mixture into a well buttered or oiled 20 x 25cm casserole dish. Sprinkle with the remaining cheese, and a little paprika if you like.

Bake at 180°C for about 45 minutes, covering loosely for the first 30 minutes. The loaf is cooked when the top has browned and the centre is firm when pressed.

Serve with baked potatoes or crusty bread, and some colourful stirfried vegetables or a crisp salad.

Convenient couscous

Couscous is a busy cook's dream come true – invaluable for anyone who wants food on the table fast! Serve it plain, or experiment with different seasonings.

SERVES 4:

1 cup couscous
2 teaspoons butter (or 1 teaspoon each: olive oil and pesto)
2 cups boiling stock (or 2 teaspoons vegetable stock powder plus 2 cups boiling water)*
freshly ground black pepper
chopped parsley or other herbs

Put the couscous in a bowl and add the butter or your favourite pesto and olive oil. Add the boiling stock, or boiling water and stock powder. Cover and leave to stand for 5–6 minutes. At the end of this time, all the liquid will be absorbed. Stir in pepper, any precooked flavourings you like, and chopped parsley or herbs. Adjust the seasonings and serve.

* When serving couscous with a 'saucy' dish alongside, add 1½ cups of stock or water instead of 2 cups, so it soaks up the sauce on the plate.

Persian couscous

Colourful and tasty, with interesting textures.

SERVES 2–4:

1 cup couscous
2 teaspoons instant vegetable stock powder
½ teaspoon sugar
zest of ½ orange (optional)
2 cups boiling water
¼–½ cup chopped almonds or pine nuts
¼–½ cup currants
2 tablespoons butter or olive oil
¼–½ cup dried apricots
2 spring onions
¼ cup chopped coriander leaves

Stir the couscous, stock powder, sugar and grated orange zest together in a bowl. Add the boiling water, cover, and leave to stand for 6 minutes.

Heat the nuts and currants in the butter or oil in a small frying pan, over moderate heat, until the nuts brown lightly and the currants puff up. Chop the dried apricots with scissors, add to the pan and heat through.

Stir the hot nuts and fruit through the couscous. Serve hot, warm or at room temperature, adding the finely chopped spring onions and coriander just before serving.

Vegetable couscous

This recipe will fill your kitchen with its fragrant aroma as it simmers.

SERVES 4–6:

1 cup quick-cooking couscous
about 1 cup boiling water
2 medium onions, sliced
2–3 cloves garlic, chopped
2 tablespoons oil
1 teaspoon each: coriander, cumin and turmeric
½ teaspoon each: chilli powder and salt
¼ teaspoon each: ground cloves and allspice
425g can whole tomatoes
1 cup cooked or canned chickpeas
2 or 3 medium-sized potatoes
2 carrots
2 cups vegetables (peas, diced kumara or zucchini, etc.)
butter

Measure the couscous into a large shallow bowl, cover with about 1 cup of boiling water and leave to soak.

Cook the onions and garlic in the oil in a saucepan or frying pan until the onion is soft and transparent. Add the spices and salt, and cook for 1–2 minutes longer, stirring continuously. Chop the tomatoes and add with the juice to the onion mixture. Stir in the chickpeas, and the potatoes and carrots cut into 1cm cubes. Cover the pan

and simmer for 15–20 minutes, adding the remaining vegetables at intervals (the slower-cooking ones first), so that all are cooked at the same time.

Drain any excess water from the couscous, and toss with a little butter. Spread the couscous over a large plate and top with the cooked vegetable mixture.

Serve along or with a selection of your favourite curry accompaniments (page 186).

Spicy roasted vegetables with couscous

An interesting combination of colours, flavours and textures.

SERVES 3–4:

MARINADE
3 tablespoons olive oil or canola oil
2 tablespoons lemon juice
1 tablespoon dark soy sauce
1 teaspoon minced garlic
1½ teaspoons each: ground cumin and coriander
½ teaspoon sugar
¼ teaspoon each: chilli powder and ground cloves

ROASTED VEGETABLES
2 capsicums (red, yellow, green or a combination)
2 medium zucchini
2 medium carrots
1 medium red onion

COUSCOUS
1 cup couscous
310g can chickpeas
1 cup boiling water or vegetable stock
1–2 tablespoons chopped flat-leafed parsley or mint
salt and freshly ground black pepper, to taste

Measure the marinade ingredients into a screw-top jar and shake to combine.

Preheat the oven to 225°C. Halve, core and deseed capsicums, then cut the flesh into strips 1–2cm wide. Slice the zucchini and carrots lengthwise into strips or ribbons 0.5–1cm thick, and cut the onion into 8 thin wedges.

Put the prepared vegetables in a plastic bag with the marinade and toss everything together so the vegetables are evenly coated with the marinade. Leave the vegetables to marinate for 5–10 minutes, then tip them into a shallow roasting pan (or sponge-roll pan) and roast them for 12–15 minutes at 225°C.

While the vegetables cook, measure the couscous into a large bowl. Add the chickpeas then the boiling water or stock. Leave to stand for 5 minutes then fluff with a fork. Cut the cooked vegetables into 1–2cm pieces, then stir these into the couscous mixture along with any remaining marinade or cooking juices. Toss the mixture together, adding salt, pepper and chopped herbs to taste, and serve.

Quinoa & vegetable one-pan dinner

SERVES 2:

1 cup quinoa
1 tablespoon olive oil or canola oil
1 large onion, cut in 1cm cubes
2 cloves garlic, chopped
2 carrots, in 1cm cubes
2–3 stalks celery, sliced
1 teaspoon each: ground turmeric,
    dried oregano and cumin
2 teaspoons vegetable stock powder
2 cups boiling water
2 cups baby spinach leaves

Quinoa is the small round seed of an ancient spinach-like plant. Prized for its complete proteins, it has an interesting, slightly crunchy texture, and cooks fast.

Put the quinoa in a bowl, pour cold water over it and leave it to stand.

Add the oil, onion and garlic to a medium-sized lidded saucepan and cook, uncovered, until the onion is transparent. Add the carrots and celery and cook for 1–2 minutes longer.

Stir the spices and the stock powder into the saucepan. Drain the quinoa and add it to the saucepan with the boiling water.

Put on the lid, leaving it ajar, and cook on medium heat for 15 minutes, until the quinoa is tender and nearly all the liquid has evaporated. Stir in the baby spinach leaves and cook for 2–3 minutes longer.

Serve piled into bowls.

Quinoa & vegetable one-pan dinner

Nearly Niçoise couscous

Nearly Niçoise couscous

This 'warm weather' recipe is an easy and colourful meal that can be made, start to finish, in about 15 minutes – or prepared before work and assembled at the last minute.

Cover the eggs with hot water, bring to the boil and simmer for 10 minutes, then cool immediately in cold water. Shell the eggs when cool enough to handle.

Put the couscous in a fairly large bowl with the pesto (if using) and the stock powder, pour the boiling water over, stir to mix, then cover and leave to stand for at least 6 minutes.

Slice the beans diagonally in 3cm lengths and cook in a little water for 2–3 minutes, then drain. Cut the tomatoes into 1cm cubes.

Shake the dressing ingredients together in a screw-top jar.

Just before serving, fluff the couscous with a fork, then fold in most of the beans, tomatoes and chopped herbs. Transfer to a serving dish or individual plates or wide shallow bowls. Cut the hard-boiled eggs into quarters. Top the couscous with the eggs, the remaining beans, tomatoes and herbs, and the olives. Drizzle with the dressing and serve, with lemon wedges if you like.

This is good served warm, if freshly made. If pre-prepared, remove from the fridge ahead of time so it is at room temperature, before serving.

SERVES 2–3:

4 eggs

1 cup couscous

2 teaspoons basil pesto (optional)

2 teaspoons instant vegetable stock powder

1½ cups boiling water

about 10 green beans

3–4 large tomatoes

2 tablespoons chopped flat-leafed parsley

2 tablespoons chopped coriander leaves

8–12 black olives

DRESSING

1 clove garlic, minced

¼ teaspoon salt

1 teaspoon basil pesto (optional)

2 tablespoons lemon juice

3–4 tablespoons olive oil

Grilled polenta

This thick, flavourful porridge is left to set, then cut into cubes and browned lightly in a non-stick frying pan. Browned cubes, threaded on skewers with vegetables, are a good barbecue option.

Bring the water and salt to the boil. Add about ½ teaspoon each of the dried herbs, or more of fresh herbs.

Sprinkle the cornmeal into the water while stirring thoroughly. Keep stirring, over low-moderate heat, for about 5 minutes, until very thick. Remove from the heat and stir in the grated cheese.

Pour into a buttered or oiled 20cm square pan, and leave to cool for about 30 minutes, then turn out and cut into 2cm cubes.

Brown on all sides in a non-stick frying pan with a little butter or oil, then thread onto skewers, alternated with vegetables, and barbecue or grill.

VARIATION: *Pour the polenta into a round pan, then cut in wedges, brown, and serve with fried eggs, mushrooms, tomatoes, etc.*

SERVES 4:

2 cups water

about 1 teaspoon salt*

fresh or dried thyme, basil and oregano

1 cup coarse yellow cornmeal

½–1 cup grated cheese (optional)

* Polenta may seem salty at first, but the saltiness diminishes on standing.

Cheesy polenta with roasted summer vegetables

SERVES 2–3:

1 tablespoon olive oil or butter

2 cloves garlic, peeled and chopped

¼–½ teaspoon chilli paste (optional)

1 cup quick-cooking or regular polenta

about 3 cups vegetable stock (or 3 cups water and 3 teaspoons instant vegetable stock powder)

3 tablespoons grated parmesan

salt and freshly ground black pepper, to taste

sundried tomato or basil pesto, or tapenade (optional)

Alison makes this meal in 15–20 minutes, 'roasting' vegetables for two in her double-sided contact grill and simmering quick cooking polenta in less than 10 minutes.

Heat the butter or oil, garlic and chilli paste in a medium-sized non-stick frying pan until it bubbles, then add the polenta and 2 cups of the stock. Stir until smooth, then cover and simmer for about 5 minutes. Add more stock until it is like very sloppy mashed potato, then cover and cook for about 5 minutes for quick-cooking polenta or 10 minutes for regular polenta. Add extra stock or water to reach a soft mashed potato consistency.

At the end of this time beat in the parmesan cheese and enough salt and pepper to bring out the mild, pleasant flavour. (For extra flavour, stir in sundried tomato or basil pesto, or tapenade.) When the vegetables are cooked, pile the polenta on individual plates or bowls and top with the Roasted summer vegetables (see below).

Roasted summer vegetables

Use amounts and types of vegetable to suit. Quarter capsicums of several colours, removing seeds and pith, cut the stems of mushrooms level with their caps, cut aubergines in 1cm slices, zucchini in 1cm diagonal slices, and small red onions into quarters lengthwise.

Brush the vegetables on both sides with olive oil, either plain or flavoured with a crushed, sliced garlic clove. Roast uncovered at 200°C for 20–30 minutes, taking out mushrooms before other vegetables if necessary. Alternatively, cook for about 5 minutes in a contact grill preheated to medium; or cook under a regular grill, for 10–15 minutes, turning halfway through. Brush the vegetables with olive oil mixed with your favourite pesto, or with Tex-Mex dressing (page 99), just before serving.

Polenta & vegetable casserole

SERVES 4:

2 cups water

1 teaspoon salt

1 cup coarse yellow cornmeal

½ cup grated cheese

TOPPING

1 large onion, sliced

3 cloves garlic, finely chopped

1 tablespoon oil

1 green or red capsicum, chopped

2–2½ cups diced or sliced vegetables (e.g. carrots, zucchini, mushrooms)

425g can whole tomatoes

1 tablespoon pesto, or 2 tablespoons chopped fresh basil

½ teaspoon marjoram

½ teaspoon thyme

salt and freshly ground black pepper, to taste

1 cup grated cheese

Polenta is like slightly grainy mashed potato – good 'comfort food'. This recipe is prepared in several stages, but they're all quite simple and you can sit down to eat the finished dish less that an hour after you start.

To make the polenta, bring the water and salt to the boil in a large saucepan. Slowly sprinkle in the cornmeal, stirring continuously. (It should form a very thick paste as you keep on stirring.) Cook for 3–5 minutes. Remove from the heat and stir in the first measure of grated cheese, then spread the mixture over the bottom of a well buttered or oiled 22cm square casserole dish or cake pan. Allow to stand while preparing the topping.

Cook the onion and garlic in the oil until soft. Add the capsicum and the slower-cooking vegetables and continue to cook for several minutes, stirring occasionally. Add the remaining vegetables, the crushed canned tomatoes and juice, and the seasonings. Simmer until the vegetables are barely tender, then spread this over the prepared polenta.

Cover with the second measure of grated cheese and bake at 175°C for about 30 minutes.

Serve alone, or with a salad and bread rolls (page 245) as a substantial meal.

Cheesy polenta with roasted summer vegetables

High in protein, beans and pulses have long been regarded as a 'mainstay' of the vegetarian diet. They provide a great source of fibre and other nutrients. There is increasing evidence to suggest beneficial health effects when beans and pulses are included in the diet.

There is a huge variety of dried (and canned) beans and pulses available – allowing you to prepare hearty and delicious beany dishes with a minimum of fuss. From chillis to stews and burgers and burritos, we think the recipes here will tempt any palate.

Beans, pulses & tofu

Cooking & soaking beans

Some types of beans and lentils may be cooked without pre-soaking (see list and table below), however, thicker-skinned beans cook faster if soaked prior to cooking.

There are two soaking methods:

1. The long soak method: Cover beans with about four times their volume of cold water and leave to stand for 8 hours or longer, in refrigerator if longer.
2. The rapid soak method: Cover beans with about four times their volume of boiling water, or bring to boil and boil for 2 minutes, then leave to stand for 1-2 hours before cooking.

Cooking beans

We usually pour off and discard the soaking liquid. Replace with about the same quantity of fresh water. Bring to boil, add a tablespoon of oil to prevent excess frothing, and simmer with the lid ajar to prevent boiling over. You can flavour beans with garlic, onion, and herbs during cooking, but you must not add salt, sugar, lemon juice or tomato products until the beans are completely tender, since these toughen the beans. Beans are cooked when they are tender enough to squash with your tongue. Beans which are undercooked will put you off recipes which are excellent if made with properly cooked beans. Nearly cooked beans are not good enough!

Approximate cooking times for the types of beans we use most frequently are given in the table. Use these as a guide only, since times vary with the age and quality of the beans.

Add about ½ teaspoon of salt to 1 cup of dried beans, after cooking. Liquid drained from beans after cooking makes good stock for soups and sauces. Refrigerate up to 3-4 days.

Type of bean	soak	cook (minutes)
moong dahl	no	20-30
red lentils	no	25-35
brown lentils	no	30-45
black-eyed beans	no	30-45
split peas	no	40-60
mung beans	no	40-50
lima beans	yes	45-90
pinto beans	yes	60-90
red kidney beans*	yes	60-90
haricot/cannellini beans	yes	75-90
black turtle beans	yes	75-90
chickpeas	yes	90-150
soybeans	yes	120-180

'Need 15 minutes of rapid boiling during cooking.

If preferred, pre-soak first six varieties and reduce cooking time.

In a hurry?

You can:

- Use drained canned beans in place of cooked drained beans
- Change bean varieties to use a quick-cooking variety which needs no soaking, e.g., black-eyed beans or brown lentils
- Use canned beans (this may also mean changing varieties)
- Soak and cook beans in bulk, in advance, then freeze them ready for use
- Use a pressure cooker
- Cook beans without soaking, remembering cooking times will be considerably longer. (The resulting recipe may differ from the original recipe, but it will usually be good, nonetheless.)

Pressure-cooking beans:

Pressure cooking dramatically decreases the cooking times of dried beans. The times we recorded with a modern pressure cooker were impressive!

- Unsoaked black-eyed beans cooked in 15 minutes.
- Black-eyed beans, rapid-soaked for 1 hour, cooked in 5 minutes.
- Unsoaked kidney beans cooked in 35 minutes.
- Pinto beans and chickpeas rapid-soaked for an hour cooked in 15 minutes to the texture of canned beans.
- Unsoaked soybeans cooked to very soft in 45 minutes.

It is obviously worth investing in an efficient pressure cooker if you eat beans often and want to speed up their cooking times.

For best results you should follow the manufacturer's instructions. If these are not available, use the following as a guide.

- Use 4 cups of water to 1 cup dried beans.
- Do not fill the cooker more than half full, since beans froth as they cook.
- Add 1 tablespoon of oil to lessen frothing.
- Let the pressure fall over 2-3 minutes.
- Cook beans without seasonings, as suggested under cooking instructions here.

Yields & costs:

- 1 cup dried beans yields 2-3 cups drained cooked beans.
- 1 can (about 400g) cooked beans contains about 1 ½ cups drained beans.
- Canned beans save a lot of time but cost 3-4 times as much as home-cooked beans.

Rapid refried beans

SERVES 4:

1 large onion, diced
2 cloves garlic, finely chopped
1 tablespoon oil
1 small green capsicum, chopped
½ teaspoon chilli powder
1 teaspoon ground cumin
½ teaspoon dried oregano
½ teaspoon salt
½ teaspoon sugar
400g can kidney beans
1 tablespoon tomato paste

Use this mixture to make delicious nachos; or serve on rice, with a shredded lettuce or tomato salad to complete the meal.

Sauté the onion and garlic in the oil in a large saucepan or frypan. Add the capsicum, chilli powder, cumin, oregano, salt and sugar. Cook, stirring occasionally to prevent sticking, until the capsicum softens, then reduce the heat.

Drain the beans, keeping the liquid, and add the beans and the tomato paste to the rest of the ingredients in the pan. Heat through over moderate heat. Mash the mixture with a potato masher or fork, or, for a smoother mixture, process in a blender or food processor. Thin down with a little of the bean liquid if desired.

Taste, and adjust seasonings to suit.

Mexican rice & beans

SERVES 4:

2 tablespoons olive oil or canola oil
1 medium onion, diced
1–2 cloves garlic, peeled and chopped
1 large green capsicum, diced
1 cup long grain rice
1 teaspoon each: ground cumin and
    oregano
½ teaspoon chilli powder
300g can tomato purée
1½–2 cups hot water
425g can red kidney beans, drained
2 tablespoons chopped coriander
½–1 teaspoon salt
sour cream and chopped fresh
    coriander, to garnish

It may not be completely authentic, but this simple and delicious one-pot bean and rice mixture certainly tastes the part!

Heat the oil in a large, lidded saucepan. Add the onion and garlic and sauté, uncovered, until the onion is soft. Stir in the capsicum and cook, stirring frequently, for 1–2 minutes longer.

Add the rice and stir until it is evenly coated with oil. Cook, stirring frequently, until the rice has turned milky white, then add the cumin, oregano, chilli powder and tomato purée. Pour in 1½ cups hot water and stir until everything is well combined. Bring the mixture to the boil, then reduce the heat to a gentle simmer and cover. Cook for about 15 minutes or until the rice is just tender, stirring occasionally to make sure the rice doesn't catch on the bottom. If the mixture looks too dry during this time, add another ¼ cup water (repeat if necessary).

When the rice is cooked, stir in the beans and coriander, and add salt to taste. Serve as is, topping each serving with a dollop of sour cream and a little extra chopped fresh coriander. Or use as a filling for enchiladas or burritos.

Cheese burritos

SERVES 3-4

SALSA
1 ripe avocado
3 firm ripe tomatoes
425g can red kidney beans
1–2 spring onions, chopped
1–2 tablespoons chopped coriander
1 teaspoon ground cumin
1 tablespoon lime or lemon juice
1 tablespoon olive oil
salt and freshly ground black pepper

about 6 flour tortillas
1–1½ cups grated tasty cheese
about 2 cups finely chopped lettuce
sour cream
hot chilli sauce

So simple, yet so good!

Turn the oven grill on to preheat, then prepare the salsa. Peel and cube the avocado, and dice the tomatoes. Stir the avocado and tomatoes together with the drained beans, chopped herbs, cumin, lime juice and oil. Season to taste with salt and pepper.

Working one or two at a time, sprinkle each of the tortillas generously with grated cheese. Place them briefly under the grill until the cheese is melted. Serve immediately, accompanied with the salsa, chopped lettuce, sour cream and hot chilli sauce.

To assemble, place a generous handful of chopped lettuce in a line down the middle of each tortilla, then add a generous spoonful or two of salsa and top this with a little sour cream and chilli sauce to taste. Fold or roll the edges of the tortilla in towards the middle to make a tube, then eat!

Cheese burritos

Bulgar & bean 'chilli con carne'

The bulgar in this sauce thickens and gives it body, and the final combination of chopped wheat, beans and rice is nutritionally well balanced too.

SERVES 4–6:

¾ **cup bulgar**
1½ **cups boiling water**
2 **large onions, diced**
2 **cloves of garlic, finely chopped**
2 **tablespoons oil or butter**
2 **teaspoons ground cumin**
1 **teaspoon oregano**
½–1 **teaspoon chilli powder (to taste)**
1 **tablespoon soy sauce**
3 **tablespoons tomato paste**
2 **teaspoons sugar**
½ **cup hot water**
juice of 1 lemon
freshly ground black pepper, to taste
425g **can kidney beans, drained and rinsed**
sour cream and spring onions or chives, to garnish

Pour the boiling water over the bulgar and then leave to stand, stirring occasionally, while preparing the rest of the recipe.

Heat the oil or butter in a large saucepan or frying pan and sauté the onions and garlic until the onion is soft and beginning to turn clear. Stir in the cumin, oregano and chilli powder and continue to cook for a few minutes.

In a small bowl or cup, mix together the soy sauce, tomato paste, sugar and hot water. Pour this purée over the onion mixture, then stir in the lemon juice, black pepper and the kidney beans.

Add the bulgar and combine everything well. The mixture should be about the consistency of a thick spaghetti sauce. If you think that it is still too thick, add a little more water.

Allow to simmer over low heat for 5–10 minutes, stirring occasionally to prevent it sticking on the bottom.

Serve over brown or white rice, topped with sour cream and chopped spring onions or chives, accompanied by your favourite salad or cooked vegetables.

Mexican beans

Based on the Mexican staple – refried beans. It is delicious with corn chips and fried tortillas, plain or folded, large or small. The mixture should be the consistency of thick spaghetti sauce.

SERVES 4:

500g **red kidney beans**
6 **cups hot water**
2 **large onions, chopped**
3–4 **cloves garlic, chopped**
2–3 **medium carrots, chopped**
2 **teaspoons whole cumin seeds**
¼ **cup tomato sauce (ketchup)**
2 **tablespoons tomato paste**
1 **tablespoon cider or wine vinegar, or 2 tablespoons lemon juice**
2 **teaspoons salt**
2 **pickled jalapeno peppers, or Tabasco sauce to taste**

Cook the beans in the water until they are tender (page 201). Do not drain.

Add the onions, garlic, carrots and cumin seeds, and cook for 30 minutes more, or until all the vegetables are tender. Add the tomato sauce, tomato paste, vinegar or lemon juice, salt and the finely chopped jalapenos or the Tabasco sauce.

Simmer for 10–15 minutes longer, then mash or purée roughly in a food processor. Taste, and add extra ground cumin, salt, Tabasco, etc., if the flavour is not as strong as you like it. Refrigerate until required, or freeze for long storage.

Mexican tortillas

Tortillas are a type of Mexican flat bread. The traditional Mexican version is made from a special type of cornmeal, but you can also buy or make wheat flour tortillas.

Tortilla terminology can be confusing! Tortillas, cut into small wedges and baked or fried, are corn chips or tostaditos. Taco shells are made by folding and frying corn tortillas until crisp. Tostadas are tortillas fried flat until they are crisp.

Enchiladas are tortillas which are warmed, spread with sauce, then rolled, folded or stacked. If you want to make tostadas, taco shells, corn chips or enchiladas yourself, start with unfried, flexible tortillas. 'Burrito' refers to any flour tortilla rolled with a filling.

SUGGESTED TOPPINGS AND FILLINGS

- **Mexican or Rapid refried beans (page 202), hot or warm**
- **grated cheese**
- **shredded lettuce**
- **chopped spring onions, or onion rings**
- **sour cream**
- **extra chilli sauce**
- **chopped olives**
- **sliced avocado or guacamole**

Family and friends help themselves to whatever they want, starting with a layer of the beans.

Red beans & rice

This dish appears on menus throughout New Orleans, and is eaten by visitors and locals at all hours.

SERVES 4–6:

2 cups red kidney beans
6 cups water
50g butter
3 onions, chopped
4–6 cloves garlic, chopped
1 green capsicum, chopped
½ cup chopped parsley
2–3 bay leaves
1 teaspoon dried thyme
12 drops Tabasco sauce, or chilli powder, to taste
1 teaspoon salt
2 cups brown rice
butter (optional)

Put everything except the salt and rice into a large saucepan. Boil vigorously for 15 minutes, then turn down and simmer for 3–4 hours, until the beans are meltingly soft and quite mushy, forming a thick sauce. Remove the bay leaves, add the salt and adjust the seasonings, adding more herbs and chilli sauce if you like.

Cook the rice so that it will be ready when the beans are cooked.

Serve the beans on the rice, with a knob of butter on each serving if you like.

If you think it needs more colour and texture, depart from tradition and serve cubes of brightly coloured capsicums to sprinkle over the top, or stir them into the beans a few minutes before serving.

Red beans & rice

Black bean chilli

- -

SERVES 4–5:

1–1½ cups small black (turtle or tiger)
   beans*
1 medium onion, diced
1 medium green capsicum, diced
2 sticks celery, diced
3 cloves garlic, crushed
1 tablespoon oil
1 teaspoon ground cumin
½ teaspoon chilli powder
1 teaspoon basil
1 teaspoon oregano
½ –1 cup tomato purée
1 cup cooking liquid from beans
sour cream and spring onions or
   chives, to garnish

Black beans come in a variety of shapes and sizes. The small black beans used for this South American recipe have an interesting smoky flavour.

Cook the beans until very tender (page 201) , then strain, reserving the liquid.

Sauté the onion, capsicum, celery and garlic in the oil for about 5 minutes, without browning. Add the seasonings, tomato purée and reserved bean liquid.

Pour the onion mixture over the drained beans. Simmer for ½ hour, stirring occasionally, adding more liquid if necessary.

Serve over rice, garnished with sour cream and chopped spring onions or chives. A dish of stirfried or raw capsicums and a green salad are good accompaniments.

* Use the larger quantity of beans and tomato purée for a more substantial mixture.

African beans

- -

SERVES 4–6:

1½ cups dry black-eyed beans
2 medium onions, chopped
2 tablespoons oil
135g can tomato paste
410g can coconut cream
2 teaspoons paprika
½ teaspoon chilli powder, to taste
½ teaspoon cumin
2 teaspoons sugar
1 teaspoon salt
freshly ground black pepper, to taste

This recipe is particularly quick because black-eyed beans cook faster than most other beans. The sauce based on tomato and coconut cream is simple, colourful and delicious.

Cook the beans following the instructions on page 201.

In a saucepan, sauté the onions in the oil until they are soft and clear. Add the tomato paste, coconut cream and seasonings, stirring until they form a smooth and creamy sauce.

When the beans are cooked, drain and combine with the sauce.

Serve immediately, or, for even better flavour and texture, leave to stand and reheat when needed. Serve on brown or white rice, accompanied by a mixed green salad.

Home-style baked beans

- -

SERVES 4:

1½ cups haricot beans (or 2 x 400g
   cans cannellini beans)
2 onions
2–3 cloves garlic
2 tablespoons oil
425g can whole tomatoes (chopped)
   or diced tomatoes in juice
1 tablespoon tomato paste
2 tablespoons sugar
1 tablespoon dark soy sauce
1 teaspoon basil
½ teaspoon marjoram
¼ teaspoon thyme
salt and freshly ground black pepper
3 cups hot water

These beans, baked in herbed tomato sauce, bear little resemblance to the more mildly flavoured canned baked beans.

Cook the beans as described on page 201, then drain well. If using canned beans, rinse and drain well.

Preheat the oven to 160°C. Chop the onions into fairly large chunks, and roughly crush and chop the garlic. Combine these in a medium-sized roasting pan or shallow casserole dish, and coat with the oil. Bake, uncovered, for 30–40 minutes, or until the onion browns, stirring occasionally.

In a blender or food processor, or with a potato masher, combine the tomatoes and juice, tomato paste, sugar, soy sauce and herbs.

Stir the cooked beans, tomato mixture, all the seasonings and hot water into the onions and garlic, and bake, uncovered, at 160°C for a further 90 minutes, stirring occasionally. If at any stage the mixture seems too thick, add more water. Taste and adjust seasonings if required.

Serve with crusty bread and a green salad or cooked vegetables, or as part of a buffet meal.

Clockwise from top right: Black bean chilli; African beans; Home-style baked beans.

Bread-topped bean casserole

SERVES 4:

1 large onion
1 medium-large carrot
2 tablespoons olive oil or canola oil
2 cloves garlic, minced
1 red or green capsicum (or ½ of each)
6 brown mushrooms
1 teaspoon sugar
1 tablespoon flour
½ cup water
1 tablespoon tomato paste
½ teaspoon dried basil
¼ teaspoon dried thyme
425g can red kidney beans, drained
½–1 teaspoon salt
freshly ground black pepper, to taste
½ loaf French bread
1–2 tablespoons olive oil
½–1 cup grated cheese

There is something very warming about the way the rich dark filling hides under a crisp golden crust.

Preheat the oven to 225°C.

Peel, quarter and slice the onion, and slice the carrot, while the oil heats in a large frying pan. Add the onions, garlic and carrot, and cook, stirring frequently, until the onions are soft and clear.

While the onion mixture cooks, deseed and slice the capsicum and quarter the mushrooms. Add the sugar, capsicum and mushrooms to the onion mix and continue to cook, stirring frequently, until the onions have browned. Stir in the flour and cook for 1 minute longer, then add the water, tomato paste and herbs. Mix in the beans and season to taste with salt and pepper. Simmer gently for about 5 minutes, then transfer it to a lightly oiled or non-stick sprayed 20 x 25cm casserole dish. (The filling can be prepared ahead to this stage.)

Cut the French bread into 1cm thick slices, and pour the oil into a small shallow dish or saucer. Lightly dip one side of each slice of bread into the oil (it should just be moistened with oil, not soaked) and arrange the slices oiled side up over the top of the filling mixture, until it is all covered.

Sprinkle the bread topping with the grated cheese, to taste, then bake at 225°C for 10–15 minutes, until the filling is hot and the crust golden brown. Serve with some lightly cooked winter vegetables or a salad, and some bread or mashed potatoes.

VARIATION: *Chop or mash the filling mixture for a different texture.*

Bean & cheese casserole

SERVES 8:

2 cups pinto or kidney beans
3 onions
2 large or 3 medium cooking apples
2 tablespoons oil
1 teaspoon chilli powder, or to taste
1 teaspoon mustard powder
1 teaspoon cumin
1 teaspoon oregano
1 teaspoon salt
freshly ground black pepper
4 tomatoes, chopped
¼ cup white wine
2 cups grated cheddar or mozzarella
  cheese

This tasty casserole is extra-rich in protein, and makes an inviting winter dinner.

Cook the beans as described on page 201, until they are as soft as you like them, then drain. Although they get baked again later on, they will not become any softer, so do not hurry this step.

Chop up the onion and apple, then sauté in the oil until the onion is transparent and the apple is tender. Add the chilli, mustard and other seasonings. Combine the beans, onion mixture, chopped tomatoes and wine in a large casserole dish. Cover and bake at 180°C for 30 minutes. Stir in the grated cheese and then return it to the oven for another 10 minutes.

Serve with several plainly cooked vegetables, such as carrots, beans, broccoli or kumara, and with crusty bread if desired.

Bean stroganoff

Using soybeans in this recipe gives it an especially high protein content, but you may find their rather crunchy texture disconcerting. If so, replace the soybeans with any other beans..

Cook the beans until tender enough to eat without any more cooking (page 201), then drain and leave to stand while preparing the sauce mixture. Heat the butter or oil in a large frying pan or heavy-bottomed saucepan, and sauté the onions until soft and golden brown. Add the mushrooms and cook until soft.

Stir in the flour gradually, to prevent lumps forming. Add the paprika, salt and pepper, and cook a little longer, stirring continuously. Gradually stir in the milk to make a thick sauce, then stir in the sherry and soy sauce.

Reduce the heat and add the sour cream, chopped parsley and cooked beans. Allow to heat through, and then serve on noodles or rice.

SERVES 4–6:

1 cup soybeans
3 tablespoons butter or oil
2 onions, diced
150g mushrooms
¼ cup flour
1 tablespoon paprika
½ teaspoon salt
freshly ground black pepper, to taste
1 cup milk
2 tablespoons sherry
1 tablespoon dark soy sauce
½ cup sour cream
1 tablespoon fresh parsley, chopped
 (or 1 teaspoon dried parsley)

Short-order curried beans

Dress up canned baked beans using this recipe – maximum reward for minimum energy.

Peel and chop the onions and apples into small cubes. Mix with the oil in a small frying pan and sauté until golden brown. Stir in the curry powder. While they cook, prepare microwave baked potatoes or toast some bread or rolls.

Add the vegetable stock powder and water to the browned onion mixture and simmer for 2–3 minutes. Add the baked beans, and bring to the boil. Either simmer until the mixture thickens, or thicken with a little cornflour and water paste. Add parsley or coriander, if desired. Taste and adjust the seasoning if necessary.

Serve on buttered toast, over split microwaved potatoes, on toasted split rolls, or on reheated rice or pasta.

SERVES 2–3:

2 onions
1–2 apples
2 tablespoons oil
1 teaspoon curry powder
2 teaspoons vegetable stock powder
½ cup water
450g can baked beans
1–2 teaspoons cornflour
chopped parsley, coriander leaf
 (optional)

Bean feast

This tasty mixture is good served hot, warm, or at room temperature. Its flavour and texture improve with standing. Haricot beans cook relatively quickly, and have a good flavour and texture.

Soak the beans overnight, then boil in the water until tender enough to squash with your tongue on the roof of your mouth (page 201). Cool the beans in their cooking liquid until you are ready to make the rest of the recipe.

Put the oil, onions, potatoes, carrots and celery in a large saucepan. Stir over moderate heat until the vegetables are very hot, then add the salt, paprika, sugar, tomato paste, basil and oregano, plus the drained beans and 1½ cups of their cooking liquid. Simmer, stirring frequently, for 15 minutes. Add the pieces of cauliflower and sliced capsicum and cook for 5 minutes longer. Remove from the heat and add the chopped parsley.

Serve reheated, warm or at room temperature, sprinkled with more parsley. Taste before serving, and adjust the seasoning if necessary.

SERVES 8–12:

2 cups haricot or other beans
8 cups water
¼ cup oil
2 large onions, quartered and sliced
2 scrubbed potatoes, cubed
2 carrots, cubed
2–3 stalks celery, sliced
2 teaspoons salt
1 teaspoon paprika
2 teaspoons sugar
¼ cup tomato paste
1 teaspoon dried basil
1 teaspoon dried oregano
2 cups cauliflower pieces
1 green capsicum, sliced (optional)
about ½ cup chopped parsley

Vegetarian shepherd's pie

This dish is popular with meat eaters as well as vegetarians. Everyone will come back for more!

Cook the beans as described on page 201 until they are tender enough to mash with your tongue against the top of your mouth, before you combine them with the other filling ingredients. Leave them to stand in their cooking liquid until required, then drain, reserving 1½ cups of cooking liquid. (You may need to add a little extra water if using canned beans.)

While the beans cook, prepare the topping. Peel the potatoes, and cook in lightly salted water. Drain, and mash with the butter, half the grated cheese, and enough milk to get a good consistency. After mashing, beat with a fork until light and fluffy.

In a large saucepan or pan, cook the onions in the butter until tender and medium-brown. Do not hurry this step. Stir in the capsicum, then the flour. Stir over moderate heat until the flour has browned slightly, then add the instant stock, herbs, paprika and soy sauce. Stir in the 1½ cups bean cooking liquid and the tomato paste, and bring to the boil, stirring constantly. Add the drained beans, taste, and adjust the seasoning if necessary. Spread the mixture on the bottom of a lightly sprayed or buttered 20 x 25cm pan. Cover with the mashed potato. Sprinkle the remaining grated cheese over the surface.

Reheat at 180°C for 20–30 minutes, or in a microwave until the bottom centre feels hot to your hand. Brown the top under a grill. (The shepherd's pie may be refrigerated at this stage.)

For easier serving, leave to stand for a few minutes before cutting. A green vegetable such as brussels sprouts, beans or broccoli is good with this. You don't need anything else, except perhaps a glass of wine or beer.

SERVES 4–6:

1 cup kidney beans (or 2 x 400g cans kidney beans)
2 large onions, chopped
2 tablespoons butter
1 red or green capsicum, chopped
3 tablespoons wholemeal flour
1 teaspoon vegetable stock powder
1 teaspoon dried basil
1 teaspoon dried oregano
2 tablespoons chopped parsley
1 teaspoon paprika
1 teaspoon dark soy sauce
1½ cups bean cooking stock
2 tablespoons tomato paste

TOPPING

1kg potatoes
2 tablespoons butter
1 cup grated cheese
milk

Corn chip casserole

The ingredients are similar to nachos, but cooked like this the corn chips soften and take on a quite different character.

Peel and slice the onion while the oil heats in a large frying pan. Add the onion and garlic and sauté for 1–2 minutes, then chop and add the capsicum. Continue to cook, stirring frequently, until the onion is soft and turning clear. Remove the pan from the heat and stir in the seasonings, kidney beans, diced avocado, coriander and lemon juice. Leave to stand while you prepare the sauce.

Melt the butter in a medium-sized pot, add the flour and stir to make a smooth paste. Cook for 1 minute, stirring continuously, then add half of the milk. Continue stirring until the mixture thickens and comes to the boil, ensuring there are no lumps. Add the remaining milk and let the sauce thicken and boil again. Remove from the heat and stir in the cheese and extra seasonings (if using).

Arrange half of the corn chips in a layer over the bottom of a shallow, 25 x 30cm casserole dish. Cover these with the avocado–bean mixture, then cover this with the remaining corn chips. Pour the cheese sauce evenly over the layered mixture, then sprinkle with the additional grated cheese and dust with paprika. Bake at 220°C for 10–15 minutes or until the top is golden brown.

Serve alone or with rice and a shredded lettuce or tomato salad.

SERVES 4:

2 tablespoons olive oil or canola oil
1 medium onion
1–2 cloves garlic, chopped
1 red or green capsicum
1 teaspoon each: ground cumin and oregano
½ teaspoon each: chilli powder and salt
425g can red kidney beans, drained
1 large avocado, peeled and diced
2–3 tablespoons chopped fresh coriander
juice of ½ lemon

SAUCE

3 tablespoons (25g) butter
3 tablespoons flour
1½ cups milk
1 cup grated tasty cheese
½ teaspoon each: ground cumin and dried oregano (optional)
150g corn chips
½ cup grated cheese
paprika, to dust

Corn & pea patties

SERVES 4:

½ cup green or yellow split peas

1½ cups water

1 clove garlic, crushed

1 teaspoon ground cumin

1 teaspoon oregano

1 tablespoon oil

450g can whole kernel corn plus liquid

2 teaspoons bouillon

2 eggs

1 teaspoon paprika

1 teaspoon curry powder

1 cup self-raising flour

oil for frying

Green and yellow split peas add extra protein to an old favourite – corn fritters.

Put the split peas, water, garlic, cumin, oregano and oil in a medium-sized saucepan. With the saucepan lid ajar, cook the split peas gently for 1 hour, or until tender. After about 45 minutes, or a little earlier if the peas look dry, strain the corn kernels and add the liquid to the peas.

When the peas are tender and most of the liquid is gone, leave to cool to room temperature. Add the bouillon powder, unbeaten eggs, corn kernels, paprika and curry powder. Mix with a fork, then fold in the flour, mixing only until combined.

Place several spoonfuls of mixture in a frying pan containing hot oil about 5mm deep. Adjust the heat so the bottom of each patty is golden brown after about 2 minutes. Turn carefully, and cook the second side similarly. Keep cooked patties hot on a paper towel in a warm oven until all are done.

Serve immediately, with several cooked vegetables and/or salads, accompanied with sauce or chutney if you like.

Dahl

SERVES 4:

1 cup red or brown lentils, or moong dahl

4 cups water

2 tablespoons oil

2 onions, chopped

2 cloves garlic, chopped

2 teaspoons cumin seeds

1 teaspoon ground turmeric

2 teaspoons grated ginger root

1 teaspoon garam masala

1 teaspoon salt

Surround big bowls of dahl and rice with little plates of sweet and savoury, raw and cooked, crunchy and soft foods.

Boil the lentils or dahl in the water until tender and mushy — about 20 minutes for moong dahl, 20–30 minutes for red lentils, and 40 minutes for brown lentils.

In a frying pan, heat the oil and cook the onions, garlic, cumin seeds, turmeric and ginger over moderate heat until the onion is tender. Stir in the garam masala and the salt and remove from the heat.

Add the onion mixture to the pulses when they are soft, and simmer together for 5 minutes, boiling fast if the mixture needs thickening, or adding more water if it is too thick.

Serve immediately, or reheat, adjusting the seasonings just before serving.

Red lentil loaf

SERVES 6-8:

1½ cups red lentils

3 cups water

1 bay leaf

2 cloves garlic, roughly chopped

2 onions, sliced

25g butter

2 eggs

2 cups grated cheese

1 cup chopped tomatoes (fresh or canned)

3 slices wholemeal bread, crumbled

2 teaspoons salt

½ teaspoon curry powder

½ cup chopped parsley

Serve this loaf with mashed potatoes, green beans or broccoli, and a fresh tomato sauce.

Simmer the lentils gently with the water, bay leaf and garlic until they are tender and the water is absorbed.

Turn the oven on to preheat to 180°C.

In a saucepan, sauté the onions in the butter until transparent. Remove from the heat and add the eggs, cheese, chopped tomatoes, crumbled bread, salt, curry powder and parsley.

Remove the bay leaf from the cooked lentils and drain off any remaining water. Stir the lentils into the rest of the loaf mixture, then spoon into a well greased or lined loaf pan (alternatively, pour into a casserole dish and serve from this, without unmoulding).

Bake, uncovered, at 180°C for about 45 minutes, or until firm in the middle.

Curried red lentil dahl

Curried red lentil dahl

- -

Dahl dishes can be a little dull, but this one is an exception!

Heat the oil in a large saucepan, add the onion and garlic and cook, stirring frequently, until the onion has softened and is turning clear. Add the bay leaf, minced chilli and other spices, and stirfry for 1–2 minutes.

Stir in the lentils, water and instant stock (if using). Bring the mixture to the boil, then reduce the heat to a gentle simmer and cook until the lentils are tender, about 20–25 minutes. Remove the bay leaf, then add salt to taste and the coriander and stir.

Serve accompanied with one or more of the following: steamed basmati rice, naan bread, poppadoms, and your favourite chutneys, relishes or pickles.

SERVES 3–4:

1 tablespoon canola oil

1 large onion, diced

1–2 cloves garlic, crushed, peeled and chopped

1 large bay leaf

1 teaspoon minced red chilli

2 teaspoons each: curry powder and turmeric

2 teaspoons each: mustard and cumin seeds

1 cup split red lentils

2 cups water

2 teaspoons instant vegetable stock (optional)

½–1 teaspoon salt, to taste

2 tablespoons chopped fresh coriander

Lentil & vegetable curry

SERVES 4:

1½ cups red or brown lentils, or
    moong dahl
2–3 cups water
2 bay leaves
2 tablespoons oil or 25g butter
2 onions, chopped
2 cloves garlic, chopped
1 teaspoon turmeric
1 teaspoon ground cumin
1 teaspoon ground ginger
2–3 cups chopped vegetables
1 teaspoon salt
1 cup hot water
about ½ cup coconut cream
    (optional)

Brown or red lentils, teamed with small amounts of several vegetables and a tasty sauce. Use leftover cooked vegetables or lightly cooked fresh vegetables from the garden.

Cook the lentils or dahl in the water with the bay leaves until tender, adding more water if necessary. Red lentils and dahl should take 20–30 minutes, and brown lentils 40 minutes. While they cook, prepare the second mixture.

Heat the oil or butter, preferably in a large non-stick frying pan with a lid, and add the onion, garlic, and spices. Cook without browning for 5 minutes.

Prepare and cut up the vegetables into evenly sized cubes or pieces, starting with those that take longest to cook. Add each vegetable as it is prepared, tossing it with the onion, and covering the pan between additions. Add the salt and hot water after the last addition, and cook until all vegetables are barely tender. Add the cooked lentils and coconut cream (if using). Taste, and adjust seasonings, thickness, etc., boiling down or thickening with a little cornflour paste if necessary.

Serve in a bowl or on rice. A salad of tomatoes and capsicums with a yoghurt or French dressing makes a good accompaniment.

Butter chickpeas

SERVES 2–3:

2 tablespoons canola oil
1 medium onion, finely chopped
1–2 cloves garlic, peeled and chopped
2 teaspoons each: curry powder and
    garam masala
1 teaspoon each: ground ginger and
    cumin
300g can condensed tomato soup
½ cup cream
310g can chickpeas, drained
200g boiled new potatoes, cubed
1–2 tablespoons chopped coriander
½ teaspoon salt

This is Simon's version of butter chicken – without the chicken. The sauce is so good it could be served with almost anything, but chickpeas, new potatoes and paneer work really well.

Heat the oil in a large saucepan. Add the onion and garlic and cook, stirring frequently, until the onion is beginning to brown. Stir in the curry powder, garam masala, ginger and cumin. Continue to cook, stirring frequently, for 1–2 minutes longer.

Add the soup, cream, chickpeas and potatoes, and leave the sauce to simmer for about 5 minutes. Add the chopped coriander and salt to taste.

Serve over steamed basmati rice, accompanied with naan bread and a selection of chutneys and/or pickles.

Chickpea & pumpkin casserole

SERVES 6:

750g peeled and deseeded pumpkin,
    cubed
1 large onion, chopped
1–2 cloves minced garlic
50g butter
6–8 drops Tabasco sauce
2 cups grated tasty cheese
½–1 teaspoon salt
freshly ground black pepper, to taste
2 x 310g cans chickpeas, drained and
    rinsed

It's hard to explain what makes this simple casserole so good, but it really is delicious.

Preheat the oven to 180°C.

Simmer the pumpkin cubes in a little water until tender, then drain well.

Sauté the onion and garlic in butter until transparent, then mash with the pumpkin, keeping the mixture slightly chunky.

Mix in the Tabasco sauce and grated cheese. Taste after adding the cheese, and add salt and pepper to taste. Gently stir in the drained chickpeas.

Spread the mixture in a large (23 x 23cm) non-stick baking dish that has been lightly oiled or sprayed, and heat through in the oven at 180°C until it is bubbly at the edges and hot in the centre.

Chickpea & spinach curry

This dish has it all – not only is it easy and delicious, it is a complete meal, and it's relatively low in fat and high in fibre.

Thaw the spinach (microwave for 6–8 minutes on Low (30%). Do not drain.

Heat the oil in a large pan. Add the chopped garlic, grated ginger and diced onion. Stirfry until the onion has softened and is turning clear. Add the curry powder, garam masala, cumin seeds (if using) and bay leaves. Cook for 1 minute, then add the spinach with its liquid and the tomatoes in juice. Crush and break up the tomatoes, then stir in the potatoes and the chickpeas.

Simmer the mixture gently for 15 minutes, or until the potato cubes are tender, adding a little of the water if the mixture begins to look too dry. When the potatoes are cooked, season to taste with salt and pepper and add the chopped coriander.

SERVES 4:

250g frozen spinach, thawed
2 tablespoons canola oil
2–3 cloves garlic, peeled and chopped
2 tablespoons grated ginger root
1 medium-large onion, diced
2–3 teaspoons curry powder (mild or hot)
2 teaspoons garam masala
½–1 teaspoon cumin seeds (optional)
2–3 bay leaves
400g can whole tomatoes in juice
2–3 medium (250g) potatoes, cut into
    1cm cubes
310g can chickpeas, drained
¼–½ cup water, if required
½–1 teaspoon salt
freshly ground black pepper, to taste
2 tablespoons chopped coriander

Chickpea & pumpkin casserole

Chickpea falafels

SERVES 3–4:

1 cup chickpeas
4 cups boiling water
½ medium onion
2 cloves garlic, peeled
½ cup chopped parsley
2 teaspoons cumin
½ teaspoon allspice
1 teaspoon salt
olive oil or canola oil to fry

TO SERVE
3–4 (20cm) pita breads
lettuce leaves
cherry tomatoes, quartered
red onion, thinly sliced

These are crunchy little chickpea patties. They are delicious stuffed into pita bread pockets with some salad and a little Tahini yoghurt sauce.

Place the chickpeas in a bowl and cover them with about 4 cups boiling water, leave to soak for 8 hours (or overnight), then drain well.

Put the onion and garlic in a food processor and process until finely chopped. Add the chickpeas and process until coarsely chopped, then add the remaining ingredients, except the oil. Process again until the mixture is about the texture of dryish crunchy peanut butter.

Divide the mixture into quarters, then divide each quarter into four smaller 'blobs'. Shape each blob into a flat, round patty about 1cm thick and 4–5cm across.

Heat 2–3mm oil over a medium heat in a non-stick frying pan, then gently add 4–6 of the patties and cook for 3–4 minutes each side until crisp and brown. (Reduce the heat if they are browning too fast; they need to be cooked through.) Drain the cooked falafel on paper towels.

Warm the pita breads, then cut them in half crosswise and open them to form pockets. Stuff a few lettuce leaves, some tomato pieces, a few slices of onion and two of the falafel into each pocket. Add a spoonful or two of Tahini yoghurt sauce or Sesame cream sauce (below) to each and serve, with napkins handy.

NOTE: *The falafel can be cooked ahead and reheated gently in a frying pan or the microwave before serving.*

Tahini yoghurt sauce

½ cup natural unsweetened yoghurt
2 tablespoons tahini (sesame paste)
2 tablespoons lemon or lime juice
½ teaspoon paprika
salt and freshly ground black pepper, to taste

Measure the first four ingredients into a small bowl and whisk until smooth, then season to taste. Serve spooned into the falafel pita pockets.

Sesame cream sauce

1 tablespoon tahini (sesame paste)
2 tablespoons lemon juice
2–4 tablespoons water
salt
few drops hot chilli sauce

If possible, make this sauce about half an hour before you want it, since its texture improves on standing. Measure the tahini into a bowl that holds about 1 cup. Add the lemon juice and enough water to mix it to a thin, smooth cream. Add salt to taste, and chilli sauce until it is as hot as you like it.

Spiced nut cutlets

Spiced nut cutlets

- -

Here it is – our version of the original 'nut cutlet'. If handled carefully, these can be barbecued quite successfully.

Place the nuts and sunflower seeds in a food processor and chop until the mixture resembles coarse breadcrumbs. Put the nuts and seeds in a large bowl. Process the bread into crumbs, and add to the chopped nuts.

Peel and quarter the onion and roughly chop the carrot. Process these until finely chopped. Add the eggs, soy sauce, spices, chopped coriander (if using) and pepper, and process briefly, then combine with the chopped nuts and breadcrumbs. Mix thoroughly.

Divide the mixture into 8 portions and shape into cutlets, wetting your hands with cold water to prevent the mixture from sticking. Heat the oil in a large frying pan and cook the patties for about 5 minutes each side, until golden brown and firm when pressed in the middle.

VARIATION: *To barbecue, brush the patties with oil, cook as above on a lightly oiled hotplate, or place in a folding wire rack (available in most barbecue shops) and cook until browned and firm. Serve in toasted hamburger buns with sweet chilli sauce or Peanut sauce (page 91) and all the trimmings!*

SERVES 8:

½ cup unblanched peanuts
½ cup cashews or almonds
½ cup pine nuts
½ cup sunflower seeds
2 slices bread
1 medium onion
1 carrot
2 eggs
2 teaspoons dark soy sauce
½ teaspoon garlic salt
½ teaspoon ground cumin
½ teaspoon chilli powder (optional)
1 tablespoon chopped coriander
    (optional)
freshly ground black pepper, to taste
1–2 tablespoons oil

Red bean burgers

SERVES 3–4:

½ small onion, quartered
1 slice firm-textured bread
1 clove garlic, minced
1 large egg
¼ cup finely grated parmesan
400g can red kidney beans
1 teaspoon ground cumin
1 teaspoon balsamic vinegar
   (optional)

COATING
3 slices stale bread (crusts are fine)
1 large egg

As long as you have a food processor, you can make these burgers very quickly. Hold your mouth the right way when shaping and coating them, because the uncooked mixture is soft.

First crumb the 3 slices of stale bread for the coating in the food processor, and put it aside in a shallow dish.

Chop the onion, 1 slice bread (broken in several pieces) and garlic in the food processor, then add the egg and the parmesan.

Tip the beans from the can into a sieve. Drain and rinse them well, since any bean liquid will make the burgers too soft. Add the beans to the food processor with the cumin and balsamic vinegar, if using. Process in bursts until the beans are fairly finely chopped (but not a smooth purée) and the mixture is just firm enough to shape into 4 large (or 6 smaller) evenly sized balls, wetting your hands with cold water to prevent the mixture from sticking.

Using a fork, beat the egg for the coating in a shallow bowl until the white and yolk are well combined.

Heat a frying pan with enough oil to cover the bottom. Turn each ball first in the crumbs, then in the egg, then in the crumbs again. Flatten to make patties about 10cm across. Place each patty in the pan as it is ready, and cook over fairly low heat for 5 minutes per side (for the 4 larger burgers), or 3–4 minutes per side (for the 6 thinner burgers). Eat straight away, or reheat on a barbecue when ready to serve.

Serve in toasted hamburger buns with your favourite hamburger trimmings, or serve with vegetarian gravy (page 149) and cooked vegetables.

VARIATION: *If you don't have a food processor, replace the bread in the burger mix with 3 tablespoons fine dry breadcrumbs, grate the onion, and mash the beans, then mix everything with a fork. Use fine dry breadcrumbs for the coating.*

Brown lentil burgers

SERVES 4–5:

½ cup brown lentils
1 bay leaf
2 medium onions
2 cloves garlic
2 tablespoons oil or butter
1 tablespoon parsley
½ teaspoon each: dried basil and
   marjoram
¼ teaspoon (a large pinch) dried
   thyme
1 teaspoon salt
freshly ground black pepper, to taste
½ cup fresh wholemeal breadcrumbs
2 eggs
2 tablespoons tomato paste
2 teaspoons dark soy sauce
½ cup flour

These burgers take a little longer to make – unless you have some cooked lentils on hand. They have a definite firm texture, much like meat burgers.

Cook the lentils in water with the bay leaf until they are tender (page 201). Remove from the heat, drain, and remove the bay leaf.

Finely chop the onions and garlic, and sauté in the oil or butter until the onion is soft and clear. Add the herbs, salt and pepper.

Put the lentils in a large bowl, add the onion mixture, then mix in the remaining ingredients. Divide the mixture into 8–10 evenly sized portions. Shape each portion into a 10–12cm patty, wetting your hands with cold water to prevent the mixture sticking. If the mixture won't hold its shape, add some more breadcrumbs or a little more flour until it does. Cook in a little oil until lightly browned on each side and firm when pressed lightly in the middle.

Marinated tofu (for burgers & kebabs)

Square slabs of marinated tofu, sautéed in a little oil, make good burgers or toasted sandwiches. Sauté tofu cubes for a few minutes on all sides, then thread them with vegetables on kebab sticks, which are then carefully grilled or barbecued.

SERVES 4:

about 500g extra-firm tofu
¼ cup corn or soya oil
¼ cup lemon juice
¼ cup dark soy sauce
2 large cloves garlic, chopped
1 tablespoon sesame oil
1 teaspoon dried oregano
hot chilli sauce to taste

Drain the tofu, cut into 15mm thick x 10mm square slices, or into 2cm cubes, and leave to stand while you prepare the marinade.

Measure the remaining ingredients into a large plastic bag, using enough hot chilli sauce to give the hotness you like.

Put the bag in a shallow baking pan and place the tofu in it so that the slices or cubes lie flat. Suck out the air, so that the tofu is surrounded by the marinade, and fasten the top with a rubberband. Leave for at least 4 hours, or up to 48 hours, turning occasionally.

Brown the drained tofu cubes in a non-stick frying pan with a few drops of oil, over moderate to high heat, for 30–40 seconds per side. Cook the drained tofu slices for several minutes per side on medium heat, since the slices will not be grilled later.

To make the kebabs, toss mushrooms, small tomatoes, red and green capsicum squares and cubes of zucchini or aubergine in the marinade, and thread onto skewers with the lightly sautéed cubes of marinated tofu. Grill at about 5cm from the heat, for about 5 minutes per side, turning once, and brushing with extra marinade if desired. Serve the kebabs on rice, noodles, bulgar, etc. They taste good with tomato sauce.

Serve the marinated tofu slices in toasted rolls or between slices of toasted bread, with tomato relish and other burger accompaniments.

Tofu burgers

This recipe serves as a good way to introduce tofu to your diet.

SERVES 4:

250g firm tofu
1 medium onion, finely diced
2–3 cloves garlic, finely diced
1 tablespoon dark soy sauce
1 tablespoon sherry (or 1 tablespoon water and dash of lemon juice)
¼ teaspoon ground ginger
1 tablespoon nutritional or brewer's yeast
¼ cup sunflower seeds
¼ cup wholemeal flour
freshly ground black pepper, to taste

Remove the tofu from its package and stand it on a sloping board for a few minutes, allowing any excess liquid to drain away. Crumble the tofu into a bowl, add the diced onion and garlic, then the remaining ingredients.

Mix together well, then, working with wet hands, divide the mixture into 8 evenly sized balls. Shape each ball into a 7–10cm patty.

Cook for 5 minutes each side, or until the burgers are golden brown.

Sweet & sour tofu

SERVES 2:

200–300g firm or extra-firm tofu
2 tablespoons oil
1 large onion
1 green or red capsicum (or ½ of each)
1 tablespoon oil
1 tablespoon cornflour
¼ cup brown sugar
2 tablespoons wine vinegar
1½ teaspoons light soy sauce
½ cup water
red food colouring (optional)

Fast and colourful, this sweet–sour mixture is ready in less than the time it takes rice to cook.

Cut the tofu into 1cm cubes and brown evenly on all sides in 2 tablespoons oil in a non-stick frying pan. This should take about 5 minutes.

Cut the onion and capsicum into 1cm pieces. Once the tofu is cooked, remove it from the pan. Sauté the onion and capsicum in the pan, in 1 tablespoon oil.

When the onion is tender, but not browned (about 5 minutes), stir in the cornflour and brown sugar, then add the vinegar, soy sauce and water, and bring to the boil, stirring constantly. Colour red with food colouring if desired. Stir the tofu into the sauce, and serve over rice or noodles.

VARIATION: *Replace the water and half the sugar with pineapple juice. Stir pineapple cubes into the hot sauce before adding the tofu.*

Oriental tofu & noodles

SERVES 4:

200g quick-cooking egg noodles*
3–4 spring onions
3 cups boiling water
2 tablespoons dark soy sauce
1 tablespoon dark sesame oil
½ teaspoon brown sugar
½ teaspoon salt
¼ teaspoon garlic powder
about 300g deep-fried tofu
385g can whole mushrooms in brine
    (reserve the brine)
185g can water chesnuts, drained
½ cup walnut pieces or roasted
    cashews

GLAZE

1 tablespoon cornflour
2 tablespoons lemon juice
2 tablespoons sherry
2 teaspoons dark soy sauce
1 teaspoon brown sugar
¼ teaspoon ground ginger
¼ teaspoon garlic powder
½ cup water
brine from mushrooms

* The noodles used in this recipe are available in stores supplying Asian foods. They do not have sachets of dried stock enclosed.

This is a very quick and simple recipe if you can buy ready-fried tofu. Deep-fried tofu is golden brown, crisp, and chewy – quite different in appearance and texture from plain tofu. To fry it yourself, cut firm or extra-firm tofu into 1cm slices, pat it dry, then deep-fry it for about 10 minutes, or until it has a golden brown, crisp crust.

Break the blocks of noodles into a large saucepan. Chop the spring onions over them. Combine the water, soy sauce, sesame oil, sugar, salt and garlic powder in a jug or bowl, pour this mixture over the noodles, then heat the saucepan until the liquid boils, and cook for 3 minutes. Cover, turn off the heat, and stir occasionally while preparing the rest of the recipe.

Cut the deep-fried tofu into slices about 1cm thick. Open and drain the mushrooms, reserving the liquid, and halve or quarter the mushrooms. Mix together the tofu, mushrooms, water chesnuts and nuts.

Combine the remaining ingredients in a small saucepan, then bring to the boil, stirring constantly, to make a lightly thickened glaze. Thin down with extra water if necessary, then gently stir in the tofu, mushrooms and nuts.

Arrange the prepared noodles (which should have absorbed all the liquid) in a shallow serving dish, top with the glazed tofu mixture, heat if necessary, and serve.

VARIATION: *Mix stirfried beansprouts, celery, etc., through the noodles.*

Eggy tofu

The tofu is sautéed until crusted, mixed first with quick-cooking vegetables, then with an egg to hold it together, and finally coated with an interesting sauce.

Heat the oil in a non-stick frying pan. Cook the tofu cubes in the hot oil until all sides are golden brown. Add the mushrooms and spring onions, and stirfry for 1–2 minutes until wilted.

Beat the egg with a fork to combine well. Add the egg to the tofu mixture in the frying pan, stirring until the egg sets.

Stir the remaining ingredients together in another container. Add this mixture to the pan, and heat until it thickens and turns transparent.

Sprinkle with chopped parsley or chives, and serve immediately on rice, toast or noodles.

SERVES 1:

2 teaspoons oil

about 100g extra-firm tofu, drained
  and cubed

¼–½ cup sliced mushrooms

1–2 spring onions

1 egg

¼ cup water

2 teaspoons Kikkoman (or other light
  Japanese) soy sauce

¼ teaspoon sesame oil

hot pepper sauce, to taste

1 teaspoon cornflour

chopped parsley or chives, to garnish

Oriental tofu & noodles

We know that you will be very popular when you cook the recipes from this chapter! Few people can resist pies and pastry, and the end results really are delicious.

You may find that it takes a while the first time you make these recipes, but after you have done it once or twice, you will be able to make these dishes remarkably quickly. Do try the self-crusting quiches – the first time we made these, we were astounded at the way a type of crust formed below the filling!

Pies & pastries

Pastry for pies

Homemade short pastry contains less fat than bought flaky pastry. It is particularly good for flans and quiches (single-crust pies). It is less likely to become soggy, and shrinks less during cooking.

One cup of flour makes enough pastry for a large single-crust pie. Double these amounts for a pie with filling enclosed in pastry (a double-crust pie).

Short pastry

MAKES 250G:

1 cup plain or wholemeal flour
60–75g cold butter
about ¼ cup cold water
1–2 teaspoons lemon juice (optional)

Traditional method: Measure the flour into a mixing bowl. Cut the butter into about 9 cubes. Cut or rub the butter into the flour, using a pastry blender, your fingertips or two knives, until the butter is in small pieces and the mixture resembles rolled oats.

Mix the water and lemon juice (if using). Add about ¼ cup of the water, a few drops at a time, tossing the mixture with a fork until it will form a ball when pressed with your fingers. Chill for 5–10 minutes before rolling out.

Food processor method: Fit the food processor with the metal cutting blade. Cut the butter into about 9 cubes. Put the flour and butter into the food processor bowl. Do not process. Add 1–2 teaspoons lemon juice to the cold water for extra-tender pastry, if you like. Process using the pulse button, adding the water in a thin stream while chopping the butter through the flour.

Test at frequent intervals to see if the particles are moist enough to press together to form a ball. The mixture will still look crumbly at this stage. (If a ball of dough forms in the processor, the mixture is too wet.) Chill for 5–10 minutes before rolling out.

NOTE: *Overmixing or too much water makes tough pastry.*

Easy 'flaky' pastry

This is not a true flaky (or puff pastry), but it is richer and flakier than a 'standard' savoury short pastry. It's very easy to make with a food processor.

MAKES 400G:

1½ cups flour
½ teaspoon baking powder
100g cold butter
½ cup cold milk
1 teaspoon white wine vinegar

Measure the flour and baking powder into a food processor fitted with the metal chopping blade. Cut the cold butter into 9 cubes and add to the flour. Process in short bursts until the butter is cut into pieces about 5mm across.

Mix the milk and vinegar. Processing in brief pulses, slowly pour in just enough liquid to make the pastry mixture look like breadcrumbs. Test at frequent intervals to see if the pastry is moist enough to press together to form a ball. Press the dough into a flattened ball and chill for about 10 minutes.

Filo pastry

Filo is fun! Although it costs more than regular bought pastry, it may be used for several different filo-wrapped foods, which will melt in your mouth in a very satisfying way. When you buy them, the sheets of filo should be quite soft and flexible, and you should be able to roll and fold them without any cracking and breaking. Always rewrap, seal, and refrigerate unused filo promptly, to stop it drying out.

Filo pastry can be used to replace bought pastry or homemade short pastry in other recipes if you like, following the cooking instructions for Avocado flan (page 229) given here. Don't be heavy-handed with the butter or oil when brushing the sheets between layers of filo – a few dabs will do. (Spray-on cooking oil makes this very easy and works well.) You can try layering filo without any butter between the sheets, if you like. The sheets will brown more quickly and be very crisp and light-textured.

Blue cheese & mushroom packages

MAKES 6–8:

1 medium onion, finely chopped
2 cloves garlic, crushed
2 tablespoons butter
200g mushrooms, chopped
250g cream cheese, softened
50g blue cheese
½ teaspoon sugar
¼ teaspoon dried thyme
spring onion, chopped
1 tablespoon sherry (optional)
6–8 sheets filo pastry
100g butter, melted

These little packages make very elegant dinner-party food. Shape them into small triangles or rectangles.

Preheat the oven to 200°C.

Sauté the onion and garlic in the butter. When soft, add the mushrooms, and cook until they begin to soften. Reduce the heat to very low, then stir in the cream cheese. (If the cream cheese is cold or very firm, it may pay to soften it by stirring or mashing first.) Crumble in the blue cheese while stirring, then add the sugar, thyme, spring onion and sherry (if using).

Remove the filo sheets from the package. Lay one sheet on a dry surface, lightly brush with melted butter and then fold the sheet in half, lengthwise for triangles or crosswise for packages. Place about ¼ cup of filling on the pastry and roll or fold it into the shape desired, completely enclosing the filling. Do not roll too tightly or the package may burst during cooking. Cut a slash on top as a further precaution against splitting. Repeat until you have used all the filling.

Place the packages on a buttered oven tray, and bake at 200°C for 15–20 minutes or until golden brown. One package per person is usually enough because of the rich filling.

Vegetable flan

SERVES 3–4:

1 uncooked pastry crust (about 250g
    pastry)*
3 eggs
½ cup sour cream
¼ cup milk
½ teaspoon salt
 freshly ground black pepper, to taste
1½ cups grated cheese
1–1½ cups cooked vegetables,
    e.g. asparagus, broccoli, corn,
    mushrooms, spinach, well drained
paprika, to dust (optional)

You can use the same basic recipe to make a flan or quiche from a wide variety of cooked vegetables, depending what you have on hand!

Preheat the oven to 200°C.

Thinly roll out the bought or homemade pastry to line a shallow 23cm or deeper 17cm flan pan.

In a medium-sized bowl, whisk together the eggs, sour cream, milk, salt, pepper, and 1 cup of the grated cheese.

Arrange the vegetables in the pie shell, then carefully pour in the egg mixture. Sprinkle the top with the remaining grated cheese and dust with paprika (if using).

Bake in the middle of the oven at 200°C for 20 minutes, then reduce the heat to 180°C and bake until the filling is set in the middle, around 10 minutes (a deeper flan may take another 10–15 minutes).

Jane's potato flan

SERVES 3–4:

150–200g homemade or pre-rolled
    flaky pastry
1 cup cottage cheese
1 egg, beaten
¼ cup sour cream
1 teaspoon salt
2 teaspoons finely chopped spring
    onion
1 cup mashed potato
about 2 tablespoons grated parmesan

This recipe, from Alison's friend Jane, is great served with a salad for lunch, or as an addition to a buffet meal.

Preheat the oven to 220°C.

Roll out the pastry until it is nice and thin, and use it to line a 20cm flan dish or pie plate.

Combine the cottage cheese, egg and sour cream in a food processor or blender (press them through a sieve if you want a really smooth mixture). Add the salt, spring onion and mashed potato and process again until combined. Turn the potato mixture into the unbaked pie crust and sprinkle liberally with the cheese.

Bake at 220°C for 30–40 minutes, until the pastry and the top are lightly browned. Serve warm with salad.

Spinach & feta pies

These very simple little pies are loosely based on Greek spanakopita. They look great, and take a minimum of effort.

Preheat the oven to 200°C.

Heat the oil in a medium-sized frying pan, add the onion and cook until softened. Stir in the pine nuts (if using) and continue to cook until these are golden brown.

While the onion cooks, squeeze as much liquid as you can from the thawed spinach. Place the spinach in a large bowl and add the crumbled cheese, then the seasonings and the onion mixture. (The quantity of salt required will depend on the saltiness of the feta – vary it to taste.) Add the egg and stir until well mixed.

Lay one sheet of filo on a dry surface and brush it lightly with oil, then fold it lengthwise to make a long, narrow rectangle. Place about ¼ cup of the filling mixture (don't be too generous) close to one end of the strip, then fold the corner up diagonally to cover the filling (so the bottom edge meets the side). Keep folding (straight then diagonally) until you reach the end of the strip. Fold any extra pastry under the package, brush lightly with oil or melted butter and place on a baking tray. Repeat until all the filling is used.

Bake at 200°C for 10–12 minutes until golden brown and firm when pressed gently in the centre. Serve hot, warm or cold.

MAKES 8–10:

1 tablespoon olive oil

1 medium onion, diced

¼ cup pine nuts (optional)

200–250g frozen spinach, thawed and drained

100–150g feta cheese, crumbled

¼ teaspoon each: dried basil and thyme

¼ teaspoon freshly grated nutmeg

¼–½ teaspoon salt, to taste

freshly ground black pepper, to taste

1 large egg

8–10 sheets filo pastry

about 2 tablespoons melted butter or olive oil

Spinach & feta pies

Easy tomato & feta 'tart'

SERVES 4:

2 sheets (about 300g) pre-rolled flaky
    pastry, thawed
2 tablespoons tomato paste
1 teaspoon dried basil or 1 tablespoon
    pesto
1 tablespoon water
½ teaspoon dried marjoram
½ teaspoon salt
grind of freshly ground black pepper
250g small ripe tomatoes
1 small red onion
½ medium yellow or red capsicum,
    deseeded
1 medium zucchini
1–2 cloves garlic, crushed, peeled and
    chopped (optional)
about 8 basil leaves, roughly shredded
2 tablespoons olive oil
100g feta cheese, crumbled
salt and freshly ground black pepper,
    to taste

This easy 'tart' is similar to a pizza. It looks and tastes great, and as it uses bought, pre-rolled pastry it is really simple to prepare.

Preheat the oven to 200°C.

Lay the first sheet of pastry on a lightly oiled or non-stick sprayed baking sheet. Brush the surface lightly with water, then lay the second sheet exactly on top. Roll or press the two sheets lightly together. Without cutting right through the pastry, run a sharp knife around the sheet about 1.5–2cm inside the edge, marking out a smaller square.

Mix together the tomato paste, dried basil or pesto, water, marjoram, salt and pepper. Spread this paste evenly over the surface of the smaller square, trying to keep the edge clean. Cut each of the tomatoes and the onion into 6–8 small wedges, and slice the capsicum into strips about 1cm wide. Halve the zucchini lengthwise and cut into thin (5mm) ribbons.

Combine the vegetables, garlic (if using) and basil leaves in a plastic bag or bowl. Add the olive oil, and stir gently until the vegetables are well mixed and evenly coated with oil.

Arrange the prepared vegetables over the paste-covered base, then sprinkle the tart evenly with crumbled feta. Season with salt and pepper to taste, then bake at 200°C for 20–25 minutes, or until the crust is golden brown.

Serve hot, warm or cold with a green salad or as part of a picnic buffet.

Cheesy onion flan

SERVES 4–6:

50g very cold butter
¾ cup flour
¼ cup grated cheese
2–3 tablespoons cold water
1 tablespoon oil
1 large onion, chopped
1 large clove garlic, chopped
1 teaspoon ground cumin
½ teaspoon dried oregano
3 large new potatoes (about 300g),
    cooked and cubed
3 large eggs
¼ cup milk
½ teaspoon salt
1 cup tasty grated cheddar cheese
pinch of paprika

This tasty flan makes a popular and economical family meal. Leftovers go well in school lunches, too.

Using a food processor, chop the butter into the flour. Add the first measure of cheese, then, with the motor running, add the cold water, drop by drop, until the mixture forms a ball.

Transfer the ball of dough to the lightly floured bench and roll out thinly. Line a 23cm pie plate or flan dish with the resulting pastry and chill until the filling is ready.

Preheat the oven to 220°C.

Heat the oil in a frying pan and add the onion and garlic. Cover and cook gently over moderate heat until the onion is transparent and lightly browned. Stir in the seasonings, then the potatoes. Mix well and cook, un-covered, until the potatoes start to sizzle. Remove from the heat.

Break the eggs into a bowl. Add the milk and salt and mix with a fork to blend. Add the potato mixture and stir to mix. Tip the filling into the chilled pie crust.

Sprinkle the surface of the filling with the second measure of cheese and dust with the paprika. Bake for 20 minutes or until the pastry is golden brown and the filling has set.

Cut the flan into pieces for easy serving. It may be eaten cold or reheat-ed, preferably with a salad.

Avocado flan

This flan has a delicate and interesting flavour, and the cooked avocado filling provides a good talking point.

Preheat the oven to 200°C.

Halve the avocado and scoop the flesh into a large mixing bowl. Mash with a fork. Add the cottage cheese, eggs and salt, and mix into the avocado. Chop the leaves as well as the stems of the spring onions. Add these, the mashed potato and the parmesan, and stir well to combine.

Remove 4 sheets of filo from the packet (reseal and refrigerate the remainder). Lightly brush the upper surfaces of 3 sheets of filo with oil and stack them up. Put the unoiled sheet on top. Ease the stacked sheets into a 23cm flan dish or pie plate, then fold the edges in and under to form the edge of the pie.

Turn the avocado mixture into the unbaked pastry shell, level the top, and bake at 200°C for 10 minutes, until the pastry is golden brown, then turn down to 180°C and bake for about 20 minutes longer, until the centre feels firm.

Serve warm, either plain or topped with overlapping thin slices of avocado (dip these in lemon juice first, to stop them browning). Easy salsa fresca (page 26) or Mango salsa spooned over each slice of pie is delicious.

VARIATION: *Replace the filo pastry with a sheet of pre-rolled puff pastry, trimming the edge to fit the baking dish.*

SERVES 3–4:

1 large avocado
1 cup cottage cheese
2 large eggs
½ teaspoon salt
3 spring onions
1 cup mashed potato*
¼ cup grated parmesan
4 sheets filo pastry
1 tablespoon olive oil or other oil
1–2 avocados to garnish (optional)
lemon juice (optional)

* For quick mashed potato, cut a scrubbed potato into 1cm cubes and microwave in an oven bag with 1 tablespoon water for 3–4 minutes, or until tender. Drain off any remaining water and squeeze the bag to mash the potato.

Cheese & mushroom flan

Flans or quiches form a good basis for a meal, and are relatively quick and easy to prepare, even if you make your own pastry.

Working on a lightly floured surface, roll the pastry out to fit a 23cm pie or flan dish, then ease it gently into the pan and trim the edges.

Preheat the oven to 220°C.

Heat the oil in a medium-sized non-stick frying pan, then add the onion, mushrooms and thyme, and sauté until softened.

Cover the bottom of the uncooked crust with the grated cheese, then cover this with the onion and mushroom mixture. Beat the eggs, sour cream, milk and salt together, then pour into the crust.

Dust the surface with paprika, then bake at 220°C for about 30 minutes or until the filling is firm in the centre.

Serve with crusty bread and a green salad.

VARIATIONS: *The possible variations on this flan are almost limitless. Try mixing the cheese with the egg and sour cream mixture; or replace the mushroom mixture with 1–2 cups of other cooked (or canned) and drained vegetables or a combination of vegetables.*

SERVES 4:

1 sheet pre-rolled short or flaky pastry, or 1 recipe short pastry (page 223)
2 tablespoons olive oil or canola oil
1 medium onion, diced
200g mushrooms, sliced
1 teaspoon fresh thyme, chopped (or ½ teaspoon dried)
1½–2 cups grated gruyère (or cheddar)
3 large eggs
½ cup lite or regular sour cream
¼ cup milk
½ teaspoon salt
paprika, to dust

Avocado flan

Leek flan

- -

SERVES 3–4:

1 uncooked pastry pie crust (about
    250g bought or homemade pastry)
3 small leeks (about 500g)
1 clove garlic, diced
1 tablespoon butter
½ cup water
3 eggs
1 cup grated emmentaler (or tasty)
    cheese
½ cup sour cream
¼ cup milk
¼ teaspoon salt
chopped herbs and paprika (optional)

This flan, freshly baked or reheated, is a popular main course for lunch or dinner.

Preheat the oven to 220°C.

Roll out the pastry thinly to line a 20–23cm flan dish or pie plate.

Carefully wash the leeks and slice into 5mm pieces. Cook the leeks and the garlic in the butter for 2–3 minutes without letting them brown, then add the water and cook until tender. Raise the heat and let any remaining liquid evaporate.

Beat the eggs, grated cheese, sour cream, milk and salt together. Remove the leeks from the heat, then stir them into the egg mixture.

Pour the filling carefully into the prepared crust. Bake at 220°C for about 30 minutes or until the filling has set in the centre. Sprinkle with chopped herbs and/or paprika before serving, if desired.

Festive quiche

- -

SERVES 6:

200g flaky pastry
400g can whole tomatoes
3 cups broccoli florets
3 eggs
½ cup cream
¼ cup milk
¼ cup grated parmesan
½ teaspoon salt

The red of the tomatoes and the green of the broccoli give this easy quiche a festive feel. It makes a great quick meal.

Preheat the oven to 220°C. Roll the pastry out thinly and use it to line a 20cm flan dish with a removable base and 5cm sides. Run a rolling pin over the top to cut off the pastry edges.

Chop the tomatoes roughly and drain well. Cook the broccoli in a little water for about 2 minutes, or until barely tender, then drain well.

Mix together the eggs, cream, milk, parmesan and salt with a fork until well combined.

Fill the uncooked pastry base with the broccoli, pour the egg mixture over it, and arrange the tomato pieces on top.

Bake at 220°C for 15 minutes, until the pastry edge has browned, then lower the oven temperature to 175°C and cook for about 10 minutes longer, or until the mixture has set in the centre.

As soon as the quiche is removed from the oven, remove the sides of the flan dish so the pastry will remain crisp.

Serve warm or reheated with a salad and bread rolls.

Country onion pie

Roasted onions are put in a crust, then surrounded with a creamy mixture flavoured with nutmeg or caraway seeds.

Preheat the oven to 200°C.

Cut the ends off the onions, then place them in a bowl and pour boiling water over them. After a minute, pour the water off and peel the outer skins off the onions; they should be soft and easy to remove in one or two pieces. (Do not peel off more layers than you need to, or you will not have enough onion to fill the pie!) Cut the onions in half crosswise.

Pour a dribble of olive oil into a heavy roasting pan. Put the onions in the pan, cut side down, and roast for 15–20 minutes, or until lightly browned.

Roll the pastry out thinly on a floured board and trim off the uneven edges to form a 25cm circle. Ease the pastry into a 20cm pie plate, turn under the pastry edges, then pinch or decorate the outer rim as desired.

Combine the remaining filling ingredients in a food processor, or mix them in a bowl, using an eggbeater. (For a stronger caraway flavour crush the caraway seeds first.) Arrange the cooked onions, cut sides up, in the unbaked pie shell. Gently pour the filling around the onions until only their tops are visible. Sprinkle lightly with extra caraway seeds, if you like.

Bake at 200°C for 15–20 minutes, or until the pastry is evenly browned and the filling is set. Turn down the heat if the crust browns too much before this time. Serve warm.

SERVES 2–3:

1 sheet pre-rolled savoury short pastry, thawed (or 1 recipe short pastry, page 223)*
12–15 small (pickling) onions
¼ cup sour cream
1 egg
¼ cup milk
¼ teaspoon salt
¼ teaspoon freshly grated nutmeg OR
½ teaspoon caraway seeds
freshly ground pepper to taste

* Pastry can be substituted for 4 sheets of filo pastry for the crust, following the instructions for Avocado flan on page 229.

Country onion pie

Self-crusting quiches

Self-crusting quiches are made without a pastry crust; they form their own fairly firm bottom layer as they cook. For best results, remember these points:

- Use a metal pie plate or flan dish with a solid (not a push-out) base, preferably one with a non-stick finish.
- Lightly oil or butter the dish before use, regardless of the finish.
- Take care not to overmix the egg mixture when you add the flour, or it may not form two layers as it cooks.
- Bake at a high temperature so the crust browns well.
- Leave to stand for 5 minutes after removing from the oven, before turning out.

Self-crusting herbed mushroom quiche

SERVES 4–6:

2 medium onions, thinly sliced
2 tablespoons oil or butter
200g mushrooms, sliced
½ teaspoon dried basil
¼ teaspoon dried thyme
freshly ground black pepper to taste
2 eggs
½ cup sour cream
¾ cup milk
½ teaspoon salt
½ cup self-raising flour
½ cup grated tasty cheese

Preheat the oven to 220°C.

Sauté the onions in the oil or butter until soft. Add the mushrooms and cook until these soften too. Add the basil, thyme and pepper, then remove from the heat.

In a medium-sized bowl, lightly beat together the eggs, sour cream, milk and salt. Sprinkle the flour over this mixture and stir just enough to combine, then add the grated cheese, again stirring just enough to mix.

Butter or non-stick spray a 25–30cm flan or pie dish. Tip in the onion and mushroom mixture, and spread it evenly over the bottom, then pour the batter evenly over this. Bake at 220°C for 20–30 minutes, until light brown and firm in the centre. Cool for 10–15 minutes before turning out.

Self-crusting potato & vegetable quiche

SERVES 4–6:

1 large onion, chopped
2 cloves garlic, peeled and chopped
1 tablespoon butter
3 eggs
¾ teaspoon salt
1 cup milk
½ cup self-raising flour
2 cooked potatoes
1 cup cooked asparagus or spinach or mushrooms or broccoli, drained and chopped
1 cup grated tasty cheese
slices of tomato or capsicum, to garnish (optional)

Preheat the oven to 220°C.

Cook the chopped onion and garlic in the butter until tender. Cool. Stir in the eggs, salt and milk, and beat with a fork until mixed. Pour this into a large bowl containing the flour, and stir with the fork until just combined. Add the potatoes cut in 1cm cubes, the well drained vegetables and the cheese.

Pour the mixture into a prepared 20–23cm pan. Garnish with sliced tomato, or thinly sliced red and green capsicums if desired.

Bake at 220°C for 20–30 minutes, until lightly browned and set in the centre.

Self-crusting lentil & tomato quiche

SERVES 4–6:

½ cup brown lentils (or 1 x 400g can lentils)
1 bay leaf
2 medium onions, sliced
2 cloves garlic, chopped
1 tablespoon oil or butter
1 tablespoon lemon juice
freshly ground black pepper, to taste
3 eggs
1 cup milk
½ teaspoon salt
½ teaspoon each: dried basil and oregano
½ cup self-raising flour
½ cup grated tasty cheese
3 tomatoes, thinly sliced
2 tablespoons grated parmesan

Preheat the oven to 220°C.

Cook the lentils with the bay leaf until they are tender (page 201) or rinse and drain the canned lentils.

Sauté the onions and garlic in the oil. When soft and clear, remove from the heat and add lemon juice and black pepper to taste.

In a large bowl, beat together the eggs, milk, salt and herbs. Stir in the flour and grated cheese, but do not overmix.

Combine the drained lentils with the cooked onions. Stir into the batter. Pour into a prepared 23–30cm flan dish or pie plate. Top with tomato slices, then sprinkle with the grated parmesan.

Bake for 25–30 minutes at 220°C, or until the centre is firm when pressed.

Three versions of Self-crusting potato & vegetable quiche

Hearty bean pie

- -

SERVES 4–6:

2 medium onions, finely chopped
2–3 cloves garlic, finely chopped
1 tablespoon oil
100g mushrooms
1 teaspoon sugar
½ teaspoon marjoram
¼ teaspoon thyme
½ teaspoon salt
freshly ground black pepper, to taste
1 tablespoon flour
1 cup water
2 tablespoons sour cream (optional)
about 2 cups cooked beans or lentils
    (page 201)
200–300g bought or homemade
    savoury short or flaky pastry
    (page 223)

The filling for this pie consists of cooked beans (or lentils) in a rich and delicious brown onion and mushroom sauce. Use canned beans when time is short, and add leftover cooked vegetables for variety.

Preheat the oven to 220°C.

Sauté the onion and garlic in the oil in a large frying pan. Add the sliced mushrooms and sugar, and cook until the onions are well browned. Stir in the herbs, salt, pepper and flour. Pour in the water slowly, stirring constantly, until the sauce is the consistency of thick gravy.

Remove from the heat and add the sour cream (if using). Stir in the cooked, drained beans. Leave to stand and cool while preparing the pastry.

Roll out two-thirds of the pastry and use it to line a 20–25cm pie dish. Spread the cooled filling evenly over the pastry. Dampen the exposed pastry edges with cold water. Roll out the remaining pastry, and lay it gently over the top, pressing it onto the dampened edge. Trim, leaving a 1–2cm overlap. Fold this under the sealed edge and decorate with a fork or by fluting the edge with your fingers. Bake at 220°C for 20 minutes, or until golden brown.

Serve with mashed potatoes and cooked vegetables for a main meal, or alone or with bread for lunch.

VARIATION: *Use this recipe to make several small pies or pastries.*

Mushroom & potato pie

- -

SERVES 4:

3–4 medium (about 500g) waxy or
    all-purpose potatoes
1 medium onion
2 tablespoons olive oil or canola oil
1 teaspoon minced garlic
200g brown mushrooms
½ teaspoon dried basil, or
    1 tablespoon basil pesto
¼ teaspoon dried thyme
½ teaspoon salt
freshly ground black pepper, to taste
1 cup sour cream
½ teaspoon salt
freshly ground black pepper
1–2 sheets pre-rolled flaky pastry
milk or lightly beaten egg, to glaze

This single-crust pie is simple to prepare, and makes a great winter meal. Its impressive appearance is matched by its delicious flavour!

Preheat the oven to 220°C.

Scrub the potatoes, then cut them into 5mm slices. Place in an oven bag or in a covered microwave dish and cook on High (100%) for 10 minutes, stirring gently after 5 minutes. Alternatively, boil the potato slices until just tender, handling them gently to avoid breaking them up.

Peel and slice the onion while the oil heats in a large frying pan. Add the onion and garlic and sauté until the onion is soft and transparent.

While the onion cooks, slice the mushrooms, then add them to the pan along with the herbs, salt and pepper. Cook, stirring frequently, until the mushrooms have wilted.

Lightly oil or spray with non-stick spray a 20 x 25cm casserole or deep pie dish. Arrange half the potato slices evenly over the bottom of the dish, then cover with the mushroom mixture and top with the remaining potato slices. Stir together the sour cream and a little extra salt and pepper, and spoon over the potato and mushroom mixture in an even layer.

Roll out the pastry (if necessary), until it will cover the pie dish. Lay the pastry gently over the filling mixture, trimming off any excess. Decorate the edge by patterning it with a fork, and puncture the pastry at 5cm intervals over the surface. Brush with a little milk or beaten egg to glaze, then bake at 220°C for about 15 minutes, until the pastry is golden brown.

Serve with a salad or cooked vegetables and some crusty bread.

Carol's vegetable strudel

This recipe was given to us by a friend. She served it to her grown-up sons who 'didn't like vegetables'. They loved it so much they asked for more!

Preheat the oven to 190°C.

Blanch the carrot, beans and broccoli separately from each other and set aside.

Heat the butter in a small frying pan and cook the leek until soft. Add the mushroom and celery and cook for a further 2 minutes, then add the bean sprouts (if used) and the previously blanched vegetables. Toss well and allow to cool.

Take 3 sheets of filo pastry and lie them side by side, long sides together with the edges slightly overlapping. Brush each sheet lightly with oil or butter. Cover with 3 more sheets and brush with oil or butter the same way. Top these with the remaining 3 sheets. You will end up with a large rectangle, 3 layers thick.

Place the prepared filling over the first third of the rectangle. Mix together the cheese, breadcrumbs, salt and basil or pesto, and sprinkle this over the vegetables. Roll up loosely. Cover the ends of the roll with tinfoil, so the filling will not fall out during cooking.

Place on an oven tray and bake for 30–35 minutes, until golden brown.

Serve immediately with a leafy green salad.

SERVES 6:

1 carrot, thinly sliced
125g green beans, sliced
150g broccoli florets
30g butter
1 small leek, finely sliced
about 100g mushrooms, sliced
1 small stick celery, sliced
100g bean sprouts (optional)
9 sheets filo pastry
oil or melted butter, for brushing
1 cup (100g) grated tasty cheese
2 slices toast-sliced bread, crumbed
½ teaspoon salt
2 tablespoons finely chopped fresh
    basil or 1 tablespoon pesto

Mushroom strudel

This recipe makes two delicious long rolls of strudel.

Preheat the oven to 225°C.

Finely chop the onions and slice the mushrooms into pieces about 5mm thick. Sauté the onion in the butter or oil over medium heat until tender, then add the sliced mushrooms. Continue to cook until the mushrooms have heated through.

In a large bowl, mix together the cottage cheese, herbs, seasonings and lemon juice. Add the mushroom and onion mixture, and stir to combine.

Lay the first sheet of filo on a dry surface and brush very lightly with melted butter. Lay the next sheet directly on top. Repeat this process until you have a stack 5 sheets thick.

Spoon half the filling in a band across the pastry, about 5cm from one of the short edges, then carefully roll up. Using a sharp (preferably serrated) knife, make diagonal slashes through several layers, 3cm apart, across the top of the roll (to prevent the roll from bursting during cooking). Repeat this process with the remaining filo and the rest of the filling. Stand the rolls on a buttered sponge-roll pan.

Bake at 225°C for 20–25 minutes, or until the pastry is golden brown and crisp. Leave to stand for 5–10 minutes before serving. Slice diagonally and serve with colourful vegetables and/or a mixed green salad.

NOTE: *If the strudel splits during cooking, slice it in the kitchen, reshape and serve.*

SERVES 6–8:

2 medium onions
250g mushrooms
2 tablespoons butter or oil
500g cottage cheese
2 tablespoons chopped fresh parsley
½ teaspoon each: dried tarragon and
    thyme
½ teaspoon salt
freshly ground black pepper, to taste
juice of 1 lemon
10 sheets filo pastry
25g melted butter

Mediterranean vegetable pie

SERVES 5-6:

2 large red, orange or yellow
   capsicums or vegetables mentioned
   in introduction (about 350g total)
2 tablespoons olive oil
1 teaspoon (1 clove) minced garlic
2 tablespoons capers or chopped
   black olives (optional)
1 cup (250g) cottage cheese
250g feta, crumbled
4 eggs, lightly beaten
½ teaspoon grated nutmeg
freshly ground black pepper, to taste
8 sheets filo pastry
olive oil, for brushing
2-3 tablespoons grated parmesan
sesame seeds or poppyseeds (optional)

*This versatile pie is good when made with roasted capsicum,
aubergine, red onion or zucchini, or a mixture of these.*

Cut the capsicums lengthwise into 3-4 large pieces. Remove the pith and
seeds. Mix the olive oil and the garlic, and turn the vegetables in this in a
shallow roasting pan. Roast, uncovered, at 200°C for about 20 minutes,
until the skin darkens slightly. (Slice and roast other vegetables similarly.)

Combine the capers or olives (if using), cottage cheese, crumbled feta,
eggs, nutmeg and black pepper. Mix well, mashing with a fork.

Preheat the oven to 190°C.

Take 4 sheets of filo pastry, brush each with a little olive oil and sprinkle
with grated parmesan. Stack them and place in a roasting pan big enough
to hold the sheets with their edges turned up about 2cm.

Pour in half the filling, then add half the roasted vegetables, the remaining filling and other vegetables.

Prepare the rest of the filo as before, and use to cover the pie. Cut the
final sheet smaller or bunch it up so it fits to the edge. Fold the edges of
the filo from the bottom of the pie over the top. Brush lightly with oil and
sprinkle the top with sesame seeds or poppyseeds if you like.

Bake for 30-45 minutes. If the pastry browns too quickly, cover with
foil for part of the baking time. Serve warm, with a leafy salad and crusty
bread.

VARIATION: *Use Quick tapenade (page 25) to replace the olives and
capers.*

Mediterranean vegetable pie

Goat cheese & olive galette

- -

A galette is somewhere between a pie (baked without a pie plate) and a pizza – the filling is spread over the top, then the pastry is folded back over the filling, so it is part open and part closed.

Prepare the pastry according to the recipe on page 223. Press the dough into a ball, flatten into a disk, wrap loosely and refrigerate while you make the filling.

Preheat the oven to 180°C.

Heat the oil in a large frying pan. Add the onion and cook over medium-high heat, stirring occasionally, for 3–4 minutes, until the onion has softened and is beginning to brown. Stir in the capsicum, tomatoes and thyme and cook for 5–6 minutes longer, stirring frequently until the capsicum is soft and the tomato pieces have lost their shape. Remove from the heat and season to taste with salt and pepper.

Working on a lightly floured surface, roll the pastry out to form a round about 45–50cm across.

Roll the pastry around the rolling pin and lift it onto an oven tray lined with Teflon or baking paper. Spread the filling mix over the middle 30cm or so of the pastry, then sprinkle the filling with the olives and crumbled cheese.

Fold the uncovered pastry edges back over the filling, making 5–6 tucks around the inner edge so it will sit flat.

Place in the middle of the oven and bake for 15–20 minutes until the pastry is golden brown. Remove from the oven and allow to cool for several minutes before serving with a simple salad.

SERVES 3–4:

1 recipe Easy 'flaky' pastry (page 223)
2 tablespoons olive oil or canola oil
2 medium onions, peeled, halved and sliced
1 medium red capsicum, cored and sliced
2 medium tomatoes, cubed
1 teaspoon dried thyme
salt and freshly ground black pepper, to taste
about 12 olives
50–100g goat cheese (feta or chèvre), crumbled

Easy pizza base

- -

Homemade yeasted pizza bases are easy to prepare, particularly if you have a breadmaker.

Making by hand: Measure the yeast into a large bowl. Combine the milk and water first, then add this to the yeast along with the sugar, salt and oil. Leave to stand for a couple of minutes, then add half the flour and stir well to make a thick batter, then add the remaining flour and stir to make a dough firm enough to knead (add extra flour if required). Tip onto a floured surface and knead for 5–10 minutes, then cover the dough loosely and leave to rise for about 10 minutes before using.

Using a bread machine: Measure all the ingredients into the machine, set the machine to the 'dough' cycle and press start. Check the dough after a few minutes of mixing; if it looks too wet, add a little extra flour, or a little water if too dry. The dough can be removed from the machine any time after about 30 minutes from the start of mixing, or, if you have time, let the cycle run through.

Turn the dough onto a floured surface and divide as required, then roll each piece into a thin (5–7mm) round shape.

MAKES 1 LARGE, 2 MEDIUM, OR 8 INDIVIDUAL BASES:

3 teaspoons instant active dried yeast
½ cup milk
¾ cup boiling water
2 teaspoons sugar
1½ teaspoons salt
2 tablespoons olive or canola oil
3 cups high grade (bread) flour
additional flour or water if required

Calzone & stromboli

If you do make your own pizza bases, why not try something a little different with these 'closed' pizzas – they're great for picnics.

Calzone: Roll the dough into 8 smaller rounds for individual pizzas. Arrange pizza fillings over one half of each base, leaving 2cm uncovered at the edge. Moisten round the edge with a little water, then fold the uncovered half over the filled half to make a half-moon shape, pressing the edges together. Bake as for pizza (this page).

Stromboli: Roll 1 recipe of the pizza base dough into 2 large (50 x 75cm), very thin rectangles. Arrange pizza toppings sparingly over each base, leaving a 5cm strip at one of the short edges uncovered. Brush the uncovered edge lightly with water, then, starting at the other short edge, roll the dough up like a sponge roll. Place the roll on a baking sheet so it sits seam-side down, then slash the top diagonally a couple of times to prevent splitting, and bake as for pizza.

Easy 'no knead' pizza

This is a really quick pizza to make. Pop it into a very hot oven and let it cook for 15 minutes, cut it in wedges and eat it!

MAKES 1:

1 cup body-temperature water
1 teaspoon Surebake or bread machine yeast
1 tablespoon olive oil
1 teaspoon salt
2 teaspoons sugar
2 cups (275g) high-grade (bread) flour
about ¼ cup extra flour, for coating

Preheat the oven on to 250°C, with a rack above the middle of the oven, and a flat metal baking tray on it. (If you have a baking stone, put it in the oven instead of the metal tray.)

Measure the warm water into a fairly large bowl, and sprinkle in the yeast, oil, salt and sugar. Mix well until everything is evenly dispersed, then add the first measure of flour (spooning the flour lightly into the cup). Mix this to a soft dough with a wooden spoon or stirrer. The mixture should be soft and slightly sticky. Sprinkle a little of the extra flour over the yeast mixture in the bowl, and form it into a ball. Leave it to stand while you find and prepare your choice of topping ingredients. The dough will start to rise while you do this.

Place a large square of baking paper, or a large non-stick liner, on another flat metal baking tray.

Assemble your choice of pizza toppings (see box). Use some or all of the suggestions. The oil, tomatoes and cheese are usually regarded as essential. The others are optional.

Now work on the pizza crust. The dough should have risen slightly. Sprinkle some of the second measure of flour over the soft pizza dough. Use the stirrer to lift the floured dough away from the sides and bottom of the bowl, and turn it onto the centre of the baking paper or the non-stick liner.

With floury hands, first shape the floured dough into a ball, then , using your fingers and hands, pat the ball of dough out into a circle 30cm across, on the baking paper or non-stick liner.

Drizzle a little olive oil on the dough and spread it fairly evenly with your fingers. Leaving the outer 2cm of the dough uncovered, sprinkle the chopped tomato over the pizza. Finely chop some red onion and slice some mushrooms, coat them with a little extra oil and spread it on the pizza too. Sprinkle the grated cheese over everything else. Place the sliced black olives on the cheese. Add the oregano or other herbs if you like. Fold the edges of the pizza in to make a 1cm rim. Drizzle a little more oil over the topping ingredients .

Turn the oven down to 225°C. Open the oven door and carefully slide the pizza, on its baking paper or liner, onto the heated pizza stone or the heated metal tray.

Bake for 15–20 minutes until the rim of the pizza is golden brown, then take it from the oven and slide the pizza off the baking paper or liner and onto a cooling rack.

Cut into pieces with a knife, pizza wheel or kitchen scissors and eat while warm.

PIZZA TOPPINGS

olive oil
chopped tomatoes, seeds removed.
finely sliced small red onion (optional)
sliced mushrooms
grated cheese, about 1 cup
sliced, pitted black olives (optional)
dried oregano (optional)

Tomato, basil & mozzarella pizza

There is something remarkably delicious about traditional Italian-style pizzas – the ingredients look so simple, yet it is packed full of taste!

SERVES 2–3:

½ recipe Easy pizza base (page 237)

about ¼ cup easy tomato topping

2 medium tomatoes, ripe but firm (or 15–20 cherry tomatoes, halved)

15–20 fresh basil leaves

100–150g mozzarella, in 5mm slices

about 1 tablespoon olive oil

freshly ground black pepper

Preheat the oven to 200°C.

Roll the dough out into an oval about 25 x 40cm. Spread thinly with the tomato topping, leaving 1–2cm uncovered around the edges (you can leave these as they are or brush lightly with water and fold them in, if you like).

Quarter the tomatoes, then cut each quarter into 3 thin wedges. Scatter the tomato wedges (or halved cherry tomatoes) over the base, then arrange the basil leaves evenly over the pizza (tearing any larger leaves into 2–3 smaller pieces).

Arrange the mozzarella slices over the surface, then drizzle the pizza with about 1 tablespoon olive oil and sprinkle with black pepper.

Bake at 200°C for 12–15 minutes or until the cheese is golden brown.

Tomato, basil & mozzarella pizza

Enjoy the different types of bread that you can make from these recipes Breads made without yeast don't have the same texture as yeast-baked breads, but they are quick to make and taste good! Don't be tempted to hurry breads raised by yeast.

The date and walnut loaf keeps well in a plastic bag and refrigerated, then sliced and buttered. Try it in packed lunches, or slice thinly and enjoy with tea or coffee, for afternoon tea or supper.

Breads & muffins

Simon's 'all-purpose' bread

Simon's 'go to' bread recipe. The dough works well as a pizza base, makes a good loaf in the bread machine, or can be run through the dough cycle and shaped into focaccia or a Vienna loaf.

The flavour of the bread is particularly good when the dough is made well ahead, then left to rest for several hours (or even overnight) before being shaped then risen again before baking.

MAKES 1 LOAF OR 2 PIZZA BASES:

¾ cup milk

½ cup hot water

2 teaspoons instant active dried yeast

½ teaspoon Surebake yeast

2 teaspoons sugar

1½ teaspoons salt

2 tablespoons olive oil

3 cups (420g) high-grade (bread) flour

Making by hand: Measure the milk, hot water, 2 yeasts, sugar, salt and oil into a large bowl with 1½ cups of the flour and mix thoroughly. Cover and leave for 15 minutes or longer in a warm place. Stir in the remaining flour, adding a little extra warm water or bread flour if necessary to make a dough just firm enough to knead.

Knead with the dough hook of an electric mixer or by hand on a lightly floured surface for 10 minutes, adding extra flour if necessary, until the dough forms a soft dough that springs back when gently pressed.

Making in a bread machine: Carefully measure all the ingredients into a 750g capacity bread machine in the order specified by the manufacturer. Set to the normal/white bread cycle, medium crust, and press start; or use the dough cycle and shape and bake by hand. You can leave the dough to sit (in the machine if the weather is cooler, or in an oiled bowl in the fridge in warmer weather) for several hours at this stage.

Shaping and baking: To make pizzas, divide the dough in 2 and shape and bake as described on page 237.

Otherwise turn the dough in 2–3 teaspoons of oil in the cleaned dry bowl. Cover with cling film and leave to sit for at least 30 minutes (you can leave it for several hours at this stage — on the bench if the weather is cooler, or in the fridge in warmer weather).

When you are ready to proceed, lightly knead the oiled dough in the bowl for about 1 minute.

Round rolls

Preheat the oven to 220°C, with the rack just below the middle. Shape the dough into about 16 round balls, dribble 1 tablespoon of olive oil onto a sponge-roll pan, and turn the rolls in this. Sprinkle with grated parmesan or other cheese, or with toasted sesame seeds, dried oregano, etc. Cover lightly with cling film and leave in a warm place until they rise to almost twice their size. Bake at 220°C for 10–15 minutes, until browned, top and bottom.

Knotted rolls

Preheat the oven to 220°C, with the rack just below the middle. Cut the dough into 12 pieces and roll each into a 25–26cm long 'pencil'. Knot each strip loosely, folding under the ends to make a rosette if you like. Put the shaped rolls on a lightly oiled oven tray. Cover lightly with cling film and leave in a warm place until they rise to almost twice their size. Brush very gently with beaten egg then sprinkle with poppyseeds, toasted sesame seeds or finely grated cheese. Bake at 220°C for 10–15 minutes, until golden brown.

Bread sticks

Preheat the oven to 180°C, with the rack just below the middle. Roll the dough into thin sticks, each about 20cm long. Place on an oiled oven tray, brush with lightly beaten egg white, then sprinkle liberally with parmesan cheese, toasted sesame seeds or poppyseeds. Allow to stand for 10 minutes, then bake at 180°C for about 20 minutes, until dried through and lightly browned. Store in an airtight container.

Pita bread

Preheat the oven to its highest temperature, with an oven tray, cast-iron pan or griddle heated in the middle of it. Cut the dough into 8 equal parts, roll each out into a 15–18cm circle on a working surface that has been well sprinkled with flour or cornmeal, then allow to stand for about 10 minutes. Slide the first circle onto a piece of cardboard, then open the oven door briefly and transfer the dough round quickly onto the heated oven tray. In 1–2 minutes the bread should rise into a ball, then deflate. Lift out with tongs after 2–3 minutes, and put the next pita bread in to cook. Once cool, store the pita breads in a plastic bag so they do not dry out.

Focaccia

Preheat the oven to 220°C, with the rack just below the middle. Lightly oil or non-stick spray 1 large or 2 small sponge-roll pans. Press the dough into the pans, leaving finger-hole depressions in the dough. Top with chopped olives, sautéed onion rings, sage or rosemary, sundried tomatoes, etc., then dribble 2–3 tablespoons of olive oil over the top. Leave to rise in a warm place for about 15 minutes, then bake at 220°C until golden brown, about 10–15 minutes. Serve warm, in rectangles.

Vienna loaf

Preheat the oven to 220°C. Turn out the dough onto a lightly floured board and roll into a 30 x 20cm oval shape. For a vienna-type loaf, roll it up into a sausage shape and place on a well oiled baking sheet or in a sponge-roll pan and leave to rise in a warm, draught-free place for about 1 hour or until double its original size. Bake as for focaccia (above).

Mixed grain bread

MAKES 1:

½ cup (85g) mixed kibbled grains*

3 teaspoons Surebake or bread
    machine yeast

1¼ cups warm water

2 tablespoons olive oil

1 tablespoon sugar

1½ teaspoons salt

2 tablespoons lecithin granules
    (optional)

1 cup (140g) wholemeal flour

2½ cups (350g) high grade (bread)
    flour

** Buy or make a mixture of kibbled
wheat, kibbled rye, and red and/or
purple wheat.*

*Precooking the kibbled grains for this recipe may seem a bit fiddly, but
it ensures a large, light-textured, moist loaf, flecked with grains.*

Place the kibbled grain mix in a small saucepan with 2–3 cups of cold
water. Bring to the boil, then simmer for 1–2 minutes. Take from the heat
and drain well in a sieve.

Making by hand: Preheat the oven to 200°C, with the reack just below the
middle. In a large bowl, mix the prepared kibbled grains with 1¼ cups cold
water. Add all the remaining ingredients except the high-grade flour. Mix
thoroughly, cover and leave for 15 minutes in a warm place.

Stir in the high-grade flour, adding a little extra water or flour if necessary, to make a dough just firm enough to knead. Knead with the dough
hook of an electric mixer or by hand on a lightly floured surface for
10 minutes, adding extra flour if necessary, until the dough forms a soft
ball that springs back when gently pressed.

Turn the dough in 2–3 teaspoons of oil in the cleaned dry bowl, cover
with cling film and leave in a warm, draught-free place for 30 minutes.

Lightly knead the oiled dough in the bowl for 1 minute. Pat the dough
into a square shape a little longer than the baking pan, then roll it into
a cylinder. Put into the sprayed or buttered loaf pan, pressing it into the
corners and levelling the top.

Leave to rise in a warm, draught-free place for about 1 hour or until
double its original size. Brush with milk or egg glaze and sprinkle with
extra kibbled grains, if you like, then bake at 200°C for about 30 minutes,
until the sides and bottom are browned and the loaf sounds hollow when
tapped underneath.

Making in a bread machine: Prepare the kibble as described above, then
carefully measure all the ingredients in the order specified by the manufacturer, including the prepared kibble combined with the measured
water, into a 750g-capacity bread machine.

Set to the normal/white bread cycle, medium crust and press start. This
is a good timer bread.

Irish soda bread

MAKES 1:

3 cups (420g) standard plain flour

1½ teaspoons salt

1½ teaspoons sugar

1 teaspoon baking soda

1 teaspoon cream of tartar

¾ cup milk

½ cup plain unsweetened yoghurt

*This is so quick to make, and so good! It is a fairly dense loaf,
but served warm from the oven, with lashings of butter, it is
simply delicious.*

Preheat the oven to 180°C.

Sift the flour, salt, sugar, baking soda and cream of tartar into a large bowl.
Measure the milk and yoghurt into a small bowl and stir to combine.

Pour the milk mixture into the dry ingredients and gently fold the
mixture together, trying to combine it evenly but without overmixing.

Tip the dough onto a lightly floured board and shape it into a ball.
Flatten a little until it is disc-shaped and measures just over 15cm across.
Place it on a lightly floured or baking paper-lined baking sheet. Using a
sharp knife, cut a deep cross into the dough (about halfway through) so it
opens nicely during baking.

Bake in the middle of the oven at 180°C for 45–50 minutes or until
golden brown and hollow sounding when tapped.

Really easy 'no knead' bread

For this bread, 5 ingredients are stirred together in a large bowl. The first, shaped and baked, chewy rolls should be ready to eat a little more than an hour after you start mixing! The rest of the dough, refrigerated in its bowl, may be taken out, shaped in any way you like, and baked at any time during the next 4 days.

MAKES 1:
2 cups warm water
2 teaspoons Surebake or bread machine yeast
1 tablespoon olive oil or canola oil
2 teaspoons salt
4 cups (about 540g) high-grade (bread) flour

Measure the warm (body-temperature) water into a large bowl. Sprinkle the yeast over the water, stir it in, then add the oil and the salt.

Stir the flour in its bag to aerate it, then spoon 1 cup of flour lightly into the measuring cup and level off the top. Tip this flour into the yeast mixture, and stir it into the liquid using a large flexible stirrer or a wooden spoon. Repeat with 3 more level cups of flour, stirring again after each one is added. At the end of this time the mixture should have formed a rather sticky ball of dough. If it seems too liquid, add about ¼ cup of flour and beat again until a sticky ball forms. Dampen the stirrer or a rubber scraper, and use it to clean down the sides of the bowl.

Cover the bowl of dough and leave it to stand in a warm place until the dough has risen to about twice its original size, usually in 15–20 minutes.

Bread rolls

For rolls to eat very soon, tilt the bowl of risen dough and let about one-quarter of the dough fall out onto a well-floured surface. You will need to cut off the amount of dough you want, using a wetted knife or a rectangular metal dough-cutter. Cover and refrigerate the rest of the dough in the covered bowl

Gently turn the soft dough over so that all its sides are floured. (It will be softer than traditional, firmer bread dough which has been kneaded.) Pat the soft dough out into a rectangle with floured hands, then fold the ends over again, and pat it down into a rectangular shape again. Cut the rectangle of soft (folded) dough into 4–8 more or less triangular rolls, with the dough-cutter or a heavy knife. We like it if the rolls have irregular shapes.

Put the shaped rolls on a floured baking tray, leaving space for rising, and leave them to stand (and rise again) for about 15 minutes (or up to 45 minutes if you are not impatient!). While the rolls rise, preheat the oven to 230°C with the rack just above the middle.

Bake the rolls for 15–20 minutes until golden brown (the crust becomes thicker with longer cooking). Remove from the oven and leave to cool on a rack.

Really easy 'no knead' bread

'No knead' heavy brown loaf with seeds

MAKES 1:

¼ cup each: wholegrain flaked oats, sunflower seeds, sesame seeds and linseed

½ cup hot water

2 teaspoons instant active dried yeast

2 cups lukewarm water

2 household tablespoons golden syrup, or 1 tablespoon golden syrup and 1 tablespoon molasses

2 tablespoons canola oil or olive oil

4 cups wholemeal flour, plus 1 extra cup

2 teaspoons salt

A dense, well-flavoured loaf. Preferably use a large (10-cup) loaf pan with gently sloping sides, so the base is smaller than the top.

Put the oats and seeds in a fairly large, dry frying pan. Heat the pan, stirring and shaking it frequently, until the contents have browned lightly and have a 'toasted' aroma. Take the pan off the stove and stir in the hot (but not boiling) water. Leave the mixture to stand until nearly all the water has been absorbed. Drain off and discard any remaining liquid.

Put the yeast, lukewarm water, golden syrup (and molasses, if using) and oil in a bowl or jug, and put this aside in a warm place for at least 10 minutes, until there is a film of fine bubbles on the surface.

While the yeast mixture stands, measure 4 cups of flour into a large bowl, and add the salt.

Pour the yeast mixture and the grain and seed mixture into the flour. Stir well, until everything is evenly mixed. The mixture should be just too soft to knead, but not runny. If it is too wet, add up to 1 cup of the extra wholemeal flour, until the dough is just firm enough to form a cylinder which you can hold on your flat hand and wrist. Gently tilt your hand and transfer the 'sausage' of dough into the non-stick sprayed baking pan, held in your other hand. Jiggle the pan backwards and forwards to form an evenly shaped loaf, the length of the baking pan. Add more flour while you do this, if necessary.

Cover the pan with cling film or stand it in a plastic bag, and leave it to rise in a warm place until the dough is almost double its size and has filled the loaf pan. This will probably take ½–1 hour. Preheat the oven to 190°C, with the rack just above the middle.

Put the risen loaf into the preheated oven and bake for about 40 minutes. It should sound hollow when tapped. Cool it on a rack. When cold, wrap and put in a cool place overnight. Slice the next day, using a sharp breadknife.

Use within 3 days, rewrapping and refrigerating it in between.

Date & walnut loaf

MAKES 2:

2 cups good quality dates, pitted

3 cups water

1½ teaspoons salt

1½ cups sugar

¼ cup canola oil or other oil

3 large eggs

about 1 cup walnuts, finely chopped

3 cups (420g) self-raising flour

OPTIONAL INGREDIENTS

finely grated zest of 1 lemon or orange

1 teaspoon vanilla

2 teaspoons mixed spice

few drops of orange oil

cream cheese, to spread*

* mix a little finely grated orange or lemon peel through it if you like.

This will keep in the fridge for a few days, or frozen for later.

Preheat the oven to 180°C, with the rack just below the middle.

Put the dates in a saucepan large enough to mix all the ingredients. Add 3 cups of water, bring to the boil and simmer for about 5 minutes, squashing the dates and breaking them up. Turn off the heat as soon as the dates have broken up, then stand the saucepan in a sink of cold water to cool.

While the date mixture is still fairly hot, add the salt, sugar and oil, and stir until the sugar dissolves. Add as many of the optional ingredients as you like, and leave to cool to room temperature.

Meanwhile, break the eggs into a small bowl and beat with a fork or whisk until combined.

When the date mixture has cooled, stir in the eggs and walnuts.

Using a fork, stir the flour in its bag to aerate it before measuring the required amount into the date mixture. Fold, without stirring more than necessary, until no streaks of flour remain in the mixture.

Spray the insides of 2 loaf pans (each of which holds 5–6 cups) with non-stick spray. Spoon the mixture into the pans, levelling the tops.

Bake in the centre of the oven for 45–60 minutes, or until a skewer poked into the centre of each loaf comes out clean. Remove from the oven and cool on a rack, removing the loaves from the pans only when they are firm enough to handle and to keep their shape.

Serve slices of loaf lightly buttered or spread with cream cheese.

'No knead' heavy brown loaf with seeds

Cheesy beer bread

MAKES 1:

3 cups (420g) self-raising flour
½ cup grated tasty cheese
1 teaspoon salt
1–2 tablespoons sugar
355ml can or bottle of beer
about 1 tablespoon of oil (optional)

This is Simon's friend Donn's recipe for a quick, no-knead bread that contains no baker's yeast. A slice or two, warm from the oven, with a bowl of soup makes the perfect winter warmer.

Preheat the oven to 180°C, with the rack just below the middle.

Measure the flour into a large bowl. Spoon the flour from the bag into the measuring cup, rather than scooping it straight from the bag, so it is not too densely packed (this can make a big difference to the total weight of flour used – too much will make a dry loaf). Add the grated cheese, salt and sugar (use the larger quantity of sugar if using a dryish beer, and less if using a sweeter, more malty beer). Toss together the dry ingredients to combine, then add the beer.

Stir everything together until the mixture looks more or less uniform and will hold together.

Oil or non-stick spray a 6–7 cup capacity loaf pan. Pour the dough into the pan, roughly levelling the top. Brush the top with a little oil for more even browning, if you like, then place the loaf in the oven. Bake for 45–60 minutes, until the top is golden brown and the loaf sounds hollow when tapped.

Remove from the oven and leave to cool on a rack for 10–15 minutes before slicing.

Cheesy cornbread

MAKES 1:*

1 large egg
1 cup creamed corn
½ cup milk
1 cup grated cheese
½ cup cornmeal
¾ cup (100g) self-raising flour
1 tablespoon sugar
½ teaspoon salt
½ teaspoon baking soda

OPTIONAL INGREDIENTS
½ cup diced red and/or green
    capsicum
1–2 sliced spring onions
½ cup cubed avocado

* Cornbread is traditionally cooked in a 20cm square pan. You can use a 23 x 10cm loaf pan, if you prefer, but it will take longer to cook (see above).

Cornbread is very popular in the southern United States. You can choose to add extras or enjoy it as is. It's good served for breakfast, and it makes the perfect accompaniment for chilli dishes.

Preheat the oven to 180°C, with the rack just below the middle.

Break the egg into a large bowl. Add the creamed corn, milk and cheese and stir to combine.

Measure the cornmeal, flour, sugar, salt and baking soda into a smaller bowl and stir to combine thoroughly.

Add the dry ingredients to the egg mixture, along with your choice of optional ingredients, and stir to combine.

Line a 20cm square pan or 23 x 10cm loaf pan with baking paper, then pour in the mixture. Bake the square loaf for about 30 minutes and the rectangular loaf for about 1 hour, or until a skewer poked in the middle comes out clean.

Spinach & feta muffins

Spinach & feta muffins

- -

Spinach and feta is a combination that always seems to work well, and these are no exception!

Preheat oven to 210°C, with the rack just below the middle.

Lightly squeeze the cooked or thawed spinach, reserving the liquid. Make the spinach liquid up to 1 cup with milk, then place the spinach, milk, cottage cheese, oil and egg in a large bowl and mix well. Add the cubed or crumbled cheese and mix lightly.

Measure the flours, baking powder and salt together into another bowl and toss together with a whisk or fork. Tip the flour mixture into the liquids, then fold gently together until the flour is just moistened. The mixture does not need to be smooth.

Spoon the mixture into 12 non-stick sprayed medium-sized muffin pans, then bake at 210°C for 15 minutes, or until golden brown and a skewer poked into the centre of a muffin comes out clean.

Remove the muffins from the oven and leave to cool in their pans for 2-3 minutes (this helps reduce sticking), before tipping out and cooling on a rack.

Delicious warm; or store cooled muffins in sealed bags to prevent drying out (freeze for longer-term storage).

MAKES 12:

½ cup (100–125g) cooked spinach, chopped (or 125g frozen spinach, thawed)

1 cup milk

1 cup (250g) cottage cheese

¼ cup canola oil

1 large egg

75g–100g feta, cubed or crumbled

1 cup wholemeal flour

1 cup plain flour

4 teaspoons baking powder

½–1 teaspoon salt

Olive, pesto & feta muffins

MAKES 12:

2 cups self-raising flour
½ teaspoon salt
100g feta, cubed
¼ cup chopped black olives
2 tablespoons basil pesto
¼ cup olive oil
1 cup plain unsweetened yoghurt
1 large egg

Like bread, fresh savoury muffins make a great accompaniment for pasta meals. They can be whipped up in just a few minutes.

Preheat the oven to 200°C, with the rack just below the middle.

Measure the flour and salt into a large bowl. Add the feta, olives and pesto, then stir until well mixed.

In another bowl, mix together the oil, yoghurt and egg. Tip the liquid into the dry ingredients, then stir gently until just mixed (stop as soon as all the flour has been moistened). Spoon the mixture into 12 medium-sized muffin pans, and bake at 200°C for 12–15 minutes, or until the tops are golden brown and the centres firm when pressed. Leave to stand for a couple of minutes, then remove from the pans and cool on a wire rack. Serve warm.

Zucchini & parmesan muffins

MAKES 12:

2 cups flour
4 teaspoons baking powder
½ teaspoon salt
freshly ground black pepper, to taste
1 cup grated tasty cheese
¼ cup grated parmesan
¾ cup milk
2 eggs
3 zucchini (250g), unpeeled, grated

These are light-textured and pretty, flecked with pale green, and perfect for summer lunches and for picnics.

Preheat the oven to 210°C, with the rack just below the middle.

Sift or fork together the flour, baking powder and salt in a large bowl. Grind in black pepper to taste (using plenty if you like), then add the grated cheeses and stir to combine.

In another bowl, whisk together the milk and eggs with a fork, then add the zucchini. Tip this mixture into the bowl of dry ingredients.

Fold together, taking care not to overmix. As soon as all the flour is moistened (but before the mixture is smooth), spoon the mixture into 12 non-stick sprayed medium-sized muffin pans or 24 mini muffin pans.

Bake at for 12–15 minutes, or until the tops are golden and the muffins spring back when pressed in the centre. Leave to stand for 2–3 minutes, then remove from the pan and cool on a rack. Serve warm, topped with cottage cheese and/or sliced tomatoes if you like.

Easy cheesy muffins

MAKES 12:

2 cups self-raising flour
2 cups (200g) grated tasty cheese
1 large egg
1 cup lager or other beer

Make this basic easy muffin recipe, or add extra flavourings to create your own version – for example, by adding pizza garnishes.

Preheat the oven to 220°C, with the rack just below the middle.

Toss the flour and grated cheese together in a large bowl, using a fork.

In another bowl, again using the fork, beat the egg enough to thoroughly mix the white and yolk. Add the beer (which can be flat or bubbly), stir to mix briefly, then pour the mixture onto the flour and cheese. Fold together until most of the flour is dampened, but do not keep mixing until the mixture is smooth.

Spoon the mixture into 12 non-stick sprayed medium-sized muffin moulds. Bake at 220°C for 10–15 minutes, until nicely browned, and until the centres spring back when pressed. Leave the muffins to stand in the pan for 3–4 minutes, until they will lift out easily.

Serve warm or cold the day they are made, or reheat the next day.

Best blueberry muffins

MAKES 12:

2 cups standard flour
4 teaspoons baking powder
1 teaspoon cinnamon
½ teaspoon salt
½ cup caster sugar
100g butter
1 cup milk
1 large egg
1–1½ cups blueberries

CINNAMON SUGAR
1 tablespoon sugar
½ teaspoon cinnamon

Cinnamon brings out the sweet berry flavour. Use free-flow frozen blueberries if fresh ones are not available, adding them before they thaw completely so they don't stain the batter.

Preheat the oven to 220°C with the rack just below the middle. Sieve the first dry ingredients into a fairly large bowl.

In another large bowl, warm the butter until just melted, then add the milk and egg, and beat to mix thoroughly.

Prepare the fresh or partly frozen berries, then put the dry mixture and the blueberries into the milk and egg mixture. Without overmixing, fold everything together. The flour should be dampened, not smooth, and the berries should keep their shape.

Divide the mixture evenly between 12 medium-sized muffin pans that have been well coated with non-stick spray. Sprinkle each with a little cinnamon sugar. Bake for 12–15 minutes, until the muffins spring back when pressed. (Muffins made with frozen berries will take about 5 minutes longer.)

Serve warm — for breakfast, morning tea with coffee, lunch or as dessert.

Best blueberry muffins

Eggless bran muffins

Eggless bran muffins

- -

Warm from the oven, these plain, old-fashioned muffins make a good, very low-fat weekend breakfast or lunch. They have a lovely golden-syrup flavour. Each muffin contains nearly 3 tablespoons of bran, so they are really high in fibre – and they contain no egg, added butter or oil.

Preheat the oven to 210°C with the rack just below the middle.

Measure the golden syrup into a large bowl (pour hot water over a ¼ cup measure, before dipping it into the tin of syrup). Add the ½ cup boiling water and stir until the syrup is dissolved. Add the milk and stir again.

Measure the remaining ingredients into another bowl (measure the baking soda into the palm of your hand, and squash it with the back of the measuring spoon to ensure there are no lumps before adding it to the bowl). Mix the dry ingredients together well, then tip them into the cool milk mixture. Fold the dry ingredients into the wet mixture until all the bran and flour is dampened. Do overmix or stir until smooth.

Using two spoons, divide the mixture equally between 12 medium-sized muffin pans that have been throroughly non-stick sprayed.

Bake for 12–15 minutes, until muffins are an attractive brown colour and they spring back when pressed. Because the mixture is fairly wet, the muffin tops may be flatter than usual. Leave muffins to stand in the pans for 3–4 minutes, then carefully transfer to a cooling rack. Put in plastic bags when cold. Freeze any muffins you do not expect to eat within 2 days.

Serve warm. Cottage cheese makes a good low-fat topping.

VARIATIONS: *Add ½ cup of small dark raisins or sultanas (soaked in hot water for a few minutes, then drained) to the syrup mixture; and/or add ¼–½ cup chopped walnuts to the bran and flour mixture.*

MAKES 12:

¾ cup golden syrup
½ cup boiling water
1 cup low-fat milk
2 cups baking bran
1 cup plain flour
1 teaspoon baking powder
1 teaspoon baking soda
1 teaspoon salt

Blueberry bran muffins

MAKES 12–15:

1 cup wheat (baking) bran
¼ cup wheatgerm or extra bran
½ cup canola oil
1 cup plain or fruity yoghurt
1 large egg
¾ cup wholemeal flour
¾ cup high-grade (bread) flour
1 teaspoon cinnamon
1 teaspoon baking powder
¾ teaspoon salt
½ teaspoon baking soda
1 cup brown sugar
1–1½ cups (150–180g) frozen
  blueberries

Here is our version of a classic American favourite. Make a batch and freeze them in ones or twos, to grab out of the freezer for a perfect lunch or snack on the run.

Preheat the oven to 200°C, with the rack just below the middle.

Put the bran, wheatgerm, oil, yoghurt and egg into a large bowl. Mix to blend everything with a fork, then leave to stand. (If you don't have wheatgerm in the house, replace it with extra bran.)

Measure the remaining dry ingredients into a medium-sized bowl, and stir well with a fork to mix thoroughly. Do not thaw the blueberries, but separate any clumps of berries. (We use half a 350g packet and find that this is a very good amount for this recipe, although you can use less.)

Tip the flour mixture into the liquid mixture, add the blueberries, then fold everything together until the dry ingredients are moistened.

Spoon the mixture into 12–15 medium or about 30 mini muffin pans that have been thoroughly non-stick sprayed.

Bake for about 15 minutes (longer than most other muffins, because of the frozen berries in the mixture), until the centres spring back when pressed. Remove from the oven and leave to cool for several minutes before removing from the pan.

Serve warm; or cool completely on a rack, then freeze the muffins in air-tight bags.

ABC muffins

MAKES 24 MINI OR 12 MEDIUM:

1 cup (2–3) mashed ripe bananas
½ cup brown sugar
¼ teaspoon salt
¼ cup canola oil
1 large egg
½ cup milk
¼–½ cup chocolate chips
1 apple, unpeeled, coarsely grated*
2 cups self-raising flour

* Use a tangy apple such as Braeburn or Granny Smith for best flavour.

A is for apple, B is for Banana, C is for chocolate! This recipe contains a good proportion of fruit; and children will enjoy them because of the chocolate chips in them. Make these in mini muffin pans and freeze some for lunchboxes or quick picnics.

Preheat the oven to 210°C, with the rack just below the middle.

Mash the ripe bananas, using a fork. In a large bowl, mix together the mashed banana, sugar, salt, oil, egg and milk until well mixed. Stir in the chocolate chips and the coarsely grated unpeeled apple.

Stir the flour in its bag with a fork to aerate, then spoon it into the cup measure without packing it down. Sprinkle it over the top of the other ingredients, then fold it in without overmixing, stopping when there are no streaks or pockets of flour visible.

Spoon the mixture into the muffin pans, which have been thoroughly sprayed with non-stick spray. Bake for 10–12 minutes or until golden brown, and until the tops spring back when pressed lightly. Leave to stand 2–3 minutes in their pans, then remove carefully and cool on a rack. Store in plastic bags when cold. Freeze any muffins that will not be eaten in 2 days.

Crunchy lemon muffins

- -

A great favourite! The sugar and lemon juice drizzled over the top of these muffins after baking gives a tangy flavour and an interesting sugary crunch.

Preheat the oven to 200°C, with the rack just below the middle.

Measure the flour and first measure of sugar into a bowl and toss to mix.

Melt the butter, add the milk, egg and lemon zest and beat well with a fork to combine.

Add the liquids to the dry ingredients and fold together until the dry ingredients have been lightly dampened but not thoroughly mixed.

Divide the mixture evenly between 12 medium-sized muffin pans that have been well coated with non-stick spray. Bake at 200°C for 10 minutes.

Stir together the lemon juice and second measure of sugar without dissolving the sugar, and drizzle this over the hot muffins as soon as they are removed from the oven. Allow to stand in the pans only for a few minutes after this, in case the syrup hardens as it cools and sticks the muffins to their pans. If this happens it may be necessary to 'lever' the muffins from the pan. Take care not to damage the non-stick finish of the pans.

Serve with tea or coffee for afternoon tea, or as a dessert with lightly whipped cream and fresh fruit or berries.

MAKES 12:

2 cups self-raising flour
¾ cup sugar
75g butter
1 cup milk
1 egg
grated zest of 1 large or 2 small lemons
¼ cup lemon juice
¼ cup sugar

Double chocolate muffins

- -

This recipe will delight chocolate lovers! The chocolate chips on the top of a chocolate muffin provide an interesting texture as well as intensity to the flavour.

Preheat oven to 200°C, with the rack just below the middle.

Sift the dry ingredients into a large mixing bowl.

Melt the butter in another large bowl, then add the egg, yoghurt, milk and vanilla, and mix until smooth.

Sprinkle the flour mixture over the liquids, and fold together until the flour is dampened, but not smooth. Divide the mixture evenly between 12 medium-sized muffin pans that have been well coated with non-stick spray (particularly important if using the chocolate chips).

If you like, sprinkle the top of each muffin with 1–2 teaspoons chocolate chips before baking. Bake for 10–12 minutes, or until the centres spring back when pressed lightly. Leave to stand in the pans for about 3 minutes before removing and cooling on a wire rack.

Serve with coffee for lunch. Make mini muffins for children's parties. Split muffins and serve for dessert with fresh strawberries or with raspberry jam and whipped cream.

MAKES 24 MINI OR 12 MEDIUM:

1¾ cups flour
1 teaspoon baking soda
1 cup caster sugar
¼ cup cocoa
100g butter
1 large egg
1 cup yoghurt
½ cup milk
½ teaspoon vanilla
¼–½ cup chocolate chips

Carrot & pineapple muffins

MAKES 24 MINI OR 12 MEDIUM:

2 cups wholemeal flour
4 teaspoons baking powder
¾ cup brown sugar
2 teaspoons cinnamon
1 teaspoon mixed spice
½–1 teaspoon salt
½ cup chopped walnuts
150g (1 packed cup) grated carrot
225g can crushed pineapple
¼ cup orange juice
1 large egg
¼ cup canola oil or 50g butter

Keep a small can of pineapple on hand so that you can make these at any time – they're so good!

Preheat the oven to 200°C, with the rack just below the middle.

Measure the flour, baking powder, sugar, spices, salt and walnuts into a large bowl. Use the larger amount of salt if you are going to use oil rather than butter. Mix well using your hands, making sure that there are no large lumps of sugar in the mixture.

Grate the carrot. (If you are not sure of the quantity, weigh the carrot before grating it, or pack the grated carrot firmly into a 1-cup measure.) Mix the grated carrot, the crushed pineapple and its juice, orange juice, egg and oil or melted butter together in another large bowl.

Tip the dry mixture into the liquids and fold everything together, until the flour is just moistened. Take care to avoid overmixing. Add a little extra orange juice if the mixture seems thicker than usual.

Spoon the mixture into 12 medium or 24 mini muffin pans that have been lightly buttered or non-stick sprayed. Bake for 12–15 minutes, or until the muffins spring back when pressed in the middle.

Extra-good straight from the oven or reheated. Pack frozen mini muffins in children's lunchboxes as a snack.

Cinnamon & apple muffins

MAKES 12:

2 medium apples (about 250g each),
    unpeeled
1 cup low-fat plain yoghurt
¼ cup canola oil
1 large egg
1 cup sugar
1 cup wholemeal flour
1 cup standard flour
½ cup chopped walnuts
3 teaspoons baking powder
2 teaspoons cinnamon
½ teaspoon salt

Cinnamon and apple go wonderfully well together. Choose a variety with a tangy flavour such as Granny Smith, Braeburn or Cox's Orange.

Preheat the oven to 190°C, with the rack just below the middle.

Grate the unpeeled apples (discarding the cores). Place the grated apple, yoghurt, oil and egg in a medium-sized bowl and mix well.

Measure all the remaining ingredients into a large bowl and stir well with a fork. Pour the liquid mixture into the dry ingredients, and gently fold together until the flour is just moistened. Do not overmix. It doesn't matter if the mixture looks a little marbled, this looks quite good in the finished muffins.

Spray 12 medium-sized muffin pans with non-stick spray, then divide the mixture evenly between them. Bake for 12–15 minutes or until the muffins are golden brown on top and spring back when pressed.

Leave the muffins to cool in the pans for 2–3 minutes, then tip out and cool on a rack. When they are cold, place the muffins in a plastic bag. Freeze any you do not expect to eat within 2 days.

Serve warm or cold anytime with tea or coffee, or include in packed lunches as a healthy treat.

Cinnamon & apple muffins

All the cakes in this chapter are very popular with our families and friends. The biscuits are not as rich as the cakes, but they always disappear remarkably quickly when put in a jar on the kitchen bench.

At the end of the chapter there are a few 'bar' recipes. We like to put a few of these firm, nutty bars in a plastic bag in the car, so we can nibble one occasionally as we drive along. Try them for yourself!

Cakes & cookies

Lemon yoghurt cake

Because you use oil, rather than butter in this cake, it is very easy to mix. It's also incredibly popular.

Preheat the oven to 180°C, with the rack just below the middle.

In a food processor, put the sugar into the bowl. Peel all the yellow peel from the lemons, using a potato peeler, and add to the bowl. Process until the lemon peel is finely chopped through the sugar.

Add the eggs, oil and salt and process until thick and smooth, then add the yoghurt and lemon juice and blend enough to mix. Add the flour and process just enough to combine with the rest of the mixture.

In a mixing bowl, put the sugar, eggs and oil in a bowl. Grate all the zest from the lemons, add it to the bowl, and beat with a handbeater, whisk or fork. Add the remaining ingredients, in the same order as above.

Pour the cake mixture into a buttered and floured ring pan. Bake at 180°C for 30 minutes, or until the sides start to shrink, the centre springs back when pressed, and a skewer inserted into the middle comes out clean. Leave to cool for about 10 minutes before turning out carefully onto a wire rack.

Sprinkle with a little icing sugar and serve, with whipped cream or yoghurt, if you like.

* Use any kind of yoghurt – plain, sweetened or flavoured. If you use flavoured yoghurt, choose a flavour that will blend with the colour and flavour of the lemon.

MAKES A 20CM RING CAKE:

1¾ cups sugar
zest of 2 lemons
2 eggs
½ cup oil
½ teaspoon salt
1½ cups yoghurt*
2–3 tablespoons lemon juice
2 cups self-raising flour

Lemon yoghurt cake

Jane's banana cake

MAKES A 21CM RING CAKE:

1½ cups self-raising flour
1 teaspoon baking soda
3 ripe bananas
125g butter, at room temperature
¾ cup sugar
2 eggs
2 tablespoons milk
1 teaspoon vanilla essence

Make this cake with overripe bananas for best flavour.

Preheat the oven to 180°C, with the rack just below the middle.

Sift the flour and baking soda together into a large bowl.

Mash the bananas roughly with a fork. Put them in a food processor with the remaining ingredients and process until smooth. Add the banana mixture to the flour in the bowl, and mix until just combined.

Pour the mixture into a 20cm ring pan that has been lined with baking paper or a non-stick liner or thoroughly non-stick sprayed.

Bake at 180°C for 35–40 minutes, or until a skewer inserted into the middle comes out clean.

Serve dusted with icing sugar, or topped with your favourite icing. The chocolate icing from Kirsten's chocolate cake (page 262) works well.

Apple & walnut cake

MAKES A 25CM SQUARE CAKE:

¾ cup corn or soya oil
1¾ cups soft brown sugar
2 eggs
1 teaspoon vanilla
1 ¾ cups wholemeal flour
1 teaspoon baking soda
2 teaspoons cinnamon
1 teaspoon grated nutmeg
1 teaspoon salt
½ cup chopped walnuts, or lightly
    toasted sunflower seeds
4 cups grated apple (6 medium
    apples), unpeeled

This is a lovely moist, dense cake which is unlikely to sit around for long! Its generous size makes it useful for a large group.

Preheat the oven to 180°C, with the rack just below the middle.

In a bowl or food processor, combine the oil, sugar, eggs and vanilla until light-coloured and creamy.

In a large bowl, toss together all the dry ingredients and the nuts or seeds with a fork until they are lightly and evenly mixed.

Grate the unpeeled apples using a sharp grater (or food processor), so they are not too mushy and wet. Press them lightly into the measuring cup.

Add the oil and egg mixture and the grated apples to the bowl with dry ingredients, stirring only until the dry ingredients are moistened.

Pour into a well-buttered roasting pan about 25cm square, and bake at 180°C for 30–45 minutes, or until the centre springs back when pressed. Cool in the pan.

To serve, sprinkle with icing sugar, and cut into generous pieces.

Wholemeal carrot cake

MAKES A 23CM ROUND CAKE OR 20CM SQUARE CAKE:

2 eggs
1 cup brown sugar
1 cup oil
2 teaspoons cinnamon
½ teaspoon salt
2 cups (250g) grated carrot
1 teaspoon baking soda
1½ cups wholemeal flour

LEMON BUTTER ICING

1½ cups icing sugar
25g soft butter
1–2 tablespoons lemon juice

A good carrot cake is always popular – for dessert, or with tea and coffee any time of the day.

Preheat the oven to 180°C, with the rack just below the middle.

In a medium-sized bowl or food processor, combine the eggs, brown sugar and oil. Beat until well combined and light in colour. Stir in the cinnamon, salt and grated carrot.

Put the baking soda and flour in another bowl and stir together well. Add to the egg mixture, and mix until all flour is dampened.

Line the bottom of a 23cm round or 20cm square pan with greaseproof paper, then lightly oil the sides. Pour or spoon the mixture into the pan.

Bake at 180°C for 45 minutes, or until the centre springs back when pushed, a skewer inserted in the centre comes out clean, and the sides begin to pull away from the pan. Leave to cool for 5 minutes in the pan, then invert onto a wire rack.

When cool, ice with lemon butter icing. To make the icing, mix the icing sugar, butter and lemon juice together.

Pineapple carrot cake

This cake is truly delicious. You can identify the different ingredients in every mouthful.

Preheat the oven to 180°C, with the rack just below the middle.

Sift the flour into a large bowl, and add the baking soda, sugar, coconut, walnuts, salt, cinnamon and grated carrot. Toss with a fork to mix well.

In another bowl, beat the eggs, oil, vanilla and pineapple, using a fork. Stir this mixture into the dry ingredients, mixing until just combined. (This mixture is firmer than other carrot cakes.)

Pour the mixture into a 23cm square baking pan, lined with baking paper or a non-stick Teflon liner. Bake at 160°C for 45–50 minutes, or until the centre of the cake springs back when pressed.

Serve with yoghurt or lightly whipped cream, with coffee or for dessert; or top with a lemon, orange or cream cheese icing.

MAKES A 23CM SQUARE CAKE:

2 cups self-raising flour
½ teaspoon baking soda
1 cup sugar
¾ cup desiccated coconut
½ cup chopped walnuts
1 teaspoon salt
2 teaspoons cinnamon
2 cups grated carrot
3 eggs
1 cup oil
1 teaspoon vanilla
225g can crushed pineapple

Zucchini chocolate cake

Chocolate and zucchini may seem a bizarre combination, but they work well in this moist, dark cake.

Preheat the oven to 170°C, with the rack just below the middle. Prepare a 25cm square pan by lining it with overlapping strips of baking paper.

Beat the butter with the sugars until light and creamy, using a mixer or food processor. Do not hurry this step.

Add the eggs one at a time, with a spoonful of the measured flour to prevent the mixture curdling. Add the vanilla and yoghurt and mix well.

Sift the dry ingredients together. Stir into the butter and egg mixture, along with the grated zucchini.

Turn the mixture into the prepared pan. Sprinkle the surface with the chocolate chips if desired. Bake for 45 minutes, or until the centre feels firm and a skewer comes out clean.

MAKES A 25CM SQUARE CAKE:

125g butter
1 cup brown sugar
½ cup white sugar
3 eggs
2½ cups flour
1 teaspoon vanilla
½ cup yoghurt
¼ cup cocoa powder
2 teaspoons baking soda
1 teaspoon cinnamon
½ teaspoon mixed spice
½ teaspoon salt
3 cups (350g) grated zucchini
½–1 cup chocolate chips or small
    buttons (optional)

Zucchini chocolate cake

Kirsten's chocolate cake

**MAKES 2 20CM ROUND CAKES OR 1
22 X 27CM RECTANGULAR CAKE:**

125g butter
2 large tablespoons golden syrup
2 eggs
2 cups flour
2 tablespoons cocoa
2 teaspoons baking powder
2 teaspoons baking soda
1 cup sugar
1½ cups milk

*This chocolate cake always arouses comment, because of its
moistness, soft texture, and flavour.*

Preheat the oven to 180°C, with the rack just below the middle.

Heat the butter until melted, then add the golden syrup. Stir to combine,
warming again only if necessary.

Put everything else in the food processor, with the eggs first, and the
milk last. Mix in brief bursts. Add the golden syrup and butter mixture, and
process for two 30-second bursts, scraping down the sides of the food
processor after the first burst.

Bake in 2 20cm round pans if you want to fill it with cream; or bake in
a 22 x 27cm pan for a rectangular, unfilled cake. Line the bottom of round
pans with baking paper, and spray or butter the sides. Line the bottom and
sides of a square or rectangular pan with baking paper.

Bake at 180°C for 25 minutes, or until the centre springs back when
pressed, and a skewer inserted in the centre comes out clean.

Ice with chocolate icing.

Chocolate icing

**1 tablespoon butter
2 teaspoons hot water
1 tablespoon cocoa
1 cup icing sugar, sifted**

Heat the butter, water and cocoa together until the butter has
melted and all ingredients are easily combined. Add the sifted icing
sugar and mix thoroughly until the icing is smooth.

Serve within 3 days.

Coffee cake

MAKES A 23CM SQUARE CAKE:

150g soft butter
1 cup brown sugar
2 tablespoons instant coffee, powder
  or granules
2 eggs
2 teaspoons vanilla
2 cups wholemeal flour
1 teaspoon baking powder
1½ teaspoons baking soda
2 teaspoons ground cinnamon
1 teaspoon ground cardamom
½ teaspoon salt
250g sour cream
¼ cup walnuts, chopped
juice of 1 lemon (2 tablespoons)

A rich, light cake for a special occasion, made with wholemeal flour.

Preheat the oven to 180°C, with the rack just below the middle.

In a large bowl, beat the butter and sugar until light and fluffy, then add
the instant coffee and mix in well. Break in the eggs and add the vanilla,
and beat well.

In another bowl, toss together the dry ingredients. Add half of this to
the creamed mixture, then mix in half the sour cream. Repeat with the
other half of the dry ingredients and the remaining sour cream. Stir in the
walnuts and lemon juice.

Pour or spoon the mixture into a 23cm pan lined with baking paper.
Bake at 180°C for 40–50 minutes, until a skewer poked into the centre
comes out clean. Leave to stand in pan for a few minutes before turning
out. Cool completely before icing (if desired).

Easy fruit & nut cake

Easy fruit & nut cake

- -

This flavourful cake makes an excellent, high-energy, nutrient-rich, healthy snack. The recipe may be modified to make a richer Christmas or other special occasion cake, too.*

Preheat the oven to 150°C, with the rack just below the middle.

Simmer the dried fruit and the orange juice in a large covered saucepan, stirring now and then, for about 5 minutes or until all the juice is soaked up by the fruit. Take off the heat and stir in the cubes of butter (the larger amount makes a richer cake), and the sugar. Stir gently until the butter melts and the sugar is no longer grainy, then stand the saucepan in cold water to cool its contents, stirring occasionally.

Chop the nuts roughly if they are in large pieces, and stir them into the cooling mixture in the pot.

When the mixture has cooled to room temperature, add the eggs, beating them in with a fork or whisk. When thoroughly mixed, sprinkle the flours over the mixture in the saucepan and stir everything together, avoiding overmixing.

Line a square 23cm pan or 2 fairly large loaf pans with strips of baking paper to cover the bottom and sides. Pour the mixture into the pan(s). Level the top, pressing on glacé cherries and whole almonds for decoration, if you like.

Bake the cake for 60–75 minutes; or the loaves for about 45 minutes. When it is ready, the centre should feel firm and spring back when pressed, and a skewer inserted into the centre (right to the bottom) will come out clean. Sprinkle with a few tablespoons of rum, whisky or brandy if desired. Leave to cool in the pan. Store loosely wrapped in baking paper or a cake tin.

For best flavour, leave the cake for 2 days before cutting.

* For a richer Christmas cake, use 1kg dried fruit, ¾ cup orange juice and 250g butter instead of given amounts.

MAKES A 23CM SQUARE CAKE:

600g (4 cups) mixed sultanas, currants and raisins (or use bought mixed fruit)

½ cup orange juice

150–200g butter, in 1cm cubes

1 cup brown sugar, well packed (or 1 cup white sugar)

about 1 cup of walnuts, pecans or almonds

4 large eggs

1 cup self-raising flour

1 cup wholemeal or plain flour

glacé cherries and whole almonds, to decorate (optional)

rum, whisky or brandy (optional)

Jaffa nut brownies

MAKES 18 PIECES:

100g butter
75g dark cooking chocolate
2 large eggs
¾ cup sugar
1 teaspoon vanilla
zest of 1 orange
½ cup chopped walnuts
½ cup flour

Make these as a treat for yourself, or to give away. For plain brownies, just leave out the orange zest and walnuts.

Preheat the oven to 180°C, with the rack just below the middle.

Cube the butter and break the chocolate into pieces. Put both into a microwave bowl and heat for 2 minutes on medium (50%) power. Alternatively, place in a medium-sized saucepan over low heat, until the butter has melted and the chocolate softened. Remove from the heat and stir until smooth and combined.

Add the eggs, sugar, vanilla, orange zest and chopped nuts and stir until well mixed. Sift in the flour and fold together, but do not overmix.

Spread into a 20cm square cake pan with the bottom lined with a Teflon liner or baking paper and the sides sprayed with non-stick spray.

Bake at 180°C for about 15 minutes or until the centre feels firm when pressed. (Don't worry if the sides rise more than the centre.)

Cool in the pan, then cut into 6 pieces lengthwise, and 3 crosswise, and store in an airtight container. Dust lightly with sieved icing sugar just before serving.

Gill's giant peanut butter cookies

MAKES 12:

100g butter, softened
¾ cup (½ a 380g jar) crunchy peanut
    butter
1 cup brown sugar
1 egg
2 tablespoons golden syrup
1 teaspoon vanilla essence
1½ cups flour
1 teaspoon baking soda
150g chocolate

Like most American cookie recipes, these are slightly chewy rather than crisp when cooked. Our friend Gill, a 'chocoholic', swears by the chocolate topping, but this is not essential.

Preheat the oven to 190°C, with the rack just below the middle.

Beat the butter and peanut butter together in a large bowl. Add the sugar, egg, golden syrup and vanilla, then beat until fluffy (4–5 minutes).

Sift in the flour and baking soda, and stir to combine.

Scoop ¼-cup measures of the mixture onto a non-stick sprayed (or Teflon lined) baking sheet, leaving some room for spreading. Flatten each pile out to about 10cm across, using the palm of your hand.

Bake for 10–12 minutes until just beginning to brown, then place 2 squares of chocolate on top of each cookie and bake for another 2–3 minutes. Remove from the oven and leave to cool on the tray for 5 minutes, then transfer the cookies to a wire rack.

Serve warm; or leave to cool and store in an airtight container.

Gill's giant peanut butter cookies

Almost-Anzac biscuits

Almost-Anzac biscuits

- -

A long-standing Australasian tradition, these biscuits are too good to forget.

Preheat the oven to 170°C, with the rack just below the middle. Line a baking tray with baking paper or a Teflon liner.

Melt the butter in a fairly large saucepan. Add the golden syrup and stir until blended. Take off the heat and add the essence, sugar, rolled oats, coconut and flour to the saucepan. Stir everything together, then add the baking soda dissolved in the warm water. If the mixture seems too crumbly to shape easily, add 1–2 tablespoons extra water.

Using your hands, shape the mixture into walnut-sized (or smaller) balls, and place on baking trays lined with baking paper, leaving room for the biscuits to spread.

Bake for about 15 minutes, until evenly golden brown. While the biscuits are warm, lift them onto a wire rack. When cold, store in an airtight container.

VARIATIONS

Add 1 cup chopped roasted peanuts or 1 cup chopped walnuts before adding the sugar.

Replace the coconut with an extra cup of rolled oats.

For more authentic Anzac biscuits, replace the rolled oats with wheatmeal, add 1 cup chopped walnuts, and leave out the essence. Use ¾ cup plain flour instead of 1 cup.

MAKES 50:

100g butter

¼ cup golden syrup

½–1 teaspoon vanilla or almond essence

1 cup sugar

1 cup instant rolled oats

1 cup desiccated coconut

1 cup standard (plain) flour

½ teaspoon baking soda

2 tablespoons warm water

Gingernuts

Gingernuts

MAKES 40-60:

100g butter
1 rounded tablespoon golden syrup
1 cup sugar
1–2 teaspoons ground ginger
1 teaspoon vanilla essence
1 large egg
1 ¾ cups standard flour
1 teaspoon baking soda

These are easy enough for even young cooks to make because you stir everything together in a pot. It's fun for children to make lots of mini gingernuts instead of big ones!

Preheat oven to 180°C, with the rack just below the middle. Line a baking tray with baking paper or a Teflon liner.

Melt the butter in a medium-sized saucepan or microwave dish. Remove from the heat when melted. Add the golden syrup (using a tablespoon dipped first in hot water), sugar, ginger (use more for a stronger flavour), and vanilla. Add the egg, then mix well with a wooden spoon. Sift the flour and baking soda into the mixture, then mix everything together again.

Stand the saucepan or bowl in cold water to cool the biscuit mixture so it is firmer. With wet hands, roll teaspoonfuls of biscuit mixture into small balls. Put these on the prepared baking trays, leaving room for them to spread.

Bake 1 tray at a time for about 10 minutes, until golden brown. While the biscuits are warm, lift them onto a wire rack. When cold, store in an airtight container.

NOTE: *If your biscuits don't spread, you have used too much flour. If they spread too far, you have not used enough flour.*

'You'd never know it' cookies

You would never know by their taste or appearance that these biscuits contain relatively little oil and are high in fibre from rolled oats and wholemeal flour.

Preheat the oven to 190°C, with the rack just below the middle.

Measure the oats into a food processor fitted with the chopping blade and process until they resemble coarse flour. Transfer the processed oats to a large bowl and add the next wholemeal flour, baking soda (make sure there are no lumps), salt, chocolate chips, sultanas and walnuts, and stir to combine.

Put the oil, egg and the sugars in the food processor and process until pale and creamy-looking. Add the vanilla and process again to mix.

Pour this mixture into the dry ingredients and stir until thoroughly combined.

Using 2 spoons, drop small walnut-sized piles of the mixture oven sheets lined with baking paper, leaving 4–5cm between each pile to allow spreading as they cook.

Place one tray at a time in the middle of the oven and bake for 10–12 minutes until golden brown. Cool the cookies on a wire rack before storing in an airtight container.

MAKES 30–36:

1 cup rolled oats
1 cup wholemeal flour
½ teaspoon baking soda
½ teaspoon salt
½ cup chocolate chips
½ cup sultanas
½ cup chopped walnuts
½ cup canola oil
1 large egg
½ cup brown sugar
½ cup white sugar
1 teaspoon vanilla

'You'd never know it' cookies

Pack-a-snack bar

Pack-a-snack bar

- -

This is a nutritious concentrated snack food.

MAKES A 18 X 28CM SLICE:

BASE
1 cup standard flour
1 cup wholemeal flour
1 cup instant rolled oats
200g chilled butter
1 cup brown sugar

TOPPING
4 large eggs
½ cup brown sugar
1 teaspoon vanilla essence
2 cups almonds
1 cup dates, chopped
1 cup dried apricots, chopped
1 cup chocolate bits or melts, plus extra for decoration
1 cup desiccated coconut

Preheat the oven to 180°C, with the rack just below the middle of the oven. Line the sides and bottom of a pan about 18 x 28cm with baking paper.

For the base, chop the flour, wholemeal flour, oats and butter (cut into cubes) together in a food processor (or grate the butter into the oats and flour in a bowl), then mix in the brown sugar and press the mixture into the prepared pan.

For the topping, put the eggs, brown sugar and vanilla in a large bowl and beat with a fork just until the whites and yolks are evenly mixed. Add all the remaining ingredients (except the extra chocolate melts), and mix together with a stirrer or spatula. Spread over the uncooked base and press down fairly evenly.

Bake for 45 minutes, covering the top with a Teflon liner or folded baking paper partway through the cooking if it browns too quickly. Leave to cool in the baking pan, preferably overnight.

When it is completely cold, cut into 4 large pieces using a sharp serrated knife. Trim off the outer edges if necessary, then cut each piece into 3 smaller bars or fingers.

Store the bars in the fridge for up to 1 week, or freeze for up to 6 weeks in plastic bags or covered containers.

Super muesli bars

- -

Muesli bars are easy to make, and homemade bars are much more economical than bought ones. Toasting the grains adds a delicious nutty flavour.

MAKES A 18 X 28CM SLICE:

1 cup rolled oats
½ cup wheatgerm
½ cup sesame seeds
½ cup sunflower seeds
¼ cup dried apricots, chopped (optional)
50g butter or ¼ cup oil
½ cup honey
¼ cup peanut butter

Line the sides and bottom of an 18 x 28cm pan with baking paper, or spray a 23cm square loose-bottomed pan.

Mix the rolled oats, wheatgerm, sesame and sunflower seeds together in a sponge-roll pan or heavy frying pan. Lightly toast the mixture by cooking about 10cm below a grill, or on the stovetop over a medium heat, until it has coloured lightly and lost its raw taste (this should take 5–6 minutes). Stir frequently to ensure they don't burn.

Briefly run the dried apricots under the hot tap, then chop them finely and set aside.

While the oat mixture is browning, measure the butter or oil, honey and peanut butter into a large frying pan. Bring to the boil over a moderate heat, stirring to blend the ingredients, then turn the heat very low and cook the mixture gently, until it forms a firm ball when a little is dropped into cold water and left for about 1 minute.

Stir the lightly browned oat mixture and chopped apricots into the syrup until evenly mixed. Carefully press the hot mixture into the prepared pan, using the back of a spoon.

Leave the mixture to cool until firm but still flexible, then turn it out and cut with a sharp serrated knife into bars. Serve in school lunches and for after-school snacks. Store in a completely airtight container, or wrap the bars individually in cling wrap (like toffee, they will soften and turn sticky if left uncovered).

Birdseed bar

This sweet bar contains many healthy and flavourful additions. Eat it with restraint – it is all too easy to keep reaching for more!

MAKES A 18 X 28CM SLICE:

1 cup sesame seeds
1 cup sunflower seeds
1 cup chopped roasted peanuts
1 cup coconut, rolled oats or crushed cornflakes
1 cup sultanas
100g butter
¼ cup honey
½ cup brown sugar

Line the base and sides of an 18 x 28cm pan with baking paper.

One variety at a time, and watching carefully to prevent overbrowning, lightly toast the sesame seeds, sunflower seeds, chopped nuts, coconut, and rolled oats or crushed cornflakes under a grill or in a large heavy-bottomed frying pan on moderate heat. Stir so that the contents brown evenly and lightly. (Do not mix before heating, since they brown at different rates.) Mix them in a large bowl after they are heated, and stir in the sultanas.

Put the butter, honey and brown sugar into a large saucepan and heat gently until the sugar dissolves, making a toffee-like mixture. Heat until a drop forms a soft ball when dropped in cold water, then tip the toasted ingredients into the saucepan. Stir well to combine, then press the mixture into the prepared pan.

Leave until lukewarm, then turn out onto a board and, using a sharp serrated knife, cut it into bars the size and shape you like.

Store promptly when cold, in an airtight container (or carefully wrap pieces individually). Serve as a healthy snack.

VARIATION: *Replace the peanuts with walnuts or almonds.*

Birdseed bar

There is something special about a delicious dessert to follow a good meal, and the recipes in this chapter are sure to make your mouth water.

If you would rather serve coffee and a sweet or two, try one of our favourite sweet recipes — both adults and children really enjoy them. Try our uncooked coconut ice recipe first. Quick and easy to make, you can put it in the refrigerator to set while you eat your main course. As the coffee brews, cut the coconut ice into cubes before serving the two together.

Desserts & sweets

Rhubarb tart

SERVES 4–6 SERVINGS:

2 cups Greek yoghurt

¼ cup cream

2 tablespoons caster sugar

1–2 sheets frozen short pastry, thawed

300g rhubarb, cut in 7cm lengths

¼ cup white sugar

½ cup white wine

5cm cinnamon stick

1 star anise

1 vanilla pod

Line a large sieve with a clean teatowel. Place the sieve over a bowl, then tip in the yoghurt. Cover the sieve, then leave the yoghurt to drain for 6–10 hours (refrigerate in warm weather).

Preheat the oven to 160°C, with the rack just below the middle.

Roll the pastry to fit a 23cm loose-bottomed flan dish. Ease it into the dish, trim the edges, then prick over the bottom with a fork. Lay a square of baking paper over the pastry, then fill it with 1–2 cups of rice or beans and bake at 160°C for 12–15 minutes or until the edges are golden brown. Lift out the baking paper and rice or beans, and leave the pastry shell to cool.

Place the rhubarb in a large pan with the white sugar, wine, cinnamon stick, star anise and vanilla pod. Heat until the mixture boils, then reduce the heat and cook for 2–3 minutes until the rhubarb is tender, but still holding its shape. Leave to cool.

Remove the vanilla pod from the rhubarb, halve it lengthwise and scrape out the pulpy seeds. Measure the cream and caster sugar into a medium-sized bowl. Add the vanilla seeds, then lightly whip the cream. Fold the strained yoghurt into the cream.

Fill the pastry shell with the cream and yoghurt mixture, then arrange the rhubarb pieces over the top. Refrigerate until required. Drizzle with a little of the rhubarb cooking syrup just before serving.

Rhubarb tart

Rhubarb cream flan

Rhubarb in party dress!

SERVES 4–6:

1 sheet pre-rolled flaky pastry or ½ quantity of Easy
 'flaky' pastry (page 223)
3–4 cups thinly sliced rhubarb
3 eggs
½ cup sugar
½ cup sour cream

Preheat the oven to 220°C, with the rack just below the middle.

Make once the recipe of the pastry. Roll the pastry out thinly and use it to line a 20cm pie plate or loose-bottomed flan dish. (There will be some pastry left over.) Fold the pastry edges back in for a pie, or cut them level with the edge for a flan.

Arrange the rhubarb slices in the uncooked crust. Combine the eggs, sugar, and sour cream until well mixed, then pour this over the rhubarb.

Bake at 220°C for 20 minutes, or until golden brown, then turn down to 180°C and continue baking until the filling is set in the middle. Serve warm.

Rhubarb cream flan

Star attractions

Of course you can make these berries and cream-filled pastries any shape you like, but stars always seem a little bit special . . .

SERVES 4:

1 sheet (about 150g) pre-rolled frozen flaky pastry,
 thawed
2 cups strawberries, raspberries or blueberries
 (or a mixture of all)
1–2 tablespoons caster sugar
2 tablespoons orange juice
250–300ml cream
1–2 tablespoons caster sugar
finely grated zest of ½ an orange
2–3 drops vanilla essence
icing sugar, to dust

Preheat the oven to 200°C, with the rack just below the middle.

While the oven heats, cut the pastry into star shapes (just cut by hand around a cardboard template if you don't have a star cutter big enough), or rounds or rectangles, or any shape you like. Arrange the pastry shapes on a baking sheet and chill until the oven is ready, then bake for 5–6 minutes until puffed and golden brown. Remove from the oven and cool on a wire rack. (You can do this well in advance if you like.)

Hull and halve or quarter any large strawberries, then place the fruit in a medium-sized bowl. Sprinkle the caster sugar over the fruit (start with the smaller amount and add more if required), add the orange juice, then stir gently to combine.

Pour the cream into a large bowl, add the second measure of caster sugar to taste, the orange zest and vanilla, then beat or whisk until softly whipped (it will just hold it shape but does not look dry).

Assemble just before serving by carefully splitting the pastry shapes into 2 layers. Place the bottom layer on a flattish plate or bowl and cover with a generous spoonful of the berries. Top the berries with a dollop of cream, then carefully place the pastry cap back on. Dust with icing sugar (put a little in a fine sieve and tap or shake gently) and serve.

Star attractions

Extra easy apple tartlets

SERVES 4:

1 pre-rolled sheet flaky pastry
2 tablespoons walnut or pecan pieces
1 tablespoon caster sugar
½ teaspoon cinnamon
2 medium apples (Granny Smith,
    Braeburn or Cox's Orange)
3–4 tablespoons apricot jam, warmed

If you use pre-rolled pastry sheets for these, the most complicated part is peeling and slicing a couple of apples!

Sit the pastry on a lightly floured board to thaw. Preheat the oven to 190°C, with the rack just below the middle.

Measure the nuts, sugar and cinnamon into a food processor or blender and process until the nuts are finely chopped.

Peel, halve and core the apples. Lie each half on a board and slice crossways into slices 2–3mm thick. Depending on the size of the apple you should have 15–20 slices.

Cut a 2cm wide strip from one side of the pastry sheet so you are left with a rectangle. Cut this rectangle into 4 equal-sized smaller rectangles and arrange these on a baking sheet. Without cutting right through, run a sharp knife 1cm in from the edge of each rectangle so it marks out a frame.

Spread 1–2 teaspoons of the sugar and nut mixture over each piece of pastry, leaving the border clear, then carefully fan out a sliced apple half on each. Warm the apricot jam (about 30 seconds in the microwave) and brush a little over the whole of each tartlet.

Bake for 15 minutes or until the pastry is golden brown. Leave to stand for 5–10 minutes, then brush with a little additional warmed jam and serve.

Filo apple strudel

SERVES 6:

¼ cup almonds or walnuts
1 thick slice bread
2 large apples, unpeeled
¼ cup sugar
1 egg
¼ cup sour cream
1 teaspoon cinnamon
½ cup sultanas or chopped dried
    apricots
9 sheets filo pastry
about 3 tablespoons melted butter,
    for brushing filo

Filo pastry makes an impressively good, easy strudel with a light flaky crust and soft fruity filling. Serve it as a special dessert, for a light lunch, or a satisfying snack at any time of the day or night!

Preheat the oven to 180°C, with the rack just below the middle.

By hand: In a large bowl, stir together the sugar, egg, sour cream and cinnamon. Add the bread, broken into pieces and leave it to soften until you can mash it with a fork. Stir in the finely chopped nuts and the sultanas or chopped apricots, then coarsely grate or finely slice the apple and stir everything together.

In the food processor: Chop the nuts and bread using the metal chopping blade, then add the unpeeled apples, cut in rough slices, and chop them to the size of peas (you may need to do this in 2 batches). Working quickly so that the apples do not brown, add the sugar, egg, sour cream and cinnamon and process briefly. Mix in the sultanas or chopped dried apricots.

Open the packet of filo only when the filling is ready. Then, working quickly, take 3 sheets of filo pastry, and lie them side by side on a dry bench, long sides together, slightly overlapping. Brush with melted butter, using about 1 teaspoon per sheet (the whole surface need not be covered). Cover with 3 more sheets, butter in the same way, then top with the remaining 3 sheets. (Wrap unused filo airtight, and refrigerate.)

Place the prepared filling along the short edge of the large filo rectangle, then roll it up loosely. Brush the whole surface evenly with more oil or melted butter. Cover the ends with foil, so the filling stays in place during baking.

Bake on an oven tray lined with baking paper, at 180°C for about 30 minutes, until evenly browned.

Serve warm or reheated, cut in fairly thick slices with a very sharp knife. Serve with ice cream or whipped cream.

Apple pie

- -

Everyone loves apple pie, so it is worth learning how to make this old favourite.

Preheat the oven to 220°C, with the rack just below the middle.

Roll the pastry out thinly and evenly on a lightly floured board, turning it often, to form 2 rounds a little bigger than a 20–23cm pie plate. Put 1 piece in the plate, with its edges overhanging, stretching it as little as possible.

Put the sugar and flour in a bowl. Coarsely shred or slice the peeled or unpeeled apples, and toss them in the sugar and flour. Pour the melted butter over the apple, add the cloves if you like, and toss to mix.

Put the prepared apple into the pastry-lined pan, dampen the surface of the remaining pastry round, and place on the apple, dampened side down. Press the 2 layers of pastry together, trim about 1cm beyond the edge of the pie plate, then fold the overhanging pastry under, pinching the layers together. Flute the edges or press with a fork, if you like. Make 1 central hole or several holes for steam to escape. Brush the top with lightly beaten egg if you want a glazed surface.

Bake at 220°C until it is golden brown and the apple is tender when tested with a skewer. Lower the heat to 180°C if the pastry browns before the apple is cooked. Serve warm, with cream, ice cream or yoghurt.

MAKES A 20–23CM ROUND PIE:

2 sheets pre-rolled flaky pastry or one recipe Easy 'flaky' pastry (page 223)

½ cup sugar

2 tablespoons flour

4–6 apples

25g butter, melted

6 whole cloves, or ¼ teaspoon ground cloves

lightly beaten egg, to glaze

Apple pie

Apple crumble

SERVES 4:

½ cup flour
½ teaspoon cinnamon
½ teaspoon mixed spice
¾ cup sugar
75g butter
½ cup rolled oats
4 medium apples (or use feijoas, peeled and sliced)

It's much quicker to make a crumbled topping than to make pastry, and in our house the crumble rates nearly as high as a pie. Leftovers, warmed in the microwave and eaten with yoghurt, make a good breakfast. Grate the apples, skin and all, instead of peeling then slicing them. It gives a 'fresher' flavour to the crumble.

Preheat the oven to 180°C, with the rack just below the middle.

Measure the flour, spices and sugar into a medium-sized bowl or food processor. Cut or rub in the butter until crumbly, then add the rolled oats.

Grate the unpeeled apples into a shallow medium-sized ovenware dish. Sprinkle the crumbly topping evenly over them.

Bake for 45 minutes, until the topping is golden brown. Serve hot or warm with cream or ice cream.

Sticky date puddings

MAKES 6 INDIVIDUAL PUDDINGS, OR 1 23CM SQUARE PUDDING:

1 cup (about 175g) pitted dates, chopped
1 cup hot water
50g butter
1 cup self-raising flour
½ teaspoon baking soda
1 teaspoon cinnamon
½ teaspoon mixed spice
¾ cup lightly packed brown sugar
2 large eggs

There is something particularly nice about being served your own little pudding for dessert.

Place the roughly chopped dates in a medium-sized microwave bowl. Cover with the water then microwave on High (100%) for 5 minutes, stirring occasionally. Stir in the butter, then set aside to cool.

Sift the flour, baking soda and spices into another medium-sized bowl, then stir in the brown sugar. Add the eggs to the date mixture, stir until well combined, then fold this into the dry ingredients.

Divide the mixture between 6 large non-stick sprayed or oiled muffin pans, or pour into a prepared 23cm square cake pan. Cover the muffin pans with foil, then place in a roasting pan containing 2cm of boiling water. Bake at 180°C for 25–30 minutes, until the puddings are firm when pressed in the centre. Leave to stand for 5 minutes before removing from pans. (Bake the large pudding uncovered for 30 minutes or until the centre is firm when pressed.)

Serve warm, topped with butterscotch sauce (below).

NOTE: *Each large muffin pan holds about 1 cup of mixture. Use other containers if preferred.*

Butterscotch sauce

1 cup sour cream
1 cup brown sugar
2 tablespoons orange liqueur, or grated zest of ½ an orange

Combine all the ingredients and heat until the sugar dissolves. (For a thicker sauce, simmer, stirring frequently, for 5–10 minutes.)

Clafoutis

Clafoutis

- -

A surprisingly simple French classic, clafoutis is traditionally made using stonefruit, but berries or a combination of stonefruit and berries also works well.

Preheat the oven to 180°C, with the rack just below the middle.

Measure the oil, sugar, eggs, milk and vanilla into a large bowl and whisk until well mixed and smooth. Add the ground almonds and flour and whisk again.

Thoroughly non-stick spray a shallow 23–25cm dish. Pour in the batter then scatter or arrange the fruit over the top.

Bake for 30 minutes until golden brown and until a skewer inserted in the middle (avoiding the fruit) comes out clean. Remove from the oven and leave to cool until barely warm.

Dust with icing sugar and serve with custard or whipped cream.

NOTE: *Can be made up to a day in advance and warmed (in the oven or microwave) before serving.*

SERVES 6:

¼ cup canola oil
1 cup sugar
2 large eggs
½ cup milk
1 teaspoon vanilla essence
1 cup (160g) ground almonds
¾ cup standard flour
About 400g fruit (cherries, plums, apricots, nectarines, raspberries, blueberries etc); quarter or slice larger fruit

Chocolate self-saucing pudding

- -

SERVES 6:

¾ cup sugar
2 tablespoons cocoa powder
1½ cups self-raising flour
1 large egg
¼ cup canola oil
1 cup milk

SAUCE

2 tablespoons cocoa powder
½ cup sugar
1¼ cups boiling water

You'd never know this delicious pudding is actually low-fat! Always popular with children and adults alike, it's really easy to make.

Turn the oven on to heat to 180°C, with the rack just below the middle. (Ignore if you're going to use the microwave instead.)

Measure the sugar, cocoa powder and flour into a 2.5-L microwave or oven-proof casserole dish and stir together well to mix evenly and make sure there are no lumps.

Break the egg into a small bowl, then add the oil and milk and whisk together. Pour this into the flour mixture and stir gently until just combined (avoid overmixing as this will make it tough).

To make the sauce, stir the cocoa powder and sugar together in a small bowl. Add the boiling water and stir until the sugar dissolves, then pour this over the pudding batter.

Place in the oven and cook for 30–40 minutes until the centre feels firm when pressed gently. Or, cover and microwave on high (100%) for 8–10 minutes or until done (until the centre is firm when pressed).

Tofu fruit whip

- -

SERVES 2-4:

175–250g fresh apricots, strawberries, bananas; or canned fruit, drained
250–300g tofu
about 1 cup orange juice, or 1 cup white wine and water, mixed
2 tablespoons brown sugar
¼–½ teaspoon vanilla essence

When you mix puréed fruit and tofu, you get a thick, amazingly smooth and delicious pudding-like mixture. Adjust the flavouring carefully, top with some toasted flaked almonds, and you have a popular, cholesterol-free, almost-nstant dessert.

Chop the fruit into a food processor or blender. Process until it forms a fairly smooth purée. Crumble in the tofu and process for about 1 minute, until very smooth, before gradually adding enough orange juice or wine and water to thin the mixture to the consistency you want. Add sugar to taste. Add the vanilla. Serve immediately, or refrigerate.

Mexican flans

- -

MAKES 12:

½ cup sugar
4 eggs
½ a 400g can sweetened condensed milk
1 L milk
½–1 teaspoon vanilla essence
strawberries and whipped cream, to serve

These caramel custards are a lower-fat version of an old favourite.

Preheat the oven to 150°C, with the rack just below the middle. Spray a tray of deep non-stick muffin pans with non-stick spray.

Put the sugar in a small, preferably non-stick frying pan and heat gently, shaking the pan to move the sugar around. Do not stir it. If the sugar starts to brown unevenly, lower the heat (dark brown caramel is bitter).

Pour the caramel into the prepared muffin pans, tilting to coat the bottoms evenly.

Beat together the eggs, condensed milk, milk and vanilla. Pour through a fine sieve into a jug, then pour into the muffin pans. Stand the tray of muffin pans in a roasting dish of hot water that comes halfway up the sides of the muffin tray.

Bake uncovered at 150°C for about 15 minutes, or until the centres feel firm and a sharp knife inserted in the middle of the custard comes out clean.

Cool to room temperature, then chill for at least 4 hours. Unmould carefully, pushing one side of the pudding down with your fingers until the pudding flips over and sits caramel-side up, on your cupped fingers. Use a sharp knife if the custards stick to the sides. Slip onto individual dishes.

Serve with the caramel liquid poured over each custard. Garnish with a fanned strawberry and a spoonful of lightly whipped cream if you like.

Instant ice cream

This ice cream is ready to eat 1 minute after you start making it. Either freeze the fruit or berry of your choice in packets containing 2 cups, or buy frozen berries. Start with strawberry ice cream, then experiment with cubed peaches and other berries.

Chop the frozen berries into smaller pieces if necessary. The fruit must be frozen hard, free-flow and in 1–2cm pieces. Tip the fruit into the food processor bowl. Work quickly to keep the fruit very cold. Process with the metal chopping blade until the fruit is finely chopped (10–20 seconds). This is a noisy operation. Add icing sugar and process until mixed.

Gradually add the chilled liquid of your choice through the feed tube, using just enough to form a smooth cream, and scraping the sides of the bowl once or twice. Stop as soon as the mixture is evenly textured and creamy. Serve immediately.

SERVES 3–4:

2 cups frozen strawberries, etc.
½ cup icing sugar
about ½ cup chilled cream, milk, yoghurt, or soy milk

Crème brûlée

Crème brûlée is an unashamedly rich dessert! It is best served in fairly small quantities. If you don't like the idea of using cream only, use a mixture of equal parts cream and milk.

Preheat the oven to 150°C, with the rack just below the middle.

Pour the cream (or milk and cream) into a small saucepan or microwave bowl. Add the vanilla pods (if using) and heat gently until it just boils.

Place the egg yolks, white sugar, vanilla essence and salt in another bowl and whisk together. Remove the vanilla pods, then pour the hot cream mixture into the bowl and whisk again. (If you did use the vanilla pods, you can split them lengthwise, gently scrape out the tiny black seeds and add these to the mixture, too.)

Pour the mixture through a sieve to remove any lumps, then carefully pour into the 4–6 ramekins, leaving a few millimetres at the top of each. Arrange the ramekins in a sponge-roll pan or roasting pan and carefully pour in enough hot water to fill to about halfway up the outsides of the ramekins.

Place the pan in the oven and bake at 150°C for 25–30 minutes, or until the custard has just set (it will still appear a little jiggly, but not runny), then remove them from the oven.

Brûlées are versatile and can be served while still quite warm in cool weather; or, in warmer weather (or if you are working in advance), cool to room temperature or even refrigerate until required. Just before serving, sprinkle the top of each ramekin evenly with 1–2 teaspoons of caster sugar (the smaller quantity for small ramekins, or more for larger ones).

Arrange the ramekins on a tray and place under a very hot grill (3–5cm from the heat) for 2–3 minutes until the sugar melts and browns. (You can do this with a blowtorch if you have one.) Remove from the heat and let the caramelised sugar cool and harden to form a crisp layer, then serve immediately.

VARIATIONS: *If you like coffee, try adding ¼ cup whole roasted coffee beans instead of (or as well as) the vanilla pod. The beans will be removed when the mixture is sieved, but you can add 2–3 of the collected beans to each ramekin before baking. The just-baked custard has a mild coffee flavour, and this intensifies on standing.*

SERVES 4–6:

2 cups cream (or 1 cup cream and 1 cup milk)
2 vanilla pods (optional)
4 large egg yolks
½ cup white sugar
1 teaspoon vanilla essence
⅛ teaspoon (pinch) salt
4–8 teaspoons caster sugar

Sour cream lemon tart

This simple tart makes an impressive finale!

MAKES A 20CM ROUND TART:

250g sweet short pastry (1 pre-rolled sheet)
½ cup sugar
thinly peeled or grated zest of ½ lemon
2 tablespoons lemon juice
2 teaspoons custard powder or cornflour
1 cup (250g) sour cream
3 large eggs

Preheat the oven to 150°C, with the rack just below the middle. While the oven heats, non-stick spray (or butter) a 20cm pie or flan dish (preferably with a removable base and fluted sides). Gently press the sheet of pastry into the pan and trim off any excess.

Measure the sugar into a food processor. Add the zest to the sugar, then process until the zest is cut finely through the sugar.

Mix the lemon juice with the custard powder (or cornflour). Add the lemon juice mixture and the sour cream to the sugar, then process until smooth and the sugar has dissolved. Add the eggs 1 at a time with the processor running.

Pour the filling mixture into the pastry base, then bake for 40–50 minutes, or until the top is beginning to brown around the edges (the middle may still jiggle a little, but this is okay). Remove from the oven and allow to cool (the middle will probably sink a little and become firmer).

Serve cut into wedges, topped with a spoonful of lightly whipped cream and sprinkled with a curl or a few grated strands of lemon zest.

Lemon–lime cheesecake

A rich, moist baked cheesecake, with a citrus twist.

MAKES A 20CM ROUND CAKE:

250g packet digestive biscuits
100g butter, melted
3 x 250g cartons cream cheese
¾ cup sugar
finely grated zest of 1 lemon and 1 lime
3 tablespoons lemon and/or lime juice
3 large eggs
whipped cream or yoghurt and passionfruit pulp, to
    serve

Preheat the oven to 150°C, with the rack just below the middle. Crush or process the biscuits into fine crumbs; or place in a plastic bag and bang with a rolling pin.

Melt the butter, then mix it evenly through the biscuit crumbs. Non-stick spray or butter a 20–23cm spring-form cake pan, then press the crumb mixture into the base and up the sides of the tin, trying to get an even thickness.

Beat or process together the cream cheese, sugar, finely grated lemon and lime zest and the juice until the mixture is light and fluffy. Add the eggs and process until evenly mixed.

Carefully pour the cream cheese mixture into the prepared base. Bake at 150°C for about 60 minutes, or until the centre is just firm. Cool, then refrigerate until ready to serve.

Cut into wedges, and top with lightly whipped cream or yoghurt and passionfruit pulp to serve.

Lemon cheesecake

SERVES 8–12:

15 wine biscuits, crushed
25g chilled butter, cubed
500g cottage cheese
1 cup sugar
2 tablespoons cornflour
2 tablespoons finely grated lemon zest
¼ teaspoon salt
2 teaspoons vanilla extract
2 tablespoons fresh lemon juice
3 large eggs
250g cream cheese

Turn the oven to 160°C, with the rack in the middle. Non-stick spray a 20–21cm round cake pan with removable base, then cut 2 squares of aluminium foil (30cm wide) and carefully fold them in a double layer, with no rips, across the bottom and up the *outside* of the tin (to ensure no water can get in during baking).

Break the biscuits into pieces, then crumb them finely in a food processor. Add the cubed butter, then process to chop it through the crumbs. Sprinkle the crumbs evenly over the bottom of the tin, then press them down evenly with the back of a spoon. Bake in the centre of the oven for 15 minutes, then remove.

To make the filling, add the cottage cheese to the cleaned food processor and whiz until it is very smooth. Add all the remaining filling ingredients except the cream cheese, and process until thick and creamy. Add the cream cheese and process again smooth.

Stand the round pan in a large roasting pan and carefully pour the mixture onto the crust. Fill the roasting pan with boiling water so it comes 1.5–2cm up the sides of the cake pan.

Bake for 30–45 minutes, or until the edges of the filling feel firm and the centre moves only very slightly when the pan is jiggled. Take the cheesecake from the oven and out of the roasting pan. Cover and leave to stand at room temperature for 1 hour, then refrigerate overnight. Just before serving, remove the sides of the pan and serve in slices, topped with strawberries or passionfruit pulp and a little softly whipped cream.

Lemon-lime cheesecake

Liqueur truffles

These truffles are the ultimate in luxury, and are very rich. Definitely not for the children!

MAKES 24:

150g dark cooking chocolate
2 tablespoons orange-flavoured liqueur
2 tablespoons butter
1 egg yolk
¼ cup cocoa powder

Break the chocolate up if necessary. Put into a micro-wave-proof dish with the liqueur. Heat for 3–4 minutes on Defrost (30%), until the chocolate is soft and will combine easily with the liqueur.

Add the butter and egg yolk, and mix until well combined (the warm chocolate will melt the butter). Leave aside 3–4 hours at room temperature, before rolling into walnut-sized balls. Roll each ball in cocoa.

Serve on very special occasions, as an after-dinner treat.

Chocolate truffles

Use crumbs from a plain chocolate cake to make these little truffles.

MAKES 48:

1 cup dried currants
2 tablespoons finely grated orange zest
¼ cup rum, whisky, brandy or orange juice
125g dark or cooking chocolate
250g (2½ cups) chocolate cake crumbs
¼ cup coarse desiccated coconut

Put the currants in a sieve and pour boiling water through them, drain and then put them into a bowl with the grated orange zest, the spirit of your choice or the orange juice.

Break up and melt the chocolate, heating it until it is liquid, either in a microwave oven for about 4 minutes on medium (50%), or in a bowl over saucepan of hot, but not boiling water. Add the melted chocolate and the cake crumbs to the currant mixture, and mix well.

Divide the mixture into 4 parts, then divide each part into 12. Roll into balls, then roll each ball in coconut. Refrigerate or freeze until ready to use.

Serve with after-dinner coffee, or package attractively for a gift from your kitchen.

Easy chocolate fudge

Chocolate fudge is always a great favourite. This version is exceptionally quick and easy and requires no beating.

MAKES 64 SQUARES:

500g dark chocolate, broken in pieces (or use chocolate chips)
400g can sweetened condensed milk
½ teaspoon vanilla essence
walnut halves to decorate (optional)

Heat the condensed milk with the broken chocolate in a heavy pot, over a low heat, or in a microwave oven on Medium (50%), stirring frequently until the chocolate is melted and the 2 are well blended.

Add the vanilla, stir well and pour into a 20cm cake pan that has been lined with baking paper or a Teflon liner. Leave until firm, then cut into 8 strips. Cut each strip into 8 squares and top each with a walnut half if you like. Cover and store in a cool place for up to 1 week.

Gift-pack by lining an attractive box or small basket and filling it with fudge.

Liqueur truffles

Left to right: Easy chocolate fudge, Fabulous fudge, Uncooked coconut ice

Fabulous fudge

This delicious soft, smooth fudge is made in a microwave. It will melt in your mouth.

MAKES 64 SQUARES:

100g butter
1 cup sugar
¼ cup golden syrup
400g can sweetened condensed milk
1 teaspoon vanilla essence

Mix all the ingredients except the vanilla in a flat-bottomed casserole dish, or a microwave jug resistant to high heat.

Microwave on High (100%) for 11–12 minutes, stirring every 2 minutes, until all the sugar has dissolved. The mixture should have bubbled vigorously all over the surface; and a drop will form a soft ball when dropped into cold water. Add the vanilla. Don't worry if the mixture looks slightly curdled or buttery.

Beat with a wooden spoon for about 5 minutes, or until the mixture loses its gloss. Spoon the mixture into a lightly buttered or sprayed 20cm cake pan.

Let stand for about 1 hour, then cut into 8 strips. Cut each strip into 8 squares.

Serve as an after-dinner treat. It makes a perfect gift as well.

Uncooked coconut ice

This is easy enough for children to make, and popular with adults, too. After several days, it becomes rather firm, but seldom lasts this long!

MAKES 64 SQUARES:

2 cups desiccated coconut
2 cups icing sugar
½ 400g can sweetened condensed milk
1 teaspoon vanilla essence
¼ teaspoon raspberry essence (optional)
4–5 drops of red food colouring
extra coconut for coating

Measure the coconut and icing sugar into a food processor or large bowl. Tip the condensed milk on top. Add the vanilla, then process in bursts or mix with a flexible stirrer, then mix with your hands.

Sprinkle some of the extra coconut on a sheet of plastic on a flat work surface. Press out half the mixture about 20cm square on the coconut. Add the raspberry essence and enough food colouring to give a pale pink colour to the mixture left in the bowl, mix it in, then tip it out and shape as previously.

Lay the pink layer on top of the white layer. Sprinkle a little extra coconut on top. Refrigerate for 15 minutes or longer, then cut into squares with a wet knife. Refrigerate until required, and eat after a few hours.

Weights & measures

Conversion charts for cooking & baking

The closest equivalent imperial measurement is given for each metric measurement.

ABBREVIATIONS

g	gram
kg	kilogram
oz	ounce
lb	pound
mm	millimetre
cm	centimetre
in	inch
ml	millilitre
L	litre
fl oz	fluid ounce
tsp	teaspoon
Tbsp	tablespoon
°C	degrees Celsius
°F	degrees Fahrenheit

WEIGHT CONVERSIONS

metric	imperial/US
15g	½ oz
30g	1 oz (= 28g more exactly)
60g	2 oz
90g	3 oz
100g	3½ oz
125g	4½ oz
150g	5 oz
175g	6 oz
200g	7 oz
225g	8 oz
250g	9 oz
300g	10½ oz
325g	11½ oz
350g	12½ oz
375g	13 oz
400g	14 oz
450g	16 oz (1 lb)
500g	17½ oz
1 kg	36 oz (2¼ lb)

Note: 1 stick butter = 4 oz (112g).

LENGTH CONVERSIONS—GENERAL

metric	imperial/US
5 mm	¼ in
1 cm	½ in
2.5 cm	1 in
5 cm	2 in
7.5 cm	3 in
10 cm	4 in
12.5 cm	5 in
15 cm	6 in
20 cm	8 in
23 cm	9 in
25 cm	10 in
28 cm	11 in
30 cm	12 in (1 foot)

LIQUID CONVERSIONS—GENERAL

metric	imperial/US
5 ml	$\frac{1}{6}$ fl oz
15 ml	½ fl oz
30 ml	1 fl oz (= 28 ml more exactly)
60 ml	2 fl oz
90 ml	3 fl oz
100 ml	3½ fl oz
125 ml	4 fl oz (¼ pint US)
150 ml	5 fl oz (¼ pint imperial)
175 ml	6 fl oz
200 ml	7 fl oz
225 ml	8 fl oz (½ pint US)
250 ml	9 fl oz
280 ml	10 fl oz (½ pint imperial)
340 ml	12 fl oz ($^3/_4$ pint US)
420 ml	15 fl oz ($^3/_4$ pint imperial)
450 ml	16 fl oz (1 pint US)
500 ml	18 fl oz
560 ml	20 fl oz (1 pint imperial)
1 L	36 fl oz (1¾ pint imperial, 2¼ pint US)

CUP AND SPOON CONVERSIONS

The metric cup (1 cup = 250 ml) is used in most countries outside the USA.

spoon/cup	metric	US metric
½ tsp	2.5 ml	2.5 ml
1 tsp	5 ml	5 ml
1 dsp	10 ml	
1 Tbsp	15 ml	15 ml
1 Tbsp (Australia)	20 ml	
⅛ cup	30 ml	30 ml
¼ cup	65 ml	60 ml
½ cup	125 ml	120 ml
¾ cup	190 ml	180 ml
1 cup	250 ml	240 ml
1½ cups	375 ml	360 ml
2 cups	500 ml	480 ml
4 cups	1 L	960 ml

OVEN TEMPERATURES

	Celsius	Fahrenheit	Gas mark
very cool	110°C	225°F	¼
	120°C	250°F	½
cool	140°C	275°F	1
	150°C	300°F	2
moderate	170°C	325°F	3
	180°C	350°F	4
moderate–hot	190°C	375°F	5
	200°C	400°F	6
hot	220°C	425°F	7
	230°C	450°F	8
very hot	240°C	475°F	9
	260°C	500°F	10

EGG SIZES (MINIMUM WEIGHTS)

	NZ	Australia	UK/Europe	US
Very/Extra Large	60g	73g	64g	
Large	7 = 62g	52g	63g	57g
Standard	6 = 53g			
Medium	5 = 44g	43g*	53g	50g
Small	under 53g	43g		
Pullet (NZ)/Peewee (US)	4 = 35g		35g	

* Western Australia sizings.

Index